WE'VE GOT PEOPLE

*From Jesse Jackson to Alexandria
Ocasio-Cortez, the End of Big Money
and the Rise of a Movement*

Ryan Grim

WASHINGTON D.C.

Cover by Soohee Cho
Cover Formatting by Paige Kelly
Book Design by Troy N. Miller

Editor: Anne Fox
Copy Editor: Alex Abbott
Managing Editor: Troy N. Miller

Printed in the United States of America
First Edition

Published by Strong Arm Press
www.strongarmpress.com
Washington, DC

ISBN-13: 978-1-947492-38-7

For Ady Barkan, Reality Winner, and all those who give everything to the fight.

And for Elizan and our kids, Iris, Sidney, Virginia, and George — may we turn this all around in time.

About This Book

If journalism is the first draft of history, then think of this one as a second draft. In the spirit of its theme, it is unfinished, and I welcome input as it is continually revised, expanded and updated. The book will be hosted digitally at StrongArmPress.com, where people will have an opportunity to comment directly on the draft. If you were involved in the events described here, or have insight into them, please offer it there. I don't know exactly when I'll publish a new edition of the book — that depends on how events unfold — but as I did in this first round, I'll benefit greatly from the wisdom and knowledge of readers.

-Ryan Grim, May 14, 2019

Contents

Prologue   7

Book One: The End of Big Money
Chapter 1: Tune Inn   13
Chapter 2: The Beginning of the Rainbow   19
Chapter 3: Pelosi's Party   35
Chapter 4: The Making of Rahm Emanuel   55
Chapter 5: The Dean Bat   61
Chapter 6: Political Genius   73
Chapter 7: Triple Rainbow   83
Chapter 8: The Dream   111
Chapter 9: Heart Attack   123
Chapter 10: Grandma Hannie   137
Chapter 11: The Public Option   145
Chapter 12: Warren v. Wall Street   175
Chapter 13: The Belt Tightens   189
Chapter 14: Senator Warren   201
Chapter 15: Occupy Washington   217

Book Two: The Rise of a Movement
Chapter 16: Orientation   229
Chapter 17: Uncorked   247
Chapter 18: Obama's Farewell Gift   257
Chapter 19: Two Nations, Indivisible   261
Chapter 20: Dead Enders   271
Chapter 21: Mrs. Hayes   285
Chapter 22: Primaries Matter   293
Chapter 23: The Zeal of the Converted   297
Chapter 24: The Year of the Woman   303
Chapter 25: Betomania   327
Chapter 26: AOC   337
Chapter 27: Which Side Are You On?   361
Chapter 28: Brett   367
Chapter 29: The Green Dream   383

Epilogue   391

Acknowledgments   397

Prologue

The ideology of slavery, for hundreds of years, was built on a set of interlocking arguments, many of which rested on the notion that the system was not a necessary evil, but in fact was beneficial to the enslaved person, a civilizing force that brought God to the godless.

And it was benevolent. Slave labor, went the argument, was morally superior to wage labor — wage slavery, as it was called — because of course a boss would treat a person he owns better than one he rents. Slavery was *good* — or, at least, it wasn't as bad as the alternatives.

White America was eager to believe the story. The country's entire economy, after all, its founding and its politics, were all built on slavery. It was too hard to see a way out of it, so it was easier to just deny the reality of it.

But there was one nagging problem: The ones who ran away.

From our vantage point today, it's difficult to understand just how deeply preoccupied the slaveholding class was with people who escaped. But it's also hard to overstate. Entire industries existed to prevent escape and to capture and return those who made it. Abolitionists made supporting fugitives central to their campaign against slavery, with the Underground Railroad the most vivid expression of the effort.

Quakers and other whites who resisted slavery created sanctuary communities, passing laws that barred state and local authorities from assisting slave catchers. Southern slavers launched raids into the North in search of escapees, often repelled in high-profile and violent fashion. The escapees who told their stories publicly up North had a dramatic effect on public opinion, exploding the narrative that slavery was ultimately a benign institution.

So the slave states turned to Congress, and made the issue of fugitives a top political priority. This culminated in the Fugitive Slave Act of 1850, which passed as the central component of the Missouri Compromise. It passed only narrowly, and if the Southern states didn't have extra members of Congress as a result of the three-fifths compromise — whereby slave states were awarded additional congressional representatives based on the number of slaves living there, but only counted as three-fifths of a person — the bill would have fallen short.

The new law required officials to arrest any black-presenting person that a Southerner swore was an escaped slave. It implemented stiff penalties for harboring fugitives and gave those arrested no opportunity to plead their case. Not only were escaped slaves captured and brought back, free blacks were, too. As the risk of slaves escaping decreased, their price rose significantly in the border states. Now that any black person was at risk of being sent into slavery, the black population of Canada exploded.

The Fugitive Slave Act forced whites in the North to reckon with slavery, to choose sides. The Whig Party, which had long been a coalition that straddled North and South and simply preferred to ignore the issue of slavery, relied for its existence on a pro-slavery party that was, for lack of a better word, moderate — one that was content to keep slavery in the South, and agree to reasonable restrictions on the trade. The Fugitive Slave Act broke apart that arrangement, making it clear that the extremists in the slavocracy were in charge in the South, and they wouldn't stop until they had achieved a hemisphere-wide slave empire. Moderation and compromise could no longer counter the far right. Only a movement bent on the full blown destruction of slavery was capable of meeting the challenge. It was the 19th Century American version of socialism or barbarism.

The Whig Party collapsed. In its place rose the Republican Party, founded on principles of abolition. The South had swung the nation in such an extreme direction that it radicalized the rest of the country in the opposite. Had it not been for those unfathomably brave people willing to risk everything to escape slavery, there would have been no realignment, and no Civil War — at least not the one we had, when we had it.

What followed came to be called the Second Founding, but has been erased from history books. Radical Republicans, as they were known, didn't just pass — and enforce, with the military — Constitutional amendments whose sweep rivaled the Bill of Rights, they went further. Voters elected black politicians as mayors, sheriffs, state legislators, U.S. senators, congressmen — even a governor in Louisiana. When the president tried to slow Reconstruction, Congress impeached him and seized power over the process. Constitutional conventions, with robust black delegations, rewrote the founding documents of states across the South. In a wide-ranging social reformation, the radicals wiped out cholera in New Orleans and integrated the police force and public transportation, established the public school system across the South, and smashed the Ku Klux Klan. If you were alive in 1871 in the South you had every reason to believe a revolution had been carried out and this was the new order. A terrorist insurgency would ultimately roll it back. But abolition, followed by Reconstruction, had briefly exposed the cynical lie — that change is impossible — upon which the system precariously resides.

Had the system of white supremacy not overreached, the rest of white America would have continued to acquiesce. But once the public became radicalized, for a brief but consequential moment, nothing less than a complete refounding and reconstruction of the country was demanded.

Book One

The End of Big Money

One

Tune Inn

Joe Crowley owned the place. It was a Sunday night in Washington in March 2010, a year and a half after a financial crisis had ripped a gaping hole in the global economy. But that night, Democrats had something to celebrate. Crowley was leading the revelry at the Tune Inn, a dive bar just down the street from the United States Capitol Building. Much to the surprise of the bartender scheduled to work the shift, Crowley, one of the top Democrats in the House of Representatives, had taken over his duties.

Making toasts and leading the bar in song, Crowley, an old school Irish pol at home in his element, poured beer from the taps and handed out pitchers and shots like they were checks from JOE PAC. That was the regular-guy name he'd given to his political action committee, which was stuffed full with campaign checks from Wall Street, pharma, big labor and all manner of private associations jockeying for influence.

Wall Street had survived the crisis, but the recovery was slow. Fifteen million people[1] were still actively looking for work and unable to find it, a number that had been flat for a soul-crushingly long time. At least another million people, probably many more, had given up looking. Some three million homeowners had faced foreclosure the year before, a number that would be matched in 2010, leading to a rise in suicides.[2] Just under 50 million people, meanwhile, had no health insurance, many of them now out of work, too many years away from Medicare, but too

---

1   According to the Department of Labor; it translated to a 9.7 percent unemployment rate.

2   The American Journal of Public Health published a study in 2014 linking foreclosures to a higher suicide rate.

close to it to be employable at anywhere near where they had been before. For people with a preexisting health condition, the only way to get coverage was to get a job that offered it — and those were in vanishingly scarce supply.

Some relief was on the way. Just hours earlier, Congress had finally passed the Affordable Care Act. The result of a 14-month battle, the bill was headed to the desk of President Barack Obama, who would put both his signature and, eventually, if somewhat reluctantly, his name on what would become the defining legislative achievement of his presidency.

Crowley at the time was known as the King of Queens, where he ruled over one of the last vestiges of the Tammany Hall–style political machines in New York. But he was also a top boss in the Democratic Party's more modern machine, the one in Washington. Crowley was one of his party's top fundraisers, which had earned him the title, at the time, of vice chair of the Democratic Congressional Campaign Committee, the campaign arm for House Democrats, and also the chairmanship of the New Democrat Coalition. The coalition grew out of the fractious 1980s and '90s, when the party split along ideological lines, and the New Dems came to represent the wing of the party that embraced corporate contributions and a business-friendly posture as a route back to power. They were the socially liberal version of Blue Dog Democrats, who were themselves remnants of the right-wing southern Democrats who had once dominated the party.

Politics was in Crowley's blood. His uncle, New York City Councilman Walter Crowley, had been a major player in the Queens machine, and when a New York state Assembly seat opened up in 1986, a 24-year-old Crowley was eased into it with little competition. More than a decade later, Queens boss Thomas Manton retired from Congress. He timed the public announcement so that only Joe Crowley's name would appear on the ballot, and thus began the career of Congressman Crowley. Two decades later, in Queens, a Christmas turkey may still have been enough to pass out to constituents, but in Washington, most of the members of Congress in the bar that night had instead gotten $5,000 each from JOE PAC. But not all of them.

Among the crush of Blue Dogs, New Dems, reporters, and befuddled regulars whose bar had been unexpectedly taken over by the House Democratic caucus, one man wasn't joining in the revelry. Raúl Grijalva, like Crowley, was a Democratic congressman. He should have been celebrating too: Democrats had just made real the century-long dream of universal health care. But unlike Crowley, he was in no mood to party. He was sitting quietly with a few of his congressional staffers at the end of the bar near the front door, a bottle of Bud and a shot of whiskey in front of him. "We're commiserating and celebrating," Grijalva told me, his mood leaning heavily toward the former.

Grijalva, an Arizonan, chaired the Congressional Progressive Caucus, the ideological rival of the New Dems, and was a regular at the Tune Inn. So much so that for weeks, a cartoon he starred in hung on a wall by the front door. It offered insight into the source of his misery. In the caricature, a shirtless Grijalva, at the beach, admires a sandcastle he's built with Lynn Woolsey, the co-chair of the CPC. Satisfied, neither of them see the menacing gang of senators marching their way, ready to stomp it into oblivion. In the unsubtle tradition of political cartoons, the sandcastle spells out PUBLIC OPTION.

Obamacare had expanded health care access, which is what Democrats from Crowley to Grijalva had wanted. But Crowley's side had won the fight over how this would be delivered, who would get rich, who would get care, and who wouldn't. The ACA left in place the country's barbaric health care and insurance system, but added new rules, markets and subsidies to drain some of the inhumanity from it. Having been unable to get single-payer considered, the left instead focused on expanding public health insurance as much as possible. The cornerstone of that effort, a Medicare-like plan that would be available to purchase in the insurance exchanges Obamacare created, had been killed. The public option cartoon, like the policy itself, had been taken down from the wall before that night in March

Yet, for all its many weaknesses, the ACA was the most significant expansion of public health care, through Medicaid, in a generation, and barred some horrific insurance industry tactics. Democrats were proud. Earlier that night, when the decisive vote flashed on the board inside the House of Representatives, signaling passage, the Democratic side of the chamber erupted in cheers, hugs, high-fives, and tears. The Republican minority responded with their own song of hope, confident that the unpopular law, which wouldn't kick in for several years, had just delivered the House majority to them. "Na, na, na, na/Hey, hey, hey/Good-bye,"[3] the Republican side sang.

Four hundred miles north, a 20-year-old Boston University student, Alexandria Ocasio-Cortez, had gone to a friend's house to watch history unfold on C-SPAN. This was a dark period for her family, as it was for

3   Democrats sang the same tune to Republicans when they passed a version of repeal through the House in 2017. I was in the press gallery for both choral performances. Republicans had previously sang the tune to Marjorie Margolies Mezvinsky, when she cast a deciding vote on Clinton's budget, which included tax increases. She did indeed lose, then ran again in 2014 and lost in the primary, despite the strong backing of both Clintons. Her son ended up marrying Chelsea Clinton.

millions. A year and a half earlier, she had gotten an emergency call from her mother while sitting in an economics class. She jumped in a taxi, took the next flight home, and went straight to the hospital to see her father just before he passed away. As the economy collapsed, without her father the family found itself "deeper and deeper underwater," she later said. They became locked in a years-long probate battle with the Westchester County Surrogate's Court, which processes the estates of people who died without a will, as Ocasio-Cortez's father had. She witnessed firsthand how attorneys appointed by the court to administer an estate enriched themselves at the expense of the families struggling to make sense of the bureaucracy, a lucrative hallmark, she would later learn, of the Queens machine. As it was, she was preparing to graduate into an economy in free fall. Perhaps she could at least get some help with health care.

The Democrats celebrating their victory in the bar that night had done nothing to alleviate the foreclosure crisis for homeowners like her mother — the Obama administration thought it was better to let it play itself out — and after an initial burst of fiscal stimulus, White House focus shifted to the debt and deficit.

The decidedly conservative nature of those partying Democrats at the Tune Inn was the result of a conscious strategy to move the party rightward in order to take back the House in 2006 and expand their majority in 2008. It worked, but it came with a price — one that was tacked onto the Affordable Care Act in the form of higher premiums and stingier care. It meant that powerful committees were stacked with right-leaning freshman and sophomore lawmakers, who weakened legislation at critical chokepoints. Many of them were posted up in the back of the bar, hooting and clinking glasses. Tom Perriello, a freshman who bucked the trend and ran as a populist in Virginia, was having fun with them. Soon as he saw me, he grabbed fellow freshman Steve Driehaus, a conservative Democrat from Ohio who'd been slotted onto the Financial Services Committee to boost his fundraising to aid with reelection. He consistently voted against the Democratic agenda. *Hey, Steve,* Perriello ribbed him, *this is the reporter who says you're corrupt and only on the banking committee so you can raise money from Wall Street.* Driehaus lost it: "How dare you! Accuse me!?" He stormed off. "That was awesome," Perriello said, in full agreement with the critique.

For all the real accomplishments of the lawmakers in that bar, liberals at the time, outside of the Tune Inn, were celebrating less than they were commiserating about a lost opportunity. In 1933 and '34 under FDR, and then again in 1964 and '65 under LBJ, Democratic majorities reshaped the country. "It is only once in a generation that a people can be lifted above material things," President Woodrow Wilson once said, perhaps optimistically. "That is why conservative government is in the saddle two-thirds of the time."

As the bill was being debated, polls showed that a significant number of voters blanched at a "government takeover" of health care. But after it was implemented — which took far too long — the surveys showed consistently that the public objected not to the reach of the health care law, but to its eye-popping premiums and deductibles, which resulted from its moderation and compromises with the health care interest groups. Those deals with the corporate powers that dominate the health-care industry slotted into a narrative that Democrats cared more about protecting the powerful than regular people. Not a single Wall Street executive of any significance was charged with a crime in the wake of the crash, despite the industry's role in fraud that brought down the entire global economy. That data point became fixed in the public's mind as a symbol of the rigged nature of the system. And the stimulus passed by the Democratic Congress, signed by Obama, was known at the time by his own advisers to be too little to fill the hole blown open by the financial crisis. It stopped the bleeding, but didn't give the economy the life it needed, so voters were left wondering who was pocketing all this federal money going out the door.

The Democrats in the bar were as oblivious to the public's frustration as they were to Grijalva's annoyance that they had taken over his haunt. The glad-handing Queens congressman left the dive to shouts of "Crow-ley! Crow-ley!" Grijalva, near the door, waved goodbye; Crowley saw him and gave the barest acknowledgement on the way out. Other Blue Dogs and New Dems gave Grijalva cursory nods at best as they headed toward the door. Grijalva stayed until after the lights came on. Filing out with the stragglers in the early morning, he said he would begin the fight again tomorrow. Though perhaps not until mid-morning.

His fight, he said, was as much against his own party leaders and its campaign arm, Crowley's DCCC, than against the GOP. Democrats play it too safe, he said. "When I give my dues to the DCCC, or when you contribute to it, you have no discretion as to where your money is going to go," he said. "And it goes to front-liners and usually Blue Dogs, and [they] usually vote against our issues. And that's a real frustration. And usually, if there's a progressive running, it's the last consideration in terms of support."

When the 2009 Congress was ushered in, talk of a permanent Democratic majority was in the air. The party, it was said, would rein in Wall Street, rewrite the rules of a rigged economy, and finally finish the unfinished business of the New Deal and the Great Society.

Instead of enjoying a permanent majority, eight months after the lights had come on that night at the Tune Inn, Democrats were swept out by the tea party wave. The party lost nearly a thousand seats nationwide in the runup to 2016, when Donald Trump won enough Electoral College votes to become president, and set about dismantling everything Democrats had built in those crucial two years. It also marked the end of Crowley, as that Boston University student launched a quixotic, insurgent challenge to the King of Queens. "Look at Obamacare," Ocasio-Cortez said[4] early in her campaign for Congress. "They really thought that a person who makes $40,000 a year can pay $200 a month in health insurance for an $8,000 deductible — and they really thought that that was insurance.

"A big piece in the election of Donald Trump has to do with the resentment — it's resentment that these people have no clue what is affordable and what's not. They really don't understand the depth of crisis that working-class Americans are in right now. They really think that their half measures are good enough when working people are drowning."

---

4   This comes from an unpublished portion of an interview Ocasio-Cortez did with my colleague Aída Chávez in April 2018.

Two

The Beginning of the Rainbow

Michigan has a way of surprising. That was as true in the 2016 Democratic primary, when Bernie Sanders stunned Hillary Clinton, as it was in the general election, when Trump stunned her.

And it was true in 1988, too.

The Michigan caucuses fell on March 27, 1988. After more than three dozen primaries and caucuses, a crowded presidential field had been winnowed down to three serious contenders: Michael Dukakis, the Massachusetts governor and presumed frontrunner; Missouri Rep. Dick Gephardt; and the Rev. Jesse Jackson, a former close aide to Martin Luther King Jr., and the public bearer of the torch of the civil rights movement.

A Missouri congressman with Big Labor backing, Gephardt was chairman of the House Democratic caucus, the position that would later be held by Rahm Emanuel and then Joe Crowley. He was running on a platform of "economic nationalism," long before Steve Bannon made the term his own. In Iowa, where the United Auto Workers were still strong, he had won an upset on the back of an issue that was resonating strongly at the time — trade.

He did it by running what became a famous ad that attacked East Asian automakers for selling cheap cars in the United States while slapping tariffs on American cars that made them effectively unmarketable there. The press pounded him for protectionism and charged him with some form of "yellow peril" racism. "He was totally demonized by the mainstream media as a protectionist, even though his description of East

Asian protectionism was precisely accurate," said Robert Kuttner, a progressive journalist who covered the election. "Gephardt was challenging the one-way mercantilism of Japan's trade and industrial policies. This had nothing whatever to do with yellow peril, but that got hung around Gephardt's neck."

The ad tapped into a genuine economic anxiety being felt around the country. After dominating the global economy since World War II, the 1980s saw foreign countries — particularly Japan, when it came to cars and electronics — catching up. Big business fought back against growing labor power in the U.S. by offshoring jobs and moving factories first to the South and then to China, Mexico or other countries with a cheap labor supply. Cities were hollowed out, crack and cocaine was pumped in.[5] Prison construction boomed. A farm crisis ravaged rural America. Amid it all, Wall Street roared and greed became a culturally celebrated virtue.

Even though he was unfairly demonized for his ad campaign, which had tapped into real economic anxiety, Gephart was a badly flawed candidate. Having earlier been an opponent of abortion rights, he made all liberals, and particularly women, nervous. And he utterly lacked charisma. After losing New Hampshire in Michael Dukakis' back yard, he had trouble raising money, and on Super Tuesday, Jackson topped him in southern primaries. Given Gephardt's hard-hat, working-class brand, he badly needed a win in Michigan. He threw everything he had left into the state.

Dukakis, too, wanted Michigan — to show that his appeal extended beyond the liberal confines of Harvard Square, and that he could win back those Reagan Democrats whose defection had cost Jimmy Carter reelection.

Jackson, meanwhile, focused on actual Democrats. And like only a candidate on the ground can, Jackson felt like something was happening in Michigan. He decided to shift his campaign schedule around so he could stay there longer to do everything he could to boost turnout.

He spent that election day touring Detroit, hitting black churches and five different housing projects. The New York Times' legendary political reporter, R.W. Apple, was on hand for the last minute push. Jackson, Apple observed in his election night dispatch, "had drawn surprisingly large crowds of both blacks and whites in the last few days," adding that despite the black establishment's support of Michael Dukakis — Detroit

---

5   My first book, *This is Your Country on Drugs: The Secret History of Getting High in America,* goes through the cultural and economic transformations that shaped this decade.

Mayor Coleman Young[6] was backing Dukakis — Jackson won some Detroit neighborhoods by 15 or 20 to one. "But the surprise was the Chicago
clergyman's powerful showing in predominantly white cities like Lan-
sing, Flint, Kalamazoo and Battle Creek, several of which he carried."

Indeed, Jackson did more than get out the black vote. Progressive
whites in the state also rallied hard to his cause. Dean Baker, who is now
a prominent progressive economist, was district director for Jackson in
Ann Arbor, and described how Jackson's team out-organized Dukakis.

Because it was a caucus and not a primary, that meant the voting
would not be held at the regular station, so Baker's team had an artist
draw a map with numbered sections that indicated where each caucus
would be held. The map was included on every piece of literature the
team distributed.

They also realized that Michigan law, which said that a voter must be
registered at the time of the caucus, meant that the voter could be registered at the caucus, or least a moment before. The state allowed "deputy
registrars," so Baker's team put enough people through training so that
a registrar could be at every caucus site in Ann Arbor and Jackson, which
was also in Baker's district.

"We advertised this in our lit, which said, 'You* can vote for Jesse
Jackson and justice, or you can vote for someone else.' The asterisk then
indicated at the bottom that even if they were not registered, they could
register at the caucus site and vote," said Baker. "On Election Day, the
Dukakis people had all their workers at the caucus sites with their lit and
their big buttons. The only person we had was a deputy registrar who
had nothing to identify them with Jackson, since it was supposed to be
a non-partisan process. The Dukakis people thought Jackson had no one
working for him (they thought the deputy registrars were sent by the
county). Meanwhile, our people were knocking on doors in the largely
black and student areas dragging people to the polls. We thought there
was no point in having people at the polls, since no one was going to the
caucus who had not already decided who they were going to vote for."

The energy of the moment comes through in the Apple dispatch. "So
dramatically did [Jackson] seize the public imagination that he was able

---

6   In September 2018, Coleman Young II ran for Congress to replace John
Conyers in an unusual dual election, one a special election to fill out his term, the
second a primary to be the Democratic nominee for that November. Young II did not
run in the special, and Councilwoman Brenda Jones edged out progressive Rashida
Tlaib. But in the primary, Young II split some of the black vote with Jones, finishing
with 12.5 percent, helping give Tlaib the win. Tlaib won by fewer than 1,000 votes,
and Jones pulled in more than 11,000. That meant that Jones became a congress-
woman for just a few weeks (and also means Tlaib's seat is anything but locked in).

to counter successfully the notion that Mr. Dukakis was the Democrat with the best chance of nomination," the Times wrote.

Jackson, after nearly 40 primaries and caucuses, was now effectively tied with Dukakis in the delegate count — a stunning moment in American politics that has gone down the memory hole.

For much of the campaign, the pundit class had been asking, *What does Jesse Jackson really want?* Surely, they reasoned, he didn't want to be president. What was his angle? A big job? Patronage? Fame? At around 2 am that night in Michigan, a news station called Baker's victory party and wanted comment. "I said that Dukakis lost the southern primaries, he lost Illinois, and now he lost Michigan. I think people have to start asking, *What does Michael Dukakis really want?*"

In 2019, speaking in Selma, Alabama, on the 54th anniversary of Bloody Sunday, Bernie Sanders was on stage. "There is a gentleman sitting right behind me whose name is Reverend Jesse Jackson," Sanders said, going on to talk about the Rainbow Coalition. "History will not forget that he talked about the imperative of black and white and Latino and Native Americans and Asian Americans to come together to fight for a nation of peace and justice."

History, of course, did forget. When we look back at election outcomes, it's easy to ascribe a certain destiny to the outcome, but that obscures what it was to live through those moments, not knowing the outcome. In some significant ways, the Jackson campaign was an answer to the question of what an alternative strategy for the party, one rooted in people rather than money, might have looked like. It was one that excited Democratic voters, but had them wondering if Jackson was truly as "electable" as the safer Dukakis. A young John Harwood, then writing for the St. Petersburg Times, asked voters in Erie, Pennsylvania what they thought of Dukakis and Jackson. "I find little enthusiasm for Dukakis, but kind of a feeling that he's a credible candidate," said Dr. William Garvey, president of Mercyhurst College.

For those in the Jackson camp, his surging campaign hadn't started in Iowa that year, but stretched back to 1983 in Chicago. The city that year underwent a fierce mayoral contest that pitted the old-school Daley machine against a grassroots coalition of progressive whites, blacks, and Latinos, rallying behind Harold Washington, a member of Congress with the backing of the Democratic Socialists of America. Washington, in Congress, had been the legislator who had managed to amend the Voting Rights Act so that courts didn't need to prove that legislators had conspired intentionally to disenfranchise blacks with a particular election policy, but only that its effect was discriminatory.

Jackson was the lead organizer for the coalition, and he got wind that liberal lion Teddy Kennedy, along with former Vice President Walter Mondale, planned to endorse the machine's pick in the primary — Richard Daley Jr., the son of the former mayor who'd arranged for Humphrey's nomination in 1968.

Kennedy and Mondale were towering figures in the party, and their intervention threatened to derail everything Jackson and Washington were working toward. Jackson told me that before the endorsement was public, he reached out to the pair, begging them not to weigh in, explaining the campaign was on the brink of something historic. But the duo told him that they were longtime friends of Daley's family. What could they do?[7]

"*Friends? What are we? Chopped liver?*" Jackson told me he thought at the time.

Yet the machine and the endorsements were no match for the coalition Jackson and Washington had built. Luis Gutiérrez, who would go on to become an iconic Chicago congressman, remembers the Washington campaign as a seminal moment in progressive politics. Gutiérrez was a social worker in his 20s, he said, and went to a Washington rally at the pavillion, the University of Illinois at Chicago's basketball arena. "With Harold Washington it was love," he said, describing how stunned he was by what he heard from the mayoral candidate. "I said, *This is a bad motherfucker*. He said he's gonna fire the police chief! Everybody thinks all this Black Lives Matter, and the police, that that's like been of our time — look at Harold Washington in 1983 saying [Richard] Brzeczek must go. Who the fuck says you're going to fire the police chief running for mayor?!"

"My story's not unique. How the fuck did Harold Washington put an army together against the Chicago machine?" Gutiérrez said, explaining how the Washington campaign became an expression of broader leftist politics. "I asked my friend...to help and she said she didn't have time, and I said, *Don't you ever fucking complain about apartheid in South Africa. Don't invite me to another rally. Don't, because I'm not coming. Because that's what they're doing here.* She looked at me and she said, *You're fucking right.*"

In an alliance with the reformed gang the Young Lords, the campaign registered a staggering 100,000 new voters. Gutiérrez credits Young Lords founder Cha-Cha Jiménez,[8] who helped organize the Hispanic community for Washington.

---

7   Daley's father, after all, had arguably made JFK president in 1960 by (gathering votes the old fashioned way) stuffing ballots. That's quite a debt.

8   The Puerto Rican New Yorkers say they started the Young Lords. That's bullshit — the Young Lords started in Chicago.

Washington stunned the city and won the primary, but the fight wasn't over, as the machine switched parties, rallying behind Republican Bernard Epton in the general election. The police chief quit just before the election, avoiding his coming termination, but also in the hopes of galvanizing white reaction against Washington. Even the local congressional delegation turned against Washington. "You and I would not be having this conversation if Dan Rostenkowski — congressman, counselor to presidents, chairman of the Ways and Means Committee, and a colleague of Harold Washington — hadn't sent a precinct captain to my house and asked me to put up an Epton poster. There are moments that just piss you off. I said, *I can't do shit about Nelson Mandela, and I couldn't help the civil rights movement*, but you just have a moment in your life where you say, *I can do something about this*."

Gutiérrez had been a supporter of Washington's in the primary, but watching the Democratic Party turn on its own nominee radicalized him. He did everything he could for Washington, who won the general·election by just four points in an overwhelmingly Democratic city. The next year, Gutiérrez primaried Rostenkowski. "I got 24 percent, but don't worry, two years later I was Harold's boy and I went to the city council," Gutiérrez said. His win ended what had been called the "Council Wars," as the machine used its council majority to block Washington's agenda. Gutiérrez's victory broke the back of the opposition.

Early in his tenure, Gutiérrez said, Washington showed that he would fight for the city's immigrants. "He [signed] an executive order barring the INS from coming on city property. That's a pretty bad motherfucker. He was the progressive — before the term had been coined and now everybody says they are one — he was one. That's pretty badass shit, to say to immigration agents, *Don't come fucking around my city*."

Washington's win was part of a wave[9] of black mayoral victories in major American cities, reshaping local political dynamics and busting up rusting machines.[10] It convinced the black community that electoral politics — beyond marching and movement building — were needed to move the Democratic Party forward. It also pointed toward a potential coalition, through the expansion of the electorate, that could take on the growing power of capital that had taken over the Republican Party and was making its move on the Democratic Party.[11]

---

9   Carl Stokes kicked it off in Cleveland in 1967.

10   It was not lost on some of those elected officials that as soon as black politicians burst through the gates, they had the privilege of overseeing the despair of deindustrialization.

11   The campaign's ability to bring new voters to the polls pointed in a strategic direction now being embraced by Alexandria Ocasio-Cortez in New York, who

"We've got to break this up," Jackson recalled thinking of the Democratic consensus forming around white-male-dominated, big-money liberalism. "This brand of liberalism is not liberating."

In spring 1983, the Black Leadership Forum — a coalition of nationally prominent and influential black leaders — met and decided to run an African-American for president in 1984. But nobody stepped forward, and Jackson eventually agreed to do it, but didn't get into the race until January 1984, the last candidate to join.

Manning Marable, one of the most incisive observers of the party realignment in real time, laid out the terrain Jackson operated on in an essay in 1985[12]:

> The defections of major electoral groups from the Democrats had reduced the party to four overlapping social blocs. The first tendency, which was clearly subordinated within the coalition, was the democratic left: African-Americans, Latinos (except Cuban-Americans), feminists, peace activists, liberal trade unionists, environmentalists, welfare-rights and low-income groups, and ideological liberals. In national electoral politics, they were best represented by the Congressional Black Caucus and a small group of white liberals in the House and Senate. To their right was the rump of the old New Deal coalition, the liberal centrists: the AFL-CIO, white ethnics in urban machines, some consumer-goods industrialists and liberal investment bankers, and Jewish organizations. The chief representative of this alignment in national politics was Minnesota senator and former vice president Hubert Humphrey. Following Humphrey's death in 1977, his protégé, Walter Mondale, assumed leadership of this bloc. A third tendency, which exhibited the most independent posture toward partisan politics, comprised what some have called the "professional managerial class" and sectors of the white, salaried middle-income strata. These white "neo-liberals" tended to oppose US militarism abroad and large defense expenditures. But on economic policies, they tended toward fiscal conservatism and a reduction of social-welfare programs. They were critical of nuclear power, and favored federal regulations to protect the environment; but they also opposed "special interests" such as organized labor. This constituency was behind the unsuccessful presidential campaigns of Morris Udall in 1976 and John Anderson in 1980. Its principal spokesman in the Democratic primaries was Colorado senator Gary Hart, who as early as 1973 had proclaimed that "American liberalism was near bankruptcy." At the extreme right of the party were those moderate-to-conservative southern Democrats who had not yet defected from the party, and a smaller number of midwestern and "sunbelt" governors and legislators who had ties to small regional capitalists, energy interests, and middle-income white constituencies. The most prominent stars of this tendency in the 1970s were Jimmy Carter, Florida governor Reubin Askew, millionaire Texas senator Lloyd Bentsen, and Ohio senator John Glenn. All of these groups, in varying degrees, opposed the general agenda of the Reagan administration. But only the democratic left, and most specifically the African-American community, mounted a sustained series of social protests against literally every initiative of the Republican president.

argues that the party's top priority should not be flipping voters from red to blue, but from non-voter to voter.

12   The essay, "Race and Realignment in American Politics," was first published in the book *The Year Left: An American Socialist Yearbook*.

Mondale quickly rounded up establishment support, winning over the AFL–CIO early, as well as most leaders in the party. A handful of racists ran to Mondale's right, and two progressives, California's Alan Cranston and George McGovern, to his left, reprising his 1972 campaign that ended with Nixon's landslide reelection.

Jackson made his case by referring to non-voters as the Biblical rocks that today's David could be slinging:

> In 1980, Reagan won Massachusetts by 2,500 votes! There were over a hundred thousand students unregistered, over 50,000 blacks, over 50,000 Hispanics. He won by 2,500. Ted Kennedy's state. Rocks just laying around.
>
> He won Illinois by 300,000 votes — 800,000 blacks were unregistered, 500,000 Hispanics, rocks just laying around! In 1980 three million high school students were unregistered to vote. Now they've registered to draft. Rocks still laying around!
>
> [snip]
>
> In 1980 Reagan won Pennsylvania by 300,000 votes, 400,000 students not registered. More than 600,000 blacks unregistered! Reagan won Pennsylvania by the margin of despair, by the margin of the fracture of our coalition.

The coalition had been well-fractured by the time Jackson got in, with most of the key endorsements already divvied up. Yet he still ran a race that drew thousands of new people into Democratic politics. He ran a thoroughly progressive campaign,[13] which was an outgrowth of the 1968 Poor People's Campaign, the King-led movement to bring together poor whites, blacks, Latinos and Native Americans to attack poverty and inequality. That movement had drawn its inspiration from the famous 1963 March on Washington for Jobs and Justice, of which the "I Have a Dream" speech is the legacy.

Jackson's campaign embraced single-payer health care, gay rights, called for ratification of the Equal Rights Amendment, free community college, reparations for descendants of slaves, gender pay equity and an end to Reagan's drug war, with a focus instead on banks who facilitate

---

13   That's not to say he was always a paragon of progressive perfection. Though his campaign was forward-thinking on women's rights, his own views were less so. "If you've got to choose between your wife, and an unborn baby — well, you shouldn't sacrifice her life," he said of his views on abortion in the 1979 book *The Tribes of America*. He went on to awkwardly explain how his personal opposition to abortion saved his marriage. "My life is very dynamic and, variety being the spice of life, alternatives keep occurring. But no outside woman could compete with my children for my affection. So my wife has kept some babies. But she kept more than that. She kept a husband and a house and some other things, too." In 2001, he acknowledged fathering a daughter with an aide of his out of wedlock.

26

money laundering.

He won five caucuses or primaries and more than 3 million votes, 18 percent of the total. Marable describes a familiar scene playing out on the convention floor, as Mondale, who had less than 39 percent of the vote, locked up the nomination. "A large bloc of convention delegates were directly selected by the party apparatus, virtually guaranteeing Mondale's nomination. In many states, the selection of convention delegates had little to do with the actual primary vote. For example, in Pennsylvania's primary, Jackson received 17 percent of the statewide popular vote to Mondale's 45 percent. On the convention floor, however, Mondale received 117 delegate votes to Jackson's 18," he wrote.

Mondale's campaign exists in our memories today as a feckless liberal effort. But in fact he ran to the center-right, applauding Reagan's invasion of Grenada; saying he'd be tougher than Reagan on the Soviet Union; and promising to cut spending and attack the deficit. The only promise he made that was traditionally associated with liberal Democrats was to raise taxes. "By the end of my first term, I will reduce the Reagan budget deficit by two-thirds," he vowed during his acceptance speech at the convention. "To the Congress, my message is: We must cut spending and pay as we go."

That political poison was injected into Mondale's speech, it would later emerge, by none other than Goldman Sachs' Robert Rubin, an archetype of the new type of Wall Street Democrat.[14]

"It was a completely incoherent campaign, relying on kind of a core of sentimental, post-New Deal liberalism, while promising to raise taxes/cut spending/eliminate the deficit," said Rich Yeselson, a longtime labor movement strategist.

While Jackson had made ending apartheid in South Africa a key moral plank in his campaign, using it as a proxy to challenge Reagan on racism, Mondale shied away from it. "Mondale took the black vote absolutely for granted, and devoted nearly his entire campaign to courting fractions of the white electorate which historically had voted for Republican presidential candidates," Manning concluded in his essay the next year.

But Reagan Republicans were not on some historically inexorable

---

14   Mondale told journalist Robert Kuttner about Rubin's influence on his speech for a 2007 profile in The American Prospect. It's also mentioned in Kuttner's book on Obama, A Presidency in Peril. Mondale lost, so Rubin had no chance to corrupt his administration, but he didn't miss the opportunity to do so with the next two. He served as Bill Clinton's Treasury Secretary and oversaw a wave of deregulation of Wall Street. His proteges, Larry Summers, Tim Geithner, and Peter Orszag, among others, would serve, to disastrous effect, in the Obama administration. Rubin went to Citigroup where he helped blow up the world economy.

glide toward a permanent majority. Tom Harkin, running on a progressive populist platform, won his first Senate race that year in Iowa. The liberal Paul Simon, who the young Rahm Emanuel was detailed to, knocked off a popular veteran Republican in Illinois. Then in 1986, Democrats re-took the Senate and made further gains in the House as the Iran-Contra scandal hobbled Reagan, leaving an expectation that the White House would swing their way in 1988.

By that year, Jackson was better prepared and organized, and the team that had formed around him in '84 knew what it was doing. His strong showing gave him credibility, which came with endorsements, including one by Burlington Mayor Bernie Sanders and another by Paul Wellstone, who chaired Jackson's campaign in Minnesota two years before he was elected senator. ("It was a big deal. I respect him very much," Jackson said[15] in 2019 in Selma.)

Catapulted by the Michigan upset, Jackson surged into Wisconsin, where he was already polling ahead. A win there would be an exclamation mark on his Midwest tour, and launch him toward the convention with a strong argument that he was well positioned to unite and inspire black voters, liberals of all races and white working-class voters ready to push back against economic oppression. At a rally outside a Chrysler plant that was due to close, Jackson zeroed in on his message that the question of class versus race missed the point, that only by uniting across race and gender in a "rainbow coalition" could the people confront the forces waging "economic violence" in the Midwest.

Gephardt surveyed the post-Michigan landscape and dropped out, leaving just Jackson and Dukakis.

Talk in the top echelons of the Democratic Party turned to panic, with David Espo of the Associated Press reporting that the establishment feared a general-election blowout if Jackson was the nominee. Plans were being drawn up, he reported, to draft New York Governor Mario Cuomo to challenge Jackson at the convention if Dukakis couldn't stop the reverend.

E.J. Dionne, then reporting for the New York Times, captured the sense of dread.

> White Democratic leaders who do not support Mr. Jackson admitted they were in a quandary, wondering how to confront the growing movement toward Mr. Jackson without appearing to be racist and without alienating the large core of activists, including many white liberals, that he has attracted....
>
> Around Washington, the words used by leading white Democrats to describe their party's situation included crisis, disarray, disaster, consternation, mess, and wacky.

15   Jackson was asked about Sanders' endorsement of his campaign by Huff-Post's Daniel Marans, who provided me the audio of the event and the exchange.

> "You've never heard a sense of panic sweep the party as it has in the last few days," said David Garth, an adviser to Senator Albert Gore Jr. of Tennessee.
>
> Mr. Garth predicted that '"the anti-Jackson constituency, when the reality of his becoming President seeps in, may be a much bigger constituency than there is out there right now."

Jackson, the Democratic political class argued, was simply unelectable, so the party should go with a winner like Dukakis. Rep. Barney Frank's sister, Ann Lewis, was working for the Jackson campaign, but Frank was backing his home state governor. He explained to Dionne that there were two reasons Jackson couldn't win. "One, there is unfortunately still racism in the country....That doesn't mean the whole country's prejudiced. It means that if there's an irreducible 15 or 20 percent prejudice against a particular group, you're giving away an awful lot," Frank said. "Two, he's still to the left of the country, especially on foreign policy."

Jackson's opponents had argued that his proximity to the nomination would paradoxically push some white Democrats away from him. It's all fine and good to vote for the charismatic black guy with the unifying message in 1988 — indeed, it was an anti-racist badge of honor — just not if he actually might win.[16] The party establishment pulled the fire alarm. I asked Jackson what kind of pressure he felt after his Michigan win. "The pressure was not on me," he said. "It was the so-called Reagan Democrats who began sowing discord and spreading lies."

The cynics were right; the polls were wrong. Dukakis won solidly in Wisconsin, stunting Jackson's momentum. Over the next month, Dukakis would win Pennsylvania, New York, Ohio and Indiana, and while Jackson continued picking off a state here and some delegates there, the nomination contest was effectively over. As is often the case, political wisdom failed the party elite, and Dukakis[17] was crushed by George H.W. Bush, on the back of a racist attack around Willie Horton.[18]

---

16   Those white voters may not have been the only ones to get cold feet about a Jackson White House. Dean Baker said that years later, in 2007, he appeared several times on television with Jesse Jackson Jr. His father, Jackson Jr. told Baker, went into a full-blown panic after Michigan. He had run to get his message out, Jackson Jr. said, but the prospect of becoming president hadn't occurred to him at the outset.

17   I was once the third person on a three-way phone call with Dukakis and fellow Greek American Arianna Huffington when the pair broke into an extended conversation in Greek.

18   Horton, serving life for murder, was released on a weekend furlough program and didn't returned. He later raped a woman before being re-arrested. The furlough program was first criticized not by Bush but by Al Gore in a debate during the primary. The Bush campaign, watching the debate, went looking for a Horton.

But with the act of forming a campaign team, Jackson had opened opportunities to people of color to enter politics.

The late Dr. Ronald Walters, a University of Maryland professor who was a deputy manager of Jackson's team, once told me he often ran into veterans of that campaign on his lecture tours.

"A number of people will come up to me and say, 'I'm a member of city council now,' or, 'I'm on the school board now.' It created a whole generation of elected officials," Walters said. Some of those officials weren't actually on the campaign. "You go to these places now and everyone was a Jackson delegate," he told me during an interview in 2007.[19] "It's kind of like a folk tale. It's become sort of an iconic moment in African-American history."

Using the political capital earned during the 1984 and 1988 presidential campaigns, the Jackson camp negotiated major rules changes that opened the party process to minorities.

His 1984 and '88 campaigns paved the way for the rise of a generation of black leaders inside the Democratic Party. "So many leaders of the African-American community have come from that campaign. He was the one," said Tina Flournoy, who has worked in the top levels of the Democratic Party and became assistant to the president of the American Federation of Teachers.

The list of those who started in or got a break from a Jackson campaign is a "Who's Who" of top minorities, most of them African American, in the Democratic Party.

Among them: Donna Brazile, the first black person to manage a presidential campaign (Al Gore's) and later the acting head of the DNC; Minyon Moore, who was President Clinton's political affairs director; Yolanda Caraway, a former top official of the Democratic National Committee and now CEO of The Caraway Group; the Rev. Leah Daughtry, a longtime veteran of the DNC who oversaw two conventions; and Alexis Herman, the first black secretary of labor (under President Clinton).

A savvy grasp of the system paved the way for Ron Brown to win the race for the DNC's chairmanship in 1989. "Ron's campaign couldn't lose. His becoming DNC chair came right out of that campaign," Jackson told me.

"Jackson opened that door," Brazile said.[20]

---

19   That story ran in Politico, where I was a reporter before joining The Huffington Post.

20   "Then we went from there to Ron Brown," Brazile added. Brown brought to the DNC, among others, Bill Morton, his top aide; Daughtry; Herman; Maurice Daniel; Harold Ford Jr., who later became a congressman from Tennessee, then an executive at Morgan Stanley and regular on "Morning Joe"; and David Mercer, who

An entire class of elected Democratic officials also graduated from the Jackson campaign, including Rep. Barbara Lee of California; Los Angeles Mayor Antonio Villaraigosa; Rep. Maxine Waters of California; Jesse Jackson Jr., who represented the Chicago district that was his father's political base; and Carol Moseley Braun, the first African American woman elected to the Senate.

The viability of the New Jacksonian remake of the coalition was demonstrated in the years after his run.[21] The 1984 campaign had registered two million new voters, most of them African American, and not coincidentally, Doug Wilder became the first black official elected statewide since Reconstruction when he won his race for lieutenant governor in Virginia in 1985.

In the 1986 midterms, those two million new voters made a big difference. Democrats netted eight seats to win control of the Senate, beating six senators who'd been elected in 1980 with Reagan. The new senators were white, but many won extremely tight races in the South and were powered by black voters. Democrats won seats in Alabama, Florida, Georgia, North Carolina and Louisiana. Harry Reid won his first Senate race that year by 14,000 votes in Nevada.

Another million voters were registered by the '88 campaign, and a wave of advances came the next two years. Wilder was elected Virginia governor by just 6,000 votes. The first African American mayor was elected in New York, Seattle and Durham, the second was elected in Cleveland.

The two then-obscure white backers of Jackson also saw surprise

---

ran Midwest operations for Brown's successful run for DNC chairman and is now owner of Mercer and Associates, Inc. Elsewhere, Brown found spots for minority operatives throughout the Democratic Party structure. Bringing in strategists whose life experience differed so greatly from their white counterparts led to a subtle change in how the party oriented itself toward its coalition, even if the dominant impulse was still to win back those boll weevils.

Brown organized the party's 1992 national convention and hired a number of black operatives in key positions: Caraway, director of site selection; Herman, convention CEO; Flournoy, general counsel; Mario Cooper, convention manager; Daughtry, managing director; and Maxine Griffin, hall manager. It was the most diverse convention organizing staff the party had ever assembled. Maurice Daniel said he and others considered themselves to be graduates of the Ron Brown school: "I try to live what Ron Brown always said: 'Reach back and lift up as you climb.'" When Brown was named secretary of commerce in 1993, he also brought his protégés into the administration, as did Moore as White House political director.

21   Thanks to Steve Cobble, a close adviser to Jackson, who compiled research on the downstream electoral effects of the '84 and '88 runs.

wins. Wellstone upset his Republican opponent, the only Senate candidate to beat an incumbent in 1990. And that same year, Vermont elected democratic socialist Bernie Sanders to the House of Representatives for the first time. The next year, as a freshman, he brought a handful of other independent-minded lawmakers together — including Lane Evans, a rural populist who managed to represent a Republican district as a leftist for 24 years; and Ron Dellums, the first DSA member to serve in Congress; Maxine Waters and Peter DeFazio — to found the Congressional Progressive Caucus.[22]

Jackson delegate Moseley Braun's Senate election came in 1992, and that year, despite Clinton's Sister Souljah moment at Jackson's convention, black voters powered Clinton to a narrow plurality.

Jackson's 1988 run is one of the great roads-untraveled in Democratic history. Could Jackson have beaten George H.W. Bush? If he had run a strong race, what would it have done to shape the soul of the party? How many more millions could the party have registered in a general election with Jackson at the top of the ticket? If the party had started organizing its grassroots base and appealing to white working-class voters[23] in economic terms rather than with racial resentment, could a workable coalition have been built? Could the rapid expansion of mass incarceration throughout the 1990s been avoided? Could the nation's rightward drift been slowed or reversed?

We'll never know, but most of the Democratic elite at the time would have said that in their hearts they were for Jackson, but in their heads they were for the more pragmatic choice of Dukakis.

But there was a lot more going on in those hearts and minds. It's common for people to say that in the 1970s the party became too liberal, and corrected by moving toward the center. But what's often left out of the conversation is the necessary verbiage, however uncomfortable it might be. The party had become more progressive not because of flower-power, the counter culture or some liberal softening of hearts. What people meant by too liberal was that it had become too cozy with blacks.

22   Waters now chairs the Financial Services Committee and DeFazio chairs the Transportation Committee. He represents a split district, but has legislated as an outspoken progressive.

23   As new research and intuition makes clear, when thinking about white working-class voters, you must separate evangelicals from non-evangelicals. The former are hardcore Republicans and not worth pursuing — indeed, research shows that attempting to persuade them only hardens and intensifies their opposition to progressivism. But among non-evangelicals, progressive messaging resonates strongly, but that phenomenon gets drowned out in the polling and the cultural conversation because evangelicals are lumped in with the rest.

The success of the black freedom and women's liberation movements accelerated a realignment of the parties — more women and people of color became Democrats, and more white racists became Republicans — but party leaders resisted this realignment until the bitter end, worried about being called too liberal.

The resistance to the realignment was chipped away at during the 1988 convention, when Jackson forced a rules change that would have a profound effect. Winner-take-all primaries were moved toward proportional representation, as long as a candidate got at least 15 percent.

Without that rule change, Barack Obama would not have won the 2008 nomination. "Barack Obama won big in 2008 with a diverse, young, expanded electorate modeled on Jackson's 1988 rainbow coalition successes," said Steve Cobble, a senior adviser to Jackson's campaigns.

But it would take two decades from his run for the party to learn that lesson. Its first order of business was to get Jesse Jackson and his coalition back in line. Four years after Jackson's run, Bill Clinton won the Democratic nomination in 1992. That summer, at the height of the general election, Clinton accepted an invitation from Jackson to speak at his annual Rainbow Coalition conference. With Jackson on stage, Clinton used the platform to rip into an obscure Bronx rapper, whose videos didn't play on MTV at the time and who had by then never topped 78 on Billboard.

"Let's stand up for what's always been best about the Rainbow Coalition, which is people coming together across racial lines," Clinton began, then made his move. "You had a rap star here last night, Sister Souljah. I defend her right to express herself through music."

Clinton then quoted Sister Souljah, making it appear as if she had recently called for black people to kill whites in the wake of the Los Angeles-Rodney King riots. In fact, Time magazine wrote then, "she was trying to explain the mind-set of black youths who have experienced so much violence at the hands of whites that murder means nothing to them."

"I know she is a young person, but she has a big influence on a lot of people," Clinton said, a statement that only became true the minute he uttered it. "If you took the words white and black and reversed them, you might think David Duke was giving that speech."

It became one of Clinton's touchstone political moments, defining the coming era of Democratic politics. It's talked about as a way for Clinton to win over white moderates and conservatives by showing he was willing to take on the base of his own party. But that misses a major purpose of the attack — it was not just a means to another end, hitting Jackson was an end in itself. The Rainbow Coalition represented the biggest threat to the Clinton wing's party dominance. Jackson demanded an apology, but never got one. It was Bill Clinton's party now.

Three

Pelosi's Party

The stench of money is so strong in politics it can overwhelm the ability to detect any other odor. That was the case in the office of Sen. John Stennis heading into the 1982 midterms. A longtime Mississippi Democrat, Stennis was facing a challenge from a well-funded and fired-up Haley Barbour,[24] then in his 30s. Stennis had been in the Senate since 1947 and had never raised more than $5,000 for a campaign.

After the thumping Democrats took in 1980, campaign consultant Ray Strother was tasked with making sure Stennis was reelected. Strother told Stennis, as part of the party's shift toward big money in the midst of the realignment, he would need $2 million to spend on television ads to fend off Barbour. The ads would show him being active and looking not-completely-decrepit, which Strother argued would be enough to get him another six-year term. Stennis told him he couldn't fathom how he could raise that amount of money.[25]

Strother later recalled, "Finally, in desperation, I reminded the old senator that he was chairman of Armed Services and had spent billions

---

24   Barbour would go on to become the state's governor as well as the B in BGR Group, a Republican lobbying shop known for representing unscrupulous world leaders and major corporations. Crowley turned to them to hold a fundraiser for him in the final stretch of his losing campaign to Ocasio-Cortez.

25   The exchange was first reported in Robert Kaiser's book *So Damn Much Money*. He drew it from Strother's memoir, *Falling Up*, and from an interview with Strother.

of dollars with the defense industry. What about LTV? I asked him. What about McDonnell Douglas?"

In other words, Mississippi's weapons makers, fattened at Stennis' hand, needed to pay up.

Stennis stopped him cold with a question. "Would that be proper?"

He answered it himself. "I hold life and death over those companies. I don't think it would be proper for me to take money from them."

Strother told him that it may be wrong, but everybody was doing it. "When I left his office he was looking at his folded hands on the table in his office that had once belonged to Harry Truman. It looked as though he was in prayer. I was very sad," Strother later said.[26]

Stennis ultimately raised the money, produced the ads and waxed Barbour. It was a good year for Democrats. With the economy tanking, the party made gains in the '82 midterms, and the shift toward corporate money was given the credit.

The Stennis anecdote is told as a tale of innocence lost in the book *So Damn Much Money,* by Washington Post reporter Robert Kaiser, and first appeared in a memoir by Strother. But the vignette overlooks a critical element of the story that puts it in an entirely different context. Stennis, principled as he may have been about campaign finance, was also a staunch white supremacist, one of the most racist senators to serve in the 20th Century.

His racism was not a political put-on. As a Mississippi prosecutor, he had tried three black men for murder even though he knew their confessions had been extracted by torture. The Supreme Court, in a landmark case, *Brown v. Mississippi* in 1936, ruled confessions by torture were inadmissible — a moment that managed to mark progress. He was an ardent and unapologetic segregationist, and fought against every significant piece of civil rights legislation he could. In 1964, he broke with LBJ and endorsed Barry Goldwater, citing Johnson's civil rights support. He was one of just two Senate Democrats to vote against the Equal Rights Amendment for women in 1972 and was instrumental in later killing it. When President Nixon was trying to stave off releasing his damning White House tapes, he offered the Stennis Compromise, which would allow the hard-of-hearing Stennis to listen to and summarize them instead.

He was still an unreconstructed racist in the 1980s, and, after winning reelection in 1982, had long since stopped being a remotely reliable member of the Democratic caucus on civil rights, women's rights or even economic populism.[27]

---

26   Ibid.

27   He did vote against Judge Robert Bork, which meant his voting record

The case of Stennis offers another layer of context to what was happening to the party in the 1980s. The perceived need for corporate cash was a direct response to the exodus of a pillar of the 20th Century Democratic coalition: the white working class, particularly in the South. In a decision that would have grave consequences for the party and the country, that money was used not to find a new coalition, but to try to salvage the old one.

The money, meanwhile, gradually transformed the message the party was able to deliver, and so having already lost on racial terms — the Democrats weren't racist enough — it lost on economic populism, too.

Rahm Emanuel would grow to become one of the greatest practitioners of the craft of blending big dollar fundraising, corporate-friendly politics and policy ideas so marginal they don't even deserve to be called incremental.

Rahm Israel Emanuel was born in November 1959, a year before JFK was elected. Stennis had already been in the Senate for 12 years. Like dozens of others in Congress, Stennis had never officially switched parties but was a Republican in all but name. He was one of a group calling themselves boll weevils, after a pest that feasted on cotton plants and was difficult to eradicate.

Stennis had first come to the Senate by winning a special election in 1947 to replace the notorious racist Theodore Bilbo. In 1948, Stennis helped lead a walkout of the Mississippi delegation at the presidential convention in Philadelphia, instead holding a rival Dixiecrat convention in Birmingham, where the renegades nominated Strom Thurmond for president.

The walkout and the Dixiecrat revolt complicate the narrative that Democrats try to tell, which is that it was the 1964 Civil Rights Act that had reshaped the parties. In reality, the realignment had started long before, yet party leaders had spent half a century, as the case of Stennis attests, trying to slow it down. Stennis finally retired — still a Democrat — in 1989.

Republican Dwight Eisenhower, in the presidential campaign of 1952 and then again in 1956, had made major inroads into the Democratic South through an alliance between Northern Republicans and Southern segregationists,[28] but he set that cause back in 1957 by sending federal troops to integrate Central High School in Little Rock (even though he

---

was at least better than Haley Barbour's would have been. Bork, though, went down 58-42, so it wasn't close. Reagan then turned to Douglas Ginsburg, who had so many problems he didn't get a vote. His third nominee was Anthony Kennedy, who was confirmed and would eventually become the Court's swing vote.

28   This was a long-running project of the National Review.

swore he was sending them only to keep the peace, not to desegregate the school or enforce *Brown*), as well as by signing the Civil Rights Act of that year.

That drove a wedge between Eisenhower and the Northern Republicans pushing for the Southern alliance, and John Kennedy in 1960 was able to win a sizable portion of the black vote. The South, though, wasn't ready to switch sides. Richard Nixon had not yet sharpened his racial rhetoric, and, in one of the moments that makes plain that progress does not march inexorably forward, he was a stronger supporter of civil rights in 1960 than he would be in '68.

Republican Nelson Rockefeller, a liberal New York governor, had run against Nixon in the primary. To head off a fight on the convention floor, Nixon traveled to Rockefeller's mansion to make peace, in what came to be known as "the Surrender of Fifth Avenue." Nixon agreed that the GOP platform would endorse the lunch-counter sit-ins going on at the time, and called for "aggressive action" against racial discrimination.

This was no platform for Dixie, so voters in Mississippi and Alabama threw their weight behind unpledged electors, rather than Kennedy and Lyndon Johnson. Those electors[29] cast their ballots for a non-existent ticket, made up of Sen. Harry Byrd, a diehard segregationist from Virginia, and Strom Thurmond.

Democrats pushed hard for progress on both civil rights and economic policy, and were rewarded at the polls. Kennedy's assassination made Johnson president, and Goldwater was delivered a sweeping rebuke in the 1964 elections. The Great Society,[30] passed largely in the 1965-'66 term, added Medicare, Medicaid and a host of other programs to the New Deal to take some of the sting out of modern life.

Emanuel's parents were actively involved in the civil rights movement and Democratic Party politics, and each new development was grist for the family's lively dinner-table debates. As progress was being made domestically, the party was slowly growing the number of men and boys stationed in Vietnam, for no clear reason that anybody could articulate, beyond the "domino theory," the nonsensical notion the U.S. had to go to war in one country to prevent some other countries from becoming communist. The war, along with the rest of the death and misery it left behind, further fractured the New Deal coalition, with white suburban men supporting the effort and lashing out at anti-war protesters and the counterculture broadly.

---

29   Thanks to the Great Migration, the number of electors assigned to those states fell throughout the century.

30   The book *The Liberal Hour: Washington and the Politics of Change in the 1960s,* is good on this.

Democrats, even as they became the party of "acid, abortion and amnesty,"[31] still nearly won the 1968 presidential election, such was the support for the party's creation of a robust welfare state.

By early 1968, the draft was in full swing and the war was a disaster; an ongoing series of atrocities and relentless carpet bombings were bringing it no closer to an end. Widespread protests against the carnage blended with a surging counterculture; drug use and crime were on the rise. Riots played out in major cities in response to police shootings and other abuses, rage boiling over. But a movement of young people, largely college students and their cohort, dove into Democratic Party politics. The insurgents of their day, they got behind Eugene McCarthy, who launched a longshot bid against LBJ on an anti-war platform. The kids shaved, cut their hair and put on their Sunday best to knock on doors in a phenomenon that came to be called "getting clean for Gene."

It worked. McCarthy came dangerously close to beating Johnson in New Hampshire. Seeing the weakness, Robert Kennedy, also against the war, jumped in the race. Johnson's internal polls showed his support fading, and in March he simultaneously announced a pause in bombing and the end of his reelection campaign.

The campaign would soon get a new contestant, sort of. When Thurmond, Stennis, and the rest of the Dixiecrats had staged their convention walkout 20 years earlier, they did so at a specific moment, as Hubert Humphrey was delivering a thundering speech on the necessity of a strong civil rights platform.[32] "My friends, to those who say that we are rushing this issue of civil rights, I say to them we are 172 years late. To those who say that this civil rights program is an infringement on states' rights, I say this: The time has arrived in America for the Democratic Party to get out of the shadow of states' rights and to walk forthrightly into the bright sunshine of human rights," he told the convention.

Humphrey was then mayor of Minneapolis and on his way to an im-

---

31   The first version of this attack ironically came from Democratic Sen. Tom Eagleton, who said it anonymously to columnist Bob Novak about George McGovern in 1972. Ironically, McGovern briefly picked Eagleton to be his running mate. After Eagleton's death, Novak outed him as the source. Amnesty had nothing to do with immigration, but rather referred to the call for pardons for draft dodgers.

32   You can find it easily on YouTube. Give it a watch. He previewed an argument that would later be used regularly by Kennedy, that the world was watching, and that if the U.S. wanted to win the Cold War against the Soviet Union it couldn't preach freedom abroad and embrace Jim Crow at home. The Soviet Union, for its part, made sure to highlight U.S. hypocrisy, just as RT never misses a chance to do today.

pressive Senate career, which would eventually include authorship of the ill-fated Humphrey-Hawkins Act, the most ambitious guaranteed jobs bill ever pushed in Congress. By 1968 he was Johnson's vice president, and declared his intent to seek the presidency. But because of the way the party was structured then, he didn't have to campaign, planning instead for the party's bosses to nominate him at the Chicago convention.[33]

So the contest went on between Kennedy and McCarthy, with Kennedy winning most of the head-to-heads. McCarthy's base of college students and upscale liberals was outnumbered by Kennedy's, which brought together black, white, and Latino working-class people. The night he won the California primary, however, he was gunned down in the kitchen after delivering his victory speech.

Humphrey, who was an internal White House opponent of the war, refused to break publicly with Johnson, and the anti-war movement stayed firmly behind McCarthy. South Dakota Sen. George McGovern entered as a last-minute candidate, and after the hostile primary season, the "Dump the Hump" forces were unable to unite to stop Humphrey. Convention boss Richard Daley, mayor of Chicago, arranged the delegates for Humphrey, as outside, a full-blown police riot played out live on television.

In most tellings of the story, Humphrey "never recovered" from the convention chaos, allowing Nixon to be elected. But that glosses over the final result, with Nixon beating Humphrey by less than a single point. As we look across history for examples of Democrats losing elections as the result of an unwillingness to stand behind a set of values, it would be hard to find a clearer example than Humphrey in '68. Historians are nearly unanimous that Humphrey's support of Johnson's war policy cost him the election. It also cost the lives of thousands more Americans and hundreds of thousands of more Vietnamese, Cambodians and Laotians, as Nixon ground forward with the war.

The back of the Democratic coalition was broken, even as it was making steady domestic progress, and for what?

As the GOP's alliance with white supremacists in the south deepened, first with Nixon and then later with Reagan, Democrats responded not by leaning into the values that made them a cohesive and coherent political coalition, but with a strategy that zeroed in on winning back those angry white men. That, they believed, was to be accomplished by attacking the New Deal and Great Society in order to prove Democrats were not spend-happy liberals. And that, in turn, opened up the spigots of big business, who saw that the Democratic Party was ready to do business.

Joe Biden, elected to the Senate in 1972, was a leading voice in the

33   This was before primaries had been reformed to give voters more of a say.

attempt to win back white working-class voters by showing them how tough Democrats could be against affirmative, school integration, and other priorities of the civil rights movement. "I do not buy the concept, popular in the '60s, which said, 'We have suppressed the black man for 300 years and the white man is now far ahead in the race for everything our society offers. In order to even the score, we must now give the black man a head start, or even hold the white man back, to even the race. I don't buy that," Biden told a Delaware weekly newspaper in 1975.[34] "I don't feel responsible for the sins of my father and grandfather. I feel responsible for what the situation is today, for the sins of my own generation. And I'll be damned if I feel responsible to pay for what happened 300 years ago."

In 1973, during a speech at the City Club in Cleveland, Biden told an audience that the Nixon-era resurgence of Republicans in the South was a good thing. "I think the two-party system," he said,[35] "although my Democratic colleagues won't like my saying this, is good for the South and good for the Negro, good for the black in the South. Other than the fact that [southern Senators] still call me *boy*, I think they've changed their mind a little bit."

Jimmy Carter's malaise-filled four years were something of an accident; progressives were dominant in the party, but Carter squeaked through as a conservative with support from just a minority of the party, thanks in significant part to a fawning profile of him in Rolling Stone by Hunter S. Thompson. The Georgia governor was barely known outside his state. Journalist Bob Kuttner was working at the Washington Post at the time, and was assigned to cover his announcement. "I was one of about five reporters to show up, and the Post put my story on the shipping page," he recalled.

Birch Bayh, a progressive senator from Indiana, was seen by the television networks as the frontrunner, and was accorded their top reporters.[36] Mo Udall, the liberal and famously witty congressman from Arizona, was also in the running. But in Iowa, Carter finished a surprising first — but with just 28 percent of the vote. Still, that was nearly double Bayh's total. Just behind him was Fred Harris, a leftist former Oklahoma senator. "Fred Harris was kind of a Bernie Sanders who didn't catch fire in 1976," said Rich Yeselson, who worked on Harris' campaign. "He was

---

34   Quote unearthed by Matt Viser in the Washington Post, March 7, 2019: "Biden's tough talk on 1970s school desegregation plan could get new scrutiny in today's Democratic Party."

35   Audio of the speech was posted by the City Club in May 2019.

36   Back then, covering a campaign was a prestigious assignment. Today, it's given to entry level reporters while the big guns parachute in when so moved.

a left-wing populist, critical of the Democratic Party's centrists, including the ultimate nominee, Jimmy Carter. But looking backward, he also was a link to Oklahoma's political history when the state had a strong socialist presence in the early 1900s."

The real winner in Iowa was nobody. Thirty-seven percent of Iowa voters simply registered "no preference." Udall, likely hurt by anti-Mormon prejudice, came in fourth. In New Hampshire a month later, Carter won again, this time with, again, just 28 percent of the vote, as the rest was split among the various liberals. Segregationist George Wallace, a remnant of the party's Dixiecrats, had by then gotten into the race but he barely registered in New Hampshire.

Carter continued winning most of the primaries and caucuses through February and March in similarly anemic fashion.[37] As the field winnowed, his numbers crept up, and he picked up momentum as the campaign swung through the South, finally cracking 50 percent in North Carolina late in March. Yet on April 6, Udall looked to have beaten him in Wisconsin. As late returns came in, Carter came from behind and won. A number of papers reported the results wrong — Udall wins! — but the final 37-36 tally for Carter gave him another jolt.

What we think of as the left still hadn't unified behind a single alternative to Carter. A heavy amount of union support was going to Scoop Jackson, who was a combination of a leftist on economic policy and a neoconservative whose aggressive foreign policy views would later be championed by folks like Dick Cheney. He won more than a million votes, and his strong showing is a reminder of Big Labor's militaristic posture during that era.[38] By not getting behind one of the liberals, labor helped clear the way for Carter.

Alarm bells started to go off among progressives, as they realized that a conservative from Georgia was on track to win the nomination with far less than majority support. An "Anybody But Carter" effort was launched, and liberals Jerry Brown and Frank Church jumped into the race late. Brown started to catch fire, beating Carter in his first primary, in Maryland.

Then there were six contests on a single day in late May: Carter won Arkansas, Kentucky and Tennessee, but Church took his home state of Idaho, as well as Oregon, and Brown won Nevada convincingly. All of a sudden, the race was alive.

---

37   Winning 30 percent of the field in a crowded primary was Donald Trump's route to the nomination, and the one Bernie Sanders hopes to take, too.

38   Unlike Cheney, Jackson was a down-the-line, strong liberal on domestic policy. In fact, maybe even more than down-the-line. His approach to the economy probably wouldn't have clashed much with that of Bernie Sanders.

Or, it might have been, if it weren't already too late. Wallace, running his explicitly racist campaign, had picked up more than 2 million votes. Carter won the nomination with just 40 percent, and easily beat the hapless Gerald Ford. Once in office, he was in open warfare with unions. "I'd love the Teamsters to be worse off," Carter adviser Alfred Kahn said bluntly.[39] "I'd love the automobile workers to be worse off. You may say that's inhumane; I'm putting it rather baldly, but I want to eliminate a situation in which certain protected workers in industries insulated from competition can increase their wages much more rapidly than the average [worker] without regard to their merit or to what a free market would do."

The landmark labor reform legislation that unions had been banking on to help them fight the tide of capital's growing strength fell just short in the Senate, with the White House barely lifting a finger to pass it. "We didn't try for revolutionary things; we pushed for things we thought we could get broad support for," said Ray Marshall who served as labor secretary in the Carter administration.

Ted Kennedy, in an effort to attack the growing strength of organized capital, began pushing a sweeping update to antitrust laws. Had it become law, the next 30 years of corporate mergers and acquisitions may have unfolded quite differently, but he ran into the determined opposition of Delaware Sen. Joe Biden, whose alliance[40] with Republicans on the issue was enough to stop it.

Carter, despite his progressive reputation, began the process of deregulation — including in the airline industry — that is normally associated with Reagan, with, perhaps just as strangely, Kennedy as the lead Democratic deregulator in the Senate. The airlines, for instance, were something of a mess. Tight regulation gave them a monopolistic attitude, and prices were high while the product was poor. The push for deregulation was broadly popular. In other industries, it wasn't what the public was clamoring for. A 1980 bill Carter signed, for instance, called the Depository Institutions Deregulation and Monetary Control Act, paved the way for mortgage-backed securities, which were at the root of the 2008 financial crisis.

Carter cut taxes for the wealthy and corporations and hiked them for the middle class. "Government cannot solve our problems, it can't set our goals, it cannot define our vision. Government cannot eliminate poverty or provide a bountiful economy or reduce inflation or save

39   As quoted in Thomas Frank's book *Listen, Liberal Or, Whatever Happened to the Party of People?*
40   This history was covered by Zach Carter in HuffPost in 2019, in an article headlined, "Joe Biden's Biggest 2020 Problem: Joe Biden."

our cities or cure illiteracy or provide energy," he promised during his 1978 State of the Union address. Later that year, he beamed himself into living rooms just ahead of the midterm elections with a dour warning: "Reducing the deficit will require difficult and unpleasant decisions. We must face a time of national austerity. Hard choices are necessary if we want to avoid consequences that are even worse."[41]

The 1978 midterms saw Democrats lose 15 seats in the House and three in the Senate. One of the newcomers was Newt Gingrich, who led the rise of what was called the New Right, a group of revolutionaries who were not interested in conserving anything, but upending the existing order.

For all of his success and well-earned popularity in his post-presidential years, Carter was, with some significant exceptions[42] for which he is rightly heralded, just bad at being president. His hostility to the left earned him a primary challenge by Ted Kennedy in 1980, though Kennedy, on some key economic issues, wasn't far to his left. Given what happened at Chappaquiddick, Kennedy was what pundits would call a flawed candidate; nonetheless, he almost knocked off the sitting president. With unions beaten down and progressives demobilized, Carter went into the general election a man without a coalition.

Carter's rejection of everything the party had stood for on economic policy was just the beginning of the party's embrace of austerity and conservative economics. One of the peculiarities of racism is the way in which it blinds the racist. Democrats saw support for the party fading, but because white men are the most visible political figures in the imagination of white politicians, as well as the media, the establishment class could only see its way out of the problem it was in by focusing narrowly on those white men. The rhetoric, policy and big money needed to win over those white men had collateral damage on the rest of the coalition, but white Democratic leaders couldn't see that, either.

While pumping big money into some races managed to save, for the time being, politicians like Mississippi's Stennis, the losses suffered in the 1980s and again in 1994 were in many ways inevitable once Democrats settled on appeasement of white grievance as the strategy. A moderate racist could never satisfy those grievances as well as an extreme one, and boll weevils were replaced by arch conservative Republicans, either through elections, retirement or, in some cases, party switching.

---

41   Both of these Carter quotes come from an October 2018 talk at Brown University by Rick Perlstein, titled, "Jimmy Carter and the Origins of the Democratic Party Cult of Austerity."

42   The Egypt-Israel Peace Treaty, for one. He was also ahead of his time on renewable energy, putting solar panels on the roof of the White House.

By focusing on a lack of big money as the cause of the party's decline and scratching and clawing to keep express segregationists in office as Democrats, the party likely slowed the realignment, and, by alienating its would-be supporters, weakened its own base and delayed the comeback.

The Democratic Party's approach to winning elections is rooted in decisions party leaders made in the immediate aftermath of Ronald Reagan's White House win in 1980. That year saw not just Jimmy Carter's surprise loss but a generation of liberal lions wiped out in the Senate. A net loss of 12 senators — many of whom had been liberal heroes for decades — from the Democratic caucus flipped the chamber to Republicans.

It's hard to overstate just how politically traumatizing that election was for Democrats. It came just two years after the rise of the New Right, the class of '78 right-wingers led by firebrands like Gingrich, and it felt like the country was repudiating everything the party stood for, which was — which was what, exactly?

And Democrats hadn't just been rejected for a moderate Republican like a Gerald Ford, but the nation had said it would rather be led by a radical like Reagan. The party that had saved the world from the Nazis, built the modern welfare state, gone to the moon and overseen the longest stretch of economic prosperity in human history was being routed by an actor.

Yet if they had to look closer, they couldn't help but admit that things had been rocky. Inflation felt out of control, wages were flat, gas lines were long and the new Islamic Republic of Iran was holding 52 Americans hostage.

The liberals of the day argued that Reagan's victory came because Carter was too conservative to deliver what people had demanded of the party, particularly to the working class in general and organized labor in particular.[43]

It was the losses in the Senate, though, that particularly rocked the party, as the slow-moving realignment jerked forward. Longtime Senators Frank Church and Birch Bayh, recent contenders for the White House, lost reelection. Mike Gravel, the anti-war hero from Alaska, didn't even win the Democratic nomination.[44] Presidential candidate George McGovern, who'd been in the Senate since 1962, fell. Warren

---

43   Jefferson Cowie's book, *Stayin' Alive: The 1970s and the Last Days of the Working Class*, is good on this, and the best book on the cultural and political shifts of the '70s generally.

44   Frank Murkowski, the father of future senator Lisa Murkowski, won the general election. Gravel is running for president in 2020.

Magnuson and Gaylord Nelson, who had collectively served for 54 years, both lost. "My timing was terrible," complained Barney Frank in his memoir, recounting his 1980 election to the House. "I had arrived at the party just when the curfew went into effect."

It wasn't just liberals who got wrecked. In North Carolina, Georgia, Florida and Alabama, Democratic incumbents — some populist, some conservative — either lost their primary or the general election. Democrats sifting through the wreckage could pick and choose data points to fit whatever analysis they wanted to make.

On the one hand, longtime liberal champions had been massively outspent, with Republicans deploying big money and negative television advertising for the first time on a mass scale.[45] On the other hand, Southern conservatives had been wiped out too, so maybe the problem wasn't that the party was too liberal. But wait: Democratic senators in Kentucky, Arkansas, South Carolina, Missouri and Louisiana had won reelection, so maybe the party *was* too liberal.

And then there was the House, where Republicans picked up 35 seats — more than Democrats would subsequently flip in their wave year of 2006. But the southern wall was too high, and the wave crashed back to the sea. Democrats came into 1981 still in control of the House.

Democrats were so confident that they would never lose the House, that the losses were easy to ignore. John Lawrence arrived in Washington as a congressional aide in 1974, washed in by the Watergate wave. After serving as Nancy Pelosi's longtime chief of staff, he authored a book on the class of '74.[46] He noted that it took Republicans ten years to get back in the House to where they were after the losses of '74, which still put them a long way from a majority. "That masqueraded the realignments that were occurring in the electorate, and the rise of really strong conservative cultural/financial/grassroots organizations that really made the conservative movement much more formidable, but not necessarily more visible in an electoral way," he said.

The party had no fear, and no drive. "There was still a sense, even after the Reagan election, even after the Senate went Republican, that the majority in the House was secure. If they had had a longer view," he said, "they would have seen that they needed to be a lot more tactical than they were." The result was "an institutional weakness in terms of building and maintaining the kind of political apparatus in the states and the districts."

45   The documentary "Get Me Roger Stone" is excellent on this turn toward negative advertising, which caught the lions sleeping.

46   *The Class of '74: Congress after Watergate and the Roots of Partisanship,* published in March 2018.

The House majority, though, was constructed with southerners who were Democrats in name only — a term that is overused today, but held real meaning then. Rep. Richard Shelby, for instance, won reelection in Alabama as a Democrat with 73 percent of the vote that year. Shelby would later be elected to the Senate twice as a Democrat, and then switch parties after the 1994 wave, going on to become the top Republican on the Banking Committee and the lead opponent of Wall Street reform. His politics never changed.

Reagan was able to ram through the bulk of his economic agenda in the first 200 days of the new Democratic Congress, which necessarily required scores of Democratic defections, and the cooperation of House Speaker Tip O'Neill, who allowed Reagan's agenda to hit the floor. In other words, Democrats controlled the House thanks to Democrats who would later become Republicans themselves or lose to Republicans eventually, most of them in the '94 Gingrich revolution. "In the House, a narrow Democratic majority included enough Southern conservatives to give the right effective control of the agenda," Frank recalled.

Harry Reid was elected to the House in 1982, a Democratic midterm as the economy slumped. Like many of his colleagues, he got along well with Reagan. "I was not a big shot at the time in the Congress, but he was easy to work with," he told me. "I can remember the first time I ever went to the Oval Office. We were there fighting about aid to the Contras and went down with three House members to the Oval Office and [Paul] Kanjorski[47] from Pennsylvania asked, *Mr. President, I'm afraid you're going to invade Nicaragua*, and Reagan, without hesitating a second said, *Don't worry about invading Nicaragua. I'm not going to, but I want those sons of bitches going to bed every night thinking I'm going to.* That was kind of Ronald Reagan. He was so easy to deal with. Every [Republican today] wants to be a Reagan Republican. I wish they were because he was one of the finest, easiest people to work with. He was a dealmaker."

The party had a few paths before it: Follow the lead of progressives, who had warned that Carter had abandoned the party's natural base, and write off the right wing Democrats who were no longer a part of a progressive coalition, or appeal to their populist natures and try to rally them to the left. A related version of that strategy, whose lead proponent had been California Democrat Phil Burton, was to disempower the conservatives but get serious about fundraising — preferably from the least objectionable sources possible — with an eye toward building real progressive power that could match the right. Or — as the party ultimately

---

47   Reagan, despite his pledge, illegally funded the Contras, right-wing terrorists in Nicaragua, by illegally selling arms to the Iranian regime, but escaped impeachment. Kanjorski was wiped out in the 2010 tea party wave.

did — try to defend the party to the last incumbent, matching Republicans dollar-for-dollar,[48] while going into a defensive crouch to protect the most basic elements of the New Deal, along with newer programs for the needy Reagan was targeting, such as Head Start.

Making the case for a robust corporate fundraising strategy was a young congressman from California, Tony Coelho, who was named head of the DCCC, at the time a political backwater. Coelho, later Rahm Emanuel's mentor, immediately began reaching out to business interests that Democrats had previously not targeted for contributions with a simple proposition: Democrats are in power in the House, so they had better pay up.

"Tony saw Democrats were not playing the aggressive game on fundraising that Republicans were developing under the rules as they emerged, following the '74 campaign finance reform act and subsequent rule changes, and felt the Democrats were simply going to get outgunned if they didn't develop a different fundraising model," said John Lawrence.

"Tony really bears a fair amount of responsibility — whether that's credit or blame, depends on where you stand — for pointing Democrats to the need for a PAC-based industry strategy for fundraising."

"With that came a lot of problems," Lawrence added. "Nobody told me they felt beholden, but obviously there were plenty of times where it was very tough to pass some of the legislation the more progressive parts of the caucus would have liked."

Pelosi was in the camp that recognized the need for conservative Democrats to keep the majority, but wanted them disempowered within the caucus. But more importantly, she was a preternatural fundraiser. The legend of Nancy Pelosi is that after raising her five children, she decided to become involved in politics. The reality is that even amid that impressive feat of child rearing, she was already heavily involved.

Phil Burton, upon seeing the San Francisco mansion she shared with her husband, investor Paul Pelosi, noted that it would make a tremendous location for political fundraisers. Pelosi, it turned out, had a gift for just that, and her fundraising prowess would eventually turn her into a power center in California politics in her own right. In 1976, more than a decade before entering Congress, she was elected as a member of the Democratic National Committee. Over the next five years, she would become chair of the Northern California Democratic Party and then the statewide Democratic Party. In 1985, she lost a bid for DNC chair.

Burton, who served in Congress for 19 years, was a transformative

48   Try the book *Prisoners of the American Dream*, by Mike Davis, if you want a closer look at this transformative period.

political figure both in California and in the education of Pelosi. Labor reporter Harold Meyerson once called him "the single most important member of the House of Representatives in the '60s and '70s."

Pelosi is often lauded for her uncanny ability to count votes, something that was also said repeatedly of Burton. He was a role model for Pelosi, someone who was enthusiastic about fundraising and took politics seriously, rather than a purist who stood aloof from what many on the left saw as a corrupt endeavor. "I'm a fighting liberal," Burton would famously say. His biographer, John Jacobs, agreed: "A ruthless and unabashed progressive, Burton terrified his opponents, ran over his friends, forged improbable coalitions, and from 1964 to 1983 became one of the most influential Representatives in the House. He also acquired more raw power than almost any left-liberal politician ever had."

Fighting meant getting your hands dirty. Burton pioneered gerrymandering in California ("My contribution to modern art," he called it; he even drew a district so that his brother John could have a House seat, too) and began what is now a common practice of spreading PAC money around to colleagues in tough races in order to build power within the caucus. He helped shape the House floor process so that lobbyists would have more ability to tweak individual pieces of legislation, uncorking contributions from K Street and helping to create the Washington ecosystem we know today. Burton encouraged Pelosi to run in one of the new districts he had drawn, but she demurred.

First elected in 1964, he took on the power of the Southern bulls, who had used seniority and one-party rule in the South to lock down control of key committee chairmanships. The sooner the party could crush its Dixiecrat wing, he argued, the better. Burton organized his liberal colleagues and reformed the process for selecting chairs, replacing it with a secret vote, which was the beginning of the end of Southern dominance of the House Democratic caucus.

In 1976, he fell one vote short in a bid for majority leader in a three-way race he had been expected to win. The progressive vote was split between Burton and Richard Bolling, allowing Texas populist Jim Wright to speak through. Had Burton been in leadership during the rise of Reagan, the Democratic response may have been far different and more effective.

In Pelosi, Burton had a ready student. If your knowledge of her comes from Republican attack ads, you know her as a "San Francisco liberal" or even "radical," but she was raised in Maryland by her father Thomas D'Alesandro Jr., the boss of the Baltimore political machine, who was by turns a congressman and mayor of Charm City. D'Alesandro's operation, like most big-city machines of the era, was linked in public to local Mafia figures, according to his FBI file.

Burton rightly saw in Pelosi that rarest of breeds, a liberal born to fight. In Burton, Pelosi found someone who knew how to make progressive change actually happen. His list of legislative achievements was long — Supplemental Security Income, a higher minimum wage, compensation for black lung, food stamps for striking workers, the abolition of the House Un-American Affairs Committee — despite or, in part, because of his legendary ruthlessness and rage.

Jim Shoch, a prominent radical activist in the 1970s, told me about the first time he met with Burton. "I think he was actually yelling into two phones at the same time when we entered his office," he said. "Part of our conversation included his recent success in favorably gerrymandering California for the Democrats. With a deeply satisfied expression on his face he exclaimed, *We fucked 'em! We fucked 'em!*"

John Burton, Phil's brother and himself a former congressman, said that Phil never quite mentored Pelosi. "I mean, Christ, this is a woman who was brought up in Baltimore politics. He wasn't working with some neophyte that all of a sudden he had to explain, *Well, here's how it works.* They got along because even though she was an 'amateur' at that time, she was still a pro,'" Burton told author Vincent Bzdek for the book *Woman of the House*. He acknowledged, though, that Phil helped "hone her skills."

They differed greatly in their outward demeanor, but internally had much the same drive. "Nancy is tougher than nails, but she's a gentle person. Phillip was just hard-ass and hard charging. He could be charming sometimes but I can't quite remember when," said John Burton.

Pelosi said that her Baltimore education made Burton easy to handle. "Actually, my family really prepared me for Phil Burton. One of the reasons I got along with Phil is because I wasn't afraid of him. I knew a lot of people like him," she told Bzdek.

It was always expected that the relatively young Burton would take another shot at leadership, and this time win, but in April 1983, at the age of 56, he died of a heart attack. Burton's untimely death cut off the potential of a counter history for Democrats. At the time, said John Lawrence, Burton was one of the few Democrats who understood that the party did not have a permanent lock on the House of Representatives, and it was that overconfidence that stunted the party's ability to think strategically about what kind of a coalition it wanted to be a post-Civil Rights era. Instead, Coelho strip-mined the majority for every corporate dollar it was worth — until it collapsed. "Would Gingrich have been as effective if Phil Burton was the foil, and not Jim Wright? There's a fair case to be made that Phil would not have been caught sleeping," he said.

Burton's wife Sala Burton won the special election to replace him. But four years later, she lay dying herself and made a parting endorsement: "Nancy."

The nod helped, but the special election was anything but a coronation. The left — made up of young people, the gay activist community, and the city's various social movements — coalesced behind city supervisor Harry Britt, who'd been appointed by Mayor Dianne Feinstein to fill the seat made vacant by the assassination of Harvey Milk.[49]

Britt was also vice chair of the city's chapter of the Democratic Socialists of America, noted Jim Shoch, who was also a member. "Pelosi's experience in dealing with the city's many Democratic clubs and factions was good practice for leading the often fractious House Democratic caucus," Shoch said.

The Los Angeles Times reported it as an establishment versus insurgent candidate. "The Democratic establishment backed Pelosi, a 46-year-old mother of five who has raised large sums for her party's candidates. Younger, more liberal activists and the city's powerful gay community backed Britt," the paper wrote.

Pelosi ran on the prophetic and on-brand slogan "a voice that will be heard," and on election night she beat Britt 36 to 33 percent, with the rest of the votes scattered among lesser candidates. In the top-two system California uses today, both Pelosi and Britt would have moved to the general election. That electoral innovation, for better or worse, was 25 years away, and Pelosi's total was enough to move her to the general against a hapless Republican. Big money and establishment power, in her first race, had beaten grassroots, leftwing energy.

When she arrived back in Washington, Steny Hoyer was waiting for her, as he'd already won a crowded special election in 1981.[50] The turn toward big money fundraising came as there was more big money around. The new tax policies enacted by Reagan and Democrats in Con-

---

49   In 1982, Britt passed domestic partner legislation, an LGBTQ milestone, but Feinstein vetoed it, saying the country wasn't ready. Feinstein is now in the U.S. Senate, and said the same thing about same-sex marriage in 2004 when San Francisco married gay couples in the "Winter of Love."

50   The two had served together as interns in the 1960s for a Maryland senator, and it hadn't gone well. More than 50 years later, the root cause of their tension is still whispered about. "There's that congressional lore that says something happened a long time ago. I had asked Steny about that, but he said doesn't recall anything in particular," said Rep. Brian Higgins of New York. "The lore is that there was some kind of personal or professional falling out very, very early, while they were interns." I talked to Higgins about this in November 2018, the day Democrats held leadership elections. Other members tell lurid stories of the rivalry, but nobody has gotten to the bottom of it.

gress made it so there were many people that had the means to pay up big. When the highest income tax rate was first introduced in the early 20th Century, it applied to just a few families. It's often said that, yes, sure, marginal tax rates were in the 90s and even as high as the 70s up through the 1970s and into the 1980s, but that's largely irrelevant because almost nobody paid that high rate. But that misunderstands the purpose of those high rates as raising revenue. The real upside was that it discouraged earning stratospheric amounts of income.

In the 1980s, the phrase "greed is good" began making the rounds. But that's not because greed was a new phenomenon. For the first time since the Gilded Age, greed was rewarded. Greed, with a 90 percent marginal tax rate, is pointless. Central to the policy goal of discouraging extreme incomes is the belief that making that much money that fast is almost always antisocial and destructive behavior. In other words, there's no genuine value a person can add to the world that is worth a million dollars a week, every week. The only way to make that kind of income is to take it from other people, leaving wreckage behind. That's why the 1980s saw the birth of corporate raiders — now renamed private equity investors — who used leveraged debt to take a controlling stake in a company, liquidate its assets and pension fund, then file for bankruptcy protection and lay off the workers.

The idea of a high marginal tax rate is not to seize money from the rich, it's to discourage private equity investors from even thinking about, say, taking over Sears and syphoning the value from it before killing it. Sure, they could do it, but with a 90 percent marginal rate on extreme incomes, what's the point?

The new policy of the 1980s was to encourage extreme incomes and rapid wealth accumulation. Top rates were cut by Reagan and the Democrats from 70 down to 50 and down under 30 percent by the end of the decade. Just as campaigns were becoming exponentially more expensive thanks to the dominance of television, a new class of super-rich were available to tap for the needed funds. Those super-rich were simultaneously using their new power to demolish organized labor — looting their pensions in the process — which exacerbated the Democratic funding gap. Political scientist Daniel Schlozman of Johns Hopkins has done some of the best research on precisely how the Democrats went from a party of workers and people to one dominated by Wall Street.[51] His conclusion is at once surprising and intuitive. As Democrats went hunting for corporate cash, most of the industries they flirted with created backlash elsewhere in the coalition, often from labor or environmentalists.

---

51   He spells it out in a 2016 paper called "Finance and the Democrats: Coalition Politics and the End of the Anti-Finance Coalition."

But Wall Street in the early 1980s wasn't the beast it is today, and so the finance industry was a relatively inoffensive source of party cash. Like any addiction, it seemed harmless at first.

Nancy Pelosi, Steny Hoyer, Rahm Emanuel, and a generation of party leaders were all shaped in their formative years by the pivot toward corporate dollars in the 1980s, though Pelosi always clung to her fighting liberal roots, taking Phil Burton's belief in building power through fundraising to the next level. Before Pelosi would meet with lobbyists or executives from a particular industry, for instance, she would flip through the print newspapers[52] that circulate in the Capitol — The Hill, Roll Call and later Politico — and check to see how many full-page ads the industry had taken out. If there were none, it reflected an unserious lobbying campaign, and an unlikely source of campaign cash for the DCCC.[53] Her focus on big money contained the seeds of her own political drift away from the left — or, perhaps more accurately, as the left developed a sophisticated critique of money and politics and set about building an alternative funding infrastructure, Pelosi stayed moored to big money, knowing no other way of doing it.

The same could be said about another progressive group that launched in the mid-1980s with a genuine understanding of power. Ellen Malcolm, an heir to the IBM fortune, invited two dozen of her friends to her home in Washington, D.C., for the inaugural meeting, in 1985, of what would become EMILY's List. When the women met, not a single woman had ever been elected to the Senate who had not succeeded her husband, and just 12 women were serving in the House. EMILY stood for "early money is like yeast," and suggested its purpose: to help women candidates get off the ground in a male-dominated game. The founding members included Barbara Boxer,[54] not yet a senator; Ann Richards,[55] not yet a Texas governor; Anne Wexler, who had already founded Wexler & Walker, a leading corporate lobbying firm; and Donna Shalala,[56] not yet Clinton's Health and Human Services secretary.

Along with help from big donors, the group pioneered small-dollar

---

52   Multiple Pelosi aides have told me this over the years.

53   The DCCC has long been run by the party's House leader, even if a deputy is nominally in charge. In the 2018 cycle, under pressure, Pelosi agreed to open it up to a caucus election, but only one person ran.

54   Boxer would win her Senate campaign in 1992, the first year to be dubbed "of the woman."

55   A populist giant who was upset by George W. Bush in a surprise election, her daughter Cecile would go on to run Planned Parenthood; Cecile's daughter Lily Adams became a union organizer and then a Democratic operative.

56   She ran for Congress in Florida in 2018, flipping a seat in Miami.

fundraising. The next year it helped elect Barbara Mikulski to the Senate from Maryland.

Many rank-and-file Democrats were uncomfortable with the shift toward business fundraising, and it's critical to remember that the pivot in that direction came relatively recently in history. The political class today sees big money as simply a natural part of politics, and anybody who suggests it ought not to be as a wild-eyed utopian. But the discomfort most Democrats betrayed at the shift is itself a signal that it was a choice and not an inevitability.

The direction taken by the party under Coelho would shape not just its strategic approach, but the outlooks of the young strategists who would later become major players. Terry McAuliffe, for instance, was Coelho's top assistant and would become the larger-than-life money-man for both Clintons. And then there was Rahm Emanuel.

Four

The Making of Rahm Emanuel

Rahm Emanuel had spent 1980 engaged in electoral politics, even though he was just 20 years old. When it came to the two paths Democrats had before them that year, he could have gone either way: He was raised to believe in the virtue of political activism. His mother was active in the civil rights movement and, according to Chicago magazine, his father had been involved in the mid 1940s, before the founding of Israel, with Irgun, Menachem Begin's underground terrorist group. "So conversations were politics with a big P and social concerns with a big S," Emanuel told the magazine in a 1992 profile. This was a family that believed politics had meaning.

He took time off from college to volunteer on his first campaign in 1980, and eventually became the chief fundraiser for a Democrat named David Robinson. The target was Paul Findley, a veteran Republican congressman known as the chief advocate for dialogue with the Palestinian Liberation Organization. It was the first campaign run explicitly on the argument that the incumbent deserved defeat because he was not in Israel's corner. The candidate, with young Emanuel's help, raised some three-quarters of a million dollars, a fortune for the time, but he still lost.[57] Ten years later, when the Gulf War broke out, Rahm Israel Emanuel would go volunteer for the Israeli Defense Forces.

57   Two years later, the then obscure pro-Israel group AIPAC recruited and financed Dick Durbin to take on Findley. He beat him, and is now the No. 2 Democrat in the Senate.

Emanuel, after the 1980 race, went back to school, where he studied philosophy and danced ballet at Sarah Lawrence College, beginning his post-college political career with the progressive organization Public Action Council. He was hired by Bob Creamer, a longtime Democratic activist. Creamer told me, "On his first day, he said, *I want you to teach me everything you know about politics.* He probably said that to everyone."

The young Emanuel was tasked by Creamer with raising money for a "progressive leadership club," which would be an adjunct of the organization, and funded by wealthy donors ideologically in line with the progressive mission, rather than corporations looking for favors.

"The idea was they would have four events a year with people from out of town they wanted to meet, and they had to pay $500 or whatever. Rahm was 22 at the time and he marched into see all these people like he was their peer," Creamer marveled.

He recalled watching him meet Philip Morris Klutznick, the former secretary of Commerce and a real estate titan in Chicago, for the first time. "*Klutznick! How ya doin', bubby?* He was quite remarkable at that. What you see is what you get, and he's been that way ever since," Creamer said.

After raising the cash for the adjunct group, Creamer detailed Emanuel to the Senate campaign of Paul Simon in 1984. "That was a seminal campaign," said Creamer, explaining that the "campaign manager got caught up in a #metoo sort of thing and he had to leave." The question was whether to go outside for a new campaign manager or look internally.

Creamer's camp won out, and they went with an internal selection, promoting a young David Axelrod, who had recently left the Chicago Tribune to be the campaign's spokesperson. They then made David Wilhelm the COO, another fateful decision.

Wilhelm would go on to work for the 1989 mayoral campaign of Richard Daley, and bring Emanuel with him. Daley subsequently recommended Wilhelm to Bill Clinton to manage his 1992 presidential campaign, and Wilhelm again brought Emanuel with him to run Clinton '92's fundraising operation.[58]

Emanuel, before getting into presidential politics, was recruited to the DCCC by Coelho when he was 24. "I had to convince him to move from cause-oriented politics to system-oriented politics," Coelho said in the '92 profile of Emanuel in Chicago magazine. "He has very strong ideals, but understands that the way to get there is to get a President in

[58]   Daley became the longest serving mayor in Chicago history, finally stepping down in 2010, when Emanuel ran to replace him. Emanuel's term expired in May 2019, after he declined to run for reelection in 2018.

the White House who shares your ideals."

In the '82 midterms, with the economy sagging, Democrats picked up 26 seats.[59] The economy rebounded and Reagan was re-elected in a landslide in 1984, but the '86 midterms, with Iran-Contra and Reagan's dawning senility, zagged back to the Democrats, as the party reclaimed control of the Senate and expanded their majority in the House. The money must be working.

The party by then had drifted firmly into the hands of big corporations, and would remain in that grip for the next three decades. Coelho claimed it was unfair to say that individual members of Congress had become corrupt, but was quick to admit that the new system itself was corrupting the legislative process.

"If you are spending all of your time calling up different people [to raise money], you all of a sudden, in your mind, you're in effect saying, 'I'm not going to go out and develop this new housing bill that may get the realtors or may get the builders or may get the unions upset,'" he told author Brooks Jackson for the Coelho biography *Honest Graft*. "That isn't a sellout. It's basically that you're not permitted to go out and do your creativity....I think that the process buys you out. But I don't think that you individually have been bought out, or that you sell out. I think there's a big difference there."

But money does play a role in how the party operates. Take Emanuel's touchstone anecdote. Pick up any profile of the pugnacious politician, and it won't be long until you come across the scene where Emanuel mails a dead fish to a rival. It's meant to prove Rahm's gangster bona fides. But peel back the skin of the story, and it stinks underneath, and reveals more about Rahm the man than he'd probably like most people to know.

The fish tale dates to the wake of the '88 election. Emanuel had lost a critical House race he was expected to win, and he blamed pollster[60] Alan Secrest for giving him erroneous information. The pollster said that the charge was bogus, but the beef between the two actually had to do with money. Secrest, during the campaign, had complained to higher-ups

---

59   Thanks to Coelho, this was a business-friendly batch, which included Tom Carper in Delaware and Bob Torricelli in New Jersey. Only the latter would be taken down for corruption. The class also included future Senators Barbara Boxer, Dick Durbin, and Harry Reid. Chuck Schumer had been elected the cycle before.

60   Secrest gladly did work against Rahm's reelection to mayor in 2019, but Rahm elected not to run. "I've always found Rahm to be willing to cut corners ethically, from my observations at least, and it hasn't really changed as his tenure as mayor," Secrest told the Chicago Tribune.

that Emanuel was giving plum party consulting gigs to his cronies.[61] So to retaliate, Emanuel sent him a dead fish. Far from being an example of Emanuel's steely-eyed ruthlessness, Rahm's touchstone anecdote merely exposes him as one more party hack doling out cash to friends — losing in the process, and going after anybody who speaks up.

The incident did little to slow Rahm's rise, and probably aided it. Emanuel's energetic approach to presidential-level fundraising — and his innovation to focus on regular high-dollar events rather than mail-driven money — gave Clinton a financial cushion that helped him weather Gennifer Flowers[62] and other scandals he faced ahead of New Hampshire. At a Little Rock retreat just before the primary, Emanuel told the campaign it had more than $3 million cash on hand, far more than Clinton's rivals at the time.[63]

Wilhelm, the campaign manager, would go on to credit Emanuel's fundraising as essential to the victory during the primary, and Emanuel kept the money flowing throughout the general election, including raising a surprisingly high number of small-dollar donations from fired-up activists, sensing victory after 12 years out of power. Over the summer, Clinton pulled in more than $7 million in small dollars against $3.4 million from big donors. "Democratic fundraisers have said they had their single best mail-solicitation fundraiser on the Monday after the Republican convention," the Times reported.[64]

Still, Election Day was not exactly a resounding affirmation that the nation was demanding triangulation and centrism: Clinton eked out a win with 43 percent of the vote, to H.W. Bush's 37 percent and Ross Perot's 19.

Coelho's star, meanwhile, was fading by then, as a 1989 corruption investigation had brought about his resignation from Congress. In classic Washington fashion, though, he quickly had a second act, aided by Rahm. Wilhelm had become chairman of the Democratic National Com-

---

61   And that's Emanuel's version of events, as it appears in Naftali Bendavid's book on the 2006 midterms, *The Thumpin': How Rahm Emanuel and the Democrats Learned to Be Ruthless and Ended the Republican Revolution*. Emanuel doesn't deny the corruption in the book, though presumably would argue that his cronies were the most effective consultants available.

62   Flowers was one of Clinton's girlfriends for 12 years, the duration of which he was married to Hillary Clinton. He was also getting hit for pulling strings to avoid fighting in Vietnam.

63   This according to Stan Greenberg's memoir, Dispatches from the War Room.

64   "Campaign Finances; Despite Economy, Clinton Sets Record for Funds," New York Times, October 24, 1992.

mittee, while Emanuel was made White House political director. Not long into his tenure, Rahm, with his door open, according to a person who overheard him from the White House hallway, was telling a reporter on the phone how instrumental he (Rahm) had been in the campaign, how powerful he was in the White House — typical Emanuel boasts — and what a horrible job Wilhelm, the man who'd gotten Emanuel his last three jobs, was doing at the DNC.

Articles began appearing questioning Wilhelm's political future, and in the summer of 1994, he announced he'd had enough and was resigning, citing the campaign against him in the press. Even in Washington, it was an extraordinary backstabbing. Emanuel's other mentor, Coelho, was brought back from the political dead to replace Wilhelm and oversee political strategy for the 1994 midterms. That was a debacle,[65] the wipeout that became known as the Gingrich revolution, sweeping Democrats from the House for the first time in a generation.

Emanuel spent six tumultuous years in the Clinton White House, before leaving to join Wasserstein Perella, an investment bank. He walked out two years later, having made more than $16 million. Emanuel ran for Congress in 2002, advocating for the invasion of Iraq, and was only a sophomore when Pelosi tapped him to run the DCCC for the 2006 cycle. Back in 1992, he had told Chicago magazine that after the Clinton campaign, he was through with raising money. "I don't want to be known as a fundraiser," he said. It wasn't the last time he'd be wrong.

---

65   Continuing to fail up, Coelho was made vice president of Al Gore's 2000 presidential campaign, all the while working simultaneously in the banking industry.

Five

The Dean Bat

The Iraq War vote was scheduled for the height of campaign season, held on a Thursday afternoon on October 10, 2002. It'd been just over a year since the September 11 attacks, and two former interns were having lunch in a House cafeteria when they saw their old boss, Congressman Ed Markey, walk in.

Markey was an old school liberal, who'd first been elected to the Massachusetts House of Representatives in 1972 and to Congress six years later.[66] He had been an opponent of the Vietnam War, and had served in the Army reserves during the height of it, avoiding getting sent over.

"My two favorite interns!" Markey exclaimed, seeing Josh Peck and Ari Rabin-Havt. Both had gone on to work for different members of Congress, but were lunching together. Markey asked for their takes on how he should vote on the Iraq War resolution, as well as a measure from Rep. John Spratt, which would have amended it to go into effect only if the United Nations approved the invasion. Markey wasn't asking because their input would change his mind, but as a continual process of educating the next generation of political operatives.

Both young men were unequivocal: Hard no on both. The arguments against were strong: The administration was run by war-hungry maniacs who couldn't be trusted to carry it out responsibly, if such a thing was even possible. It would destabilize the region and breed anti-American sentiment, only giving Al Qaeda exactly what it wanted. And Sen.

66   He was elected to the Senate in 2013.

Ryan Grim

Bob Graham, a Democrat from Florida, had been warning everybody that the so-called intelligence about weapons of mass destruction was garbage. He had served on the 9/11 Commission and sat on the Intelligence Committee, and was one of the few people who'd read the raw intel. That he didn't believe it was enough for the interns. Dressing it up with the Spratt amendment made it no better.

There was, quite simply, no reason to invade, they both said.

Markey didn't dispute any of the reasoning, but countered with an argument that shook the idealistic young staffers. All of that may be true, he said, but Democrats couldn't afford to look weak on defense, not in the shadow of Vietnam, and in the wake of the attacks of September 11. The politics of the moment demanded that he vote to authorize the war. The midterms were coming, after all.

"He's such an incredible champion on so many progressive things," said Peck. "His view was Democrats needed to demonstrate strength. This was a thousand years ago when the paradigm around Democrats being weak on the military was a little more salient."

That they were hearing this from someone they both admired was particularly difficult to stomach. "We all knew it was fucked. There was nobody who was saying, like, *This is the right thing.* That was what was what killed me on the Democratic establishment," Rabin-Havt recounted. "Nobody was like, *This is the moral war, this the right war, this is a good thing to be doing.* Everybody kind of knew it was a screwy situation. Everyone knew the weapons of mass destruction thing was kind of crap because Graham from Florida was saying it."

It would have been at least understandable if the party believed the war was a good idea. But on what could hardly be a matter of higher moral import, the party was cowering. "It was kind of an awakening about, *God, the Democratic establishment sucks.* They're going to be for us getting into this war," he said. "It was the Democratic establishment saying we have to do this thing that was incredibly evil."

It was a particularly dark moment for the Democratic Party. The 9/11 attacks and the Iraq War that followed would shape world history to come, but the events also played a pivotal role in the evolution of the left and the party. Throughout the '90s, as Clinton hewed to the center, ended welfare and humiliated his supporters with his Oval Office escapades, energy on the left coalesced around what came to be called the anti-globalization movement, which burst into public view in Seattle in November 1999 and then in Washington, D.C., in April 2000.

The first demonstration shut down a meeting of the World Trade Organization and the second[67] targeted annual gatherings of the Interna-

67   I was a senior in college and showed up in my flannel and bandana for the

tional Monetary Fund and World Bank. The movement had a strong anarchist component — socialism still had a post-Soviet Union branding problem — and brought together labor, environmentalists, anti-capitalists, and activists from the developing world protesting exploitation being carried out in the name of globalization.

That energy flowed not into the campaign of Al Gore, but to Ralph Nader, a cranky, proto-Bernie candidate who packed stadiums across the country, filling young people with hope of a better world.[68]

A new anti-globalization demonstration had been planned for fall 2001 in Washington, and it was expected to be the largest ever. Then September 11 hit, and the question facing organizers was whether to cancel the event. The decision was to press ahead — but to make it instead an anti-war march, and so ended the anti-globalization movement, even as its anarchist roots would sprout again with Occupy Wall Street a decade later.[69]

While the political parties and the major media were largely in agreement that invading Iraq was the thing to do, the action in the streets said something different entirely, with millions taking to the streets around the world.[70]

---

one in Washington, which was known as A16, and got blasted with pepper spray while seated on the street in a frigid rain. It was thrilling.

68   Much energy has been spent since debating whether Nader's presence on the ballot swung the election to George W. Bush. To me, the numbers are clear that it most certainly did, but it's the wrong question to ask: Why was there so much energy around Ralph Nader in the first place? The Green Party, after all, existed in 2008, but the youth energy flowed to Obama. In 2016, Jill Stein didn't win enough votes to be credited or blamed with tipping the scales, but why was she even a thing?

69   Indeed, many OWS organizers had been leaders or foot soldiers in the anti-globalization push, such as Jonathan Smucker, David Graeber, Winnie Wong and Claire Sandberg.

70   I was a graduate student at the University of Maryland at the time, and doing camera work for mayor and council meetings in Chestertown, Md. As the minutes still reflect, I turned the camera on myself during one meeting and asked for the floor, then proposed a resolution that the conservative village of Chestertown, population roughly 5,000, go on record as opposed to the war. The motion was politely tabled. I did help the UMD Graduate Student Government, however, pass such a resolution. Yet somehow the advice and counsel of such an august body had little impact on the thinking of President Bush. It did impact my own thinking about journalism, though. After a day in the streets with several hundred thousand anti-war marchers, I'd wake up the next morning to see a tiny story buried deep in the Washington Post about it. That was my first inkling that maybe I should be a reporter so I could fix that imbalance.

On the eve of the invasion, Iraqi President Saddam Hussein made a sweeping offer to swear off weapons of mass destruction — of which he had none — and allow inspectors full access. Neither the public opposition nor the collapse of the public rationale did anything to slow the war. Bush invaded in March 2003, and ran his reelection campaign on patriotism, war-fever, xenophobia, and homophobia.

Rabin-Havt, witnessing the power public polling had on members of Congress, decided he needed to become a pollster. Polling had found that the invasion wasn't actually popular, yet that fact had never broken through. He figured he could do it better, so he googled to find the most influential one in the business. The answer he landed on: Mark Penn.

Penn, today a much-reviled figure across much of the Democratic spectrum, was a key figure in the rise of Bill Clinton, and is a lead strategist for the dark money group No Labels, which relies on a handful of billionaires to support Republicans and conservative Democrats under the guise of good government. At the time, and still, a large portion of Penn's income came from corporate work, with Democratic Party politics on the side.

Rabin-Havt's most memorable experience from his time at Penn's firm came after he accompanied Penn and Al From to a briefing on Capitol Hill. From was a co-founder of the Democratic Leadership Council, the effort that began in the 1980s to drag the party to the right, which had its first major success with the election of President Clinton.

On the way back from the Capitol, From asked the driver to drop him off at the Capital Grille. As he got out of the car, Rabin-Havt, who'd been sandwiched in the back with From, reached out to shake his hand to say goodbye. It was a fatal error for a junior staffer in Washington.

Later that day, his boss found him. "Did you try to shake Al From's hand? Mark is furious," he was told. If you haven't spent much time in Washington, this story may sound implausible. But if you told it to people who *have* worked a long time in the city's politics, their reaction would be: *I can't believe he tried to shake his hand. What was he thinking?* It's rooted in Washington's concentrically organized power structures; the White House or the party's leader is at the center, and power radiates out. It's verboten to reach inside a circle you (or your parents) are not part of.

In any event, Rabin-Havt left the polling firm to try something different. By this time, he'd begun to realize the potential of internet organizing, and approached Wes Boyd, a founder of MoveOn.org, which was still a rather obscure organization. It had begun in the midst of the Clinton impeachment fight as a petition arguing that Congress should simply censure Clinton and "move on." In the years immediately after, the original organizers, who fortuitously had both a tech and a direct mail background — understood the power of a mailing list and used it for a variety of liberal causes, but it hadn't caught on as a major force yet.

In the final weeks of the 2002 midterms, MoveOn had sent out an email asking members to thank four politicians who had pledged to oppose the war and follow through, focusing on Paul Wellstone, then in a tight reelection campaign in Minnesota. The reaction stunned people in MoveOn's leadership. In the type of email that would later become familiar, the group wrote back to its members with news that startled the political world: "Amazing. You blew away all our goals with an incredible $1,250,000 raised in three days, from more than 30,000 individual donations."

It was the first indication that money — real money — could be raised from small donors on the internet. The euphoria didn't last — days later, a small plane carrying Wellstone went down, killing one of the era's legendary progressives. Democrats swapped in an aging Walter Mondale, and MoveOn rapidly pumped money his way, but he was beaten by Norm Coleman.[71]

By 2003, MoveOn was all in for the presidential campaign of Howard Dean, and Rabin-Havt and a friend, Ben Brandzel, pitched Boyd on digitally organizing college students. Boyd bit, funding a group called MoveOn Student Action, which had the alternate — and, in hindsight, kind of embarrassing — name of Click Back America. Brandzel went to work for the Dean campaign, as did some MoveOn organizers, such as Zack Exley, while Rabin-Havt launched Click Back America.

Peck was also inspired by Dean, particularly for his anti-war stance, and Peck decided to quit the Hill and go work for him, leading to a moment that was just as absurd-yet-telling as Rabin-Havt's ill-fated handshake. Peck was then working for Steven Rothman, a Democrat from New Jersey whose politics didn't align with his, and who had backed the war. He was a legislative correspondent, or an LC, one of the young people who answers constituent letters and is paid so meagerly they forage for food and drinks at every free event in Washington they can find.

Peck told Rothman's chief of staff that he was leaving to join the Dean campaign. "At the ripe old age of 25, he told me I was committing career suicide leaving my LC job to work on the Dean campaign," Peck recalled.

For people who know Howard Dean fifteen years later as the corpo-

---

71   Who was himself beaten by Al Franken in 2008 in an election that went to a months-long recount. Franken, who was friends with Wellstone, was driven to challenge Coleman for the way he exploited Wellstone's funeral for political advantage.

rate lobbyist who trolls the left on social media, it may be difficult to absorb just how path-breaking his campaign in 2003 and '04 was. He ran as an anti-war candidate and, as a doctor and governor of Vermont, made providing universal health care the centerpiece of his campaign. He had long been a centrist in the mold of Bill Clinton, and nodded to that instinct with his promise to balance the budget and "pay for" his health care program. But he unapologetically attacked President Bush on every front, giving progressives the fight they'd been looking for, but not getting, from party leaders.

Though he personally had no idea how it was happening, and not a lot of interest in it at first, his campaign pioneered small-dollar fundraising and using the web to facilitate grassroots organizing. His was the first campaign to be substantially financed by, and ultimately organized around, regular people in the age of the internet.

"Involvement in the Dean campaign was one of those uniquely intense personal experiences that, like sex or a profound religious conversion, are hard to describe and often look odd or pathetic to those not sharing in it," wrote Thomas Streeter in the introduction to a book he co-wrote and edited with Zephyr Teachout, a fellow Dean alum, called *Mousepads, Shoe Leather, and Hope.* "And, we suspect, experiences like these are of a piece with deep social change, and will be a component of any successful effort to build a more democratic society in the future."

Much like the 2016 Sanders campaign, it was overwhelmed with enthusiastic supporters and had to find new ways to harness the energy. Some of it found ways to harness itself, thanks to the nascent blogosphere. A leading figure in that world at the time was Jerome Armstrong, writing at the site MyDD, which was short for "my direct democracy." In January 2003, he posted a link to a "Meetup for Dean," using the then-budding social media site called Meetup.com. There was as yet no such thing as Facebook or Twitter, and Armstrong was acting independently of the campaign, but Meetups would soon become synonymous with Dean. Crucially, the campaign's leadership recognized that this new base of supporters needed to be treated as more than just wells to be tapped for money, but that the key was to use the internet to organize them in the real world.

The longshot Dean was also quick to recognize that the internet energy was his path to viability, and he leaned into it. In February 2003, he gave a speech at the Democratic National Committee that would define his campaign. It came to be known as the "What I want to know..." speech, in which he blasted establishment Democrats for cozying up with President Bush. This was just weeks before the invasion of Iraq. "I'm Howard Dean, and I'm here to represent the democratic wing of the Democratic Party," he said, harkening back to the late Wellstone's famous line.

Dean, to his credit, was rolling with it. "What happened was very different than what we'd expected," he later said.[72] "We had intended to run this as a traditional campaign — an underdog campaign, but a traditional campaign. But then the internet exploded and became this enormous, growing phenomenon, and with the growth also came growing pains. I had people who had been around me for a long time, and traditional campaign staffers, and then twenty-somethings who were completely comfortable with the internet, and we had to fit it all together."

Dean understood that what was happening online was simply a technological aggregation of real people who, if treated with respect and dignity, and given something to believe in, could respond in explosive ways. "Most people even to this day don't fully understand what we learned about the internet. Most politicians, and even the press, treat the internet as a shorthand for an ATM," Dean said.[73] "The grassroots and the netroots are really one and the same. I think too many people fail to understand that about the internet. And if you don't, you are going to find it tough to successfully use the internet for campaigns. The internet is about community building and the fundraising has to be secondary."

Yet the fundraising capacity was what would change politics in the Democratic Party. It was the Dean Bat that ushered the new era. As each quarter closes in, rumors about how much each campaign has raised begin circulating, often spread by the campaigns themselves to intimidate rivals or set low expectations that can then be beaten. The rumor that summer was that both John Edwards and John Kerry would raise about $5 million. The campaign's finance director, Stephanie Schriock,[74] had managed to raise about $2 million.

The campaign cranked up its emails and pushed to about $2.5 million. There was only one way to hit $5 million in just a few days, Exley argued to campaign manager Joe Trippi, and that was to risk failing. Be honest with supporters, Exley suggested, and tell them exactly how much money we have, how much we need, and why.

"That would be crazy," Trippi told him. If they came up short, they'd look feckless.

"Yes, but you're crazy," Exley reminded him.

Trippi took the idea to Schriock and other higher-ups in the cam-

---

72   Interview is from *Mousepads, Shoe Leather, and Hope: Lessons from the Howard Dean Campaign for the Future of Internet Politics*, 2007.

73   Ibid.

74   A great high-dollar fundraiser, she would go on to run EMILY's List.

paign, and they were good with it. Nicco Mele, the campaign's webmaster, built a red bat — a Dean Bat — that would fill up as donations came in.

The next morning, Exley saw an email from the campaign in his inbox. "I was like, *Oh shit, he actually did it,*" Exley recalled. "That was the moment that changed politics."

Social media was still virtually non-existent. Mark Zuckerberg was busy running FaceMash, a terrible site that rated college students on their attractiveness, and he wouldn't pivot and rename it "The Facebook" until February 2004. But moments could still go viral, and this one did. Bloggers began writing about the Dean Bat challenge and driving their readers to the page, which had to be updated manually by Mele. Money poured in, and the mainstream media began writing about the phenomenon, with the will-he-or-won't-he-make-it suspense capturing national attention. "On the last day we were in striking distance of $5 million and it just went wild. People realized this guy might just do it," Exley said. "Friends at the Kerry and Edwards campaigns kept hitting refresh, crying and refreshing."

The energy was contagious. The finance director for Carol Moseley Braun, who was also running for president, got caught up in the moment and donated to Dean, Exley recalled. When that became public, she was fired and went to work for Dean. (Braun later dropped out and endorsed Dean.)

The netroots took Dean from a longshot to a contender, but ultimately that wasn't enough to get him all the way there. With the war not yet extremely unpopular, Democrats thought they'd have a better chance of winning with a war hero, Senator John Kerry, than with an antiwar candidate from the hippie-state Vermont. In December, ahead of the Iowa caucuses, Dean scoffed at the capture of ousted Iraq President Saddam Hussein, saying that it wouldn't make the U.S. or its troops any safer. He was pilloried.

Dean himself said he started to realize he was going to lose in Iowa about three weeks before the caucus. Fundraising was still gangbusters, and he was drawing enthusiastic crowds, but he started noticing some familiar faces from town to town. And that wasn't good. "All of a sudden I realized I was going from event to event with these enormous crowds and it was like being the Grateful Dead, it was the same crowd," Dean said. "I'd go to the next rally and there'd be a huge crowd of a thousand people, and they'd be the same people. When I saw that, I realized what was happening was *this was not about ordinary Iowans.*" Indeed, some of those Deanheads weren't Iowans at all, just enthusiastic supporters of Dean who'd come from out of state. "I knew what was going to happen before it happened," he said. "I wasn't surprised."

When Kerry emerged the winner, his campaign drew no lessons whatsoever from the Dean campaign. In a staff shakeup, David Horne, one of the few on the campaign who understood the blogosphere and digital organizing, was pushed out, and went to MoveOn. He told the staff there that the Kerry campaign, despite his firing, or, perhaps, because of it, needed digital help, and Exley volunteered. Rabin-Havt, doing Click Back America, had largely been working out of Exley's apartment in Adams Morgan. When Exley left for the Kerry campaign, Rabin-Havt joined him.

"We spent a year screaming about swift boats, and nobody would listen to us," Rabin-Havt said, referring to the right-wing smear that Republicans used against Kerry, claiming that he wasn't actually wounded very badly in Vietnam. It was backed by a group of veterans who had been Kerry's antagonists for decades, and for a long time, the mainstream media didn't bite on the story, but Exley and Rabin-Havt were pushing for a response regardless. They proposed hitting Kerry's email list with a message signed by Wesley Clark, a retired general, with the subject line, "There's no such thing as not being wounded badly enough."

Because the issue wasn't leading the news, the campaign bosses concluded, Kerry could safely ignore it, which was smarter than dignifying it. "The online people were all screaming about this very early on. We just kept getting told there wasn't an issue," Rabin-Havt said, adding that Kerry senior adviser Peter Daou, who spent a lot of time reading right-wing blogs, also saw it. "Daou, not that I want to give Peter Daou credit for anything at this point, but he does deserve it — he was the loudest voice that wasn't being listened to," said Rabin-Havt.

Daou, in fact, had been brought onto the campaign for just that purpose. At the time he was an anti-war activist and progressive critic of the Democratic Party, which may be hard for people to conceptualize, who only know him as the ruthless and relentless online warrior for Hillary Clinton he later became. In late 2003, Daou approached Kerry at a fundraiser in the Hamptons and handed him an unsolicited 15-page memo laying out precisely why Dean was galvanizing progressives online, and what Kerry needed to do to match it. Instead of trashing it, Kerry read it, was impressed, shared it with his aides, and brought Daou on board.

The toxic, aggressive battles that now happen on Twitter and, to a lesser extent, Facebook, Daou said, were at the time raging in two key places: Democratic Underground and Free Republic.

Daou confirmed Rabin-Havt's version, saying that he saw the attacks bubbling on Free Republic and other right-wing sites in the winter of 2004. The higher-ups, he said, sent him to the veterans portion of the campaign, though he kept pushing it higher.

"I started saying, *Look, there are sites called wintersoldier.com and Free Republic that are all talking about his military record and you guys better pay attention*," Daou recalled. "It was at the incipient moment of things buzzing online and then turning into a news story. There was not an appreciation of how quickly that brushfire could turn into a full raging inferno, which it did, months later, about five months after my warnings."

Daou said that he recommended handling it publicly, going to the press to rebut the disingenuous and false charges. Getting that conversation out of the way in March would have taken the air out of it later, he argued. Instead, it dominated September and October, and fed the Bush narrative that he was strong while Kerry was weak. Of course, Kerry had enlisted, and Bush had been AWOL, but none of it mattered. Bush was eminently beatable, but he won fairly easily.

Two years earlier, Rabin-Havt had realized that the leaders of the Democratic Party were soulless, when they decided to back an invasion they knew was the wrong thing to do. Now he realized they were hacks, too. "That was the moment," he said, "where you realized how fucking incompetent all these people were."

Not only had Republicans re-elected Bush and held the House and Senate, they had ousted the party's Senate leader, South Dakota's Tom Daschle. Rabin-Havt, looking for his next thing, made another unusual move, going to work for Senate Minority Whip Harry Reid of Nevada in December 2004, a month before he was elected to replace Daschle as leader. Rabin-Havt, a lefty with roots in the blogosphere, wouldn't seem like a match for Reid, who was thought of at the time as something of a political conservative, and certainly not somebody with his thumb on the pulse of the younger generation.

But Reid was souring fast on the war he had supported and excited by the energy he saw in the netroots. He brought in Rabin-Havt to bring him closer to it, fueling one of the most consequential political evolutions in a generation. Reid began regular conference calls with bloggers where the lines were open, producing a real give and take. In 2006, he brought in Josh Orton, whose background was in the blogosphere and liberal talk radio, followed by another lefty, Murshed Zaheed.

That year, the first national blogger convention, called Yearly Kos, was held in Las Vegas, and Reid gave the keynote address. "I remember I was at the first Daily Kos conference. I frankly — let's see, how to phrase this? — I didn't fully understand the impact, but I knew the strength of that networking was just starting, and I felt I should be in in the beginning rather than try to jump in in the middle," Reid said.

I asked Reid why he was able to evolve with the time politically, but many of his colleagues remained stuck in the 1980s. "First of all I had a wonderful staff who was very — I listened to them," he said. "My thought process changed on many different issues."

Reid became the first co-sponsor of Sen. Russ Feingold's radical-for-the-time, anti–Iraq-war legislation. He slammed Bush as a "liar" and a "loser," later apologizing for the latter but pointedly adding that he stood by the liar charge. While Rahm Emanuel and House Democrats recruited the most conservative Democrats possible in the 2006 election cycle, Reid and Chuck Schumer, surprising everyone, were willing to recruit and support populists and progressives, which helped bring to the Senate Jon Tester of Montana and Sherrod Brown of Ohio.[75]

Many of the veterans of the Dean campaign went to work for Ned Lamont in Connecticut, who was challenging Joe Lieberman in the primary. Bloggers wanted to make an example out of Lieberman, who routinely allied with Republicans, was among the most war-happy members of either party, and was the strongest voice in the caucus on behalf of the insurance industry, which has a dominant presence in Connecticut. Lamont stunned Lieberman in the primary, but Lieberman ran in the general election anyway, under the banner of a party he created, narcissistically named "Connecticut for Lieberman."

Democrats went from a 55-45 minority to a 51-49 majority on election night.

In 2007, Reid moved the Nevada caucuses to the front of the presidential primary calendar, for the sole purpose of getting Democratic presidential candidates on record against using Yucca Mountain to dispose of nuclear waste. The party then scheduled a a presidential primary debate in Las Vegas and named as the television partner Fox News.

Bloggers erupted in fury, and MoveOn launched a campaign to get it shut down. Adam Green, a MoveOn staffer, told Reid's aides that if the Senate leader didn't get it taken off of Fox, MoveOn would bring a world of pain down on him. It turned out that Green was freelancing, and MoveOn had no such plans, but the pressure campaign was real. Reid's staff was split, with veterans insisting the debate go forward, and the newer staff with links to the movement urging him to call it off. Reid asked his staff to organize a conference call with bloggers on an unrelated issue,

---

75   The DSCC, according to Guy Cecil, actually preferred John Morrison in Montana, the state auditor, on the recommendation of Sen. Max Baucus, over Jon Tester, the populist, anti-war farmer, and even tried to nudge Tester out of the race. But as it went on, Cecil said, the party committee realized what a "caricature of a politician" Morrison was, and that Tester had something special going on. The DSCC began privately urging donors to support Tester, and never officially endorsed Morrison. Tester beat Morrison, won the general election and has been re-elected twice.

but, Orton, suspecting Reid really wanted to talk about the Fox debate, called Markos Moulitsas of Daily Kos to make sure he'd join, as he had a habit of skipping such calls.

On the call, Fox came up immediately, and the bloggers told Reid he was making their lives harder. Fox News was not yet completely understood to be right-wing propaganda, and Democrats were legitimizing a network, they argued, that was hellbent on destroying them. Reid, they said, was undermining them in the messaging war they were waging on behalf of him.

The call was persuasive — exactly what Reid wanted. After he hung up, he told his top aides, "These are my friends. We don't treat our friends that way. Fix this."

His aides dragged their feet, and one of Reid's best skills was always follow-up. He couldn't be slow-walked by subordinates. So he called the presidential candidates themselves and told them Fox was out as the sponsor.

Fox did not take the news well. "News organizations will want to think twice before getting involved in the Nevada Democratic Caucus, which appears to be controlled by radical fringe, out-of-state interest groups, not the Nevada Democratic Party," Fox Vice President David Rhodes said in a statement released when the news was undeniable. "In the past, MoveOn.org has said they 'own' the Democratic Party. While most Democrats don't agree with that, it's clearly the case in Nevada."

I asked Reid if his own political evolution was influenced by his relationship with the bloggers. "I think that's a fair statement, and here's why," he said. "We had MoveOn. We had Daily Kos, and on and on with the early days of all this, and I think that they were on the cutting edge of a new generation of ideas. And I think that's where the Democratic caucus became more involved in new ideas, it came from them."

Six

Political Genius

Rahm Emanuel is a political genius — just ask him. Or, better yet, read the book that defined Rahm's role in the 2006 midterms, the year that Democrats recaptured control of the House. By Naftali Bendavid, a Chicago Tribune reporter, it's called *The Thumpin': How Rahm Emanuel and the Democrats Learned to Be Ruthless and Ended the Republican Revolution.*

When conditions finally aligned in 2006 for Democrats, the playbook from the 1980s and 1990s was the one put into action. And nobody could have been a more enthusiastic field leader for it than Emanuel.

The thesis of *The Thumpin'*, based on fly-on-the-wall access to Emanuel — who goes by the nickname Rahmbo — over the two-year period leading up to the wave election, is that Democrats took back the House on the force of Rahm Emanuel's will, and on the back of a hard-edged strategy of recruiting moderate and conservative Democrats, many of them veterans, in Republican-held districts, who could raise big money and out-war their opponents.

"Emanuel was fighting a weak, feminine image that had long haunted the Democratic Party, in part from its ties to women and gays, apart from its perceived weakness on national defense," writes the author of *The Thumpin'*, channeling Rahm.

John Lapp, the executive director of the DCCC under Rahm, explains in the book the plan to recruit veterans: "That's the stuff I love — tough, macho Democrats taking on the Republicans." Lapp's deputy on the

73

campaign, Ali Wade, is now Ali Lapp, and runs House Majority PAC, the Democratic super PAC that works in alliance with the DCCC.

The 2006 strategy remains, to this day, the model for Democratic victory. That's partly because many of the party's leading operatives, now in their 30s, 40s and 50s, were shaped in their formative political years by the experience of winning that cycle under Rahm. Christina Reynolds, for instance, ran the research department under Rahm in '06, and in 2018 ran communications for EMILY's List. Ali Ward, a Rahm deputy in 2006, ran House Majority PAC in 2018, the super PAC that backs DCCC candidates. Almost all of the staff at the committee in that 2006 cycle are now consultants who work with the DCCC or the candidates it backs.

That strategy has also been locked in because Emanuel is gifted at working the media, and was close friends with key reporters and editors at the Washington Post and New York Times, which were essentially unrivaled at the time in setting the agenda. The Huffington Post had only launched in 2005 and had yet to hire an actual reporter by 2006, relying wholly on aggregation and outside bloggers writing for free. Politico, which changed the nature of political reporting in Washington, launched in 2007. Outside of host Keith Olbermann, MSNBC wasn't liberal, and wasn't much of a force; "The Rachel Maddow Show" didn't debut until 2008. The Nation was largely ignored in Washington, and The New Republic was caught up in counterintuitive cleverness and war mongering.

The blogosphere was the only real place a counter-narrative could get told, but it had little mass penetration; Twitter, launched in March 2006, hadn't caught on yet. By 2018, the online, explicitly left-ish press had a robust, if financially precarious, presence, with everybody from The Intercept and HuffPost to The New Republic, BuzzFeed, New York magazine and a host of others able to influence the conversation.

But without that countervailing influence, Emanuel was able to spin his yarn unchallenged. Personnel and propaganda aside, the belief in the '06 strategy also comes because there was effectively no other win to look back on. Republicans took over the House in 1994 — the Gingrich revolution, the Contract with America — and in the 24 years since then, Democrats have known almost nothing but failure. Before 2018, the party had lost every single election for House control other than 2006 and, with Barack Obama at the top of the ticket, 2008.

For Rahm and other advocates of his approach to winning, it is extraordinarily important that his strategy be seen as the *reason* Democrats won the House. Rahm knew he was putting himself in place to be lifted up. "If I make gains — and I'm not talking about one or two seats, I mean, make gains — I'll be seen as part of it. Your ability in the House just grows if you're part of people getting closer to being able to accomplish your objective," he says in the book. Indeed, he parlayed the win into the fourth-ranking spot in leadership, putting him in line to become Speaker.

In other words, power comes with being seen as being responsible for the win. That's why it's even more important to explore what actually happened in 2006. A closer look reveals that Rahm's strategy cost Democrats seats in a number of races, and certainly had electoral costs down the road — as Rahm's class of new members watered down and opposed Obama's agenda, helping slow the economy and make health care reform less popular, ultimately feeding later Democratic losses.

It was his ability as a fundraiser that led Nancy Pelosi to tap him to helm the DCCC in 2006. And when it came to raising money, he didn't disappoint. But a closer look at his political performance quickly undermines the narrative he later set. Let's start with one of the first anecdotes held up in *The Thumpin'* as evidence of Rahm's ruthless effectiveness.

> To get the right candidate, Emanuel was more than willing to fight with other Democrats. He was looking for a candidate in a tough district in North Carolina, for example, and Congressman Brad Miller, a North Carolina Democrat, pleaded with Emanuel to back a protege of his. But Emanuel thought the man was too liberal for the district and refused to support him, leading to shouting matches between Emanuel and Miller. Instead, Emanuel recruited a more conservative attorney named Tim Dunn, who had served with the Marines in Iraq.

In the book, it's the last we hear of that North Carolina race, and for good reason. The story of the shouting match, according to Miller, is true. "Yep. I proved to Rahm that I knew every conjugation of the verb 'to fuck' that he knew," Miller told me, adding that he was never interviewed for the Rahm book.

Here's how it actually unfolded: Miller and other members of the North Carolina congressional delegation had recruited Rick Glazier, a Fayetteville attorney who by that point had won four elections in a conservative area, two for school board and two for state House. He was flown up to Washington to meet with Emanuel and Rep. Chris Van Hollen, a Democrat from Maryland who was Emanuel's deputy and would take over the DCCC in 2008.

But when it became clear Emanuel wanted somebody else, Glazier stepped aside. "I'm the guy who's progressive but won in a conservative district four times. But if Rahm wants to go another way that's okay," Glazier said, reflecting on the whiplash experience 12 years earlier.

The first time Dunn met with a Democratic audience, his campaign effectively collapsed. Among the views he shared: abortion rights encourage promiscuity; the Constitution should be amended to ban same-sex marriage; contracts between gay partners to create some legal basis to their relationship should be void. And so on. He also had significant financial liabilities Emanuel had apparently been unaware of, and wasn't able to run a real campaign.

Dunn quickly dropped out, so Rahm called Glazier just before the filing deadline. Glazier was blunt in his rejection, he told me, telling Rahm: "I keep my promises and commitments, which was meant to be a fairly significant cut on what the DCCC had done."

So Rahm walked away from the district, declaring it, in his political wisdom, now unwinnable.

"In the middle of all that I got a dunning call about my DCCC dues," Miller said. "I told them to perform an anatomically impossible act. They then cut off my DCCC services. I spent a couple of hundred dollars to buy my own blast fax machine — remember those? — and used my Washington fundraiser's lists for my Washington events. Rahm did step in to end that and said he understood that I might be unhappy. Rahm revels in his image as a tough guy. Tough guys punch up. Rahm only punches down."

A high school teacher named Larry Kissell got into the race and, with support from effectively nobody, wound up in a close race at the wire. Miller alerted the netroots, and MoveOn pumped money into the contest at the last minute. After multiple recounts, Kissell conceded, losing by just 329 votes.

"I mean no disrespect to Larry, but Rick [Glazier] would have won that year without doubt," said Miller. "Rick already had a solid reputation and an obvious base. He wouldn't have made Democrats think that they might as well keep the Republican incumbent. Larry started from scratch."

Kissell immediately announced he would run again in 2008, and this time, with the backing of the DCCC, he proved the district was winnable, by winning it handily.

But while Kissell was sworn in as a Democrat, he rarely voted with the party — opposing Obamacare, climate change legislation and most spending bills that came to the floor.

Glazier, on the other hand, was publicly supportive of the Affordable Care Act at the time, telling me it would have been improved by inclusion of a public option, though he understood the political decision-making that led to its exclusion. He became a champion of the law in North Carolina, and urged both Kissell and Rep. Mike McIntyre, another Blue Dog who opposed it, to rethink their approach. "I would never have hesitated in fully supporting that," he said, adding that Democratic weakness on the issue was blood in the water for the right. "I thought the candidates who wavered early on gave the tea party the impetus to grow."

Had Glazier been the nominee instead, he'd have been a reliable Democratic vote. Given that the major Democratic priorities were watered down heavily for each single Blue Dog vote leadership needed, that matters. "Rick would have been a great member, not just a reliable vote," Miller noted.

Glazier is now the executive director of the North Carolina Justice Center, after serving 13 years in the North Carolina House. In 16 elections, he never lost once.

In New Hampshire that same year, Emanuel's DCCC backed state House minority leader Jim Craig over local activist Carol Shea-Porter, in a classic establishment-versus-grassroots campaign. The conventional wisdom suggested that Craig's endorsements, his moderation, and his ability to fundraise were what was needed in the district. Instead, Shea-Porter took a firm stand against the war in Iraq and organized an army of foot soldiers on the ground.

Vastly outspent, she smoked Craig by 19 points in the primary. The DCCC, again in its wisdom, wrote her off, declining to spend a dime on what they saw as a lost cause. She spent less than $300,000 and, on the back of progressive enthusiasm and her robust ground game, won the general election. Once in Congress, she voted for every Democratic priority without apology.

In California, the DCCC backed Steve Filson against Jerry McNerney, whom Emanuel believed was hopelessly liberal. Filson, a conservative and an airline pilot, fit Emanuel's mold of what a tough candidate should look like. After McNerney beat Filson in the primary, a peeved Rahm said the DCCC wouldn't be helping him in the general. A coalition of environmental groups and other progressives got behind him instead, and McNerney won anyway, without party help. Bloggers built a Say No To Pombo website that drove local media coverage and shifted the dynamics of the race.

In Upstate New York, Emanuel went with Judy Aydelott, a former Republican who was a tremendous fundraiser. She was crushed by environmentalist and musician John Hall, after which the DCCC shunned the race as unwinnable. Hall won.

Emanuel also ignored Dan Maffei, who lost in a recount by roughly 1,000 votes. With DCCC support the next cycle, he won in 2008.

On election night, Emanuel was stunned when John Yarmuth, a liberal in Kentucky who had founded an alt-weekly magazine and was thought to be a lost cause, was one of the first to be declared a winner. He's remained a solid progressive in Congress ever since; in 2019 he became the chair of the House Budget Committee, a position once held by Paul Ryan. Shea-Porter retired in 2018. Strong environmentalists, McNerney and Loebsack are both now senior members of the powerful Energy and Commerce Committee.

Outside Pittsburgh, MoveOn and some elements of organized labor heavily backed Jason Altmire in his western Pennsylvania race. "He was elected with the support of independent groups and he would not have won in 2006 without them," said strategist Tom Matzzie of MoveOn. He followed Altmire's race closely when he was the Washington director of MoveOn because he grew up in Altmire's district. Collectively, MoveOn and the AFL-CIO raised more than a million dollars for Altimire in 2006, the bulk of his money.

"We literally did not know Jason Altmire's name until a couple of weeks before the election," Bill Burton, the DCCC's communications director in 2006, recalled to me years later. "Jerry McNerney and the [Richard] Pombo seat, Carol Shea-Porter, Dave Loebsack in Iowa, all of those candidates, the thing that they had in common was they had strong grassroots energy and raised the threshold amount of money to get their name out there, not that dissimilar to what Alexandria Ocasio-Cortez had going for her."

Even on Rahm's own terms, his candidates often failed to perform. The top three highest recipients of DCCC cash all lost. Emanuel spent several million dollars backing Tammy Duckworth in a primary against a candidate that local and national progressives were backing. Duckworth didn't live in the district he wanted her to run in, and *The Thumpin'* reports that neither Durbin nor Emanuel were even sure if she actually was a Democrat. But as a helicopter pilot in Iraq, she was shot down and had lost both her legs, which had both men giddy at the prospect of her as the face of the '06 class of Democrats.

The DCCC's millions were barely enough to squeak her through the primary, 44-40, but she lost the general election, a close race that might well have been won by the candidate with local support. Duckworth ran again in 2012 and went on to win a Senate seat in 2016.

Emanuel's approach was in sharp contrast with the one that other strategists were lobbying for. Rahm, looking to keep expectations low, initially planned to target no more than 15 seats, barely enough to win the majority if he ran the table. A handful of outside strategists with unions and progressive groups, including Matzzie, Mike Lux of American Family Voices, and Larry Scanlon, political director at AFSCME, argued that the party should go big, and rope in anger at the Iraq War with the theme of corruption, while running on economic populism in upwards of 70 House districts.

The biggest challenge from within the party to Emanuel's way of doing politics came from former Vermont Gov. Howard Dean. Dean, having run for president in 2004 on an anti-war platform, pioneered the strategy, quite by accident, of marshalling small-dollar resources into big money. Act Blue, in fact, hadn't even been created when he popularized the idea of a money bomb — his "Raise the Bat" campaign — an effort to raise an eye-popping amount of money in a short time for the twin purposes of raising that money, and also demonstrating broad support. His run attracted many of the same sorts of progressives who had backed Jesse Jackson's campaigns, or Eugene McCarthy before him. And some of those people turned out to be among the most talented in politics. As I covered in chapter five, he lost to John Kerry, but went on to become DNC chair, arguing for a 50-state strategy which clashed with Emanuel's narrow focus.

The arguments grew increasingly heated, and eventually the progressive coalition, frustrated at Rahm's minimal ambition, set up a separate operation to go bigger, while staying in touch throughout the cycle.

Lux, a veteran Democratic operative, and Emanuel had a long working relationship dating back to 1982, but an unpublished memo Lux circulated around Washington after the 2006 election put an end to that friendship.

He committed the sin of putting down on paper what was largely going unsaid: the DCCC, which was being lauded for taking back the House, had in fact screwed up.

In the memo, he noted that Rahm spent more than $2 million defending three incumbents — Melissa Bean, Leonard Boswell, and Chet Edwards — who won easily, by six, seven, and 18 points, respectively. "In an overwhelmingly Democratic year, with three incumbents who have won elections in the past, even in Republican years, did we really need to spend that much to help these incumbents win? If you look at the margins by which they won, I would say the answer is probably not," Lux wrote in the December 2006 memo, which has not previously been published. "In a Democratic wave year like 2006, I probably would have let those incumbents take care of themselves."

He then looked at 17 races where the DCCC spent at least $1.5 million, mostly on TV ads. In five of those 17, the Democrat won by less than five points, meaning the investment made tactical sense. In seven of them, the Democrat lost a reasonably close race, coming within at least seven points.

But in another five races, the Democrat won by at least 10 points, in one case by as much as 24 points. The party spent more than $10 million on those five races.

Compare that to 12 races that were decided by six points or less where the DCCC stayed completely out. These were races they deemed unwinnable, but the progressive coalition rallied around anyway. Three of those were won.

Out of a field of 65 competitive races, the DCCC, in other words, got 18 of their targeting decisions wrong. Of the first 22 candidates Emanuel got behind, just nine won. Targeting — the process of choosing which districts to fight in — isn't a science, and it's understandable to miss some. But blowing your targeting on 28 percent of the races is a whopping miss. "So given that Rahm and his team at the DCCC are incredibly smart folks (and they are), what happened?" Lux asked in his memo, before answering his own question. "When you look at a lot of the races we didn't put money into, most of those candidates were anti-establishment, generally more populist progressive folks who I'm guessing the DCCC just didn't trust to run good campaigns or win. When you look at races like the Kentucky race where we dumped $2.7 million and lost by seven, that was a former congressman, very conventional, very conservative Democrat that Rahm probably just assumed would do well in that district. This was a year for anti-establishment, strongly anti-Bush candidates, and the DCCC did not, in general, do a particularly fine job of supporting those kinds of candidates, and I think that skewed the spending and targeting decisions."

Emanuel had dug in on the 18 seats in districts John Kerry had won in 2004 but still were represented by Republicans. Those seats were toss-ups, but even there he did barely better than flipping a coin, winning 10. That partly comes down to talent — politicians who consistently hold swing districts or seats where the opposite party wins the presidential election tend to be unusually good at connecting with voters.

In 2006, Democrats won 10 seats in districts George W. Bush had carried with between 50 and 55 percent of the vote. They won seven in races where Bush pulled in 55 to 60 and won three upsets where Bush had won 60 percent or more of the vote just two years earlier. In other words, one-third of all Democratic pickups came in races where the party had been crushed two years prior and was paying little attention this time around.

"Back in 2006, a strong argument can be made that Rahm was in the right place at the right time with the wrong strategy," said Mike Podhorzer, the AFL-CIO's strategist who worked on the '06 campaign, and was among those urging the DCCC to go big early.

The legend of Rahm is ultimately constructed not by real success but by a clever trick: profanity, which Rahm famously deploys loudly and with abandon, to friends and enemies alike, creating the impression of some serious fucking toughness, man. Rahm applies that approach to donors and has found it wildly effective, bludgeoning money out of the rich and transferring it to Democratic coffers.

"The first third of your campaign is money, money, money," Rahm told a group of staffers in one scene in *The Thumpin'*. "The second third is money, money, and money. And the last third is votes, press, and money." Notice that field organizing, door-knocking or having an inspiring message doesn't make it onto the list.

If everything is about money obtained via wealthy donors or business PACs, that rules out running a populist campaign that might threaten the people and corporations who have most of that money. Nor does it allow for trying to raise necessary campaign funds through grassroots donations. Lux, in his book *How to Democrat in the Age of Trump*, describes meetings with campaign consultants who go over polling that shows populist messages performing best, yet talking the candidate out of pursuing those messages, lest donors get spooked.

So the DCCC, then and now, hunts for poll-tested policies it can run on without offending that base of donors. In 2006 it was "Six for '06," a Rahm-created marketing exercise that offered six promises to voters:

1. Raise the minimum wage
2. Reform pensions
3. Make college tuition tax deductible
4. Negotiate for lower drug prices
5. Invest in alternative energy
6. Adopt the recommendations of the 9/11 Commission

But Rahm's ambitions couldn't be contained in such a short list; he wrote Nancy Pelosi a memo in early 2006, describing two more ideas he thought would bury Republicans: stem cells and a focus on the debt.

Rahm's approach is often described as politically agnostic or even nihilistic — he advised taking no position on the Iraq War or anything other than opposition to Republican corruption — finding meaning only in winning, or putting "points on the board." But whenever he finds himself in a political argument, it is always, without exception, battling the left. "We took on the communists in the party," he quips in *The Thumpin'* after Duckworth barely beat the liberal candidate in an Illinois primary.

In 2006, Rahm's greatest antagonist outside the party was what was known then as the blogosphere. One of the loudest and most effective critics at the time was David Sirota, who was then just a few years removed from working as a senior aide for Dave Obey, the top Democrat on the Appropriations Committee.

He's quoted prophetically, though passingly, in *The Thumpin'*. "For many, many years, the DCCC — under Rahm's leadership especially — seemed to think that having no ideology, no convictions, is a winning

formula," Sirota offered. "Even if you do win [in 2006] under that sce-
nario because the Republicans have screwed up so much, you have created an extremely tenuous majority, one that might set you back many,
many years."

The advances Democrats made during their two years in power were
just enough to infuriate and invigorate the right, while leaving much of
the rest of the country unsatisfied. It led to the loss of roughly a thousand seats across the country in the next decade, and the election of a
fascist-curious reality TV star running against The Swamp, promising to
fix a broken system through force of personality.

The centrist and conservative candidates were nominated not because they were best for the district, but because Rahm liked them the
best, particularly for their ability to raise and spend their own money,
but also because they aligned with him ideologically.

"The most important thing to the DCCC then was if you were
self-funding," said Podhorzer of the AFL-CIO. "That moved candidates
toward business centrists and their ability to last after that election was
not that great. And it set the stage for Obama's Democratic majority not
being as aligned with his policies as a more progressive majority might
have."

That's the generous interpretation. Alternately, Obama and his chief
of staff, Emanuel, may have gotten just the Congress they wanted. Those
Blue Dogs that packed the Tune Inn the night Obamacare passed, after
all, hadn't crashed the party. They had invites.

Seven

Triple Rainbow

The following chapter was written and reported with Kerry Eleveld, the author of Don't Tell Me to Wait: How the Fight for Gay Rights Changed America and Transformed Obama's Presidency. *I met her while she was covering Obama on the campaign trail and later in the White House. She interviewed him three times, including once in the Oval Office. Eleveld now works as Senior Political Writer for Daily Kos.*

Barbara Boxer was in the fight of her political life when President Obama joined her at a Los Angeles fundraiser in April 2010. But the night would not be about the four-term California senator. Amid the crowd of some 1,400 people gathered at the California Science Center was a handful of activists from a recently formed pro-LGBTQ direct action group called GetEQUAL.

The group's members were frustrated with the White House's foot dragging on gay issues, particularly after the many promises Obama had made to queer Americans on the campaign trail in 2008. They were also well aware that Democrats would likely lose control of at least one congressional chamber in the upcoming midterms, leaving a narrow window in which to pass any key LGBTQ legislative priorities before Republicans took over. Repealing the military's ban on lesbian and gay soldiers serving openly, a 17-year-old law known as "don't ask, don't tell," was foremost on their minds. To them, Obama was the key—the repeal effort would live or die by whether it was a top priority for the president and they were going to make sure it was top of mind for him that night.

"Hello, California!" Obama answered to cheers from the adoring crowd. "I am fired up!" But a couple minutes into Obama's speech, the GetEQUAL activists began a popcorn-style interruption in which one person would start chanting and, as soon as they were silenced by the Secret Service, another would pick up the chant from a different place in the room. Obama, who was usually expert at handling hecklers, was distracted. Finally, Dan Fotou, who had planted himself just 30 feet from the stage, landed a direct blow. "It's time to repeal 'don't ask, don't tell!'" he yelled, locking eyes with Obama, who abruptly broke from his script. "We are going to do that!" Obama responded, glaring and pointing at Fotou. "Hey, hold on a second ... We are going to do that," he told the crowd, getting a brief respite.

But shortly after Fotou was removed from the space, the chanting began anew, continuing for several minutes. Obama, flummoxed, stepped away from the podium and out of frame from the cameras entirely to privately ask Boxer how she had voted on the gay ban in the early '90s. She'd first been elected to the Senate in 1992 — the most recent Year of the Woman — and was pushing for a fourth term. When he returned, Obama reported, "I just checked with Barbara—so if anybody else is thinking about starting a chant, Barbara didn't even vote for 'don't ask, don't tell' in the first place."

By the time GetEQUAL activists had been entirely removed, they had hijacked the president's speech for close to seven minutes. Following the event, Obama was "unusually surly," as the National Journal later depicted Obama's mood, and let some expletives fly in front of his point man on repeal, White House aide Jim Messina, Rahm Emanuel's deputy.[76]

The tension between Obama and the activists grew out of a decades-old dynamic between national Democrats and LGBTQ voters, who had become a critical part of the Democratic coalition. Democrats needed gay support both at the ballot box and financially, but the party had also grown wary of hot-button LGBTQ issues that had given Republicans a cudgel to wield in the last several election cycles. Democrats had developed a habit of courting gay voters during election season while delivering next to nothing for them once the votes were counted. That wasn't going to cut it anymore. LGBTQ Americans were done with waiting around patiently for Democrats to decide the political climate was safe enough to engage on their issues.

Marriage equality, in particular, had been an issue bedeviling the Democratic establishment since it burst onto the national stage with the made-for-TV "Winter of Love" — a 29-day marathon of marriages in February 2004[77] during which more than 4,100 same-sex couples from across the country flocked to San Francisco's City Hall to finally get the chance to say *I do*. Then-mayor Gavin Newsom, a telegenic rising star, kicked off the rolling nuptials on February 12 when he ordered city clerks to begin issuing marriage licenses to same-sex couples. Exuberant cou-

76   Eleveld, *Don't Tell Me to Wait*, 134-141.
77   I (Ryan Grim) was a graduate student at the University of Maryland. At an

ples pitched tents outside of City Hall to wait their turn while flower bouquets flooded in from anonymous donors around the world to greet the stream of newlyweds.

One month later, California's Supreme Court halted the marriages and, by summer, invalidated every single one of them. But the marriage spectacle wasn't isolated to California. Another liberal bastion, Massachusetts, became the first state to begin legally marrying same-sex couples in May that year after the Commonwealth's high court ruled in 2003 that same-sex couples had the constitutional right to marry. A political firestorm over gay rights burned on both sides of the country that would ultimately force national Democrats to live up to their political commitments to LGBTQ Americans over the next several election cycles.

But getting Democrats to do the right thing by a loyal constituency that contributed sizable sums of money to their campaigns would take a monumental effort by LGBTQ activists, both inside and outside of Washington. They would have to convince Democratic lawmakers of a bigger electoral price to pay for failing to advance gay issues than for pushing them. And that cause suffered a major blow after the 2004 election cycle, which left the party believing that embracing LGBTQ rights too forcefully was tantamount to political suicide.

Following the 2003 Massachusetts court ruling and the nationally televised Winter of Love in California, Republicans labored to make gay marriage a central issue in the reelection bid of President George W. Bush. Shortly after San Francisco's wedding fest, Bush used his bully pulpit to call for a federal constitutional amendment banning same-sex marriage. Bush's chief strategist Karl Rove and his campaign manager Ken Mehlman fanned the flames of hysteria to land measures banning same sex marriage on ballots in eleven states that November. Republicans cast the marriage battle in the starkest of terms, with Bush calling it "the most fundamental institution of civilization." *Allowing same-sex couples to marry*, they argued, *would not only sully the institution, it would lead to the downfall of America and indeed civilization itself.* Mainstream reporters routinely spoke of Rove in a reverential tone, applauding as political genius his push for bigoted ballot measures in swing states.

---

event on campus with then-Second Lady Lynne Cheney, I stood up and asked her about the controversy. Her daughter, Mary, was an out lesbian, and I asked if Cheney would attend the wedding if it happened that weekend in San Francisco. She stood up and walked off the stage. I was detained by campus police and charged under the student code of conduct, along with two other students, with disrupting the event. The incident made national news — my first 15 minutes — and the school dropped the charges. The LGBTQ press was particularly interested in the story, I was told, because I was straight and had no obvious reason to care about the issue.

The Democratic presidential frontrunner, Massachusetts Senator John Kerry, suddenly found himself in a squeeze. Kerry was one of 14 senators who had been good on the issue previously, having voted against the 1996 federal Defense of Marriage Act, which defined marriage as being between a man and a woman and therefore prohibited over a thousand federal benefits from flowing to same-sex spouses regardless of whether they had a state-sanctioned marriage. But on the eve of such marriages commencing in his home state, Kerry reiterated his support for gay civil unions, trying to sell them as an equal alternative to marriage.

"I personally believe marriage is between a man and a woman — and in extending our rights under the Constitution in a nondiscriminatory manner," Kerry told a reporter just days before the Commonwealth's first same-sex weddings commenced on May 17, 2004.[78] He also stood opposed to Bush's constitutional marriage amendment but said he supported such a ban in his home state. Kerry preferred that state lawmakers pass a civil unions law, which he argued would "advance the goal of equal protection."

It was a lot of incomprehensible legalistic pretzel twisting. The "separate but equal" argument Kerry was advancing may seem preposterous by today's standards, but four years later Democratic nominee Barack Obama rolled out almost exactly the same position during the '08 cycle.

When Kerry ultimately lost his '04 election bid, the political class quickly laid blame on the marriage issue that had roiled Kerry and other Democrats during the cycle. Some Democrats stewed over Newsom's embrace of it. "I believe it did energize a very conservative vote," California Sen. Dianne Feinstein said of the same-sex marriages in San Francisco. "I think that whole issue has been too much, too fast, too soon," she added. "And people aren't ready for it."[79]

Every single anti-gay marriage amendment had passed at the polls, and pundits and journalists alike theorized the ballot measures had increased turnout among conservative voters in those states, thereby delivering the election to Bush. The specious logic caught fire in the Beltway and quickly settled in as the conventional wisdom still embraced by many political junkies to this day.

But even as the marriage myth solidified, Rove, the mastermind behind the entire venture, acknowledged the amendments themselves likely weren't the driving force behind Bush's win. The anti-gay initiatives had passed by large margins everywhere including in both Michi-

---

78   "Kerry Again Opposes Same-Sex Marriage," Washington Post, May 2004.
79   "Some Democrats Blame One of Their Own," New York Times, November 2004.

gan and Oregon, Rove noted a week after the election, yet Kerry had won both states.[80] Rove instead observed that there was "a broad consensus" on marriage in both parties, claiming the issue was simply part of a bigger narrative where "moral values ranked higher than they traditionally do" in most elections.

As political scientists studied the turnout and voting trends more closely, they would prove Rove at least partially correct. Later that month, a gathering of pollsters and professors at Stanford concluded the ballot initiatives had increased turnout across party lines — producing about a three percent higher turnout than in 2000 in the 11 states with measures. But the increased turnout had not resulted in significantly more support for Bush in those states, as Rove noted both at the time and later in his memoir, *Courage and Consequence: My Life as a Conservative in the Fight.* Plenty of those people who came out wound up voting for Kerry.

Instead, the election had largely turned on post-9/11 national security issues. "[Bush's] image of leadership, his focus on security, the fact that 9/11 hasn't happened again within this country's borders convinced Americans, especially women with families to protect, that this president should be returned to the White House," Gary Langer, director of polling for ABC News, told attendees at the 2004 American Presidential Election: Voter Decision-Making in a Complex World.

Nonetheless, the marriage myth became lore, and it reinforced for many Democratic operatives exactly what they came to believe during the early years of Bill Clinton's presidency. Clinton had been the first major-party presidential nominee to openly court lesbian and gay voters, accept bundled money (to the tune of several million dollars — real money in those days), and explicitly name-check "gay" Americans in major speeches.[81] Over the course of the Democratic primary, he had competed to win LGBTQ support, and one pledge he had made to gay donors was that he would push to end the ban on lesbians and gays serving in the military. But what Clinton never imagined was that the military's gay ban would accidently become the very first policy initiative of his presidency. That was exactly what happened just a week after the '92 election. Following a Veteran's Day speech he delivered in Little Rock, Arkansas, Clinton responded to reporters' questions about whether he planned to keep his promise on the gay ban.

"Yes, I want to," Clinton replied, adding that he hoped to "consult with military leaders" about how to do it. "My position is we need ev-

---

80   "Moral Values' Carried Bush, Rove Says," New York Times, November 2004.

81   Kerry Eleveld, *Don't Tell Me To Wait: How the Fight for Gay Rights Changed America and Transformed Obama's Presidency*, (New York: Basic Books, 2015), 3-4.

erybody in America that's got a contribution to make that's willing to obey the law and work hard and play by the rules."

Clinton's stance, which hadn't received much mainstream attention on the campaign trail, put him immediately at odds with top military brass who vehemently opposed the change. The next day, the New York Times ran two A1 above-the-fold stories about the ban declaring: "Clinton to Open Military's Ranks to Homosexuals." The young President-elect and his team were suddenly knee-deep in their first policy declaration, which would consume them straight through the transition and into his nascent presidency.

Top Clinton aide George Stephanopoulos would later write in his memoir *All Too Human* that the issue "overwhelmed" their first week in office, adding, "It was the last thing we wanted." The thorny debate wouldn't be fully put to rest until six months later when President Clinton, following the military's lead, announced the "don't ask, don't tell" policy, which would purportedly allow gays to serve so long as they hid their sexuality. It was a compromise that pleased no one — least of all the gay activists who had supported Clinton's campaign. A couple of weeks later, about 30 top gay rights advocates, including Clinton's longtime friend and closest gay ally David Mixner, sat for arrest in front of the White House.

To Clinton's top aides, including Rahm Emanuel, the high-profile skirmish with the gay constituency had done nothing but weaken Clinton's hand in the opening months of his presidency. Though they caught a break while a six-month review of the issue ensued, it had tripped them up coming out of the gate, strained their relationship with the military, taken the American public by surprise, and produced a political rift with a key but controversial constituency. As the imbroglio unfolded, they had been trying to fill critical Cabinet posts, begin work on a major health care overhaul, and finally generate some positive press through accomplishments like signing into law the Family and Medical Leave Act, which had been blocked by successive Republican presidents.

The gay ban debacle became another data point for Emanuel and other like-minded centrist Democrats that social issues like guns, gays, immigration, and reproductive rights were political losers. That ethic would inform the recruiting and strategy he'd do in 2006 as chairman of the DCCC, as well as his role as Barack Obama's initial chief of staff during his first two years in office, which would also prove to be the most productive and consequential of Obama's two-term tenure.

Although more than 15 years had elapsed between the time Clinton stumbled over the gay ban and Obama's transition team was prepping for his arrival at the White House, one would have never known it by the posture Team Obama adopted. For Democratic candidates in the '08 presidential election, lesbian, gay and transgender issues had played far more prominently than in any previous election. Despite the fact that Republicans had gleefully stoked same-sex marriage as a wedge issue in both 2004 and 2006, the hard-fought primary battle between Obama and Hillary Clinton for the Democratic nomination had forced both candidates to court every last voter they could find.

By that time, gay and transgender Americans had become a force in Democratic Party politics, putting their issues in the spotlight as both Obama and Clinton duked it out for the time, money, votes, and devotion of LGBTQ voters. Both candidates played it safe by supporting civil unions over marriage equality, but they also made high-profile pledges to pass hate crimes and employment protections along with overturning "don't ask, don't tell" and the Defense of Marriage Act — both of which were explicitly discriminatory byproducts of the Clinton administration.

While gay marriage was still hotly debated nationwide, public opinion on other LGBTQ issues had moved forward considerably. Expanding federal hate crimes protections to include sexual orientation and gender identity (along with gender and disability) was so noncontroversial, it had cleared both Democratic-led chambers in the previous Congress but died under a veto threat from President George W. Bush. Passing workplace protections for lesbian and gay employees had enjoyed majority support since the '70s and by 2008 polled at anywhere from 70-90 percent approval, depending on how the question was asked.

But in 2007 a rift had developed within the LGBTQ community over whether to include transgender Americans in a federal workplace protections bill. Ultimately, the Washington advocates and lawmakers who had lobbied to exclude transgender workers — including then-Rep. Barney Frank, who suggested they could be added later but were political poison at the moment — had largely been excoriated. Transgender individuals would likely never be left out of subsequent federal legislation, but the internecine political skirmish left Washington lawmakers somewhat uncertain about the path forward.

Meanwhile, the debate over allowing gays to serve openly in the military had progressed considerably since Clinton's early stumble. As reports had trickled out over the years of mission-critical lesbian and gay service members being discharged while the military was engaged in combat in both Iraq and Afghanistan, Americans had soured on the gay ban. The original argument against allowing lesbians and gay men to serve openly — that it would hurt unit cohesion and combat readiness — fell apart when Americans learned the military was expelling service members like Arabic-speaking linguists simply because they were gay.

By 2008, the issue was regularly polling at anywhere from 65 percent well into the 70s in support of repeal, depending on the way the question was phrased.

Obama and Clinton had also promised to overturn the Defense of Marriage Act. It was considered a heavier lift than the other measures because it touched on the hot-button issue of marriage, but here Democrats deployed a states' rights argument normally embraced by conservatives. While both candidates said they believed marriage was between a man and woman, they also said it should be litigated at the state level since defining and regulating marriage had effectively been left up to the states since the nation's founding. Because the crux of DOMA prevented federal benefits from flowing to same-sex couples with state-sanctioned marriages, the law infringed on the right of the states to regulate marriages and should therefore be eradicated, they argued.

Among gay and transgender advocates inside Washington, a generally agreed upon hierarchy of priorities developed heading into Obama's presidency, ordered by what they assumed would be easiest to most difficult to achieve: first passing hate crimes, then employment protections, followed by repealing the gay ban and DOMA. But that didn't account for many factors, including what would organically bubble up from advocacy at the state level. Making federal benefits available to same-sex couples with valid marriages, for instance, was an issue that was becoming more prominent by the month in the early days of Obama's presidency. By the time Obama was sworn in, both Massachusetts and Connecticut were performing gay marriages and within his first 100 days in office, three more states — Iowa, Vermont, and Maine — would legalize same-sex marriage. So Obama's promise to make federal benefits such as qualifying for the Family Medical Leave Act, Social Security survivor benefits, or equal treatment under taxation and immigration laws available to same-sex spouses quickly became a matter of real-world consequence rather than a theoretical exercise in ideology.

But what is perhaps most important to remember about one of the most prominent advances for the LGBTQ advocates during the Obama era — the advent of marriage equality nationwide — is that a political path had to be paved on the way to making that legal victory possible. While Supreme Court deliberations are, or at least were, sometimes idealized as existing beyond the politics of the day, the justices nonetheless exist in the same world as their fellow Americans. They consume the same headlines, talk to their peers and family members, and live their daily lives in the same political realities as the rest of America. And although they have occasionally done so at pivotal junctures in history, the justices are generally not prone to delivering decisions that prove so disruptive to the masses that they cause widespread chaos.

When Obama entered office, support for same-sex marriage stood at about 40 percent, well under a bare majority of the nation. Notably, not a single piece of major pro-LGBTQ legislation had ever been signed into law, even though early versions of the hate crimes and workplace protections bills had first been introduced in the mid- to late '90s. That deficit of political progress was going to have to shift in a positive direction. LGBTQ Americans needed to prove they were tolerated, accepted, and embraced by enough of their fellow citizens that granting same-sex couples the freedom to marry wouldn't upend the national order.

Of course, what's clear in retrospect wasn't a regular point of discussion among advocates going into Obama's presidency, partly because no one really imagined such a cataclysmic marriage decision was just over a handful of years away. But with the benefit of hindsight, it's difficult to imagine the high court delivering that 2015 marriage equality decision without at least some demonstration of pro-gay political will serving as a down payment on those freedoms. Legal scholars could disagree on this point given the many bold civil rights decisions that flowed from the court led by Chief Justice Earl Warren in the 1950s and '60s. But there's no disputing the fact that the high court headed by Chief Justice John Roberts today is nowhere near the vanguard of civil rights that the Warren Court of the 20th Century was.

It was also true, however, that political progress for gay and transgender Americans wasn't so much a matter of *if* rather than *when*. Despite the dearth of accomplishments at the federal level, cultural acceptance and even celebration of the LGBTQ community was steadily growing. Beloved comedian Ellen DeGeneres had busted out of the closet on a Time magazine cover in 1997 and her career not only survived, it ultimately thrived; the hit comedy "Will & Grace," featuring two gay male lead characters, had graced America's living rooms from the late '90s to the mid-aughts; and prior to the passage of about two dozen anti-gay marriage amendments from 2004-2006, support for marriage equality had steadily risen some 15 points, from a quarter of the country in the mid-'90s to around 40 percent a decade later in Gallup tracking polls. The queer-themed hits would keep rolling right into Obama's presidency, with shows like "Project Runway" and "RuPaul's Drag Race," which debuted in February 2009.

Nonetheless, LGBTQ citizens had little to show for all that cultural goodwill. Democratic lawmakers, meanwhile, had helped raise the profile of the LGBTQ community but done next-to-nothing concrete to advance their cause otherwise. The dynamic that hatched during the Clinton administration was still very much in play on the eve of Obama's presidency. Democratic politicians were great at sending the right signals to court lesbian, gay, bisexual, and transgender voters, but once the votes were counted, LGBTQ issues immediately took a backseat to everything else. The pattern is a classic conundrum for civil rights advocates.

This was the dilemma LGBTQ activists faced at the outset of Obama's presidency. As a candidate, especially during the primary, Obama had worked hard to earn their votes and made lots of promises along the way. But once he set foot in the Oval Office, the young president and his advisers would have to be convinced that putting energy into advancing LGBTQ policies would benefit them politically. And unfortunately, the most recent data points all suggested the opposite. Whether it was Clinton and the gay ban or John Kerry and the marriage amendments, national Democrats perceived those political battles as costing them a lot with little to no payoff.

And here's where a rift began between the LGBTQ advocates who were Washington insiders and queer advocates on the ground. The insiders were accustomed to the slow grind of governing that would allow Democrats plenty of space to deliver little more than good intentions, at least in the early part of Obama's tenure. So the gay advocates who made their living in Washington were primed to both accept and perpetuate an exceedingly gradual arc of change. In fact, many of them came up in the Clinton era and shared the conventional wisdom that pushing LGBTQ issues too fast would doom both Obama and Democrats in the next election.

Meanwhile queer activists on the ground were hungrier than ever for advances following three election cycles of gut-wrenching attacks on the very core of their humanity at the ballot box. The moment that pushed them past their breaking point came on election night in 2008 with the passage of California's Proposition 8, which summarily banned same-sex marriages in the state. What made Prop 8 unique from other marriage bans that had swept the nation was that it actually took away rights that already existed for same-sex couples in the Golden State.

Following the San Francisco marriage frenzy of early 2004, state advocates had passed two marriage equality bills through the state legislature only to have them vetoed by Gov. Arnold Schwarzenegger. In May 2008, California's high court finally ruled that prohibiting same-sex marriages violated the state's constitution, about a month after anti-equality activists certified enough signatures to put the issue on the ballot later that year. In the intervening months between legalization and reversal, some 18,000 same-sex couples wed only to watch their hard-won right be stolen out from underneath them on the same night Barack Obama was elected the nation's first African American president.

Amid the elation of most liberal-leaning Americans over one of the nation's most stunning civil rights achievements, many queer Americans found the night profoundly bittersweet. Prop 8, then the most expensive social-issue measure in history with a combined $106 million in spending from both sides, had become a national referendum on the fundamental freedoms and indeed the humanity of lesbian and gay Americans. Losing in California, a liberal bulwark and home to the iconic Castro District that helped birth the gay rights movement in the '70s, was both unthinkable and unacceptable. It could not stand. And the grief and disbelief queer activists experienced that night steeled them for action. They needed Obama to champion the civil rights movement he had promised, and to make that happen, they were — perhaps more than any progressive movement — primed to go to war with the administration and the man most of them helped elect.

The first sign that the loss of Prop 8 might not be business as usual wasn't necessarily the tens of thousands of protesters who poured out into the streets in cities across the state. What signaled that something even bigger and more sustainable was afoot was the swift organization of hundreds of rallies across the country and even internationally. After activists Amy Balliet and Willow Witte built an interactive site on which people could post and publicize marriage rallies, on November 15, protests launched in all 50 states, eight countries, and some 300 cities around the world. As one marriage equality activist noted, a "democratic monster" had been unleashed.[82] The organic outpouring of grief, anger, and resolve was a response to the vote itself, of course. But it was also directed at the more than a dozen LGBTQ insiders who had organized the unsuccessful statewide campaign against Prop 8. These were people who supposedly knew what they were doing but had failed miserably. And in the view of many frustrated activists, it was time to get them out of the way.

"I realized that all the organizations that were built to protect us were in the pocket of the Democratic machine," grassroots organizer Robin McGehee recalled of the Prop 8 loss. McGehee, who lived in Fresno, had fought hard to promote the "No On 8" campaign while also knocking on doors for Obama. Her work was centered in the middle of the state, which was largely ignored by both campaigns. "We had put so much effort into getting Obama elected in areas where he had no chance," McGehee said. But after the Prop 8 loss, she felt like Obama's team quickly moved along. "It was like, *Well, we'll do our best, but we can't promise anything,*" she remembered. "I felt very disenfranchised." That was the

---

82   "Protests, boycotts erupt in the wake of Prop. 8's passage," San Jose Mercury News, November 2008.

moment she realized that she had to "fight the machine" to advance LGBTQ rights. McGehee organized a post-Prop 8 rally called "Meet in the Middle 4 Equality," and she would later help found the direct-action group GetEQUAL that dogged both the White House and Democratic lawmakers, particularly during President Obama's first term.

The first sign that Obama and his top aides planned to maintain the status quo was when his inaugural committee announced pastor Rick Warren would deliver the invocation at Obama's inauguration. Warren wasn't just any pastor — he was an anti-marriage-equality warrior who advocated for the passage of Prop 8, even posting a video message urging his evangelical flock at Saddleback Church in Southern California to vote for the measure.[83] Warren had also sponsored a candidate forum at Saddleback between the GOP nominee, Sen. John McCain, and Obama several months before the election. When he asked Obama to "define marriage," Obama uttered what would become his most prominent pronouncement on the matter the entire campaign. "I believe marriage is between a man and a woman," he said to cheers from the crowd, reiterating the stance he had taken throughout the election.

"Now, for me as a Christian," Obama added, "it's also a sacred union. Ya know, God's in the mix." The implication was that marriage was too "sacred" to include the apparently unholy unions of same-sex couples. Obama's words were ultimately repurposed by Prop 8 supporters into robocalls urging people to vote for the measure. While no one can say definitively how Obama's pronouncement affected the final outcome, it was a gift to the "Yes on 8" campaign, which badly needed to peel off Obama voters to support the discriminatory measure. Sure enough, Obama carried the state by an overwhelming 24 points on election night, yet enough of his voters also favored Prop 8 to pass it, 52 to 48 percent. And now the "holy" man who helped strip same-sex couples of their dignity would be blessing Obama's presidency.

The second and perhaps more subtle sign Obama had learned the lessons of the Clinton White House too well came when reporting surfaced within weeks of the 2009 inauguration that the White House planned to work with the military to study the issue of repeal. Whatever might happen on the gay ban, it wasn't going to happen quickly and probably not for a year or more. "Study" meant one thing in Washington — delay. In fact, the issue had been studied repeatedly over the last several decades with the bulk of the research pointing to one conclusion: Allowing gays to serve openly would not significantly harm military readiness and unit cohesion and might even improve them.

Studies aside, the White House's intentions on the stickier LGBTQ

---

83   Eleveld, *Don't Tell Me to Wait*, 32-33.

issues became clear — they were going to stall. Along the way, they would enlist advocates from many prominent gay groups like the Human Rights Campaign, the largest organization nationally, to counsel patience to queer activists across the country. The problem for the White House was that gay and transgender issues continued to percolate nationwide. Within several months of Obama's swearing-in, the number of states that had legalized same-sex marriage had more than doubled to five. And after the White House had paid nothing but lip service to LGBTQ issues in Obama's first 100 days in office, a prominent former gay White House advisor to Clinton would pen a piece in the Washington Post titled, "Where's Our 'Fierce Advocate'?" — a reference to Obama dubbing himself a "fierce advocate of equality" following criticism over his Warren pick for the inauguration.

Within weeks, another gay former Clintonite, insider-turned-outsider David Mixner, would call for an equality march on Washington, appealing to young activists in particular to organize it if the Beltway groups failed to do so. The White House and other LGBTQ insiders like HRC thought they could buy themselves some time and good will if they secured passage of the expanded hate crimes bill, which had been languishing for over a decade. But passing hate crimes was taking more time than they thought and they had wildly misjudged the impatience in the streets. Queer activists were looking for a lot more than stiffer penalties and help from federal investigators if someone beat them to a pulp while hurling anti-gay epithets.

The standoff between Washington insiders and grassroots activists would finally come to a head one October weekend in 2009. It was, for Washington insiders, an event that epitomized their version of progress President Obama would keynote the HRC gala. The following day, hundreds of thousands of LGBTQ activists and allies would take part in the National Equality March on Washington. Organizers outside of D.C. had collaborated for months on putting the march together with next to zero help from the established and well-funded gay groups inside Washington. The president's attendance at the HRC fundraiser on Saturday, confirmed just a week in advance of the event, was a clear response to the displeasure that some 200,000 marchers planned to express about his leadership.

Obama's speech wasn't even an advance. It promised nothing new to the community. He previewed the fact that hate crimes legislation would pass later that month, but when it came to other priorities, all he did was recommit himself to previous pledges. "I will end 'don't ask, don't tell,'" he told that crowd of about 3,000, "that is my commitment to you." But he offered no timelines or benchmarks even as the clock was starting to work against activists.

Obama would never have as much power or as many votes to get things passed in the next Congress. That meant repeal would have to happen in 2010, a midterm election year and a time when lawmakers get notoriously gun shy about taking any votes that might scuttle their reelection chances. Repealing the military's gay ban — despite polling in the 60s and 70s — was exactly the type of vote many Democratic lawmakers feared. Congressional Democrats would need to see real resolve rather than mere rhetoric from Obama if they were going to prioritize repeal. The president would offer a glimpse of that resolve several months later during his 2010 State of the Union address, pledging that he would work with Congress "this year" to end the policy. But again, no details emerged beyond the applause line.

In the weeks that followed, the Chair of the Joint Chiefs, Admiral Mike Mullen, would testify at a Senate hearing that he personally supported repealing the measure as a matter of "integrity." Mullen's testimony was a significant shot in the arm for repeal. At the same hearing, Defense Secretary Gates would announce a plan to undertake a massive study, surveying hundreds of thousands of active-duty troops in order to explore how repeal would affect military readiness. Finally, something concrete had emerged. But Secretary Gates set the date for completion of the report for December 1, 2010, and quickly began stressing that no votes should be taken on legislation before the study was completed. That timing seemed a death knell for repeal that year — there wouldn't be time to shepherd repeal legislation through both chambers of Congress in less than a month.

The White House stayed silent on the timeline until Press Secretary Robert Gibbs was grilled on it during a briefing. He said that Obama had "set forward a process" with the Pentagon that he believed was the best way to move forward toward repeal.[84] In fact, Gates later said that both President Obama and Rahm Emanuel "promised — unequivocally and on several occasions — to oppose any legislation before completion of the review."[85]

But what the White House, Democratic lawmakers, and even gay Beltway advocates never counted on was having the post-Prop 8 rage from the streets arrive at Washington's doorstep. Indeed, the relatively small but dedicated group GetEQUAL grew out of the National Equality March. Throughout the rest of Obama's first term, the group would serve as an inconvenient reminder of what LGBTQ Americans expected after helping elect the strongest Democratic majority government in generations.

84   Eleveld, *Don't Tell Me to Wait*, 143-144.
85   Robert M. Gates, *Duty: Memoirs of a Secretary at War*.

GetEQUAL activists hijacked HRC events, interrupted congressional proceedings, and staged protests targeting key Democratic lawmakers like House Speaker Nancy Pelosi and Senate Majority Leader Harry Reid. But in 2010 in particular, they directed some of their most effective actions straight at the White House. Several times that year, lesbian, gay, and transgender veterans handcuffed themselves to the fence surrounding the White House, using the spectacle to alert the ubiquitous White House Press Corps and the nation that a key Democratic constituency was losing patience with President Obama. GetEQUAL activists also showed up in unexpected places to stage organized interruptions of Obama's speeches, such as they did at a televised fundraiser for Boxer.

In July 2010, the annual Netroots Nation conference was held in Las Vegas, Nevada, largely because Harry Reid had agreed to keynote the marquee gathering of bloggers and activists he'd grown close to. As he spoke, former Lt. Dan Choi, an Iraq War vet who'd recently been kicked out of the military due to his sexuality, approached the stage to present his West Point ring to Reid. In an emotional exchange, Reid accepted it, and promised to return it only after he had successfully repealed the DADT policy.

LGBTQ activists were the first progressive constituency to vocally and overtly register their discontent in the early days of Obama's presidency. Like the suffragette and civil rights activists who came before them, queer rights crusaders had learned that major civil rights advances never came without a fight. Indeed, one of the most painful lessons for the gay rights movement came in the '80s and '90s when politicians and the federal government turned a blind eye to an epidemic that was killing gay men by the tens of thousands. Faced with a virtual death sentence that national leaders desperately wanted to ignore, gay men and their allies concluded rightly that "Silence = Death," which ultimately became the rallying cry of one of the most tenacious direct action groups in modern American politics. From its founding in 1987, ACT UP, which stood for AIDS Coalition to Unleash Power, browbeat lawmakers and federal officials into finally developing effective treatments for HIV. Some 15 years and more than 300,000 deaths after the first news reports of a "rare cancer" in gay men surfaced in 1981, lifesaving drugs would finally be approved by the U.S. Food and Drug Administration in the mid-'90s.

At the height of the AIDS crisis, ACT UP activists proved to be fearless — and they struck fear in the hearts of politicians. They were committed, creative, media savvy for the era, and totally undaunted by societal norms. In December 1989, they staged what would become a definitive protest at St. Patrick's Cathedral in New York after Cardinal John Joseph

O'Connor had denounced condom use as a way to counteract the spread of HIV and AIDS. As about 4,500 protesters flooded Fifth Avenue outside the church, some ACT UP members staged a "die in" inside the Cathedral while others chained themselves to pews. Finally, one protester who had gotten up to take communion crushed the wafer symbolizing the body of Christ and let it drop to the floor. The protest inspired worldwide outrage, including a rebuke from the New York Times editorial board, which wrote that the action had "turned honorable dissent into dishonorable action." Internally, ACT UP members had debated the action for months before staging the protest and some feared they had gone too far in the wake of the blowback. But the takeaway externally was worth its weight in gold: If ACT UP would take on the Catholic Church, they would take on anyone.

These were the stories GetEQUAL activists drew inspiration from decades later. Group leaders even visited New York in early 2010 to brainstorm with some of ACT UP's originating and most influential members, such as founder Larry Kramer and journalist Ann Northrop.[86] Though the present-day activists weren't watching a plague ravage their community, they were once again confronting government indifference that systematically ignored and erased their very existence.

The impatience and pressure these hungry activists brought to Washington didn't necessarily force Obama to do something he didn't want to do. He wanted to be good on the issues and viewed himself as a champion of civil rights. In fact, Defense Secretary Gates would also write in his memoir that repealing the gay ban was "the only military matter" on which he "ever sensed deep passion" from Obama. But the president was also an incrementalist at heart who had forged his identity through working to make change within the confines of America's institutions. What the activists did was disrupt those confines to speed up the timeline on repeal. They were the catalyst that initiated the chemical reaction, but they never would have succeeded without the other elements in place: a cultural shift toward acceptance of LGBTQ Americans, a willing president and Congress that just needed a convincing push, a decades-long legal advance in the courts that was finally ripening, and an assortment of pro-repeal lobbyists, lawmakers, and legislative aides using whatever leverage they had to push repeal through before the close of the 111th Congress.

All of these critical components made possible what was nothing short of a series of small miracles from the spring of 2010 to the waning days of December. In spite of the agreed upon process from the White House and the Pentagon, a May vote in a key Senate committee attached

---

86   Eleveld, *Don't Tell Me to Wait*, 113-116.

the repeal measure to the military's must-pass budget bill, giving repeal a fighting chance for passage before the end of the year. Though the vote appeared to be a silver bullet, the budget bill languished into December, reflecting the continued reservations of both Pentagon officials and the Democratic caucus, which had no appetite for passing the legislation prior to the midterms. But heading into the lame-duck session, the repeal effort scored two game-changers that would turn Gates into a sudden and urgent booster of overturning the ban.

The first came on October 12, when a federal judge who had ruled "don't ask, don't tell" unconstitutional a month earlier placed a worldwide injunction on the ban in a case that had originally been filed in 2004, *Log Cabin Republicans v. United States.* The order sent shockwaves through the Pentagon as officials rushed to issue new worldwide guidelines that would normally be months in the making. A little over a week later, an appellate court temporarily suspended the injunction while it reviewed the decision, forcing the military to shift course on the policy twice in the span of eight days, with the threat of more abrupt disruptions down the road.

Gates suddenly understood: if Congress didn't repeal the gay ban legislatively, the courts were going to overturn it, and likely sooner rather than later. Legislative repeal had all sorts of built-in structures that would allow the military to make the changes methodically over the course of many months of planning. But having the policy under review in the courts could leave the military in limbo possibly for years. The instability on such a consequential personnel matter would be intolerable for an institution that thrives on order, discipline, and churning recruitment.

Just a couple of short months after that ruling, Gates would become a fervent and vocal supporter of legislative repeal. His evolution was helped along by the results of the massive study the military had undertaken on "don't ask, don't tell." The final 250-page report found the risk of repealing the ban "to overall military effectiveness is low." In fact, 67 percent of the some 115,000 active-duty service members said repeal would either be "a positive" or have "no effect" at all on the readiness of their units; only 12 percent predicted a negative impact. After the results were released in late November, Gates would begin his final push to convince lawmakers to repeal the ban before the end of the 111th Congress.

After the tea party wiped out Democrats in the November 2010 midterms, congressional Democratic leadership met on December 4 with Obama in the Oval Office to talk about the agenda for the lame duck — the last shot Democrats would have at unified control. Obama made clear a nuclear weapons treaty he had negotiated with Russia, called New START, was his top priority. Nuclear arms control was one of the issues Obama cared about both personally and as a legacy item. In the 1980s, as Obama came of political age, he had marched against nuclear weapons, and he grew up under the fear of global annihilation at the press of a button. "The administration's first, second, and third priority was getting this START treaty ratified," said one person in the room.

After the meeting, Reid stayed behind to talk to the president one on one. Reid had never been a vocal champion of LGBTQ rights, but throughout the 2000s, as he grew closer to the party's activist base, his politics on social issues had been swinging left. It had also become personal: Reid had a niece who was a lesbian, he would later tell reporters.[87] Her coming out had just the kind of political effect that '70s-era activist Harvey Milk had presciently promised it would decades earlier.

The majority leader would never make a threat to Obama in front of anybody else, and he wasn't about to do it that day. The two wandered over to the Oval Office window to chat. "Reid put the screws on him.... Reid in so many words made it clear to the president that he wouldn't get his START treaty ratified if he didn't get on board with repealing 'don't ask, don't tell,'" said the person who'd previously been in the room, and was told about it afterward. "Let's put it this way: 'don't ask, don't tell' became a priority for him."

Repeal hit the Senate floor on December 9, 2010, tucked into the Pentagon spending bill. Reid had reasoned that Republicans lacked the votes to strip it and surely wouldn't be craven enough to block an entire annual defense bill — which would mark a first in decades. Reid had been wrong. They were quite willing to take it down. "Eventually these people will vote against the Iraq War," Rep. Barney Frank (D-Mass.), a lead proponent of repeal, told me at the time.

The bill went down, with several Republicans withholding their support, claiming they wanted to force a vote on other priorities first—a tax cut, chief among them. Dan Choi, the West Point grad whose ring was in Reid's possession, would soon check himself in for mental health treatment, collapsing under the weight of the defeat.

Within minutes of its demise, Sen. Joe Lieberman, the lawmaker spearheading the repeal effort, hastily arranged a press conference to resurrect the stand alone bill that had been attached to the budget bill earlier that year. Lieberman, who sat on the Senate Armed Services

---

87   "My niece is a lesbian," Reid told a handful of reporters in 2013, including my HuffPost colleague Jen Bendery, who wrote about it at the time. "She's a school teacher. Her employment shouldn't be affected with that. We should have a law that says that, not just the good graces of wherever you work."

Committee and was deeply invested in ending the ban, repeated something he had been saying for weeks: he had the sixty votes necessary to pass repeal, if only Reid would bring the bill to the floor *after* meeting the GOP's demand to vote on tax cuts. It all came down to a matter of priorities — would Democrats prioritize repeal as they had repeatedly promised or would they use it as a pawn in a much larger game of chess?

Throughout the year, Reid had been working unusually closely with House Majority Leader Steny Hoyer (D-Md). Hoyer, the relative conservative in leadership, had value in the way he could work with the military and with Blue Dog Democrats, pulling them into the fold or at least turning down the volume on their complaints.

Reid planned to recess for the year on Friday, December 17. With basically one week left, the Senate needed to vote on a tax bill, a massive government funding bill for the coming year, and START. By midweek, the tax cut measure had passed, but Reid was still publicly hedging on repeal. On Wednesday, the House passed its repeal bill, leaving only the Senate remaining. "I don't know if I'll bring it up [for a vote] before Christmas," Reid said, suggesting that technically the session extended into early January. At the other end of Pennsylvania Avenue, White House Press Secretary Gibbs was finally acknowledging that they had the votes to pass repeal, but added, "if we have time."

It was looking grim. Advocates had managed to build enough support for ending the gay ban to pass repeal on its own merits and yet the White House seemed content to let the clock run out as Republicans took control of the House. Worse, White House aides were pressing Reid and Pelosi to back off, what one person on the receiving end of it called "a pretty fierce lobbying effort to get him to back off of it," arguing that the votes weren't there and that the focus should be elsewhere.

Neither backed down. In the meantime, a giant trillion-dollar budget deal collapsed, leaving a hole in the voting schedule while alternate plans were worked out to keep the government funded. On the night of December 16, Reid called Obama in the Oval Office to tell him he planned to put repeal on the floor. Obama made a strong case against it, convinced it would fail and derail the remainder of the lame-duck agenda. It was a familiar argument from the Rahm Emanuel camp—that losing on one issue was contagious and would infect the rest of the agenda, that it was better to put "points on the board" with certain victories. The DREAM Act was scheduled for a vote on the same day, and the thought of two losses was just too much to bear. Reid heard him out before delivering his response "Well, Mr. President, sometimes you just gotta roll the dice," Reid said, and then he hung up.[88]

88   I (Grim) wrote a profile of him for HuffPost in 2010 called "Harry Reid, The

Reid quickly slotted in a floor vote on repeal and passed it with 63 votes, three more than the 60-vote threshold necessary to advance the bill. On final passage, it picked up two more, going to Obama's desk after passing the Senate 65-31.

Later that day, with hunger-striking young immigrants watching from the gallery, Reid put the DREAM Act on the floor. It fell five votes short of the 60 needed to overcome the GOP filibuster. Good to his word, after DADT was repealed, Reid put the START treaty on the floor and successfully ratified it. Top White House advisor David Axelrod would later write in his memoir *Believer: My Forty Years in Politics* that President Obama had gotten nearly everything "on his list" during the lame duck session, including START, among other bills, and "to our mild surprise and great relief," the repeal of the military's gay ban.[89]

Going into the 111th Congress, not a single piece of major pro-LGBTQ legislation had ever been enacted. After it, the words "lesbian, gay, bisexual and transgender" had been entered into the U.S. Code for the first time with the expansion of the hate crimes law, and explicit government-sanctioned discrimination of lesbians and gay men risking their lives to protect America's freedoms would come to an end.

And, no, people didn't march in the streets following the demise of "don't ask, don't tell," as the Rahm Emanuels of Washington had feared. For all the blood, sweat, and tears it took to drag repeal across the finish line, the ban fell with the whimper it should have, given the overwhelming public support for ending it. In that respect, "don't ask, don't tell" repeal — which had struck fear in the hearts of many Democrats — marked a profound change in momentum on gay and transgender issues in Washington. In fact, every time the White House took a step to advance equality for LGBTQ Americans, the political goodwill and praise it received in return consistently proved to far outweigh any blowback. And pushing freedom forward for a new chapter in America's civil rights

---

Man Who Never Says Goodbye." That he hung up on Obama was entirely in character, and wasn't the first time he had done so. He simply does not say goodbye, seeing the formality as superfluous. When the conversation with Reid is over, it's over. After I learned of this moment, I interviewed Reid, who confirmed it. "I told the president, I understand how important the START Treaty is, and I'll do everything I can to help with that. But I said, I'm going to go ahead and 'roll the dice,' exact words, 'roll the dice,' on don't ask, don't tell. I said, I think it should turn out well for both of us, but I'm rolling the dice. It turned out well for both of us," Reid said. In Obama's defense, Reid said, the vote was legitimately in doubt. "I was a little worried myself," he said. "I wasn't sure I had the votes."

89   David Axelrod, *Believer: My Forty Years in Politics*, (New York: Penguin Press, 2015), 430.

story also had the benefit of putting President Obama exactly where he envisioned himself in the arc of history. As one White House aide would later observe, every new win on gay issues just got easier and easier.[90]

The next domino to fall was the Defense of Marriage Act, which barred the federal government from respecting state-sanctioned same-sex marriages. Several solid cases had been filed challenging the law and a federal court ruling in one of them had struck it down as unconstitutional, though it had not yet made its way to the Supreme Court. It was an issue that had escalated considerably during Obama's first two years in office as states continued to legalize same-sex marriage and the administration was put in the awkward position of continuing to deny legally married couples federal benefits while defending that discrimination in court.

The White House had taken a lot of heat regarding its continued legal defense of DOMA. The Department of Justice filed its first brief in defense of the discriminatory law in June 2009, sparking grassroots outrage, a united denunciation from pro-LGBTQ legal advocacy groups, and a good number of powerful gay donors dropping out of an annual Pride month fundraiser for the Democratic National Committee. Millionaire donor Bruce Bastian, for instance, told the gay publication the Washington Blade, "I don't think blanket donations to the Democratic Party are justified right now."[91]

With "don't ask, don't tell" off the books, DOMA became easier to handle. After internally debating the constitutional merits of the law for more than a year, President Obama, along with his White House attorneys and lawyers at the Justice Department, all concluded separately that DOMA was unconstitutional when reviewed under the more rigorous standard of scrutiny usually applied to laws targeting disfavored minorities.[92] On February 23, 2011, shortly after repeal passed, Attorney General Eric Holder announced the administration no longer deemed the law constitutional and therefore would not continue to defend it in court.

Announcing that conclusion got a heck of a lot simpler after the legislative victory on "don't ask, don't tell," a law the administration had also been defending in the courts.

Far from the sky falling, repeal had been a win. There were no angry protests from either the public or the military, and the enthusiastic response to what was arguably the most pristine progressive win of Obama's first two years in office heartened the administration. Passing

90   Background interview by Kerry Eleveld with former White House aide to President Obama, September 25, 2014.

91   Eleveld, *Don't Tell Me to Wait*, 88-89.

92   Eleveld, *Don't Tell Me to Wait*, 196-220.

health care reform may have been the president's most consequential legacy, but the Affordable Care Act wasn't nearly as aggressive as many liberals had hoped it would be. Overturning "don't ask, don't tell" was a promise kept, plain and simple.

The pieces for full marriage equality were coming into place. The military's ban on lesbians and gays serving openly had been the first. Once it was gone, the march toward the freedom to marry became politically viable, as it had for so many of America's allies abroad that embraced open military service in advance of legalizing same-sex marriage.

The fact that a robust legal advance was pushing the issues forward in courts across the country also helped force the issue in Washington. As much as the White House would have preferred to leave issues like the gay ban and DOMA for another day, they were continually forced to take stands on the laws in the judicial setting. And in the early days of the administration, those public-facing stands stood in stark contrast to the portrait candidate Obama had painted of himself on the campaign trail.

Once the administration had repealed the gay ban and stopped defending DOMA, Obama would be forced to reckon with his position in support of civil unions — one that he had held fast to since his 2004 run for U.S. Senate. Similar to DOMA, legal cases challenging marriage bans in the states were in process. In fact, two all-star lawyers, conservative Ted Olson and liberal David Boies, were tag-teaming a high-profile assault on California's Proposition 8 that had reached the 9th Circuit Court of Appeals by winter 2010.

Although Obama had embraced civil unions over marriage equality in his bids for federal office, he had also signed a statement during his 1996 run for Illinois State Senate supporting the freedom to marry. "I favor legalizing same-sex marriages, and would fight efforts to prohibit such marriages," read a typed statement signed by Obama, responding to a survey from a gay Chicago newspaper, then called Outlines. But that revelation, in complete contradiction to his oft-repeated assertion during the '08 cycle that marriage is "between a man and a woman," didn't surface until January 2009, between the election and Obama's inauguration. It caused a brief stir in the media, but the presidential transition was on the move and Obama and his aides managed to escape any serious scrutiny of the questionnaire until early 2011. It was as if the younger, more idealistic Obama had gotten out ahead of the more calculated politician he would become. But his split personalities on same-sex marriage (and by extension full equality for LGBTQ Americans) were on a collision course heading into his 2012 reelection bid. Not only had support for same-sex marriage risen about 10 points over the previous decade, the issue had also become a moral imperative for many liberal voters in the same way that denying marriage rights had long been for conservative voters.

Some of the credit for that shift belongs, accidentally, to Karl Rove and Bush's 2004 campaign chairman Ken Mehlman. By turning the issue of gay marriage into an electoral weapon, they made it a partisan issue and made Democrats pick sides. Like Obama and Kerry, most had been content to squat the middle position of civil unions and just move on to more comfortable terrain. But if Democrats are forced to take sides on a civil rights question, the bulk of them, particularly in the grassroots, will come down on the right side.

Rove and Mehlman forced that decision, and by early 2012, Pew Research found that 59 percent of Democrats supported marriage equality, an increase of nearly 20 points from 40 percent in 2004. But nearly three-quarters of liberal Democrats favored it. And perhaps most important, urgency on the left was meeting urgency on the right head on. In April 2012, Pew wrote: "22% say they strongly support allowing gays and lesbians to marry legally; an identical percentage (22%) strongly opposes gay marriage. In 2008, there was about twice as much strong opposition to as strong support for gay marriage (30% vs. 14%)." The 2012 numbers were a significant turnaround from 2004, when 36 percent of Americans "strongly opposed" same-sex marriage while just 11 percent "strongly favored" it.

President Obama finally announced his public support for marriage equality in May 2012, right as his bid for a second term was beginning to heat up. "I've just concluded that for me personally it is important for me to go ahead and affirm that I think same-sex couples should be able to get married," Obama told Robin Roberts of ABC News in a nationally televised interview. Longtime Obama aide Axelrod made headlines when he asserted in his memoir *Believer* that Obama had favored the freedom to marry all along, but what the moment truly reveals is how little it matters what a politician believes in their heart.

"For as long as we had been working together, Obama had felt a tug between his personal views and the politics of gay marriage," Axelrod wrote, acknowledging Obama's endorsement of marriage equality in the '96 questionnaire.[93] "I had no doubt that this was his heartfelt belief," he continued. "[A]s he ran for higher office, he grudgingly accepted the counsel of more pragmatic folks like me, and modified his position to support civil unions rather than marriage, which he would term a 'sacred union.' Having prided himself on forthrightness, though, Obama never felt comfortable with his compromise and, no doubt, compromised position."

---

93   Axelrod, *Believer*, 446-447.

It wasn't exactly a good look in the rear-view mirror to find out that the first African American president had used religious bigotry toward an unpopular minority as a stepping stone to higher office. In fact, President Obama was quick to deny Axelrod's assertion in a subsequent interview with Buzzfeed News.

"I think David is mixing up my personal feelings with my position on the issue," Obama said. "I always felt that same-sex couples should be able to enjoy the same rights, legally, as anybody else, and so it was frustrating to me not to, I think, be able to square that with what were a whole bunch of religious sensitivities out there." The rather convoluted answer cleared up little other than the fact that the president still wanted to have it both ways — always having been a supporter of equal rights for LGBTQ Americans, yet earnest in his embrace of civil unions. How promoting a separate-and-unequal institution counts as a blow for equality will forever be hard to "square," to use Obama's framing, but certainly he will try to do so in his inevitable memoir.

In 2008, however, when 70 percent of lesbian, gay, and bisexual voters cast their ballots for Obama, most of them had accepted that his civil unions stance was the electoral necessity Axelrod had suggested it was. In fact, even before Obama completed his political evolution on the matter, a hot debate was raging within gay political circles about whether a flip-flop on the issue would doom him at the polls in 2012. Many LGBTQ advocates still believed it would, especially those in Washington.

But the truth of the matter, and where Obama and his aides ultimately came down, was that it had become impossible for him to package himself as a "fierce advocate" for equality if he didn't evolve. One key attribute that voters had attached to Obama during his 2008 campaign was that he was a guy who stood on principle. At least one of his confidants advised him in 2011 to forget about the polling — he simply couldn't afford to head into his reelection campaign with an air of disingenuousness.[94] That confidant was Obama's former Harvard Law classmate and RNC chair Ken Mehlman, who had come out in 2010 — to the great aggravation of many LGBTQ activists — and begun to advocate for the freedom to marry. In some ways, the Obama administration had become a victim of its own successes. Queer issues had been increasingly mainstreamed amid all the high-profile advancements taking place. In the process, marriage equality had become a broader progressive cause rather than a constituency issue important solely to LGBTQ voters.

While so much of the public discussion about President Obama's evolution on same-sex marriage has revolved around what really lay in Obama's heart, the more salient political lesson is that LGBTQ activists

---

94   Eleveld, *Don't Tell Me to Wait*, 235-237.

had managed to make his evolution a political necessity in a matter of four short years. While Obama saw civil unions as the winning electoral position in 2008, he also concluded that he had no choice but to embrace marriage equality in 2012. It was a political gamble — and clearly the right one — but it wasn't one any normal politician would choose to take in the heat of a reelection bid unless they concluded they had run out of options.

And while the polling had improved on the freedom to marry, Democratic operatives had also slowly but surely come to see an upside to pushing LGBTQ equality forward. In fact, a post-election battleground state poll commissioned by the pro-gay conservative group Mehlman founded, Project Right Side, found that 73 percent of Obama voters said his support for marriage equality made them "more likely" to vote for him, with almost half of them saying it made them "much more" likely to support him. In addition, a majority of voters in those eight battleground states, including 58 percent of independents, favored same-sex marriage. Obama's support for marriage equality had undoubtedly helped him win a second term.

But beyond the electoral benefits, Obama's evolution also gave the marriage cause an unqualified boost. Pro-equality activists logged wins in all four of 2012's marriage-related ballot measures — defeating a marriage ban in Minnesota and affirming gay marriage rights in Maine, Maryland, and Washington. It was nothing short of a sea change in the states after marriage bans had prevailed at the ballot box in some 30 states. The president's announcement also cleared the way for his administration to be on the right side of history when the issues of both DOMA and marriage equality reached the Supreme Court. Likewise, LGBTQ legal advocates benefitted from having the full weight of the executive branch on their side even as congressional Republicans weighed in against same-sex marital rights and the federal benefits included therein.

When challenges to both DOMA and Proposition 8 were reviewed by the high court in 2013, the Department of Justice filed amicus briefs in both cases — *United States v. Windsor* and *Hollingsworth v. Perry* — arguing that the laws were discriminatory and their constitutionality should be reviewed under a more rigorous standard known as "heightened scrutiny." When DOMA was finally ruled unconstitutional, it sparked a wave of legal decisions in the states overturning gay marriage bans. And when the question of same-sex marriage reached the Supreme Court again in 2015 in the landmark case *Obergefell v. Hodges*, the Obama administration unequivocally advocated for striking down all marriage bans nationwide, calling them "facially discriminatory" and arguing they relegate same-

Ryan Grim

sex families to "second-class" status.

None of this is to take anything away from the legal advocates, Roberta Kaplan and Mary Bonauto in particular, who argued these cases at the Supreme Court, along with the many other attorneys who have nudged gay and transgender rights forward, case by case, district by district, and circuit by circuit over decades. Instead, it's an affirmation of the intermingling between the legal and the political and how each can push the other forward.

The people, ultimately, are the genesis of all movements toward freedom, something President Obama captured on June 26, 2015, the day the Supreme Court finally struck down marriage bans nationwide. The court's action was, he said, "a consequence of the countless small acts of courage of millions of people across decades who stood up, who came out, who talked to parents — parents who loved their children no matter what."

The president called those courageous truth tellers "countless, often anonymous heroes" and said they deserved our thanks: "What an extraordinary achievement. What a vindication of the belief that ordinary people can do extraordinary things."

It was as if he was channeling the spirit of gay rights legend Harvey Milk, who gained attention in 1977 after becoming one of the nation's first openly gay elected officials when he was voted on to the San Francisco Board of Supervisors. A year later, Milk and then-Mayor George Moscone would be shot by a disgruntled colleague who had resigned his supervisor post. But Milk's infectious energy lived on after he famously encouraged gay people everywhere to come out for themselves and the sake of the movement.

"Gay brothers and sisters," he began, addressing a crowd on June 25, 1978, Gay Freedom Day in San Francisco, "you must come out. Come out... to your parents... I know that it is hard and will hurt them but think about how they will hurt you in the voting booth! Come out to your relatives. I know it is hard and will upset them, but think of how they will upset you in the voting booth. Come out to your friends... if indeed they are your friends. Come out to your neighbors... to your fellow workers... to the people who work where you eat and shop... once and for all, break down the myths, destroy the lies and distortions. For your sake. For their sake. For the sake of the youngsters..."[95]

In a recording Milk made to be played in the event of his assassination, he again called on every gay doctor, lawyer, architect, and others to come out. "That would do more to end prejudice overnight than anybody would imagine," he asserted.

95   Randy Shilts, *The Mayor of Castro Street: The Life and Times of Harvey Milk,*

The power of the LGBTQ movement and its relatively quick reversal in fortunes over a decade on marriage equality laid in the millions of Americans who risked their jobs, their livelihoods, and even their lives to own their truth. While people who identify as lesbian, gay, bisexual, or transgender account for a rather small percentage of the U.S. population — typically anywhere from 3-5 percent in polls — they also exist in every community of the country. LGBTQ individuals are a part of every race, gender, culture, religion, political party, and socio-economic group in the nation, making it impossible for people to completely otherize them as somehow not one of their own. It is a unique dynamic for a minority in America, and one that helped queer activists gain outsized impact among their fellow countrymen. In fact, a 2011 Gallup poll found that, on average, U.S. adults estimated that gays and lesbians accounted for 25 percent of the population.

Milk's call to come out gained renewed and heightened urgency as nearly a generation of gay men fell to the AIDS epidemic while the federal government barely lifted a finger. Along with AIDS activists, the up and coming generation of Gen Xers seemed to conclude that living in the shadows simply wasn't an option anymore. Coming out became an ethic, a necessity, an essential affirmation of life. Each new person who took that step advanced the march for equality. Eventually, the politics in Washington began to follow the cultural revolution emanating from neighborhoods across America.

But the work of equality is far from over. The administration of Donald Trump is busy attacking nearly every one of the gains that was made under President Obama. Trump officials have taken particular aim at transgender individuals, undermining their service in the military, their access to public spaces, and their safety and dignity in schools. In addition, no federal law exists that provides explicit "gender identity" and "sexual orientation" protections in the workplace and public accommodations. Though federal courts have increasingly concluded that transgender and gay individuals are covered by the prohibition of "sex" discrimination under Title VII of the Civil Rights Act of 1964, it is not a matter of settled law.

The work of securing these protections will be bolstered by the coming age of activism from Millennials and Generation Z, by far the most welcoming and queer-friendly generations to date. The increasing acceptance and inclusion of LGBTQ Americans is a self-reinforcing trend that has been built generation by generation. And while the queer rights movement is suffering the inevitable setbacks that any movement does after making great gains, the irrepressible work of progress will con-

---

(New York: St. Martin's Griffin, 1982), 368.

tinue — expanding into a political landscape that is virtually unrecognizable from the one that existed 100 years ago, 50 years ago, or even a decade ago, when a young and progressive president promising "Hope and Change" was still advocating for civil unions. It was the anonymous heroes through the ages that forever changed that political landscape.

Eight

The Dream

For people who have come to understand politics in a post-Great Recession era, the immigration debate during the mid to late 2000s would be entirely unrecognizable. In 2005, President George W. Bush teamed up with Senators John McCain and Ted Kennedy on a push for comprehensive reform, and there was genuine optimism it could happen, giving a path to citizenship for people here illegally, as it had happened under Reagan just two decades earlier.

In some ways, having Bush in the White House was better for reform's prospects than under Clinton. In the 1990s, Democrats had been the party of immigration enforcement, with Rahm Emanuel urging Clinton to get as tough as possible. Bush, waging war around the globe and clearing brush on his ranch with a cowboy hat, was confident in his reputation for toughness, so he didn't mind compromising on the issue. As a border state governor, he also had a better understanding of the realities of the immigration system. As a pro-business Republican, his fealty to the Chamber of Commerce pushed him further toward reform.

While the Senate worked on its proposal, Republican hardliners were whipping up their own hysterical bill in the House, led by Wisconsin Rep. Jim Sensenbrenner. Co-sponsored by Peter King (R-N.Y.) it was a preview of the rightward lurch of immigration politics to come. It included no pathway to citizenship, no protections for people already in the country, not even a guest worker program. It criminalized immigration violations that had long been civil affairs, turning even a visa overstay into an "aggravated felony," empowering local and state police to become immigration enforcement officers. It also made it a felony to aid someone in the country illegally in any way, and funded new fencing on the border and a surveillance and monitoring regime in the interior of the country.

As the vote approached, the Congressional Hispanic Caucus met to talk strategy. One of its most conservative members, John Salazar, who represented a swing district in Colorado, gave a rousing speech, saying that this was a moment to stand together. He pledged to oppose the Sensenbrenner bill.

"For the first time, Latinos were going to vote as a caucus, not talk smack, but actually go out and vote," said one CHC member who was in the room.

But the unity wouldn't last. "Rahm went to Salazar and told him, don't expect any money from the DCCC, or my help, if you vote against Sensenbrenner," the CHC member said. It was a painful choice to make. "Salazar's wife was like, *This is a piece of shit legislation*, I remember her saying that."

Emanuel, serving by then as chair of the DCCC, saw an opportunity for a win-win. Bush wasn't going to sign the bill, and the Senate would never pass it, he argued, so it was essentially a free vote. He urged moderate and conservative Democrats to back the bill, including Chicago freshman Melissa Bean, whom he had helped elect in 2004. That would burnish their conservative credentials, but there would be an added benefit for the party, too. The bill was so vicious and racist that it would prompt an outpouring of anger from the Latino community, which Emanuel could then channel into votes in the 2006 midterms.

"I remember immediately after that, he was like, *We're gonna take the majority over*. Rahm was gonna do what Rahm was gonna do. If that meant telling Latino members of Congress to vote against their conscience, that's what he was gonna do," said the CHC member.

The move helped unleash a wave of nativism that has only grown more powerful as the years have gone by, culminating in the election of Trump in 2016.

Emanuel was right that the immigrant rights community would respond forcefully. The bill passed in December 2005 with just 203 Republican votes, fifteen short of the 218 needed. But 36 Democrats put it over the top, including Bean and Salazar. The name Sensenbrenner became profanity on Spanish-language TV and radio, and the community mobilized millions in mass demonstrations.

The protests began in Chicago, with 100,000 taking to the streets in March. Then more than a million people rallied in Los Angeles. In April, simultaneous protests erupted in 102 different cities. On May 1 — May Day, honoring workers and unions — millions again took to the streets.

As the protests grew, so did the backlash. Right-wing radio was obsessed with Mexican and Central American flags being flown at the rallies, and counter-protesters began burning Mexican flags at their own demonstrations. Membership in the Minutemen, an anti-immigrant militia, surged. States and cities passed their own draconian laws, such as Arizona's notorious SB 1070. Immigration and Customs Enforcement (ICE) responded by stepping up raids. Emanuel may have thought letting the legislation pass was harmless, but deportations soared in the final two years of the Bush administration, with ICE feeling emboldened to hit back organizers of and participants in the demonstrations.[96] ICE has been on a war footing since.

But Emanuel did get this slight uptick in the Latino vote share. Hispanics were more likely to vote[97] in the 2006 midterms because of the Sensenbrenner bill.

The surge in nativism had come just as — and, indeed, because — the immigrant rights movement had been making real progress. When Ana Maria Archila, a young activist in Queens, first got involved in the movement in 2001, the focus was on building capacity so that they could push Congress to act. That summer, the existence of secret negotiations between the U.S. and Mexican governments over sweeping immigration policy reforms broke into public, and Congress moved quickly to put them into law. But like with the anti-globalization movement, the attacks on 9/11 derailed that.

So the movement went back to building capacity, and, strategically, decided to focus on winning over Big Labor, and by 2002, had pulled it off. That summer, the AFL-CIO passed a resolution saying it had "officially embraced the cause of immigrant workers in the United States" and would lobby for executive action and legislation that would legalize residents.

The strategy and the message, said Archila, were both dictated by, and aimed at, the power structure that the movement thought it had to win over. "The framework that got developed at the time was comprehensive immigration reform, which was based on an analysis of power, which continues to be similar today, that in order to win any kind of legalization, we had to get the votes of congressional leaders and members

96   ICE's response to the demonstrations is covered in *Rallying for Immigrant Rights: The Fight for Inclusion in 21st Century America*, edited by Kim Voss and Irene Bloemraad (2011).

97   Juan Andrade, "Immigration and Its Impact on Latino Politics," *The Almanac of Latino Politics* (2008).

that are in parts of America that are quite conservative," she said. "In order to win legalization for some, we needed to accept, essentially, the entrenchment of the enforcement apparatus, the growth of the deportation machine, and all of that, *and* satisfy the needs of business."

To get there, the movement leaned on an assimilation-heavy strategy that rhymed with the approach taken by the LGBTQ community: there's nothing scary about us; we're just like you. "The narrative that we deployed at the time, in the 2000s, was, *We are good people, we are family people, we share the values, we're not criminals. Don't you fucking know we pick your tomatoes, goddammit? Like, don't you like those?*"

Bush had first proposed some sort of amnesty in 2001, and the backlash that exploded in the midst of the 2006 demonstrations had been lit back then. Rep. Luis Gutiérrez, shortly after Republicans re-took Congress in the 2002 midterms, mocked the idea that the good immigrant should live side by side with the notion that amnesty is off the table. "Don't say *amnesty*," he mimicked critics.[98] "*Ay Dios mio. Pardon me for working, for picking your grapes, for cleaning your bathroom, for raising your kids. Sorry.*"

That message necessarily required some whitewashing of American history. "It was very much appealing to this narrative of America, the melting pot and the good immigrant, we are all immigrants — but a narrative that really did not hold the complexity of the history of this country, and excluded the experiences of black people in this country and didn't insinuate any analysis or race really," she said. "It was more like, *We are workers and you need us, and we're good, we're going to be fine, you don't need to be scared* — basically speaking to white America."

The Sensenbrenner bill had spit in the face of that strategy. It was the House of Representatives saying that it didn't care about your values, your love of God, didn't care about your work ethic, didn't care that you picked the tomatoes.

But when Democrats took over in 2006, there was new hope that reform could get through. The Sensenbrenners had been repudiated, leaving Democrats to negotiate the details with Bush.

The 2007 compromise was ushered by Kennedy and Sen. Jon Kyl, a Republican from Arizona. Kennedy's rotating partners on immigration reform are themselves a window into the evolving politics. In 2001 and 2002, his lead ally had been Kansas Republican Sam Brownback, who fought hard for protections for refugees, asylum seekers, and for a pathway to citizenship. His immigration work would cause him reelection

---

98   This comes from the extraordinary documentary series "How Democracy Works Now," a project that filmed immigration reform advocates and opponents for more than a decade.

problems, and he'd eventually become governor, leading "the Kansas experiment," a radical project of budget and tax cuts that wrecked the state.

In 2004, his partner, the AFL-CIO, turned on him, bucking reform, which Bush used to his advantage for reelection, winning 40 percent[99] of the Hispanic vote, enough to win him reelection.

Next, he'd worked with McCain, but as McCain began thinking about running for president, he couldn't be seen doing immigration reform, which left Kennedy with Kyl for that 2007 push.

They put together a package that was typical of the genre — more border security, more agents, more verification at job centers in exchange for a reformed guest worker program, fixes to the thoroughly broken immigration system broadly, and a pathway to citizenship for those here without papers.

The bill had the tenuous backing of immigrant rights groups, big business and labor, but also faced a lot of opposition from activists for its overly harsh approach.

It also had to run the gauntlet of the Senate floor. It was put there using one of the most arcane rules the Senate has ever devised, known as the "clay pigeon." A significant number of amendments to the bill are allowed on the floor for a vote and are fired into the air like a clay pigeon. If any single one of them wins, the whole thing shatters, the amendment process ends, and the Senate moves immediately to a cloture vote — which is a measure that requires 60 votes to end the debate and move toward final passage. The purpose is to impress upon senators that the deal crafted and sent to the Senate floor is extraordinarily fragile, and even though any particular amendment may seem mundane or helpful, its addition to the bill breaks the clay into pieces.

So opponents of the bill try to add popular-seeming language to it in the hope of taking it down, and the bill's backers defend it against all amendments. It also provides cover for people who want to publicly back it, but had private reasons to oppose it — say, because they were running for president and didn't want to alienate key constituencies who fairly believed the bill was too punitive on the enforcement side and not generous enough on the legalization side.

The clay pigeon was launched in June 2007. "Barack Obama played virtually no role in the negotiations," Kyl recalled to me years later. Obama, then a senator running for president, however, would play a major role on the floor. Amendment after amendment was fired up into

---

99   Exit polls put him at 44 percent, but a subsequent study found that the pollster had oversampled the heavily Republican Cuban population. Adjusted, it fell to 40 percent.

the sky, with opponents missing their shots and the pigeons landing softly in the grass.

Obama had co-sponsored a key amendment that greatly weakened the employee verification process along with Sens. Max Baucus (D-Mont.) and Charles Grassley (R-Iowa). The Baucus-Grassley-Obama measure was considered a major threat by the Kennedy-Kyl coalition, and a GOP lobbyist who worked on it recalled that she expected it to pass if it got a vote.

It never came up because the previous amendment, sponsored by Byron Dorgan, did pass. Dorgan's passage shattered the clay pigeon and was followed by a vote on cloture.

The documentary crew cameras were in the offices of the Essential Worker Immigration Coalition, an offshoot of the Chamber of Commerce, as the votes were unfolding. When news broke that Obama was backing the Dorgan amendment, the lobbyists knew it was over.[100] *"Presidential candidate kills immigration bill* — there's a headline for you," lobbyist Craig Silvertooth said to nobody in particular. The Dorgan amendment passed by a single vote, 49-48.

It was at least the fifth time that day that Obama had voted against Kennedy on amendments. While that may have been the shell that took it down, it appears that the fix was already in, even if the bill had made it through the amendment process unscathed.

The Chamber of Commerce had been optimistic that it had the support of Senate Minority Leader Mitch McConnell (R-Ky.). But on the cloture vote, he wasn't with them. "That's the whole thing," said one business lobbyist in the film as McConnell cast his critical no vote. Republicans voted against it by a margin of 37-12, making clear they saw the direction the issue was headed. "This is about as right-leaning a bill that's conceivable. It just shows that the party is in the grip of the nativists in a way that it wasn't," added another lobbyist.

The motion got 46 votes, 14 shy of the 60 it needed, with 16 Democrats, including independent Bernie Sanders, voting no. Sherrod Brown of Ohio also voted no from the left, as did Byron Dorgan.

Kyl, meanwhile, said that his experience heading the 2007 negotiations has left him concerned that today's Congress won't be able to come

---

100   Dorgan told me that it's unfair to consider his amendment a deal-breaker. "I know the supporters called my amendment a poison pill, and it's because they were worried about losing the Chamber of Commerce support," Dorgan told me. "It's always the case that when an agreement is reached, those who reached the agreement are determined to prevent it from being amended, so they call every amendment a killer. They always claim it is like a loose thread on a cheap suit — pull the thread and the arm falls off."

to agreement. He said that despite the progress he and Kennedy made, major issues remained largely unresolved.

"It's easy to say, *You have to go to the back of the line*," Kyl said, but the line is so long for some nationalities with limited quotas that it becomes impractical. "For Mexicans and El Salvadorans, which are a large part of what we're talking about, they'd be dead by the time they got in," Kyl said. To manage that problem, he had agreed to allow the millions at the front of the line to be expedited, but that would then cause its own problems, including a massive influx of new immigrants who would need to be assimilated and absorbed into the labor market, he argued. How to resolve that conflict, he said, was never resolved.

Nor, he said, were the critical details of the guest worker program, a major element of any comprehensive package. Kyl said that no agreement could be reached as to who would be considered a guest worker, what the levels would be, how those levels would respond to economic conditions and which federal agency would oversee the program.

The backlash and the failure of comprehensive reform transformed the politics of the immigrant rights movement. For years, the position among activists was that the so-called Dreamers — people brought to the country as children without papers — should not be broken off separately, but needed to be part of the comprehensive reform. They were the most publicly sympathetic cases, went the argument, and cleaving them off would leave everyone else — including their parents or grandparents — stuck behind. Gutiérrez had first introduced the bill back in 2001 and it had triggered an intense debate within the community, but Dreamers had played ball with the broader movement. Now they were getting restless.

When Obama became president, it soon became clear that his promise to move quickly on immigration reform wasn't going to be kept, particularly as the tea party protests rocked the summer recess of 2009. "There's always a sense that no matter how hard we work, to get through the White House, we have to get through Rahm," said Grijalva in 2010.[101] "I would like immigration not to be part of the chief of staff's portfolio. It would make our ability to convince and access decision-makers in the White House a lot easier."

"It's going to be much easier for this issue to move after Rahm Emanuel leaves the White House," said Simon Rosenberg,[102] head of the New Democratic Network. "Rahm has a long history of a lack of sympathy for the importance of the immigration issue."

Dreamers began to put pressure on the White House and on the

---

101   Quote comes from Peter Nicholas, writing in the Los Angeles Times.
102   Ibid.

immigrant rights community itself. The formed the group United We Dream in 2009, pulling together disparate youth organizations that had been shut out of the larger infrastructure.

In May 2010, a more radical group, The Dream Is Coming, took what was the first step on the path the movement has taken since. Five undocumented people sat down in the office of McCain, demanding he support the DREAM Act, as he had before. Four were arrested, with three given deportation orders.[103]

The sit-in exposed a split within the Dreamer movement. Though the young people had broken off from the larger movement, and were pressuring it to get behind them, instead of the other way around, they were still embracing the good immigrant narrative, led by valedictorians and Stanford students. Protesters wore caps-and-gowns and engaged in a "study in" in a Senate cafeteria.

In July, New York Dreamers pressured Chuck Schumer with a ten-day hunger strike. In November and December, a 43-day hunger strike in San Antonio pressured Senator Kay Bailey Hutchison, a Republican who had previously backed the DREAM Act but was now wobbly.

In November, Democrats were washed out of the House by the tea party wave, and lost six seats in the Senate (in addition to the one they had already lost to Scott Brown in January in the special election). The lame duck was the last chance. Activists flooded phone lines, staged sit-ins and launched new hunger strikes. The bill passed the House, still controlled by Pelosi, and got a Senate vote on a Saturday morning in December.

It carried the day by a vote of 55-41, but because Democrats hadn't eliminated the filibuster, it needed 60 to pass. It fell five short, with six Democrats against it.[104] "This bill is a law that at its fundamental core is a reward for illegal activity," crowed Sen. Jeff Sessions, then a senator from Alabama, who would go on to lead the most viciously anti-immigrant Justice Department in modern memory.

On December 21, with the window for legislative action closed, Obama reached out to Luis Gutiérrez,[105] the Chicago congressman. "He calls and he says to me, 'We lost the House, and we're weaker in the Senate. So now I have to defend immigrants, and we need to defend them together.'

103   Daniel Altschuler, "The Dreamers' Movement Comes of Age," *Dissent*, May 16, 2011.
104   That was West Virginia Sen. Joe Manchin, Kay Hagan of North Carolina, Mark Pryor of Arkansas, Ben Nelson of Nebraska and both Montana Democrats, Jon Tester and Max Baucus. Only Tester and Manchin remained in the Senate after 2018.
105   As told to Brian Abrams, in an unpublished portion of an interview for his oral history of the Obama years.

So he says to me, he says, *Luis* — I remember exactly the words — *I want you to put your thinking hat on. I know you're going to Puerto Rico. You know I'm going to Hawaii* — it's kind of jovial, right? — *and when we get back, give me your best ideas on how we protect them.*"

From there, Gutiérrez said, came the drafts of the coming executive orders and memos on prosecutorial discretion that would reverse the administration's approach to immigration. But it did not come naturally to White House officials. "I come back [in February 2011] and I meet with [new chief of staff] Bill Daley," Gutiérrez said. "Bill Daley's response was, *Well, wouldn't Mexicans just cross the border en masse to find American citizens to get married to?* And I almost fell under the table. *Uh, yeah, some really poor Mexican migrant workers are gonna find willing American citizen women to just marry them. Uh, I think we have a little problem here.*"

The same day that the DREAM Act failed, the military's "don't ask, don't tell" policy was repealed, and immigration activists noticed, and compared what the LGBTQ movement had done to what they had done.

The assessment led to several different conclusions. In the wake of the defeat, some Dreamers began to rethink the strategy of aligning their struggle with a mythical American Dream narrative, and began linking immigrant justice with other efforts to combat oppression. "'Unafraid and here to stay' is the motto of Dreamers now, and there is a much clearer race analysis, and they look at the system of immigration enforcement as an extension of the criminalization apparatus," said Archila. "So it's not a separate thing from mass incarceration, but it's a core component of it."

The new activists' "politics were shaped by the movements of the last ten years, Occupy, the Movement for Black Lives, the resistance itself," she said. "And so they transformed the narrative from one of appealing to a kind of construct of American history, to one that is much more unapologetic. Like, *I am undocumented, I am here to stay.*"

Others saw the LGBTQ success on the cultural front as key to their victory, and decided the culture war had to be won before the political battle could be. People like Ai-jen Poo, executive director of the National Domestic Workers Alliance, argued that the fight had to be won in cultural spaces like Hollywood.[106] In 2011, Pulitzer Prize–winning journalist Jose Antonio Vargas[107] came out publicly as undocumented, as part of

106   Netflix's "Roma" came directly from that effort.

107   In late 2008, I interviewed with Arianna Huffington for my eventual job as congressional reporter for The Huffington Post. Because she's Arianna Huffington, it was scheduled in the evening at the Four Seasons bar in Washington. When I arrived, she was already there with Vargas, then at the Washington Post, who, I eventually realized, would be sitting in on my interview, for no particular reason I could

that effort to win cultural hearts and minds, later going on to launch a media platform aimed at telling stories of immigrants.

Rahm Emanuel left at the end of 2010 to run for mayor of Chicago, and Obama still had hopes for comprehensive reform. In a pattern that would play out from issue to issue, he believed that if he showed some toughness and compromised with Republicans early, they'd buy in to his approach. Toward the end of his presidency, he came to realize the futility of the strategy, but in 2010 and 2011, was still wedded to it. He pushed ahead with deportations and border security, in an effort to bring Republicans to the table.

That's how Obama eventually came to be known as the "deporter in chief," but in at least one way, the label was a bit of a mirage. The spike in deportations had largely been a numbers game Obama played. Under the Bush administration, if somebody was caught trying to cross at the border, they'd be put on a bus and sent back, but they weren't tabulated as a deportation. Obama changed that policy, and the accounting move made it appear as though a surge of deportations was under way.[108]

Obama won reelection with strong Hispanic support, and the Republican National Committee, in its autopsy, concluded that it needed to embrace immigration reform to stem the loss of Latino support or be relegated to permanent minority status.

By a vote of 68–32, the Senate in 2013 finally passed comprehensive reform, which included a pathway to citizenship and staggering amounts of money for border security. House Speaker John Boehner had promised Obama the bill would get a vote on the floor, where it had the votes to pass. But the right-wing of the party pushed back hard, and as he deliberated, his deputy, Rep. Eric Cantor, lost his Virginia primary in a stunning upset. His opponent, Dave Brat,[109] had wielded the "amnesty" in the bill as a weapon against Cantor. Immigration reform was dead, and Boehner never put it on the floor.

---

discern. Luckily, because we were both journalists in our late-20s/early-30s in the same small town of Washington, I was friendly with him already, and his presence probably made the interview go better for me. I got the job, and we eventually hired Vargas, too. He later told me he also had no idea why he was there for my job interview, but I'm glad that he was.

108   One lingering consequence of that statistical move is to mask the barbarity of what Trump has done. Border crossings have plummeted under Trump, yet deportations have been flat, meaning that Trump is rounding up an equivalent number of people from the interior of the country to match the numbers Obama was previously doing at the border. The numbers then appear flat from one administration to the next, but that obscures the reality.

109   He was swept out in 2018 by Democrat Abigail Spanberger.

More than a decade of failure and stepped-up enforcement had left the movement without a clear path forward. "There's the people who insist on legislative change, the people who say the whole system has to be rebuilt, and the people who say, well you need to actually appeal to people's hearts and minds, otherwise we're never gonna win something that is dignifying for us," said Ana Maria Archila. "There isn't a unifying demand or a unifying strategy anymore."

Nine

Heart Attack

Sweat poured down Hank Paulson's rapidly whitening face. It was a Sunday night in October 2008, the global financial system was in free fall, and Paulson — George W. Bush's treasury secretary and a former CEO of Goldman Sachs — was in the Capitol with Senate Leader Harry Reid in search of a bailout.

But it was Paulson, Reid thought to himself, who was in the most urgent need of rescue. This man was dying in front of him. Reid, Paulson, and Reid's aide Jim Manley were off in a sideroom in the House Speaker's office waiting for Nancy Pelosi, who was late, as was her practice.[110]

Under normal circumstances, a treasury secretary having serious health problems — Reid and Manley were sure it was a heart attack — in the middle of an important congressional meeting would be newsworthy. But at the moment, in October of 2008, this kind of news could be catastrophic. Paulson was not only in charge of the response to the billowing global crisis, but was one of the few competent members of the Bush team.

Paulson's time as a top CEO on Wall Street gave him real insight into the globe's financial plumbing, which he knew operated heavily on confidence. If word got out that Paulson was collapsing under the weight of

110   All involved, from her allies to her adversaries, say that Pelosi's chronic tardiness — she regularly made Presidents Bush and Obama wait — was a power move. Pelosi's ability to understand and use power is what separated her in those years from most Democratic politicians.

the crisis, that confidence could vanish, and the bottom could fall out.

So the Senate majority leader huddled with Manley and they gamed out how they could get the Capitol's doctor into the Speaker's office without being seen by the press, and thus by the world. A nearby elevator might work, but it was just around the corner from the scrum of reporters. Perhaps a side door?

The week before, the House of Representatives had rejected Paulson's request for a $700 billion bailout of Wall Street, and now congressional leaders were supposed to be figuring out a new path forward. Before Reid and Manley had devised a plan, Paulson began to recover, life returning slowly to his face. The pair agreed to keep the heart-attack scare, or whatever had happened, secret.

Paulson, who had just recently been chairman and CEO of Goldman Sachs, would later tell Reid he had been suffering from the flu, but his body may also have been overwhelmed by an excess of metaphors coursing through his veins. The Wall Street crash was the bookend of an era of deregulatory politics that had begun some 30 years ago. It would create the conditions that have shaped our global politics in the decade since.

Paulson, after a meeting that went terribly, left through a side door at around 2 in the morning. I spotted him and managed to position myself at his side as he weaved his way out of the Capitol, my tape recorder in his face. By then a practiced politician, he said nothing in response to the first few questions I and the other reporters threw at him.

We needed something for our copy, so I tried a different tack. What, I asked him, should people know when they wake up tomorrow morning?

"It's Monday," he said.

A camera snapped, and the resulting photo graced the next morning's front page of the New York Times. Everybody was laughing.

The crash, along with John McCain's uncertain and peripatetic reaction to it,[111] and Bush's sub-30 percent approval rating, combined to turn what had been a closely contested presidential campaign into a breezy win for Barack Obama, the first time a Democrat had won a majority of votes in the general election since 1976. And it opened the possibility of a progressive reformation of the country for the first time since the 1960s. It also opened darker possibilities. Obama surged into Washington on the back of a movement of historic proportions. Anger at the Iraq War and fury at the incompetence, at best, of George W. Bush was tipped into a landslide by the financial crisis that struck just weeks before the

---

111   He claimed he was suspending his campaign until the crisis was over, which made little sense, then followed by siding with House Republicans who were only stoking the crisis further. It came just after he had said the fundamentals of the economy were strong.

election.

Obama had long been gathering crowds of astonishing sizes, and he raised hundreds of millions of dollars from regular people moved by a message of hope and change. The Republican Party was in freefall, its ideology thoroughly discredited by the Wall Street meltdown. "I made a mistake in presuming that the self-interests of organizations, specifically banks and others, were such that they were best capable of protecting their own shareholders and their equity in the firms," said longtime Federal Reserve Chairman Alan Greenspan that October, flatly admitting that his life's work had been in error.

Obama's wave had brought the number of Democratic senators to 58. When Harry Reid persuaded Pennsylvania's Arlen Specter to switch parties, that made it 59. In Minnesota, Republicans were battling furiously to drag out a recount between Al Franken and incumbent Norm Coleman, knowing that every day that passed was a day without a filibuster-proof majority. In July, Franken was finally declared the winner, bringing the number to 60. In the House, there were 257 Democrats, a 79-seat majority.

The country, as Bush left office, was losing more than 500,000 jobs a month, creeping close to a million in January. The nation was ready for change. Gallup put Obama's approval rating at his inauguration at 67 percent, with just 13 percent opposed and the rest undecided. It stayed in the 60s well into the summer.

Majorities were strongly supportive of a New Deal–level intervention in the economy, an entire refounding of a system exposed as dangerously broken. Time magazine put Obama on its cover, rendering him to look like FDR. Nationalizing major banks was being talked about by typically conservative financial analysts. Long-sought universal health care was in sight, as was a reorganizing of the economy around a green-jobs revolution that would combat climate change.

As Obama clinched the nomination, he marked the occasion with language that seemed both aspirational and, in the moment, entirely plausible: "I am absolutely certain that generations from now, we will be able to look back and tell our children that this was the moment when we began to provide care for the sick and good jobs to the jobless; this was the moment when the rise of the oceans began to slow and our planet began to heal; this was the moment when we ended a war and secured our nation and restored our image as the last, best hope on Earth. This was the moment — this was the time — when we came together to remake this great nation so that it may always reflect our very best selves, and our highest ideals."

To meet this challenge, Obama had wanted to make sure he had a team ready to go. The vetting began as early as August, leaked emails later showed. "John," wrote Michael Froman to John Podesta, "Our vetting process begins on Tuesday." He included a list of people the team would be going through, and promised more to come. Froman's email was sent from his work account — at Citigroup. Unsurprisingly, the administration was stacked with Wall Street veterans.

One of the first tests for the White House came when Rep. Baron Hill, a Blue Dog from Indiana, phoned Emanuel the day before the stimulus was set to come up for a vote in the House that January. The Dogs had met that morning and they were threatening to vote against it. Hill knew he had an ally in the White House. He had been an early endorser of Obama and had campaigned with him. "I feel like I am a Blue Dog, Baron," Obama had told him multiple times.[112]

Obama's top economic advisers had started from the premise that there were limits to what was politically possible. When the incoming head of the Council of Economic Advisers, Christina Romer, suggested that $1.8 trillion was needed to fill the hole in the economy, Obama's top economic adviser, Larry Summers, rebuffed her, calling the figure impractical politically.

Romer pared her proposal down to a $1.2 trillion stimulus, but Summers still considered it too heavy a lift to get through Congress. The memo Summers finally presented to the president listed $800 billion[113] as the top figure.

Summers was out of his lane, play-acting as a pundit, guessing what was politically feasible. Rahm Emanuel was doing the same thing, though at least that was part of his job description. He pushed to lower the figure, too. "You were literally shedding hundreds of thousands of jobs a month. You didn't have to artificially create a sense of urgency," Emanuel said.[114] "The harder challenge was getting the policy people and the political people [on the same page], and this was what happened with any big policy. What can the political system absorb?"

They had pushed it below $800 billion and the Blue Dogs were still yelping. Emanuel rushed to the Hill for an emergency meeting with the coalition that he himself had built with his strategy to recruit conservative Democratic candidates. Now they were threatening to humiliate him. "You guys can't do this," implored Emanuel. "You can't embarrass

---

112   The line and the meeting is recounted in Bob Woodward's book, *The Price of Politics*.

113   The paucity of the approach, if it wasn't obvious at the time, was made clear when Donald Trump later pushed through a $1.5 trillion tax cut just because.

114   Interview appears in Brian Abrams' *Obama: An Oral History, 2009-2017*, published in 2018.

the president right out of the gate."

The Blue Dogs demanded that the stimulus be trimmed. It included some spending they didn't like, and they also wanted a policy called PAYGO reinstated. That meant that any new spending by the government would need to be offset by cuts somewhere else. This came even as the Labor Department reported that 598,000 people lost jobs that month, putting more than 11 million people total out of work, not counting those who had given up looking. Each one of those was a life upended, and the response from the Blue Dog wing of the party was to do less.

The president did venture outside the Beltway to sell the stimulus, making a trip to Florida to stand alongside one of the few supportive Republican lawmakers, then-Gov. Charlie Crist. But he did not travel to Maine to pressure Republican Sens. Susan Collins and Olympia Snowe to back the measure, as progressives urged him to do.

"We did put pressure on them. We did go out and campaign. We went down to Florida and stood with Charlie Crist and he was almost never heard from again," said Axelrod.[115] "We made the case that we needed to intervene [to save the economy]. But as a political matter there was an upward limit for what was sellable."

It was during the stimulus that the myth of Rahm Emanuel ought to have been exposed as just that. If he were truly the hard-knuckled operator, the crass pragmatist who knew how to wield power that he claimed to be, he would have had levers he could have pulled. Or, alternately, perhaps Emanuel was just fine with a limited response to the crisis, shaped as he was by the Clintonian ideology that the era of big government is over.

His approach can be seen most vividly in the passive way that he describes the politics at the time. He doesn't see himself as a political actor, but rather that politics are acting on him. "That number kept growing until it got to, I think, just shy of $800" billion, he said,[116] "because I think at that point there was a political argument you couldn't go north of 800, even though the policy people would have liked to have seen overwhelming force at all levels."

The month that Obama was sworn into office, the country lost more than 800,000 jobs, a number that is difficult to fathom ten years later, pushing the number of people looking for jobs and unable to find them at nearly 12 million. Governors around the country — Republicans and Democrats — were desperate for help. Obama was ready to

115   Axelrod made these comments in an interview with my HuffPost colleague Sam Stein for a story we wrote together on Obama's political strategy, or lack thereof.

116   Same oral history from 2018.

offer that help, and could have demanded that any Republican governor who wanted stimulus money for their state had to publicly support the package and pressure the state's members of Congress to back it. He could have made threats directed at particular back-home interests or pet projects. He could have demanded Republicans support the bill in exchange for the tax cuts, and taken the tax cuts out if they didn't. He did none of that.

As the White House negotiated, Republicans stole a page from the Democratic playbook and took their arguments to the American people, organizing rallies around the country. "We used their model, and what surprised me was they stopped using their model," RNC Chair Michael Steele said.

"I always thought that Obama would actually do both, that he would play the inside game while he was building up the outside strategy of more of a global network that he could pull the trigger on, push a button and, you know, thirteen-hundred-people-would-respond-in-10-minutes type thing," said Steele. "I was actually absolutely surprised."

When Maine Sen. Susan Collins decided that the stimulus could include no money to upgrade schools, said Jared Bernstein, Vice President Joe Biden's economic adviser, the White House decided not to fight her on it. "The idea that the president would then go to Maine strikes me as a questionable strategy and one we chose not to follow," he said.[117]

Of course, another option was to put a strong stimulus on the Senate floor and let Collins go ahead and vote against it with the economy losing roughly a quarter million jobs every week. If Democrats put a big stimulus on the floor and it was blocked by Republicans and a handful of Democrats, the markets might tank and job losses would continue. That's precisely what happened when Congress voted down the Wall Street bailout. But the pressure from the collapsing economy pushed Congress to approve it not long after rejecting it, which would likely have happened for the stimulus, too, if Obama had tried to go big. That's not the route he took, and so schools got nothing toward upgrades, and the dollar value was kept arbitrarily low.

Michael Grunwald's book *The New New Deal* makes the case that the stimulus was a historic investment in reshaping the U.S. economy along the lines of what took place under FDR. Grunwald, who would go on to ghost-write Tim Geithner's biography, is a proponent of the idea that Obama wanted to do more, but he simply couldn't, due to political restrictions — and also that what he did do was very good. But economists have documented how insufficient the Recovery Act was in filling the

117   Bernstein said this to Sam Stein for an article we wrote together in The Huffington Post.

hole the recession created. And for many Democrats, the failure to fight on the ground for a policy that met the moment remains a fatal error. Rep. Jerry Nadler (D–N.Y.) told me that losing Congress was "baked in the cake" from the moment Congress passed a stimulus that wasn't big enough to fill the hole.[118]

The cake was put in the oven in Steny Hoyer's office in the Capitol, as Emanuel and the Blue Dogs cursed and shouted at each other that January day. Emanuel, after dishing out his typical dose of profanity, gave the Blue Dogs everything they asked for, and even offered them a meeting with Obama later to air further grievances. Emanuel's toughness was all theater.

The pattern was established. The White House would be taking marching orders from the conservatives on the Hill, and the left — the "professional left," Robert Gibbs would later dub them — would take its orders from the White House.[119]

Obama during the campaign had pledged to close Guantanamo Bay, and as a Constitutional law professor, it was likely one of the things he genuinely cared about. He brought in Greg Craig to oversee the transfer of prisoners and closure of the prison, but it went nowhere. Craig[120] "didn't have Rahm's trust early, and that obviously ended up costing him his job," said a White House official. "He wasn't integrated into the political decision making process in the White House, and so was trying to make substantive decisions in a political vacuum which is never a successful [way] forward." The main problem was that moving each prisoner meant a headline — Terrorist To Be Moved To San Diego Prison! — and those events had to be managed diplomatically. The administration couldn't afford to lose a vote on health care reform or the stimulus by angering a member of Congress who was facing questions about a new prisoner in their district. "The problem was the Counsel's office didn't have the political capacity to integrate the congressional priorities of the White House in addition to the legal," the official said. "I think that the president cared a great deal about it and if the Counsel's office had sort of been integrated into the political decision making, you could

118   This is not 20/20 hindsight. I wrote an article for HuffPost on March 11, 2009, for instance, called "Why The Stimulus Is Too Small," quoting prominent economists who deemed it way, way too little. They were right.

119   On a conference call with bloggers and progressive media, Susan Madrak once asked David Axelrod if he knew what hippie punching was. "We're the girl you'll take under the bleachers but you won't be seen with in the light of day," Madrak, a blogger with Crooks and Liars, told Axelrod on a September 2010 call.

120   After Craig flamed out at the White House, he cashed in, doing foreign lobbying work, In 2019, he was indicted in connection with it.

Ryan Grim

have seen a deal happen in the early days. But because it was devoid of that, we were proposing prisons in districts that did not make sense. But [the counsel's office didn't realize where] Rahm [and others] were making other decisions, and that made it complicated."

In late March, three conservative Democratic senators — Evan Bayh, Tom Carper, and Blanche Lincoln — took to the Washington Post op-ed page to call for President Obama to slow down. "Many independents voted for President Obama and the contours of his change agenda, but they will not rubber-stamp it. They are wary of ideological solutions and are overwhelmingly pragmatic. Many of them live in our states and in the states of the other senators who have joined our group," they offered.

That was too much for Bob Borosage and Roger Hickey. Leaders at the progressive group Campaign for America's Future, Borosage and Hickey launched a campaign called "Bird Dog the Blue Dogs," an early version of the Indivisible technique of organizing constituents to hound members of Congress at public events.

CAF put headshots of the Blue Dogs on its website, and Hickey went on Chris Matthews' MSNBC program on March 24, 2009, to talk about it. "The Blue Dog Democrats are about to be dogged themselves. I'm talking about those nervous Democrats who are skittish about President Obama's big agenda of health, education and energy," Matthews said, introducing Hickey.

The MSNBC appearance led to an invitation to the White House, though not necessarily the kind they wanted. The pair was summoned to meet with Jim Messina, Rahm Emanuel's deputy. "We want you to stop this," Messina ordered.

"Well, we're an outside group," responded Borosage. "We're actually fending off an attack on Obama."

"We can fend off our own attack," Messina promised.

"We're allies, not footsoldiers," Borosage pushed back.

Messina looked at Roger Hickey. "Your friend doesn't seem to get this," Messina told him.

"We're not opposing you on this; we're defending you," Hickey insisted.

The meeting was disorienting because political tactics and style are an expression of values. Obama was thought by progressives to be one of them, to be of the people. But here he was acting like a top-down royalist, uncomfortably with even sympathetic dissent.

Disobedience would be met with banishment from the inner circle. Hickey recalled Messina making the message clear: *If you guys don't lay off, you're not going to be invited to this operation we're setting up to commu-*

130

nicate with the liberals.

The operation was known as Common Purpose, and would later be brilliantly dubbed by blogger Jane Hamsher as the "veal pen." It was a once-a-week private gathering between senior administration officials and outside progressive groups, billed as a place to plot strategy, but in reality a way for the White House to deliver marching orders and, more importantly, stroke egos.

An invite to the meeting came with more than psychic benefits. Wealthy donors ideologically aligned with Obama would be impressed, and write bigger checks. It was, theoretically, an opportunity to influence policy at the highest levels. It took no effort to rationalize making compromises to keep that access.

"Since we really weren't doing much in the way of active pressure on the Blue Dogs — it was basically just me and a website — we basically agreed that we would take that down," said Hickey. "We wanted to be part of this thing, Common Purpose [which was] quasi-independent, but really totally run by the White House."

The message went out not just to CAF but to all of the hopeful occupants of the veal pen. The reasoning was that pressure on the Blue Dogs would backfire — it would push them into the arms of the Republicans and also weaken them at home, costing them reelection in 2010. Obama and Emanuel, who had built relationships with many of them, felt like they could handle them on their own, no help needed.

The White House practiced what it preached. During the campaign, Obama's biggest weapon had been the millions-strong army that door-knocked, donated and turned out to vote. After the election it was converted into a new group, called Organizing for America (OFA) and merged with the Democratic National Committee, which was run by executive director Jen O'Malley.[121] That army was fired up and ready to go, but Obama put it on ice.

"It could have been so much more," said one former top official at OFA, who envisioned an alternate reality in which Obama, on his euphoric election night, or a few weeks later, rallied his troops and stormed into Washington, pledging, "I'm going to bring before Congress this package of legislation that's going to fix health care and fix the environment and I want ten million people to sign on to show their support for this legislation so Congress knows we mean business. Had that happened, I think he could have crushed that number. Members of Congress were terrified of him. The terror would have been more pronounced."

Joe Rospars, who'd been "new media director" on the 2008 cam-

121   Who would become Obama's deputy campaign manager in 2012 and Beto O'Rourke's campaign manager for the 2020 cycle.

paign, cashed out, jumping to the digital firm Blue State Digital. In January, Mitch Stewart was named to run OFA. Both he and O'Malley's backgrounds were in field, not digital. "The funny thing is none of these people had any interest or involvement with digital during the campaign, and then everyone got real interested," recalled Shant Mesrobian who was on the campaign's digital team but quit in frustration in spring 2009. "Jen had zero digital experience. I remember her saying at the outset that digital was not going to be like it was on the campaign — it wasn't going to be a metrics-driven, results-oriented program. Which was her way of saying that we wouldn't run it based on what the list/movement responded to or prioritized. It would be a top down, admin-driven tool.

If the movement was taking orders from the White House, the White House was taking its from Wall Street. In early March, it emerged that AIG executives planned to give themselves several hundred million dollars in bonuses. This was the financial conglomerate that had been rescued by the government after recklessly destroying itself, and nearly taking the global economy down with it. AIG had just days earlier cashed a government check worth $30 billion, bringing their total handout to $170 billion. They had also just announced a $62 billion quarterly loss. Now they wanted bonuses? The public was apoplectic, and politicians reached for the most over-the-top rhetoric they could find. As was often the case, Iowa GOP Senator Chuck Grassley won that contest, calling for the executives to "either do one of two things: resign or go commit suicide."

It soon became clear that the bonuses had only been possible because of Geithner, Larry Summers, and Rahm Emanuel. Geithner concluded that the bonus-clawback provision would be unconstitutional, because it would apply to contracts already inked. Banking Committee Chairman Chris Dodd had held his ground. "Tim Geithner felt that there were constitutional issues with a clawback. We disagreed," Dodd said.[122] "And I recall very vividly going to some meeting in the basement of the Dirksen garage, and my old friend Rahm Emanuel — he spent 15 minutes working for me in 1992 — and we had a shouting match. Rahm was arguing very strenuously that he wanted that whole [retroactive] provision out, and I vehemently disagreed. Anyway, the administration didn't give up and, unbeknown to me entirely, they convinced a person on the staff to delete a section of that sentence of the amendment. I never knew about it."

Dodd has never fingered who precisely in the administration went around him to his staff to change the bill, but Emanuel is widely known to be one of the few principals in Washington comfortable going directly to the staff of other principals.

Nevertheless, fury was now heaped on Dodd, Geithner, and Summers, and Dodd eventually announced he would not run for reelection in 2010. "I paid the price for it," Dodd said.

"Chris Dodd is not one percent charged with that. It was not his fault. People don't understand how difficult it is to stop bad things from happening in a massive bill and it got by all of us," Harry Reid told me, adding that he didn't think it was Emanuel. "I think it was in the bowels of the Treasury Department."

As Congress contemplated ways to seize the bonuses through tax policy, the White House was finally feeling pressure to get tough on Wall Street. On March 11, Summers phoned Sheila Bair, then the head of the Federal Deposit Insurance Corporation,[123] to ask what specifically it would take to break up, wind down and restart Citigroup, which continued to hemorrhage and was sitting on a pile of toxic mortgages. Its share price was floating under a dollar. He and Christina Romer,[124] another top economic adviser, had decided to push for a nationalization of Citi. Bair, without knowing why precisely Summers was asking, walked him through the details. On March 15, 2009,[125] Obama sat down with his economic team to discuss the ongoing crisis with Citigroup and the rest of Wall Street. The president, too, had been intrigued by the idea of using bailout funds to nationalize failing banks and break them up into safer, component parts.

Geithner battled it out with Summers and Romer in a packed Roosevelt Room, with Obama as the judge and jury. Geithner argued that the smartest way forward was to give the biggest banks "stress tests" to determine how healthy they were. With that score card out, investors would have confidence in the banks, and because the U.S. had vouched for the test, there would be implicit assurance that the banks would not be allowed to fail. The plan to nationalize banks, Geithner warned, could spark a run and a fresh financial crisis.

Romer and Summers laid out the idea of taking over a few failing institutions and splitting them into "good banks" and "bad banks." The bad bank would separate out the toxic assets, putting them in a publicly run institution. Freed from pressures to foreclose, the mortgages, which were far under water, could be renegotiated with the homeowner. Fewer foreclosures would slow the collapse of the housing market broadly,

---

123   Her account appears in her memoir, *Bull by the Horns.*

124   Romer was an expert on the Great Depression and the most progressive and least volatile of Obama's economic advisers.

125   The meeting is recounted in Ron Suskind's 2011 book *Confidence Men.*

which was continuing to ravage the economy, and it would be a lifeline for the millions of people caught up in the crisis. It would also be a major signal that Obama intended to do something serious and lasting in the wake of the crisis.

Obama framed it in moral and political terms, saying at the meeting that the Summers–Romer idea would "strike a blow for prudence" and "begin to change the reckless behavior of Wall Street and show millions of unemployed Americans that accountability flows in both directions."

While the debate went on, Obama got up and left. "Look," he said, "I'm going to get a haircut and have dinner with my family. You've heard me. When I come back I want this issue resolved."

Emanuel waited until the boss left the room. "Everyone shut the fuck up. Let me be clear — taking down the banking system in a program that could cost $700 billion is a fantasy," he said. "Listen, it's not going to fuckin' happen. We have no fucking credibility. So give it up. The job of everyone in this room is to move the president, when he gets back, toward a solution that works."

Romer felt like she'd been "punched in the stomach," she later said.[126] "Right there, Rahm killed it."

When Obama returned, Summers told him about Emanuel's political concern and acknowledged it was real. But, he added, there was $200 billion left in the bailout account, and it could be used to break up and resolve Citigroup. When that went well, they'd be able to go to Congress to repeat it with other institutions.

At the same time, Emanuel added, Geithner could continue with his stress tests and his "support" for the banks — in other words, the Fed and Treasury would pump them full of as much money as needed to keep them afloat.

It was agreed. The president may have been judge and jury in the room, but he wasn't the executioner. He tasked Geithner with drawing up plans to resolve Citigroup.

Back at the Treasury Department, Geithner met with his economic team. Much as Trump's advisers have done to him, Geithner simply ignored Obama's order. "I don't want even one molecule of energy spent on anything other than the stress tests!"[127]

Alan Krueger, Geithner's top economist, pushed back — sort of.

"I believe energy is measured in 'ergs,'" he said gently.

126   Ibid.
127   This exchange also comes from Suskind, and appears to be sourced to Geithner aide Alan Krueger, one of the more gifted and compassionate economists of his generation. In March 2019, Krueger, a widely respected and compassionate economist, took his life at the age of 58.

"Okay," Geithner clarified, "not one erg of energy."

Later, Krueger told author Ron Suskind, who first reported on the meeting, that Geithner simply thought Obama, Summers, and Romer were wrong. "The bottom line is Tim and others at Treasury felt the president didn't fully understand the complexities of the issue, or simply that they were right and he was wrong, and that trying to resolve Citi and then other banks would have been disastrous."

The unresolved financial crisis would go on to spawn a rise of right-wing populism around the globe, which would ricochet back to the United States on election night in 2016. Suskind, in his interview with Obama, asked what the president thought of Geithner's slow-walking of his bank plan. "Agitated may be too strong a word," Obama offered.

That same month, March 2009, the administration faced another pivotal decision: whether to bailout the auto industry. After the election, Bush had made a small loan to the industry that was enough to get it through to the next year so that the decision would belong to the next president. At the critical meeting, David Axelrod presented polling on how much the public hated bailouts. Tim Geithner, of all people, pushed back, noting that polls always show animosity toward bailouts, but the public changes its mind too late. Everybody wanted to just let Lehman Brothers die, and the Fed did, but when it blew up the global financial system, attitudes changed about whether it should have been rescued. His advice was unusually wise: ignore the polls and do what's right. Others in the meeting noted the tens of thousands of jobs at stake in the auto industry. That's when Rahm Emanuel interjected with his own thoughts: "Fuck the UAW."

It was quintessential Rahm, using profanity to disguise an act of utter cowardice in tough-guy bravado, all while being blindingly wrong about both the politics and the substance.

Obama's best decisions were made when he did the opposite of what Emanuel advised. The auto bailout became key to his reelection.

Ten

Grandma Hannie

Elizabeth Warren's first political memory is from around the time she was six years old, listening to stories about the Great Depression in Oklahoma from her grandmother, Hannie Crawford Reed. "They lost money when those banks closed up," she said of her grandparents and extended family. "They watched these little towns shrivel up when the bank was gone. There was no money, there were no jobs. So my grandmother used to say one thing that was political that I can remember. She'd say, *Franklin Roosevelt made it safe to put money in banks, and she would say, And he did a lot of other things, too.*"

The Depression loomed especially large in her family lore. "I wasn't born until long after the Depression, until after World War II, but I grew up as a child of the Depression, because my grandmother and grandfather, my aunts, my uncles, my mom and my dad, all my older cousins had lived through the Depression," she said. "And it was such a searing experience in Oklahoma, that the Depression hung around our family like a shroud. It was always there."

If she had to guess, she said, she would say that her parents were populist Democrats, fond of FDR, but they never discussed partisan politics. Her mother, she said, would volunteer as a poll worker and bring her along, giving her a sense as a child that politics, whatever it was, mattered.

Her politics today have been heavily informed by her childhood experiences — not just by Grandma Hannie's stories of FDR, but also of her family's Native American background. Her parents eloped at a young age, she was always told, because her father's parents objected to him marrying Pauline Reed, citing her Native American roots, which dated back to Hannie's own grandmother, O.C. Sarah Smith Crawford.[128]

---

128   There's some speculation that O.C. came from etsi, the Cherokee word for mother. The only evidence that has ever emerged showing O.C. to have Native Amer-

Whether family lore is rooted in truth or in myth has little influence on how it is received by a child and later incorporated into an adult's story of herself. The family's financial difficulties, however, have not been challenged. Warren often talks about her father, Donald Herring, having a heart attack and being unable to work, the family nearly losing their home. It was only when her mother landed a minimum wage job at Sears that catastrophe was averted, and she has regularly talked about how different a time it was, that a single minimum wage income could support a family of three. (Her older brothers had left the house by then and joined the military.) The experience marked a starting point in her narrative of the destruction of the middle class over the next several decades, as workers' wages fell in real terms and capital seized the growth from their increasing productivity.

Warren escaped Oklahoma by winning a debate scholarship at George Washington University but got married at 19, dropped out and moved to Texas to finish college. Partisan politics was not a part of her 20s or 30s, either. Warren was just 21 when she had Amelia, who'd later become her co-author.[129] At the time, the responsibility of caring for her new daughter was an obstacle between Warren and her plans to go to law school. Amelia was two when Warren started at Rutgers University.

That experience, too, became part of her 2020-cycle stump speech, as she has talked about her furious determination to potty-train Amelia by age two, so that she could get her into daycare. She recalls driving Amelia home after class with one hand shaking Amelia's foot to keep her awake in the car so that the girl would nap at home, the only chance Warren would have to study.

Next came Alexander, and the family moved to Texas, where Warren tried her hand at homemaking. It was not her thing. Washing dishes one night, she turned to her husband and said simply, "I want a divorce."

While Bernie Sanders and Warren may have wound up in similar spots on the ideological spectrum, at least in the public eye, they took very different routes to get there. Sanders took a traditional leftist path, reading Marx and throwing himself into the civil rights, anti-war, and environmental movements, followed by support of indigenous and revolutionary movements in Central America in the 1980s. He kept an arms-length relationship with the Democratic Party, engaging in electoral politics — often unsuccessfully, in the beginning — but not on the party's terms. He was elected mayor of Burlington, and later to Congress

ican roots is a marriage certificate, but that document, after having been reported on by an amateur genealogist, has never been found and may not exist.

129   The mother-daughter duo co-wrote the 2003 book *The Two-Income Trap* and 2005's *All Your Worth*.

and then the Senate, as an independent, calling himself a democratic socialist, caucusing with the party while in the House and Senate but never fully joining.

Warren, by contrast, was for decades what a political consultant might refer to as an infrequent voter, often missing midterms and primaries. And, despite her formidable education and intellect, she was a low-information one at that.

Critics of Warren from the left have long flagged the fact that she was registered to vote as a Republican up through the 1990s. But her first presidential vote, in 1972, was cast against Richard Nixon, whom she disliked passionately. But reflecting how little she had paid attention to day-to-day politics at the time, she couldn't immediately recall who had been running against him when I asked. When told it was Democrat George McGovern, she said, yes, she would have voted for him but didn't have any specific memory of having done so. (She was living in New Jersey at the time.)

Nixon was re-elected that year, of course, but resigned and was replaced by Gerald Ford. Warren said she had voted Ford in 1976, believing that "Ford was a decent man."

But she was happy with Jimmy Carter, who beat him. "I thought he [also] was a decent man," she said, transferring her then-standard for what she wanted in a politician from Ford to Carter. "He was a really good man."

As the decade wore on, Warren's career as a law professor had taken off. She got a job teaching at Rutgers law school, then, in 1978, at the University of Houston Law Center, and began what would become her landmark research on bankruptcy in 1981, with Jay Westbrook and Terry Sullivan, a study that continues to the present day. When Warren started it, she was still a believer in free-market orthodoxy, and influenced by a conservative law school ideology called "law and economics." She approached the research from a right-wing angle, expecting to prove that people filing for bankruptcy were trying to bilk the system.

The results of the research woke Warren up politically, and she rejected the law and economics ideology she had tried on. "When we went into the whole consumer bankruptcy thing," Westbrook said, "I think her attitude was very much balanced between, on the one hand, *No doubt there are people who have difficulties and they're struggling and so forth*, and on the other hand, *By golly, you ought to pay your debts, and probably some of these people are not being very committed to doing what they ought to do.*"

Warren said that doing the work changed her politics. "Terry and Jay went into that with a pretty sympathetic lens that, *These are people, let's take a look, give them the benefit of the doubt that they had fallen on hard times,*" she said. "I was the skeptic on the team."

"I had grown up in a family that had been turned upside-down economically, a family that had run out of money more than once when there were still bills to pay and kids to feed — but my family had never filed for bankruptcy," she said. "So I approached it from the angle that these are people who may just be taking advantage of the system. *These are people who aren't like my family. We pulled our belts tighter, why didn't they pull their belts tighter?*"

But then she dug into the stories of those who had. "Then we started digging into the data and reading the files and recording the numbers and analyzing what's going on, and the world slowly starts to shift for me, and I start to see these families as like mine — hard-working people who have built something, people who have done everything they were supposed to do the way they were supposed to do it," she said. Now they "had been hit by a job loss, a serious medical problem, a divorce or death in the family, and had hurtled over a financial cliff. And when I looked at the numbers, I began to understand the alternative for people in bankruptcy was not to work a little harder and pay off your debt. The alternative was to stay in debt and live with collection calls and repossessions until the day you die. And that's when it began to change for me."

Westbrook, who has spent years in bankruptcy courtrooms, said that the same phenomenon routinely happens with judges. Even an attorney who spends their career before the bench as a lawyer for creditors gradually shifts, he said, under the weight of seeing, day after day, good families destroyed by bad luck.

The research the team produced is widely cited around the issue of bankruptcies driven by medical emergencies, but it contains a less-heralded, though no less poignant finding: Many bankruptcies were caused by families moving to better neighborhoods than they could afford to get better schools for their kids.

From there, said Warren, she zoomed out from the particular stories of hardship she was encountering and began asking why she was seeing so much more of it in the 1980s than she had before.

"This happens over the space of a decade, I began to open up the questions I asked. I started with the question of the families who use bankruptcy. But over time it becomes, *So why are bankruptcies going up in America?*" she said. "What was changing in the 1980s and 1990s? What difference was there in America?"

The answer to that question, she said, led her to become a Democrat. "I start to do the work on how incomes stay flat and core expenses go up, and families do everything they can to cope with the squeeze. They quit saving. They go deeper and deeper into debt, but the credit card companies and payday lenders and subprime mortgage outfits figure out there's money to be made here, and they come after these families and pick their bones clean. And that's who ends up in bankruptcy. So that's how it expands out. And by then I'm a Democrat," she said.

What to do with that epiphany wasn't clear. At the time, the two parties had yet to separate entirely along ideological lines — some deeply conservative and racist Democrats still held office, particularly in her part of the country. And despite the Reagan revolution, some genuinely liberal Republicans survived for a generation after him.

In the fall of 1987, she moved to Pennsylvania and registered there as a Republican. She said she couldn't quite remember why she did it but that she was a fan of Republican Sen. Arlen Specter. "Again, I thought he was a decent man," she said. She couldn't recall whom he ran against. (His Democratic opponent was Lynn Yeakel.)

That GOP registration, though, set off speculation over the years that one of the Senate's most progressive champions may have at one time been a Ronald Reagan backer. So I asked her: *Is it true? Is it possible the champion of the regulatory cops on Wall Street voted for the man who made deregulation a hallmark of his presidency?*

No.

In 1984 and 1988, Warren voted for Walter Mondale and then Michael Dukakis but, in 1992, split her ticket, voting for Republican Arlen Specter for Senate and Democrat Bill Clinton for president. Specter was a good example of the one-time flexibility of the party system and the politicians within it: He began and ended his career as a Democrat, but was a Republican for much of the middle of it.[130]

In 1980, she said, she was a registered independent living in Missouri City, Texas, and cast her vote to re-elect Carter. When Reagan won, she wasn't happy, but not crushed the way she was on election night in 2016. "I was disappointed and didn't like him, but I wasn't deeply worried for the country, not anything like when Trump was elected," she explained. If she could go back in time, she said, she would tell herself "this was a far more pivotal historical moment than you understand."

---

130   His party-switch in 2009 enabled Democrats to achieve their 60-vote supermajority in the Senate. Specter had been promised he wouldn't face a primary in the next election, but Joe Sestak didn't feel bound by the deal. He knocked Specter out, but then went on to lose to Pat Toomey in the tea party wave year of 2010. Sestak spent the next five years preparing for a rematch, building a broad base of support across the state. But party leaders were livid with Sestak for 2010, and spent several million dollars boosting Katie McGinty instead. She won a three-way primary and went on to underperform Clinton in the general, losing a winnable race against Toomey, who is up again in 2022. Specter died in 2012.

Indeed, her most recent book divides the 20th century into two pivotal epochs, 1935 to 1980 and 1980 to 2016. As that history was unfolding before her, she became increasingly aware of what was going wrong with the country.

By the mid-'90s, she had accepted a job at Harvard and by then was a full-fledged, registered Democrat, a claim backed up by voter registration records.

Westbrook pinpointed her turn toward becoming a partisan Democrat to her appointment to the National Bankruptcy Review Commission in 1995. Being a part of that panel, he said, put her into contact with high-level politics in a way that she'd never been before.

Becoming a partisan is difficult for a scholar, Westbrook said. Academic researchers start with a question, collect data, analyze it, and form a conclusion. Partisans start with a conclusion — say, taxes are too high or spending on infrastructure is too low — and find data to back it up. That could partially explain why Warren has not, in fact, proved to be a reliable partisan, willing to criticize President Barack Obama for being too soft on Wall Street, or Clinton for voting the wrong way on bankruptcy reform.

The bankruptcy commission, and her activism that came after it, had given her a first taste of national politics, and also her first run-ins with Hillary Clinton and Joe Biden,[131] then both senators. Biden was the chief advocate for the credit card companies, and Warren clashed with him often. Warren lobbied Clinton hard to oppose the bankruptcy bill, and thought that she had her word that she was against it. When Clinton ultimately voted for it, Warren felt betrayed.[132]

It was the financial crash, just a few years later, that brought her to Washington for good. Congress finally approved its bailout of Wall Street in early October, and one of the conditions tacked on was that a commission would be established to audit how the money was being spent. The elections in November came and went, and Washington forgot about that provision. So the Treasury Department's inspector general took matters into his own hands, and told the Washington Post that the bailout was "a mess" and there was nobody watching the billions of dollars go out the door.

131   Clinton was elected in 2000; Biden in 1972.
132   When her vote became a liability in the 2016 race, she instructed her staff to find evidence that she had supported the bill because women's groups had asked her to do so after she won some concessions, according to hacked emails dumped online by Wikileaks. Her advisers searched the record and found that it wasn't true, that women's groups were strongly opposed and had wanted to oppose it. Clinton said it anyway.

Reid and Pelosi scrambled, but Reid had somebody in mind: the Harvard professor he remembered from the fight over bankruptcy.

Reid phoned her at home in Cambridge in mid-November 2008. She was about to host a barbeque for law students when the call came. "Harry Reid," the soft voice said.

"Who?" she asked.

"Um, Harry Reid," he repeated softly, pausing. "Majority leader, U.S. Senate."

"Oh," she said.

He asked her to chair the commission that would oversee the bailout funds, and with no clue what that entailed, she said yes on the spot. Reid, who does not do small talk, simply hung up

"I found her, put her on the debt commission. I read one of her books on poverty. She was a Harvard professor and she was just good from the get-go," Reid told me.

The commission was virtually powerless, but Warren demonstrated an ability to create power where it didn't exist before. As chair of the commission, she used the platform to brutalize Treasury Secretary Tim Geithner every time he came before her. The exchanges went viral, and earned her an enemy for life. She wasn't thinking of her long-term career. "Growing up, I never saw an appetite for politics. Even now, I don't think she really likes Washington or politics. She's just there to do this one thing," her daughter, Amelia Warren Tyagi, told a Vogue reporter in 2010.

The gavel also put her in closer contact with members of Congress, and she used the proximity to push her idea for an agency dedicated to regulating consumer financial products, which she had first spelled out in an essay published in the journal Democracy in the summer of 2007. Its title, an homage to Ralph Nader's consumer protection days, was "Unsafe at Any Rate."[133]

When she sat down with Barney Frank, then the House Financial Services Committee chair, he told Warren that he wanted to regulate the banks before turning to her consumer bureau. She told him about Grandma Hannie. "One of the earliest conversations we had about how to think about financial reform in the wake of the 2008 crash was, *What goes first? What's the first thing we need to think about?* And Barney wanted to start with the nonbank financial institutions," she said, "and stronger regulations over the largest, too-big-to-fail banks."

Warren agreed that the argument made sense on a policy level, but politically, it was important to win people's trust. "I argued back to Barney that we needed to start where the crash had started, and where fam-

---

133   Nader's transformative book is titled *Unsafe at Any Speed.*

ilies understood it and felt it and that was, *family by family, mortgage by mortgage, how those giant banks had taken down the economy.* He and I were kind of going back and forth and then I said, *Barney, let me tell you about my grandmother*, and I told him that story," she said. "Once he made it safe to put money in banks, my grandmother trusted Franklin Roosevelt. And so my argument to Barney was, *Start where people will understand what we're trying to do. And that's with the consumer agency.* And you know Barney, he has the quickest mind on earth — he cocked his head, took about three seconds and said, *You're right. We'll start with the consumer agency.*"

It was uncanny insight for a politician, if she could be called one by then, and it was made possible, perhaps, by the decades she spent before becoming one. If Warren's launch into politics can be pinpointed to 1995 with her commission appointment, that would mean that well into her 40s, she was still living, voting, and thinking, politically speaking, at least, like a regular person.

She still seemed like a regular-ish person when I first encountered her on April 10, 2009, at a Capitol Hill press conference where she joined a handful of House and Senate Democrats in introducing a bill to create something then called the "Financial Product Safety Commission."

I quoted her at length in an article in The Huffington Post that day. Finally, here was someone talking in plain English about how the banks had caused the financial crisis by ripping off regular people, and how it could be stopped: "If there had been an agency, like the Financial Product Safety Commission, that had said, *You just don't get to fool people on pricing*, then what would have happened is there would have been millions of families who got tangled in predatory mortgages who never would have gotten them."

Without all those predatory mortgages that quickly imploded, she continued, there'd have been no housing bubble to pop. "It never would have been as profitable for mortgage brokers and others in the financial services industry to market these products, because they would not have been such high-profit products," Warren explained. "If we never would have started at the front end, we never would have fed them into the financial system."

Eleven

The Public Option

There was a time when the Center for American Progress was a force capable of driving the Democratic Party in a progressive direction. The center-left think tank today works to produce more moderate versions of popular policies like Medicare for All or a Green New Deal — worried that big ideas will scare swing voters in the next election. But in the 2008 cycle, it saw its role differently, acting to broaden what was considered possible. The critical role it played in the health care debate is still being felt today.

The device the think tank used to stretch the political window[134] was a March 2008 presidential candidate forum on health care in Las Vegas. The event meant that Hillary Clinton, Barack Obama, and John Edwards would all have to show up with health care plans, ones designed to impress liberals who were active in primaries. Edwards, then running on his theme of "two Americas," stole the show with a well-thought-out plan, the centerpiece of which was a public insurance option that would be similar to Medicare and would compete with private plans. Clinton showed up with a technocratic plan based on the Massachusetts model implemented by Mitt Romney, the drivers of which were a mandate

---

134   It's often referred to as the Overton Window, which I find pretentious, because it describes something so simple it doesn't deserve to be named after a thinker. It's merely the idea that by proposing and advocating for a big idea, advocates can change the public conception of what is possible. Does somebody named Overton really need credit for that?

that everybody buy insurance and a promise that the government would help make it affordable. Obama came basically empty handed, save for principled opposition to the mandate. He left the forum embarrassed by Edwards' success, and instructed his staff to put together a robust plan. Playing Obama, Edwards, and Clinton off of each other, the group Campaign for America's Future, along with other progressive activists, pushed each campaign to endorse the public option. Obama eventually, if reluctantly, included it in his health care plan.

When the primary ended, some of Clinton's key staff merged with Obama's. Clinton's adviser Neera Tanden took a leading role in health care policy for the Obama campaign. Suddenly, claimed CAF's Roger Hickey, the public option disappeared from Obama's campaign site.

Hickey said he called Tanden to find out what had happened. "She treated me like an idiot. *Oh, of course it's still part of the plan.* We literally spent hours on the phone that day demanding to know where the fuck it had gone. Finally she put it back onto the website. So there were early-on indicators that we were going to have to push and push and push," he told me.[135]

The presidential plans would go on to shape the congressional approach. That was particularly clear in a meeting called by Sen. Ted Kennedy in October 2008, before Obama had been elected. Kennedy himself, ailing with a brain tumor, couldn't make it, but he had instructed key health policy staff to bring together the major stakeholders in the health care field and find a consensus on how to move forward. Dubbed "the Workhorse Group," the gang included some activists, such as Ron Pollack of Families USA, representatives of labor groups such as the Service Employees International Union, as well as every major industry group: big insurance, pharma, for-profit hospitals and medical device makers.[136]

John McDonough, Kennedy's top health policy staffer, led the meeting in the Dirksen Senate Office Building, and laid out three avenues that Congress could go if and when Democrats took control in January.

The first was called Constitution Avenue, a full break with employee-based coverage, either to single-payer or to a kludgy scheme cooked up by Sens. Ron Wyden and Bob Bennett. The second was Independence

---

135   "That is entirely made up," Tanden said. "He didn't call me." I told Hickey that Tanden denied he ever called, and he said he was surprised, having expected her to say that it was a web glitch or a misunderstanding. "Guess she doesn't think I'm important enough to acknowledge," Hickey said.

136   The meeting is recounted in a memoir/policy treatise, Inside National Health Reform, by John McDonough, a top Senate health staffer who helped write the ACA and also interviewed scores of key players.

Avenue, a small-ball approach that involved state-based high-risk pools and other fiddling at the edges. Then came Massachusetts Avenue, which would take the model implemented by Romney, and developed by the conservative Heritage Foundation, and take it national.

After an hour-and-a-half of debate, a vote was called. Zero hands went up for Constitution; zero went up for Independence. Of the roughly 20 participants, 15 hands went up for Massachusetts.

It was the most seriously single payer would be taken on Capitol Hill for the next eight years. The consensus among those who mattered — the people in that room — was clear.

Obama and his advisers made a set of strategic decisions that would define the subsequent health care reform process. The first was that it couldn't add to the deficit, meaning cuts elsewhere or tax hikes would have to balance it out. There was little appetite from Obama for more deficit spending after the Wall Street bailout, the stimulus, and the auto bailout. The second was to grant Congress a huge say over the legislative process.

Leaving Congress alone, for the White House, also meant getting the public off lawmakers' backs. Obama made the decision not to rally the public for the strongest health care bill possible. He had come to Washington with soaring approval ratings, the ability to fill stadiums with supporters, and an email list of tens of millions of people engaged and ready for action. He shut it all down. "When he became president, he did a smart thing, he got experienced and smart people to advise him on how to transition in," said one Democratic official who watched it happen. "The problem with skilled and experienced people is they they fundamentally don't have any experience with a grassroots theory of change. That very very critical tool of his campaign, that could do whatever they wanted, got sidelined."

There was a fear that somehow the bill wouldn't live up to expectations, and people would grow disappointed and cynical and not turn out in the 2010 midterm elections. Along the way, it would infuriate key constituencies in the health care industry who would funnel money to Republicans. Better, went the reasoning, to leave it to Chief of Staff Rahm Emanuel and his deputy, Jim Messina, who would negotiate directly with key senators, who would negotiate with Republicans.

It was the most consequential political decision of Obama's presidency, putting on ice the movement he had helped stoke. OFA, his campaign arm, still existed, and tried at times to exert pressure. At one point, OFA emailed its millions of supporters a flyer and urged them to print it out and drop it off at the offices of their local member of Congress. The flyer called on the representative to support the strongest possible health care bill, and more than 10,000 people started showing up at congressional offices. Pretty quickly, angry calls from members of Congress started coming to Jen O'Malley, the DNC's executive director. Elected Democrats felt like they were being shown up, that the action suggested that they were somehow not progressive or strong enough on the issue. The reaction, one OFA official told me, was baffling, and got organizing completely backwards. These were the kinds of people any liberal congressional office should want to have a relationship with, the kind of folks who care enough to be active. "Instead they were saying, please don't come to my office anymore," said the OFA official. O'Malley made the decision to call off the flyers.

Nathan Kosted was the field director for OFA in Montana, Baucus' home state. He told me his boss, the state director, gave him the orders from on high: leave Baucus alone, and give his office a heads up if any organizing around health care reform was contemplated. He was told that if he posted support for the public option on social media he'd be fired. Molly Moody was state director for Health Care for America Now (HCAN), the well-funded[137] progressive coalition pushing for reform. She showed up at a Baucus office in Montana with a group of protesters demanding he support the public option. She was banned from the office.

That type of approach left the White House with one path through Congress, to cut deals with some of health care reform's traditional opponents to try to buy their support — or at least dull their criticisms. The key industries then, as now, were the drug makers, the insurers, the device makers and the hospitals. The first to come on board was the Pharmaceutical Research and Manufacturers Association (PhRMA), then led by former Louisiana Rep. Billy Tauzin, as pure a distillation of Washington as possible. Once a Democrat, he switched parties and led the controversial 2003 GOP drug bill.[138] After muscling the bill through

---

137   In an odd twist of history, HCAN was heavily funded by Atlantic Philanthropies, which was set up in Bermuda by Chuck Feeney, who became a billionaire through domination of the duty-free shopping market and set about giving his entire fortune away.

138   The bill, rammed through by Tom DeLay, known as "The Hammer," put Medicare on the hook for prescription drugs, but with a gap in payments known as "the donut hole." Democrats opposed it, but seniors greatly benefited from it, and the legislation, an entitlement created by Republicans, has saved countless lives. The process of its passage was a travesty. The vote was called at 3 am, and it was defeated, but Republicans kept the vote open while they made threats and promises. Some of it led to House ethics committee reprimands, but one incident hasn't previously been told: Rep. Jerry Moran, who later became a Kansas senator, had told GOP leadership he was a yes, but voted no on the floor and fled. Bob Ney, who was

Congress, he immediately resigned and went to work as the top lobbyist for PhRMA.

PhRMA, in secret talks, agreed to chip in $100 billion over 10 years toward health care reform in exchange for an expanded pool of customers. The $100 billion would come through lower drug prices, rebates, and other means of lowering costs. The administration promised not to use its purchasing power to lower prescription drug prices, and to oppose the re-importation of cheaper drugs from Canada and elsewhere, key PhRMA priorities.

When it became public that PhRMA had inked a deal with the White House, reform picked up momentum and the other industries began panicking, worried they'd be steamrolled. The hospitals came to the table, represented by three different groups — public, private, and Catholic non-profit. The Federation of American Hospitals — the private, for-profit ones — was run by Chip Kahn, a figure who struck fear into Democratic hearts, as he had been the health care lobbyist in the 1990s who was the brains behind the brutal "Harry and Louise" (two married mopes fretting about Hillarycare in a TV ad) which, in Washington legend, tanked Clinton's health care reform effort.

Democrats wanted Kahn on board for both symbolic and substantive reasons. The hospitals' key demand was that coverage be broadly expanded. The uninsured patients showing up in emergency rooms were killing hospitals, and they were willing to cut costs if that problem could be dealt with. The White House may not have known how ready the hospitals were for reform.

Two years earlier, Kahn had been at a hospital lobby conference when he was summoned into a raucous meeting. "Staff told me I had better get into the room fast because everyone is angry. My members told me they were sick and tired of incremental health reform measures. They wanted universal coverage *now*. I said, 'We won't get it.' They told me they wanted the Federation to stand for this right away," Kahn said.[139] "They felt the path we were on was unsustainable with the levels of uncompensated care and the expectation that hospitals would take care of everyone, plus this byzantine financing scheme."

They struck a deal. The device-makers, too, cut a deal. The insurers

then chairman of the House Administration Committee, ordered the Capitol Police to break into Moran's office to find him. He wasn't there, but a Republican eventually found him hiding in the House gym. He fled on foot, escaping with his no vote in tact. At 5:53 a.m., the vote board showed a slight lead, and Republicans gaveled it to a close. Ney later went to prison, the result of an unrelated scandal.

139   He told this to Senate staffer John McDonough, who included it in his book *Inside National Health Reform*.

did not, and fought it until the end.

Those deals were initially cut in private, but details leaked out. In the summer of 2009, I obtained a document that laid out to the decimal point precisely what Big Pharma had agreed to and what they'd gotten. Then reporting for The Huffington Post, I emailed both PhRMA and the White House, and waited for a reply.

Several years later, GOP investigators on the House Energy and Commerce Committee subpoenaed the White House for emails related to the PhRMA deal and stumbled on my correspondence. It showed officials at the White House and PhRMA swapping ideas on how best to deny the existence of a deal.

"Clearly, someone is trying to short circuit our efforts to try and make health care reform a reality this year," wrote Ken Johnson, a top lobbyist for PhRMA, in an email to the White House's top health care communications official, Linda Douglass.

Johnson and Douglass settled on a strategy of denying the memo's accuracy, and both the White House and PhRMA denied it on the record. I replied that I was confident in my sources and planned to run the story anyway.

Told of my plan, Douglass asked Johnson how it was that a news outlet could print something with both sides denying it, noting that other reporters had inquired about the details but backed off in the face of denials. The Huffington Post, Johnson explained to Douglass, doesn't follow normal journalistic rules.

In their on-record denials, they had both been lying, and the final bill released by the Senate Finance Committee followed the agreement almost precisely.

On the Hill, the chair of that Finance Committee, Sen. Max Baucus[140] (D-Mont.), had long been the patron of Jim Messina, Rahm's deputy. Baucus sat down and began months of endless negotiations with Republicans on his panel. Those talks dragged on as the public — with a heavy assist from congressional Republicans — soured on reform. Throughout the summer of 2009, angry crowds at town hall meetings berated Democratic lawmakers on everything from government overreach to death panels.

That summer, both Mike Enzi and Chuck Grassley, GOP senators

---

140   I once called Baucus' office in the midst of the negotiations, asking for spokesman Scott Mulhauser. "Are you going to shut our phone lines down again?" the intern answering the line asked. I asked him what he meant, and he explained that my story the previous day about Baucus going wobbly on the public option had blown their phones up so badly they stopped working. "Well then, yes, I probably am," I told him. "Haha, good," the kid told me, before patching me through.

Baucus thought he could win over, publicly trashed the bill. Enzi even told a Wyoming audience that he was purposely dragging the talks on in the hopes of killing it. "If I hadn't been involved in this process as long as I have and to the depth as I have, you would already have national health care," he told a conservative audience angry at his participation in talks. That wasn't long after Grassley had warned an Iowa crowd that Obamacare would "pull the plug on Grandma." And this from two of the three Republicans actively negotiating with Baucus back in Washington.

The White House, including even Baucus' protegé, Messina, grew impatient with the negotiations, and began pressuring Harry Reid to simply bypass Baucus. Emanuel "could see how well I knew those guys and how close I was to them. He could also tell that I was on Obama's side," said Messina.[141] "I wasn't going to be a whore for Senate Dems."

Whatever Messina wanted to do, Reid told them, you simply couldn't go around Baucus. Under Senate rules that Democrats had no intention of changing, 60 votes were needed to move the bill. Franken had only just arrived, bringing the caucus to 60, but that meant they couldn't lose a single vote. And by engaging the committee process — not only Finance, but the health committee was hard at work, too — rather than trying to ram it through as a leadership project as Mitch McConnell might do, Reid couldn't do much about Baucus.

"Don't you remember what he did to Daschle?" Reid asked the White House.[142]

In the House, an entirely different process was under way. Health care reform was mostly running through three committees, Ways and Means,[143] chaired by Charlie Rangel; Energy and Commerce, which was supposed to be chaired by John Dingell, but won in a coup by Henry Waxman;[144] and Education and Labor, chaired by George Miller. Waxman

---

141   Abrams, *Obama: An Oral History*.

142   Former Senate Democratic Leader Tom Daschle had been an Obama mentor and the two remained close friends. Obama wanted Daschle to be Health and Human Services secretary, but Baucus and Daschle had hated each other for years. Baucus, as Finance chair, got access to Daschle's tax returns, and scorched him for not paying taxes on what Baucus said should count as income, the use of a car and driver to ride around town. Baucus was right; Daschle, humiliated, withdrew.

143   I played for several years for the Ways and Means softball team, called WAM, because my friend Jeff Hild, an aide to subcommittee chairman Pete Stark, played on the team. My HuffPost colleague Arthur Delaney also played, and because Democrats controlled the committee in the years we played, he joked that we were literally going to bat for Democrats.

144   Chairmanships are doled out by seniority, and nobody was more senior than Dingell. But Waxman argued that Dingell was too old to handle what would

and Miller both came in during the post-Watergate wave of 1974, which swept in a new class of technocratic liberals.

The Congressional Progressive Caucus had been around for just under 20 years, but members thought of it more as a book club and debating society than a genuine political force. But as activists on the outside began agitating for progressives to make sure the health care bill was as strong as possible, the CPC set up a structure that could channel that energy. It was called Progressive Congress and run by an insurgent candidate who had come up short, Darcy Burner. Her deputy was Shaunna Thomas.

Burner and Thomas had deep ties with what was then called the netroots, the network of bloggers who could trigger thousands of phone calls or emails at a moment's notice, as well as to the online activist infrastructure that had developed since the Dean campaign.

They launched what they called internally the "kill the hostage" strategy. The argument from Blue Dogs was that progressive demands should be ignored, because their bleeding hearts would never allow them to kill a bill that would do some good for some number of people if it passed. Blue Dogs, they argued, had no such compunction, so they should be the ones to negotiate it.

So Burner, Thomas, and the bloggers[145] organized a letter signed by progressives saying that if the bill didn't include a "robust public option," they'd vote against it.

Raúl Grijalva and Lynn Woolsey, the caucus co-chairs, worked their colleagues for signatures, and once they had a decent number, Grijalva leaked the list of progressives who had committed to voting against any bill that didn't include a robust public plan to Daily Kos blogger Joan McCarter. With that list in hand, the blogosphere pressured those who weren't on it to make the pledge, and it eventually grew into the dozens — more than enough to form a swing bloc on the House floor. It was the first real show of force progressives had muscled in a generation. They took their letter to Pelosi, who authorized an official whip check — a canvassing of House Democrats to see if there was enough support in the party for a health care bill with what was now routinely referred to as the

---

be a historic amount of legislation, and, more importantly, that his ties to the auto industry — he represented Detroit — made him too resistant to addressing climate change. Waxman beat Dingell and used his perch to pass Waxman-Dingell through the House, a bill that would cap carbon emissions. It never got a vote in the Senate, while Dingell would go on to become a Twitter celebrity before dying in 2019. His seat was subsequently held by his wife, Debbie Dingell, a lead co-sponsor of Medicare for All.

145   Led by Jane Hamsher at FireDogLake.

"robust" public option.[146]

In the middle of October 2009, Woolsey climbed aboard the Speaker's military plane in San Francisco bound for Washington, D.C. On the flight back, they swapped intelligence, a journey that marked the highest the progressives would ascend in a generation, but one that would quickly come back to earth. The two went over the survey results one by one, with Pelosi offering her savant-like insight into each member's position: *He's not voting for it. She's for it. She told you that? Don't believe it.* By the time the aircraft touched down, it was clear that the robust public option was a handful of votes shy.

Woolsey saw the glass half full; Pelosi found it empty. "We compared notes, and it was very clear that the robust public option totally had as much support as most plans have around here before they go to the whip operation, but we didn't have the 218 that we needed. But usually, outside of the whip organization, you don't need to go and get 218 votes," recalled Woolsey. "That's why there's a whip organization."

In other words, the soft survey — a whip check, rather than a full-on whip — is used to gauge a baseline level of support. If it's within striking distance, the whip team goes out and breaks arms, begs, pleads, makes promises or threats, until the votes are there.

In this case, the whip office would only be brought in to deliver the bad news. Majority Whip James Clyburn, a leader in the civil rights movement who represents a district in South Carolina, met with Woolsey and her co-chair, Grijalva, to go over the survey document. With 47 "no" votes out of 256 Democrats, that left them nine short. It's not going to happen, Clyburn told them. The whip list was quickly leaked to the press.

Clyburn called Grijalva into his office and asked if he had been the leaker. After initially denying it, he copped to the breach. He eventually confessed it to me, too. "It didn't help," Grijalva acknowledged, pausing to reflect on his decision.[147] "It didn't help. It was some level of desperation ... and frustration."

The first leak to Daily Kos had paid off, but this one backfired. The caucus had lost the trust of Democratic leaders and the push for the public option had been dealt a major blow. "That was the end of it. Because no longer were we team players," concluded Woolsey.

Clyburn told me he felt burned. "It had a very negative impact on the effort," he said. "That was a low point in this whole process."

---

146   Basically, "robust" meant that the plan would pay Medicare rates plus an additional 5 percent.

147   This quote appeared in a story in The Huffington Post written with Arthur Delaney in 2010, called "Power Struggle."

"We're much more protective of our whip [sheet] after that. We've started telling people what the numbers are, rather than showing them," Clyburn said. "I can't see myself doing that again."

By October, the White House had long since given up on the public option, even as progressive pressure continued to build. Late that month, Jesse Lee, a White House official whose job it was to deal with progressive reporters, bloggers and netroots groups, lashed out at Murshed Zaheed, a former Reid staffer who was by then working for Media Matters. "Here's the deal," Lee emailed him, "you, along with Reid's guys have been waging a fullout assault on the President for the last two days based on the premise that Reid is a few votes away from getting [a] public option and Obama's deliberately fucking it up...[Y]our incessance on this, propagating grassroots hatred of Obama, is going to hurt everybody from Reid on down in the long run. Given that the premise of your assault is bullshit, I suggest you consider yourself to have gotten away with one for your 'boss' and cut it out."

"Reality here is that WH folks don't buy Reid's math," he added. "They don't believe he is 'one or two votes short' and btw it's not like there are 'one or two' they haven't called. I'm not gonna go out on a limb to defend this position, but the reason [Maine Republican Olympia] Snowe is important is not to wax glossy about bipartisanship, it's because there are several Dems who have said they won't vote yes unless a Republican does."

Zaheed pushed back, a preview of a political gulf that would only widen between Reid and Obama over the years. "I know for fact that Reid wants PO ... badly. He is feeling good about where he is. However, it will help if we get clear statements from the WH," he replied. "I appreciate your take. But I need to stick up for my boss, because he is doing the right thing, pushing for the right thing."

After two consecutive wave elections, the Congressional Progressive Caucus had one of its own former members as Speaker of the House, and a roster that was 83 strong. They'd been organizing since 1991. Yet the most aggressive advocate of a public option was Harry Reid? What happened?

It's not pretty, but the story of the CPC in 2009 and 2010 is one of a caucus whose leadership was riven with internal strife, and whose membership was largely disorganized and checked out of the bloc. On a deeper level, its dysfunction was more structural. For a caucus to be effective it needs both carrots and sticks — a way to reward members — either of the caucus or leadership — who stay in line, and a way to punish those who stray. The right-wing Freedom Caucus, for instance, rewards its members with conservative branding that protects them against a primary, and punishes leadership by taking down bills it doesn't find strong enough — or, in the case of John Boehner, would later take down the Speaker himself.

For Democrats in 2009 and '10, primaries generally weren't a concern. Alexandra Rojas, who would become director of Justice Democrats in 2018, when primaries started to matter, was just starting high school. The CPC didn't have a big base of small donors that it could drive toward allies, and it was far too large to make credible threats about bloc voting. Nobody believed that dozens of progressives would vote no on universal health care no matter how compromised the legislation was.

The leadership fight was personal — longtime CPC leader Woolsey simply did not like her new co-chair and the feeling was mutual — but it was also about competing political visions. Woolsey had unveiled contempt for outside groups that organized to pressure the CPC, and Grijalva saw them as allies.

Grijalva is and was well-liked by his colleagues, which matters, but his ability to make credible threats in negotiations was not typically well respected. Woolsey, as had apparently been the case on the Petaluma City Council as well, was not well-liked, nor was her organizing ability respected. That, however, was the leadership with which the CPC went into the breach that was the 2009 and 2010 Congress.

Grijalva is a first-generation American who didn't learn English until the fifth grade. "Growing up, you were made to believe that the fact that you spoke another language or you came from another culture, that there was a bad stigma to that," he said. "I watched my parents go through a lot of stuff, not all of it good, to take care of their family, and it can't help but shape your values."

Grijalva's start in politics came when he volunteered with the farm-workers union in the early '70s, where he met legendary labor leader Dolores Huerta, who is often described, in a typically patriarchal way, as the female Cesar Chavez. Their friendship lasted. In the run-up to the final health care vote, Huerta was in Washington, D.C., cracking heads: she gave two hold-out congressmen from California — Dennis Cardoza and Jim Costa — a stern lecture, she said. Both came around. "Raúl is the kind of person that, when you first meet him, you always think it's the guy that's standing next to him that is the politician," said Huerta, who is based in Arizona, where Grijalva's politics were forged.

Like Obama, Grijalva began as a community organizer, the type of experience that teaches much about how power operates and the art of a specific kind of compromise. "I'm very proud of being a progressive, but I'm also a pragmatist," Grijalva said. "I understand that you take your victory and you build on it. And I think sometimes we on the left tend to think an issue to death as opposed to do an issue. We learned that through the civil rights movement, the farm workers movement, how you get this contract and you work on it. Community organizing, OK, you get the street lights in the neighborhood, then you move to the bigger things: the schools, no health services. But you give everybody a taste of what a victory feels like, and then you get much more help after that."

Eve Shapiro is a pediatrician in Tucson and a member of the Physicians for a National Health Program, a national group that has long championed a single-payer program like Medicare for All. Grijalva persuaded Shapiro that his strategy made sense because it was achievable, but he also persuaded her that supporting the public option did not mean giving up on single payer.

"As long as people see it as a work in progress, and that's how Grijalva saw it, that's why we felt comfortable in supporting what he was going to do," she said.

The work on the ground, Grijalva said, instills in him the idea that he is representing the progressive community. Asked why he and Woolsey can't agree on whether to work with outside groups, he said: "I don't know, I think it's a question of backgrounds. I, Keith [Ellison], Donna Edwards, and some of the other people that have come in, we realize that a big reason that we're here is because of the support we have from progressives in the base, and we grew up with that. Maybe that's it."

But Grijalva had his problems. As one progressive leader who worked closely with the CPC put it: "It's one of those untold stories that none of us can ever tell — how many years of effectiveness we lost to Raúl occupying the co-chair position at the CPC."

But it's important enough to be told. Grijalva drinks — a lot. Throughout the debate over the Affordable Care Act, I had a reporting rule with myself that I would never quote him in an article if we spoke after roughly 5 p.m. It was no accident that he was at the Tune Inn that Sunday night that Democrats were celebrating the passage of Obamacare. My colleague at HuffPost, Arthur Delaney, was also a regular there for years, and when I told him that Grijalva was as well, he told me that wasn't true, that members of Congress came there often, but none were there on a daily basis.

Later, we were at the bar and I saw Grijalva and introduced him. Delaney, after meeting him, said he had never realized he was a congressman and that, yes, he was nearly always there.

In July 2018, I met Deb Haaland, who'd recently won a House primary in New Mexico, for coffee on a Thursday afternoon. Grijalva had endorsed her primary opponent but quickly gotten behind her once it was over, and the two were friendly. Walking down Pennsylvania Avenue, I spotted him sitting at the sidewalk table outside the Tune Inn, his typical round of a shot of whiskey and a beer in front of him. I pointed him out and Haaland, publicly in recovery herself, stopped to say hi.

Grijalva, even though he was sitting outside, seemed embarrassed. "End of the day," he said sheepishly, though it was 2:45.

In 2017, it emerged that he had paid a $48,000 settlement to an employee who accused him of being drunk regularly in the office and creating a hostile environment. The next year, as Grijalva clashed with Interior Secretary Ryan Zinke, Zinke tweeted that Grijalva's investigation shouldn't be taken seriously because of all the time the congressman spent at the Tune Inn. It was mid-afternoon, and Grijalva was at that very bar when Zinke fired off the tweet.

Back in Arizona, questions about Grijalva's drinking had chased him since a DUI in 1985. In January 2018, he was asked about his drinking by a local news station. "I dealt with it and I feel very comfortable that I got past that," Grijalva told News4Tucson in a lengthy interview. "And it was a period of my life in which other things were affecting me and affecting me personally, and once you wrestle the demons, and you beat 'em, you beat 'em. And I feel very comfortable that that demon's beat."

Like Grijalva, Woolsey's origin story was impressive: she was a mom on welfare at one point, and she stumbled into Congress. In 1992, called "the year of the woman," Barbara Boxer left her Northern California seat to run for Senate. Woolsey was on the Petaluma City Council at the time, and word around the House was that her colleagues there were so annoyed by her approach to politics that they all agreed to endorse her for Congress if she would just leave the council. Apocryphal or not, it led to a nine-way primary, with seven of the candidates coming from Marin County. They split the Marin vote and she squeaked through with roughly a quarter of the vote.

As co-chair of the CPC, she actively discouraged outside progressive groups from organizing to push an agenda. In June 2009, Amy Isaacs went to see her old friend Woolsey to tell her that she was retiring after a long organizing career that included 20 years at the old-school liberal organization Americans for Democratic Action. Isaacs wanted to introduce her to the succeeding director and to offer help with her agenda. It was a fairly pro forma meeting, but she had no idea what she was in for. Isaacs described the meeting that ensued as "what has to have been the most bizarre conversation with a member of Congress that I've had in 40 years." Woolsey made it clear that one of her top priorities was making sure that Grijalva didn't win out in his effort to ally the CPC with outside organizations. "Those aren't quite the words she used, but that was certainly the meaning she conveyed. And it was odd. It was very odd,"

Isaacs told me, explaining that Woolsey made clear that she wanted the CPC to be left alone.[148]

Woolsey didn't want help from outside groups, but she also didn't want them praising her rival. When MoveOn sent a mass email into districts represented by members of the CPC, asking them to thank Grijalva for his work on the public option, Woolsey lost it. "They just sent out this universal thing and dropped the member's name in it," Woolsey complained to me. "And they've actually apologized to me profusely for doing that. They were chagrined that they would've done that to me. But they just didn't think. It was a mistake. They shouldn't have done it."

Woolsey said she would rather wage an internal struggle free from interference. "They're outside groups and they belong — it is not their job to give direction to the progressive caucus, who are working, all 83 of us, at breakneck speed, to get things as progressive as possible," said Woolsey. "To go to the most progressive members of the House and tell them they're not progressive enough is not healthy."

Grijalva had the opposite view. "Politically, we think it's not a question of influence, it's a question of coalition-building," Grijalva said when asked about Woolsey's concern about the influence of outside groups. "Somebody needs to knock on the door, and knock hard sometimes," he said. "This is not an intellectual exercise, this is a political exercise, and you need political backing."

I asked Woolsey how the co-chair setup had been going. She paused. "It's hard," she finally said. "I think now the progressive caucus might be mature enough that in the next Congress, we should be looking at having a single chair."

Even with all of its tactical screw-ups and structural flaws, the progressive effort had forced the public option back into the conversation after the Obama administration had left it for dead.[149] In the bill's final hour, it was Scott Brown, paradoxically, who opened the door for the revival of the public option.

When Ted Kennedy died in August 2009 of brain cancer, his passing created a Senate vacancy that was filled by a placeholder while a special election was organized.[150]

On December 24, 2009, Paul Kirk cast the 60th vote to break a filibuster and pass the Senate version of the Affordable Care Act, a slightly

---

148   Even more strangely, Woolsey would become president of ADA in 2010, serving there until 2016. She retired from Congress in 2012.

149   It's just "a sliver of reform," Obama said at one point, downplaying its significance to the overall bill and repeatedly expressing frustration at how fixated the left was on the public option.

150   Kirk was the man who beat Nancy Pelosi in the 1985 race for DNC chair.

more corporate-friendly plan than the one that had passed the House on November 7. That bill, shepherded through by Pelosi, included a public health insurance option to compete with private plans in the marketplaces that would be created by Obamacare. It was not the more robust version of the public option that the Congressional Progressive Caucus had pushed for, but the bill was broadly considered more aggressive, and the two chambers planned to hash out their differences in a conference committee.

Two weeks earlier, Democrats had held a Senate primary contest in Massachusetts, to nominate a candidate to replace the late Ted Kennedy. The race pitted Rep. Michael Capuano from Boston against Attorney General Martha Coakley. Former President Bill Clinton, EMILY's List, and other party leaders got behind Coakley early. The only statewide official in the race, she easily dispatched Capuano in the December primary. "They said that women don't have much luck in Massachusetts politics," she declared at her party that night. "And we believed that it was quite possible that that luck was about to change."

Assured of victory in the coming January general election, she tried that luck and departed for a two-week vacation in the Caribbean. Yet Capuano returned to Washington shaken by what he'd seen on the campaign trail. He was invited to brief a private gathering of House Democrats in the basement of the Capitol.

He leaned into a standing microphone, looked around the room at his colleagues, and, according to one of the lawmakers present, delivered a two-word speech: "You're screwed."

As the gathered House Democrats gradually realized they had heard the extent of his speech, the silence was punctuated only by soft, nervous laughter. Later, Capuano elaborated on the theme to me. Everywhere he went in Massachusetts, he said, he met people who were absolutely livid at the anemic approach to job creation in the wake of the crisis. That rage, he warned, was going to be turned against Democrats at the polls if they didn't deliver.[151]

Coakley, still on the beach, saw it too late. In January 2010, she was dealt an upset that was stunning to everyone but Capuano. The health care reform effort appeared buried amid the rubble.

The night of the special election, three progressive groups — Progressive Change Campaign Committee, Democracy for America, and MoveOn — fielded a poll of a thousand people who voted for Obama in 2008 but either switched to support Brown for Senate or decided not to vote. More than 80 percent of both groups favored a public option.

---

151   Capuano was later felled by a version of that rage, losing a 2018 primary to insurgent challenger Ayanna Pressley.

Nobody listened to Capuano's assessment that the sagging economy was driving public rage, and conventional wisdom had formed that the push for health care was too aggressive, and the vote represented a backlash. But even that was flimsy, according to the survey.

A plurality of people who switched from Obama to Brown — 48 percent — or didn't vote — 43 percent — said that they opposed the Senate health care bill, the poll financed by the coalition of progressive groups found. But it's not enough to know simply that they were against it. Among those Brown voters, 23 percent thought it went "too far" — but 36 percent thought it *didn't go far enough.* Another 41 percent said they weren't sure why they opposed it.

That means that roughly one-third of voters who wanted stronger health care reform than Congress was delivering switched from Obama to Brown. Given that Brown won by just five points, it could have made the difference. The drawn-out process, the compromises with industry, the gradually weakening bill, fed a cynicism that Washington wasn't working for regular people, a suspicion strengthened by the still battered economy.

It may seem counterintuitive to express anger at a weak bill by voting for somebody who only wants to kill it, but our electoral system only gives voters two choices, and voting can often be more emotive than it is rational.

The decision for some Obama voters was to not vote at all. Among those who didn't vote and said they opposed health care, a full 53 percent said they objected to the Senate bill because it didn't go far enough; 39 percent weren't sure and only 8 percent thought it went too far. So one-fifth of Obama voters who stayed home were upset that the bill wasn't strong enough. Had Coakley been able to turn out just a fraction of them, she'd have won.

Her upset deprived Democrats of their 60-vote supermajority.

That meant that any bill that would emerge from conference committee would need at least one Republican to support it, or Democrats would have to nuke the filibuster. But it would take 50 votes to end the filibuster, and there were no more than a few who'd have gone for it. That meant the health care bill would need 60 votes, and it wasn't at all clear where they'd be coming from. The fate of the bill was suddenly in doubt.

Curiously, Democrats still had several weeks before Brown was sworn in to agree to a compromise and pass the bill with their filibuster-proof majority, but there was no sense of urgency in the conference committee. "We had a huge blow-up over graduate medical education provisions," said Kate Leone, who was Reid's health care staffer in the negotiations with the House. It was completely disconnected from reality. While Mitch McConnell would have given his party 24 hours to get it done and onto the floor, Democrats were frozen. Even if the conference committee had rapidly come to an agreement, Democrats like Kent Conrad, the Budget Committee chairman, would have demanded that the Congressional Budget Office analyze and score the legislation, even if it meant taking more time than they had. The Democrats' commitment to legislative norms prevented them from even considering rushing the bill through.

Instead, Democrats, including Pelosi ally Barney Frank of Massachusetts, began writing the bill's obituary. Offered Frank in the wake of Coakley's loss:

> I feel strongly that the Democratic majority in congress must respect the process and make no effort to bypass the electoral results. If Martha Coakley had won, I believe we could have worked out a reasonable compromise between the House and Senate health care bills. But since Scott Brown has won and the Republicans now have 41 votes in the senate, that approach is no longer appropriate. I am hopeful that some Republican senators will be willing to discuss a revised version of health care reform. Because I do not think that the country would be well served by the health care status quo. But our respect for democratic procedures must rule out any effort to pass a health care bill as if the Massachusetts election had not happened. Going forward, I hope there will be a serious effort to change the Senate rule which means that 59 are not enough to pass major legislation, but those are the rules by which the health care bill was considered, and it would be wrong to change them in the middle of this process.

"If [Coakley] loses, it's over," said Rep. Carolyn Maloney (D-N.Y.), before the votes were tallied. Reid, facing his own reelection, was inclined to back burner the ACA, with New York Sen. Charles Schumer, the No. 3 Democrat in the Senate at the time, urging him to move to a jobs bill.

But even on election night, there was at least one politician who wasn't giving up.

"We don't say a state that already has health care should determine whether the rest of the country should," Pelosi said. "We will get the job done. I'm very confident. I've always been confident."

The reaction from White House chief of staff Rahm Emanuel had been the opposite, and he began pushing to back off the ACA and instead do piecemeal reform focused largely on expanding care for children. The White House, Obama included, began sending mixed signals about whether it wanted to go big or small, with Obama endorsing a plan that included "the core elements" of reform.

"I would advise that we try to move quickly to coalesce around those elements of the package that people agree on," Obama said in one interview.

Pelosi, in a conference call later that month with House leadership, dubbed Emanuel an "incrementalist" and mocked the small-ball idea as "kiddie care."

The House would be going big, she said. To do it, the lower chamber would pass the version of the ACA that had already moved through the Senate. And the Senate would use the reconciliation process, which requires just 50 votes but is only available for legislation that impacts the budget, in order to make some changes to the original bill.

"I was a mid-level staffer on the Hill during the original ACA fight," recalled Ezra Levin, who would later become a co-founder of Indivisible, a progressive political organization. "I vividly remember the feeling on Capitol Hill the week after Scott Brown won — suddenly the wheels were coming off. People were talking about scuttling a major bill and doing something piecemeal."

He said that he and his eventual Indivisible co-founder Leah Greenberg, also a Hill staffer at the time, drafted an op-ed they never published, since Pelosi's push made the issue moot. The unpublished piece argued that "abandoning the ACA would turn off millennial idealists like us from the possibilities of politics. Why work in government, policy, and politics if the result of a generational win like 2008 resulted in barely anything at all? But Pelosi saved it. She demonstrated serious leadership at a time of real uncertainty. It was, corny as it sounds, inspirational. And tens of millions of Americans got health insurance as a result of that leadership in that moment."

The Affordable Care Act, even the House-passed version, was a flawed piece of legislation for a host of reasons, some that can be laid at Pelosi's feet and some that can't. But as an act of legislative prowess, her revival of it remains a signature accomplishment. "With the help of Nancy Pelosi, we were able to [rescue the ACA]. It was hard though. It was really very, very hard," Reid said, adding that he was much less confident than her. "We had to go back and use reconciliation and do some pretty tricky things to get it done. So that certainly didn't spur my enthusiasm. It was a pretty dark time."

Just ahead of the final vote, Pelosi sat down with progressive reporters and bloggers for a last pre-passage interview. She relished her victory over Emanuel and the incrementalists. "My biggest fight was against those who want to do something incremental versus those who want to do something comprehensive. We have won that," she said proudly.

"In our midst, there's the small-bill crowd — here," she said, referring to the Capitol, then added, gesturing out the window behind her, where Pennsylvania Avenue stretched to the White House, "and there."

But having won the fight to go big, she had to get it over the line. In a meeting that Pelosi held for Democratic rookies the week after Scott Brown's surprise victory, one of the freshmen, Rep. Jared Polis of Colorado, suggested reviving the public option. The Senate was in the process of considering the use of the reconciliation procedure, which would require only 50 votes and eliminate the need to placate public option opponents such as Sen. Joe Lieberman. If only 50 votes are needed, Polis argued, let's go for it. It's what people want.

It was an approach not often taken by Democrats: attack, rather than retreat. The idea had come from outside Congress, pitched to Polis by Adam Green.

Green had met Polis at an event put together by Darcy Burner, and remembered that Polis had been enthusiastic about the public option. Green had left MoveOn to co-found the Progressive Change Campaign Committee earlier in 2009,[152] along with Stephanie Taylor, launched as an antidote to the Democratic Congressional Campaign Committee. They put together a letter as an organizing tool, and Polis recruited Chellie Pingree, a progressive freshman from Maine, a state represented then by two moderate Republican senators. The pair began circulating a letter calling on the Senate to use reconciliation to pass a public option and finish health care reform.

Shaunna Thomas was still at Progressive Congress, the organization that was directly linked to the CPC, and used her connection on the Hill to round up as many signatures as possible.

The PCCC had taken a confrontational stance toward the administration from early on, challenging it to live up to the campaign rhetoric that got Obama elected. The group's most high-profile move had come the previous summer, prompted by comments made by an anonymous "se-

---

152   I wrote a story on January 7, 2009, announcing the launch of the organization, and at HuffPost we linked to it regularly, seeding it with hundreds of thousands of members. The headline, "Dem Activists Plan 'PCCC' to Back Progressives," was followed with: "A group of progressive operatives from MoveOn and labor circles have teamed with a prominent Internet pioneer to try to give the Sam Bennetts of the world the final push they need — and send even more [Tom] Perriellos to Congress. The organization will be the first of its kind exclusively to focus on electing progressive Democrats in congressional elections." Bennett, a progressive, had lost a close but flawed 2008 race in Allentown, Pa., while Perriello won an upset in Virginia. Stephanie Taylor, who ran Perriello's field campaign, was a co-founder. The "prominent Internet pioneer" was Aaron Swartz, who later died by suicide under the weight of a viciously unjust prosecution at the hands of Boston's U.S. Attorney Carmen Ortiz. Another top Perriello aide, Leah Greenberg, went on to found Indivisible.

nior White House adviser" to the Washington Post. "I don't understand why the left of the left has decided that this is their Waterloo," said the senior somebody. "We've gotten to this point where health care on the left is determined by the breadth of the public option. I don't understand how that has become the measure of whether what we achieve is health care reform."

So Green and Taylor organized hundreds of campaign staff and volunteers to sign a letter declaring that yes, in fact, they did want a public option as part of reform, and they were not merely the "left of the left." They ran the letter as a full-page ad in the New York Times. "Since we were a scrappy tiny unfunded startup, that ad basically took all our money," Taylor recalled. But it got a ton of press, and forced the administration to continue to grapple with the public option.[153]

The PCCC began working with Pingree and Polis to organize around the letter. They were joined by Democracy for America, launched from the 2004 Howard Dean campaign; MoveOn; and CREDO Action,[154] a millions-strong online progressive outfit, in pushing for outside support, generating calls into members' offices asking that they sign on. The blogosphere lit up, cataloging each new signatory to the letter. Thomas, perhaps the only lobbyist on the Hill at the time funded by small donors, stalked the halls with the implicit carrot of support from small donors, and the stick of opposition from that same public if they stayed on the sidelines.

More than a hundred members signed on. The reactions from Grijalva and Woolsey to the Pingree-Polis initiative were as different as you'd expect. Grijalva encouraged them and urged each member of the CPC to sign the letter. He also engaged outside groups, hoping to give it an extra boost. Woolsey was dismissive of the project from the start, approaching Pingree to tell her it wasn't a useful move. "I wouldn't say she was chastising me or anything else, but saying that those [are the] kinds of things the progressive caucus is happy to do together," Pingree told me. (Other lawmakers who heard about the conversation claim that it wasn't as gentle as Pingree described it.)

Polis enlisted the support of Sen. Michael Bennet, a freshman Democrat from Polis' home state of Colorado facing pressure from a progressive primary challenger, and in need of some cred. New York's freshman Sen. Kirsten Gillibrand also signed on, her first big break in the Senate

---

153   Even though we now know it had already been traded away to the hospital industry.

154   Then run by Becky Bond, who would become a senior aide on Bernie Sanders' 2016 campaign and Beto O'Rourke's 2018 Senate run and, briefly, his 2020 presidential campaign.

with her Blue Dog roots in the House. With freshman Sen. Jeff Merkley (D-Ore.) and sophomore Sen. Sherrod Brown (D-Ohio), the four put out a Senate version of the Pingree-Polis letter.

The effort caught fire in the Senate, where more than 40 senators eventually made the commitment, and more than 50 said they would vote for it if it were on the floor.

"The netroots advocacy effort made an enormous impact. When Chellie Pingree and I launched the letter, we didn't know if we'd have a dozen, two dozen signatures, and that's probably what we would've had, absent a strong netroots effort," Polis told me at the time. "Without even knowing that it was going to occur, there was a strong netroots push by Adam Green and others to raise money for Chellie Pingree and I, and it raised over $25,000 for my reelection campaign and similar numbers for Chellie Pingree."

The groups would go on to raise even larger sums for Bennet and Gillibrand on the Senate side. And while the total dollar amounts were small, each candidate picked up the names and addresses of thousands of progressive donors who can be tapped again and again. Bennet and Gillibrand, both of whom had been viewed with suspicion by the Democratic base, were given a boost, with Bennet's primary opponent left only to argue that Bennet hadn't fought hard enough for it. Stepping up and pushing a progressive priority had proven to be a winning political strategy.

The letter gave despondent grassroots Democrats something to organize around, and they began calling their senators and members of Congress and demanding they sign the letter. As names piled up, the new endorsements created new stories, articles that then fed the outside activism.

As the number of senators joining the effort had expanded, it generated leadership support, with Schumer and Bob Menendez (N.J.) getting behind it. With genuine momentum behind it, Harry Reid was the next to jump on board.

"Senator Reid has always and continues to support the public option as a way to drive down costs and create competition," read a statement his office put out on Friday, February 19. "That is why he included the measure in his original health care proposal. If a decision is made to use reconciliation to advance health care, Senator Reid will work with the White House, the House, and members of his caucus in an effort to craft a public option that can overcome procedural obstacles and secure enough votes."

The White House didn't appreciate the new energy. A few hours after Reid's office put out its statement in support of the public option, Rahm met senior Reid aide Jim Manley and a few reporters from the Washington Post and the New York Times[155] for dinner and drinks at Lola's, a Capitol Hill bar and grill. Seeing Manley, Emanuel offered a response to Reid's gesture with one of his own: a double-bird, an eerie sight given his severed right finger.

It wasn't exactly the storming of the Bastille, but it was a startling turn of events, a reminder of how fast things can change. "There are decades where nothing happens; and there are weeks where decades happen," Lenin once said.[156]

The public option, left for dead, had been revived, not in a White House meeting, but by two freshmen members of Congress with the help of millions of people organizing online.

Reconciliation was in fact used — which Republicans later employed as a justification to use the same 50-vote threshold to repeal it, as if they needed one — but the public option was not included. Privately, efforts by Reid staffers to persuade the White House to bring back the public option were rebuffed. "The word kept coming back, too many promises have been made. It's over," said one senior Reid aide.

As the final details of the bill were being worked out, a national public option was still alive; Reid and his aides were trying to work through the details of what type of public expansion would be agreeable to the caucus, and the two senators they needed to go through were Ben Nelson and Joe Lieberman. Both would take the offers back to representatives of the insurance industry for feedback, Reid aides said.

Connecticut's political economy has long been dominated by insurers, who were major supporters of Lieberman. Nelson, meanwhile, simply *was* the insurance industry. He had been an executive at Central National Insurance Group of Omaha, before becoming the state's insurance commissioner. After his stint in public service, he went back to the insurance company, eventually becoming the firm's president.

"We had the votes, it just didn't last very long," said Reid. "We had the votes on public option for 24 hours and a number of votes changed. Where the pressure came from, I don't know, but it came and we were unable to get it done."

In public, it was dropped in exchange for allowing people 55 and over to buy into Medicare, itself a huge step forward, as the ten years before Medicare kicks in can be the most trying both professionally and in terms of health complications. The expansion of Medicaid was itself ex-

---

155   The Times reporter was Carl Hulse, a dean of the Capitol Hill press corps who has been close with Rahm dating back to the '80s.

156   He was also a psychopath and a mass murderer, on the scale of a Henry Kissinger.

panded, bumping it up from 133 percent of the poverty line to 140, which would have made millions of more people eligible. Both were demands made by Pingree and Polis.

Emerging from a meeting with Reid and other Democratic leaders, Sen. Jay Rockefeller, a progressive Democrat from West Virginia,[157] was positively beaming. He was so pleased with the deal, he said, he wanted to hear his conservative colleague, Kent Conrad of North Dakota, explain it to reporters instead. Conrad did.

But the deal was soon dead. Joe Lieberman went on "Face the Nation" to say that he wouldn't support any bill that had a Medicare expansion in it. Chuck Schumer, who watches the Sunday shows, called Harry Reid, who often didn't. "Lieberman seemed to draw a line in the sand," Schumer told Reid.[158] "You should check in with him. He seemed to rule out supporting the bill if it has the Medicare buy in."

Reid called his aide Manley and asked for a transcript. "He just wasn't honest with me," Reid said, seeing it in black and white.

Reid called Emanuel, who was driving his son home from a bar mitzvah class, and told him to get over to the Capitol; he called Lieberman, too. Reid had previously considered kicking Lieberman out of the party or stripping him of his seniority on committees — the near-final straw for him had come when Lieberman spoke at the Republican National Convention and questioned whether the country would be safe with Obama as president — but had backed down. Now he wanted to call Lieberman's bluff.

But Emanuel told him to cave. "We need to get it done," Emanuel told him.

I asked Lieberman later whether he had been willing to give up his committee gavel in the fight over health care, a punishment that Reid could have doled out. "Oh, God, no. Nobody's asking me that," Lieberman said. In fact, when Obama addressed the Democratic caucus at the height of the debate, as the public option and Medicare buy-in were teetering on the brink, Lieberman told me the president asked him simply to work it out. "When he came to the caucus he said, 'Just try to work this out as you get to the end here.' And I said, 'OK,'" explained Lieberman.

I also asked Reid about that meeting with Emanuel. "I think when people write about health care it's hard to write what really happened, because what really happened was not an evenly flowing river," he said. "What we had was something like — I floated the Colorado once through

---

157   Yes, such a thing existed in the not-distant past.

158   Most of this exchange comes from a 2010 story by Sam Stein in HuffPost, fleshed out later to me by Manley.

the Grand Canyon, and that's what health care was kind of like. *Oh, it's so nice,* and then *bang!* you hit those rapids and it throws you up in the air and *Oh man, I'm glad I'm alive.* That's kind of health care. So that was just a minor bump. We had a lot of bumps."

As health policy staffer John McDonough wrote in his memoir, when the health care debate began and it looked like Democrats might be able to get a caucus of 60 senators, "some Democrats even thought a fifty-eight or fifty-nine vote margin was preferable to sixty — a level triggering unrealistic expectations among the Democratic base."

On the House side, the insurance companies worked their will through the Blue Dogs and New Democrats. The first sign that Blue Dogs would have their way, and be allowed to stand in for Republicans, came in the summer of 2009, on the House Energy and Commerce Committee, when Chairman Henry Waxman agreed to their demand for a "weak" public option, where rates could not be tied to Medicare. After several weeks during which the Blue Dogs were hailed by the media for successfully leveraging the size of their bloc to get what they wanted, it seemed progressives might be able to do the same. But they didn't; despite the threats made by progressives, when it came time to vote, the strong public option had not been revived, and all but two CPC members voted for it.

This is a reality that activists will need to remember in 2021 if Democrats make a new push forward — centrists have an undeniable structural advantage when it comes to gaming out the vote. Barney Frank, never one to buy into my legislative analysis, flipped the script. "They are able to put the brakes on to some extent, but we're driving the car," he told me. Frank regarded the agenda of House Democrats as essentially a progressive one, and in his view, to think of Blue Dogs and New Dems as more "effective" than progressives is to miss the point.

"The progressive caucus is behind these things coming up at all," he said. "You take that for granted. We have had basically liberal bills in health care, financial regulatory reform — we got an independent consumer agency....Your definition of effectiveness is for people being able to modify the basics, but you forget about the people who got the basic thing through. Can you not see that? You start when the movie's four-fifths over."

Frank did acknowledge that the more conservative caucuses are good at what they do. "It's easy to be effective if you're in the middle," he said. "What's our tactic? We threaten not to vote for the bill?"

That's exactly what the PCCC tried to organize four or five progressives to do. Because the bill was so close at the end, reasoned PCCC's Stephanie Taylor, a reasonable demand, coupled with a credible threat to sink the bill, would have to be met. The plan was to demand an up-or-down vote on the House floor to add a public option to the bill. There was an elegance to the proposal: if it didn't have the votes, then no harm, no foul. If it did, the Senate would have to re-pass the bill, but because it was using the reconciliation process, only 50 would be needed, and it would be a make-or-break vote. If the parliamentarian somehow ruled it out of order, well, there was nothing stopping the House from reverting to the original bill and passing it.

"We tried to convince a bloc of four or five House members to at least stand together and withhold their vote on the final bill unless they got an up or down vote on the public option — we were convinced we had the votes," said Taylor. "We couldn't find a bloc of four members to do it."

Taylor had competition on the lobbying front. A week before the vote, Obama told Rep. Dennis Kucinich that he just happened to be flying to Ohio on Air Force One, and if he wanted a ride, he'd be happy to take him. Kucinich boarded as a public "firm no" and landed a yes. It wasn't the plane flight that did it, Kucinich told me years later, but the recognition that there was nothing more to be gained by holding out any further. He had voted against an earlier version for not being good enough, and he had dragged it as far left as he could.

"I wrote a lengthy, as yet unpublished account of my decision, immediately after I met with the president on Air Force One," he said. "My decision to support the legislation was not based on anything the President promised or said to me, either before, during or after the meeting. I had a rather complicated relationship with the Obama administration, but an uncomplicated relationship with my constituents. I voted the pleas and the interests of my constituents of the 10th District of Ohio, mindful that the few identifiable benefits they would receive would, in the long run, be insufficient. People were hungry for some relief. I would have preferred to deliver the whole loaf instead of three slices, but I wasn't running the bakery."

Since then, Taylor thinks progressives have built much stronger capacity. "Today we could definitely put together a bloc of four or five, and possibly a block of twenty to twenty-five, in a similarly high stakes fight," she said.

At the time, it was a more credible threat from the right. Bart Stupak, a New Democrat from Michigan, successfully led a gang of forty anti-abortion-rights Democrats who threatened to block the health care bill in November if they were not given an opportunity to have a floor vote on an amendment to restrict funding for abortion.

I asked Stupak how he got his way while the progressives failed to get theirs.

"You have to pick your fights at the right time," said Stupak, pointing out that Pelosi knew from a previous appropriations fight in July that he would be willing to block a bill. "You can't be crying wolf all the time because you lose your wolfiness. You lose your credibility. So I'm not going to lose my credibility. So you use it at certain times when it's appropriate."

In March, Stupak and his gang of anti-choice dissidents eventually came around to a compromise on abortion and voted in favor of the bill. During the floor debate, a Republican shouted "baby killer" at Stupak while he spoke.

As the voting process began that Sunday evening, the lights in the House chamber dimmed and projectors displayed individual members' votes on the wall above reporters' heads in the press galleries. Several anxious faces peered upward from the floor, but not Pelosi's — she made her rounds, hugging Democrats and signing copies of the bill before the tally even neared 216. (After all, a vote on the "rule" to proceed to the bill succeeded with 224.) She spent several minutes in a friendly conversation with Stupak. Stupak ultimately voted for Obamacare and partied with Crowley that night at the Tune Inn.

Both knew the bill was in the can. "We knew who the 219 were," said Hoyer. Having Stupak on board gave cover to the members deciding the vote based on politics. Several Democrats, such as Rick Boucher of Virginia, had not announced their intentions and refused to reveal them until the last minute. Boucher was one of several members who voted only after 216 yeas had already piled up.

But allowing some Democrats to retreat made it harder for the ones who had the courage to stand and fight. Immediately after the vote, and repeatedly throughout his re-election campaign, the National Republican Congressional Committee used Boucher's vote to blast his neighbor Perriello, whose energetic defense of health care reform during 21 town halls in August 2009 was the counterattack the administration had desperately needed. "Boucher: Perriello's Obamacare vote will hurt seniors," read a typical missive from the NRCC. Perriello had to defend his vote not only from GOP attacks, but also from Democratic ones.

Both Clyburn and Hoyer say that they probably could have whipped enough votes to offset the loss of Stupak. "I think we could have," Clyburn said, who also adds they had the votes for the public option. "But I would much rather have 219 than try to eke out 216." Hoyer agreed: "I think we could've done it," but getting that 216 would've forced more Blue Dogs to take a hard vote, something leadership would rather avoid.

"We would've had to get more marginal members," he said, "the

Blue Dog and other caucuses — I guess the Blue Dogs primarily."

Stupak, as savvy a vote-counter as anybody in the House, saw it, too. "Speakers never bring a bill to the floor unless they have the votes. And they always have a few in reserve," Stupak explained to the Catholic News Agency in a post-vote interview. "I had a number of members who thanked us after, because they could vote no."

But the votes Stupak delivered did not bring the bill to the necessary 216[159]; it was already there. When Rep. Zack Space (D-Ohio) announced the day before the vote that he'd be opposing it, Republicans and other Hill observers saw it as a sign that Pelosi had the votes and was now releasing vulnerable members. But the Stupak group was made up of public option supporters. With him back on board, Pelosi now had at least the 216 votes for a reconciliation package with a public option in it. But she didn't want 216. She wanted more. The public option died so that Rick Boucher could vote no — and then lose in a landslide.

We'll never know how the politics of Stupak's maneuver would have played back home. Two weeks after the Affordable Care Act was signed into law, Stupak, who'd been representing Michigan's Upper Peninsula since 1992, announced his retirement.[160] Republicans have held the seat since.

Regardless, the Pingree-Polis effort cemented public health care as a key legislative priority in the future, paving the way for the surge in support for public health care ideas like Medicare for All.

It also did something leadership never expected: Going for broke and coming up short didn't deal the party a setback; it galvanized activists and changed what had been a defeatist conversation into one of deter-

---

159   Because of vacancies, only 216 were needed for a majority, not the standard 218.

160   Stupak's top health care aide switched parties, going to work for Sen. Chuck Grassley of Iowa. Her husband, who'd been a top Republican staffer on the Energy and Commerce Committee, went to work for BGR Group, a major GOP lobbying firm, where he represented health care clients. In 2018, Democrat Matt Morgan decided to take a run at the seat, and sat down with Stupak to get his endorsement. Stupak asked about his position on abortion, Morgan told me. Morgan told him he was pro-choice, and believed in a women's right to make her own reproductive decisions. But he added that his goal on a policy level was the same as Stupak's, to reduce the number of abortions. The best way to do that, he argued, was by preventing unwanted pregnancies, through education and access to contraception. "I agree with you," Stupak told Morgan, and endorsed his candidacy. Morgan was kicked off the ballot by a Republican-led election board, but got back on with a historic write-in campaign backed by Michael Moore. Morgan, though, lost by 12 points on Election Day, turned back by historic Republican turnout.

mination. It helped save Obamacare at a moment when its life hung in the balance.

"It helped a whole lot," Clyburn, the man in charge of whipping votes, told me of the Pingree-Polis letter. "The base getting fired up helped a whole lot. We could feel it out there." Majority Leader Hoyer, reflecting on the letter, told me the same thing. "It added energy to the effort to get to where we wanted to get," he said in an interview in his office the week the House passed the final piece of reform.

The ultimate failure to include a public option led the PCCC to rethink its approach. "The end game, when six Stupak people exerted leverage to get what they wanted and we couldn't get a bloc of six progressives to do the same made us realize we needed Hill infrastructure," Green said, "leading to P Street."

Its full name was the P Street Project, a wink at Tom DeLay's K Street Project. The former Republican Majority Leader, known as The Hammer, had demanded that K Street stack its lobby shops with Republicans, rather than follow the corporate bipartisan tradition. The goal of the P Street Project was to get in the trenches on Capitol Hill and battle the corporate lobbyists in hand-to-hand combat. It was another piece of progressive infrastructure being built from scratch. They poached Thomas from Progressive Congress and made her the lobbyist, essentially, for the netroots. At the CPC-linked organization, she'd been able to nudge members of Congress in the right direction, but without independence, she couldn't make serious threats or deliver real rewards. Now she could.

The Pingree-Polis letter had helped save reform itself. While the Democratic establishment was lying flat on its back, progressives had played offense. That organized effort was one of the first glimpses into the progressive resurgence taking shape independent of the White House and the party establishment, as the movement realized that Obama would need to be forced to bring about the change he promised.

Obama himself deserves some credit for the last-minute revival of his signature effort. With the bill on the brink, he broke with his inside game playbook and used his bully pulpit in one of the more effective ways a president ever had. His aides demanded that cameras record his appearance before the House Republican Caucus retreat in Baltimore, during which he publicly called out those lawmakers for knee-jerk opposition and intellectual dishonesty. It was a viral sensation. A month later, he held open meetings at the Blair House, debating congressional Republicans on the merits and shortcomings of their pieces of reform.

The Blair House summit was deemed a draw by the Capitol Hill press, but what the media missed was that Obama had redirected the nation's attention to health care and away from the Scott Brown victory in Massachusetts. The momentum shifted. The party decided to move forward with reconciliation. Democrats re-created the space they needed to get the Affordable Care Act passed.

Though the public option was lost, the organizing left behind infrastructure and energy that was ready for the next fight; a few years later, as it would work to put Elizabeth Warren in Scott Brown's Senate seat. A few years after that, the same organizers worked to draft her to run for president against Hillary Clinton. When she rejected the entreaties, and Bernie Sanders ran instead, the emails and activists organized by the draft-Warren effort were handed over to Sanders, helping launch his campaign. The most prominent group, Ready For Warren, renamed itself People For Bernie.[161] The Sanders campaign looked like it had burst from nowhere, but its roots lay in the organizing outside the Democratic establishment that had been going on for the past six years.

---

161   The group's co-founder, Occupy Wall Street organizer Winnie Wong, coined the pun "Feel the Bern."

Twelve

Warren v. Wall Street

By the fall of 2009, the Wall Street reform bill that would come to be known as Dodd-Frank was being dragged through Congress by Elizabeth Warren's consumer agency. The law professor and blogger worked the halls of Congress with her longtime aide Dan Geldon, who had previously been her law student. Warren and Geldon, who would become her presidential campaign manager in 2019, both had an understanding of her ability to drive media coverage toward a particular element of the debate. She cultivated relationships with members of the blogosphere and progressive media in a way that few politicians — though she wasn't quite one yet — were doing at the time. But she also met privately with as many lawmakers as she could.

In the summer of 2009, Warren and Geldon stopped in for a meeting with Chicago's Melissa Bean, who expressed interested in Warren's idea for a consumer financial protection agency, but raised an objection. Warren answered it, and Bean raised another, and another, and another, running through what Warren recalled as about half a dozen qualms. "Well, she didn't agree with much of anything, but at least she was talking. Maybe we have a shot at persuading her," Warren told Geldon. "For a moment, Dan looked like he was weighing whether to give me the bad news," Warren later recalled. The bad news was that Bean had just run through, in order, every talking point that had been included in a press release sent that morning by the American Bankers Association.[162]

162   The meeting is described in Warren's memoir, *A Fighting Chance,* but the

175

By October, the bill started to make its way through the House Financial Services Committee. It's worth taking a look at a single debate on a key amendment to get a flavor for the way Washington worked that year. Facing a pivotal vote, the 42 Democrats and 29 Republicans on the panel faced a straightforward question that day: *Should the lending practices of auto dealers be regulated by the consumer financial protection bureau?*

Auto dealers seemed like an obvious target for the new agency; nearly every time someone buys a car, the dealer also sells them an auto loan, complete with promises like zero percent interest and a pile of cash back. Americans held some $850 billion in car debt at the time and dealers are responsible for marketing roughly four-fifths of that amount. They pocket lucrative commissions with little oversight, steering customers — disproportionately from the black and brown working class — into predatory loans for overpriced cars. The committee seemed poised to change that.

Enter Rep. John Campbell, a Republican and a former Saab dealer from Orange County,[163] who according to his financial disclosure statement was still collecting rent from some of his former auto dealer colleagues. Campbell downplayed the importance of his industry partners and proposed an amendment to the bill exempting dealers from the new agency's purview. On October 22, it came up for a vote.

As usual, the members filed into the high-ceilinged first-floor hearing room in the Rayburn House Office Building. Committee Chairman Frank oversaw the vote atop four tiered rows of seats, a full story above the witnesses and the audience. The longest-serving Democratic members of the panel — informally known as the banking committee — sat to the right or just below the chairman; it can take years, if not decades, for a freshman representative to ascend up the risers.

The clerk called the roll, starting from the top. Senior Democrats roundly rejected Campbell's amendment. It appeared as if the Democrats would beat back the effort and apply the same standard to car dealers that was applied to everyone else.

Then came the bottom two rows, the place where progressive policy goes to die. The freshmen and sophomores who sat lower down, most of them representing swing districts and holding their seats thanks to big money from DCCC, began weighing in with yes after yes after yes — followed by unanimous ayes from the GOP side.

Then, once it became clear that auto dealers were getting their way,

---

identity of the lawmaker is withheld. I can confidently report that it was Bean.

163   In a delicious irony, Campbell's former seat was won in 2018 by Katie Porter, a former law student of Warren's, her co-author and an expert on consumer bankruptcy. Campbell decided not to seek reelection in 2014.

those senior Democrats — not wanting to get on the bad side of a powerful industry for a losing cause — actually started switching their votes from no to yes, pretending that they voted in error the first time around.

As confusion spread and more votes were changed, Frank tweaked his colleagues with a subtle dig. "Can I ask this? Would members please vote loudly, especially if you plan to vote differently than the clerk anticipates?" The chamber echoed with laughter.

To add some theatrics to the ruse, several members asked the clerk how they were recorded before asking to switch their votes — shocked to learn they had mistakenly voted to regulate auto lending, but quickly rectifying the error. After Rep. Dennis Moore (D-Kan.), a senior member of the New Democrat Coalition and a subcommittee chairman, employed this technique, Frank put a stop to it. "I would also say, at the same time, if you know how you're recorded, don't ask the clerk. Just change your vote," he said. This time, there was no laughter.

Despite the opposition of the powerful chairman and nearly every consumer group in the country, the Campbell amendment passed by a 47-21 margin. Auto dealers would remain safe from the CFPB.

The banking committee is the second-largest in Congress — the Transportation and Infrastructure Committee had just three more members in 2009 — having grown in size to better siphon money from Wall Street, like a host adapting its shape for a parasite. Brad Miller, then a committee member, had his share of battles with the bottom two rows. Many of "the Blues and News," as he called them, are hamstrung by a "dependence on contributions from the industry. That traditionally has been one of the reasons to get on the committee. It was seen as a money committee."

The Democratic leadership chose to embrace this concept, setting up the committee as an ATM for vulnerable rookies. Eleven freshman representatives from conservative-leaning districts, designated as "frontline" members, were given precious spots on the committee. From that perch, they raised on average twice as much as the average House Democrat.

Because the frontline members faced the possible end of their careers in November, their skittish voting habits made the Democrats' 13-seat advantage on the committee weaker than it appears. If seven members break with the party on a vote, the GOP wins. Rep. Luis Gutiérrez, who retired in 2018, referred to them as "the unreliable bottom row." The second row is little better, populated by the Democrats from red-leaning areas who first took office after the 2006 election. "Maxine [Waters] says she has the same problem," Rep. Judy Chu, a California Democrat, told me of Frank's successor at the top of the committee.

In short, by setting up the committee as a place for shaky Democrats from red districts to pad their campaign coffers, leadership made a choice to prioritize fundraising over the passage of strong legislation. "It makes it difficult to corral consensus," said Rep. Stephen Lynch (D–Mass.), a subcommittee chairman, of the unwieldy panel.

As the House leadership set up committees for the 111th Congress in early 2009, Frank pushed to shrink the size of his own panel to better meet the historic challenges presented by the financial collapse and bailout, said several members of the committee, including Reps. Mel Watt (D–N.C.), Miller, and Lynch. Instead, it got bigger. "He was obviously outvoted," quipped Lynch. "Either that or he missed the meeting."

Frank didn't conceal his distress at the size of his panel. "I had no part in setting up the committee. That was all the Speaker," Frank said when I asked about the front-row frontliners. Then, without prompting, he added: "It's also very large, which is a problem. We're the second-largest committee, but the transportation committee does not have ideological issues."

The size and makeup of the committee were a challenge even for Frank, a chairman not lacking in confidence or energy. "It's been very hard work. The committee used to be a very good little committee, because it had the urban constituency. But it's become a somewhat more desirable committee for people," he told me. "There are a large number of people who have marginal seats, and it obviously makes me have to work harder and is a constraint on what we can do. We start out with what I want to do, but what's relevant is what I can get a majority for."

By "urban constituency," Frank is referring to the passion, aside from LGBTQ rights, that animated his career: housing policy, and particularly assistance to the poor in affording housing. He was elected in 1980, and played defense against the Reagan revolution for the bulk of his career, working in and around Wall Street, but reluctant to take it on squarely. On its own, affordable housing policy is noble and important work, but it's also an insight into the narrow politics of Frank's generation. It sanded down some of the financial system's rougher edges. The new members who joined the committee were uninterested in affordable housing, and instead wanted contributions from the elements of the system that were making housing unaffordable. That was the tension Frank alluded to and never resolved. In 2015, after retiring, he joined the board of New York–based Signature Bank.

The sheer size of the panel could sentence reform to death by a thousand cuts. Each member of the majority, no matter where he or she falls on the political spectrum, had political interests back home. If those interests are affected by the bill, they've got someone on the panel to carry their concerns about "unintended consequences" to the chairman. And those members in the "marginal seats," put on the committee by leadership not because of their expertise or party loyalty, but because they can wring cash from it, were Frank's most difficult.

Frank denied that the big banks controlled his committee members; he actually claimed that the big banks' backing of legislation was so toxic that he didn't want their public support. "Goldman [Sachs] has no influence down here. Bank of America doesn't. Bank of America was ready to support the consumer policeman," Frank said in an interview in his office at the time, referring to the Consumer Financial Protection Bureau. That support, he said, was politely declined.

There was some truth to Frank's point; groups like the auto dealers didn't bring with them to Capitol Hill the public-relations baggage of Wall Street or Goldman Sachs. "The local auto dealers are very popular in their districts," Frank said. The more an interest group could make an issue district-specific and the more it could relate on an everyday level, Frank argued, the better it would do. "That's why the realtors always beat the bankers. The bankers sit and they go" — Frank made a dour face, leaned back in his chair and tightly folded his arms, miming an aloof posture — "the realtors are out there joining the Kiwanis and sponsoring little league."

The same was true with John Deere, dairy farmers and other back-slapping boys from back home. But the big banks figured this out, too — and they used precisely such groups to poke holes in the reform effort. Over the previous year, they'd drafted an army of credible little guys to walk the halls of Congress and push the interests of brokers, swaps traders and Wall Street bankers. And they showed that they didn't need big loopholes to slip trillions of dollars through.

"What's happening now is the pro-regulation forces are being out-grassroots'ed by the antis," Frank said. One member, he said, represented tons of title insurance companies. Another came from the headquarters of credit unions. A third district is home to LexisNexis; another to Equifax. Each of those entities received special treatment because their representative sits on the committee — and the more members on the committee, the more special treatment is needed.

"I have not had a problem because of campaign contributions. The problem is democracy," said Frank, "it's people responding to people in their districts: community bankers, realtors, auto dealers, as I said, end users, insurance agents." Later on, when the bill was on the House floor, Frank and Watt, a subcommittee chairman, tried to narrow the auto dealer exemption but failed. The lopsided committee vote had sapped the strength of the opposition.

The general makeup of the committee dated back to January 2007, when Democrats reclaimed control of Congress. It was a different world than the one after the global financial crisis of 2008. "No one knew when this committee was appointed that the U.S. economy, the world economy would walk to the precipice, and therefore put the eyes of the world on that committee. Nobody could have foretold [that]," said Rep. Emanuel Cleaver (D–Mo.).

The legislation's failure to tightly regulate the derivatives market, however, was a crippling weakness. And the frontliners took credit for that.

Democratic Rep. Jim Himes, a frontliner and a New Dem, knocked out moderate Republican Chris Shays in Connecticut in 2008, after Shays survived a well-funded challenge in 2006. A former banker, Himes quickly became an influential member on the committee. "The list of [New Dem] principles for financial regulatory reform, I was intimately involved in that, because I co-chair the New Dem Financial Services task force with Melissa Bean," Himes told me. Bean, along with retiring Rep. Dennis Moore (D–Kan.), was a New Dem ringleader on the committee.

Both Bean and Himes were Rahm Emanuel favorites, and boosted heavily by Joe Crowley. The DCCC spent more than one million dollars on Bean in 2004 and 2006. The conservative incoming members repaid Emanuel by making him caucus chair, the fourth-ranking position, before he left in 2009 to become Obama's chief of staff. They rewarded Crowley by making him chairman of the New Democrat Coalition, and later lifted him to caucus chair, Emanuel's old job.

Bean, a New Democrat from Illinois with a clear pro-business bent, got well over $200,000 from EMILY's List over the span of her career, far more than from any other source (though, collectively speaking, nobody gave more to Bean than Wall Street). But it's complicated. Bean won her suburban Chicago seat in 2004 from the ultra-conservative Republican Phil Crane, founding chairman of the Republican Study Committee and longest-serving Republican in the House at the time of his defeat. Toppling Crane was no small victory for Democrats across the spectrum, and was especially sweet for the Chicago-based Emanuel, serving as a dry run for the 2006 campaign.

With Bean, progressives got yes votes on health care, cap and trade, and financial regulatory reform — but not quite the regulatory reform they wanted. Bean is a case of House dynamism in effect. Though just one member and only in her third term, she was able to use her solid grasp of financial issues and genuine intellect to carve out a leading role on the committee — often doing the handiwork of Wall Street.[164] In the

164   Crane, meanwhile, would have been one more Republican vote against

fall, Bean, as chair of the New Democrats' financial services task force, led a bloc of New Dems in a revolt against a sweeping financial reform bill as it was about to come to the House floor for amendments and a final vote. Progressives wanted to allow states to pass tougher laws to protect consumers from abusive bank practices — things like inactivity fees and excessive overdrafts. Bean threatened to take down the entire bill unless party leadership allowed a vote on her "national standard" amendment, which would allow state attorneys general to prosecute nationally chartered banks but not to enforce state laws that might be tougher than the national law.

Bean, confident in her support, deftly navigated the rabbit warren of committees and power centers in Congress. She faced off with Treasury Department officials in Nancy Pelosi's office, negotiating a compromise that disappointed consumer advocates but gave bank lobbyists a "glimmer of hope." She'd outmaneuvered progressive Democrats, who in the Financial Services Committee had likewise threatened to tank the entire bill if her amendment had been included. She pulled her amendment in committee but secured a promise from Frank that she could have a vote on the amendment when the bill reached the floor. The promise gave her leverage in the negotiations in the speaker's office, and the resulting compromise was added to a catch-all "manager's amendment" that was easily approved.

To the Bean camp, a candidate in a red district like hers simply can't afford the luxury of being progressive on financial reform. And donors know it. "She is terrifically progressive about some things, not as progressive as I like about other things, but I understand why," said Matt Flamm, a Bean campaign volunteer and candidate for state representative in Bean's district. "When it comes to choice, when it comes to gay rights — 100 percent. When it comes to fiscal issues, she is more conservative than I am. If she weren't, she couldn't get elected."

"This is incredibly hostile territory," Flamm said of the district. Indeed, Emanuel had spent big so she could come back to Congress, weaken Wall Street reform, and then lose in 2010.[165]

Bank lobbyists looking for the seven votes needed to upend legislation knew where to start. Bean and 15 other New Dems had effective veto

---

financial regulatory reform. One more Republican wouldn't have been a problem, but with too many more, the Democrats lose the House.

165   She was beaten in a razor-thin race by eccentric tea partier Joe Walsh. The district was then redrawn by Democrats, and Walsh was beaten by Rahm's old friend Tammy Duckworth by ten points in 2012. When Duckworth ran for the Senate in 2016, Raja Krishnamoorthi, a Democrat, easily won her seat. Bean went on to work for JP Morgan Chase.

power on the committee and were sympathetic to their interests. Six of the committee's New Dems were frontline freshmen that year. The panel was also home to seven Blue Dogs, another faction of business-friendly Democrats, three of which were also New Dems. Two of the Blue Dogs were frontliners, including Rep. Walt Minnick, a freshman Democrat from Idaho who worked to beat back the pro-consumer finance authority in committee and pushed an amendment on the House floor that would have gutted it. Both efforts failed, but Minnick was nonetheless singled out for praise by the American Bankers Association in a post-vote memo. It didn't matter. He lost in 2010 in a landslide.

Some of the Blue Dogs and New Dems described their experiences working as bankers as an advantage. "I worked in the industry for many years, and so it's been very exciting for me to probably play a more engaged role than a new member ordinarily would," said Himes. "Scott Murphy and I and two or three others really drove the creation of the derivatives bill. Nobody understands it, but it's one of the more important aspects of the regulatory reform. And looking at it as a former businessperson, I think we've really struck a good compromise. I don't think the bill is in any way heavy-handed."

Murphy (D-N.Y.) was a venture capitalist who won a special election to replace Kirsten Gillibrand when she ascended to the Senate. A Blue Dog (as Gillibrand mostly was while in the House) Murphy wasn't on the committee, but on the House floor he punched a gaping hole in the derivatives portion of the bill — which was already riddled with gaps. Unregulated derivatives, which are largely ways for investors to speculate with other people's money, introduce dangerous risk into the financial system and, thanks significantly to the frontliners, remained unregulated in the House reform bill.

To get a sense of just how tilted toward Wall Street the House was that cycle, consider that Dodd-Frank got stronger after the House passed its version and the Senate got to work. Since Democrats had declined to bust the filibuster, the Senate needed 60 votes, which by then meant getting some Republicans, plus all of the red-state Democrats.

And it still got stronger.

Warren, organized labor, the blogosphere and the Progressive Change Campaign Committee deserve some of the credit for that.

In Arkansas, they prodded progressive Bill Halter, who was then the lieutenant governor, into the primary to challenge Blanche Lincoln, largely for her betrayal on labor's key priority, the Employee Free Choice Act, but it wound up impacting Dodd-Frank, too. "We spent months trying to get everybody behind him to secure the money that could tempt him into the race. We knew that that was critical. And that just needs to happen on an ongoing basis," FireDogLake's Jane Hamsher told me at the time. "We talked about having monthly parties for members of Congress in liberal electorate groups. And then it sort of broke down — [then-SEIU President] Andy [Stern] and I had, last year —and then it broke down into, *Well, we don't want to challenge the White House*, and that sort of ended that. But that coalition is happening again because the labor unions and MoveOn were so profoundly let down by the alliances that they made."

Lincoln had joined with Bayh and Carper to form the Blue Dog faction, intent on driving policy to the right. She was chair of the Agriculture Committee, which had jurisdiction over derivatives, because the financial products had started as corn futures and the like.

Lincoln was expected to introduce a bank-friendly title of the Dodd-Frank that would take a hands-off approach. But under pressure from her left, she did an about-face, writing a bill that forced big banks to spin off their derivatives trading operations, as aggressive an approach as was being contemplated at the time.

The language largely survived, in part because Schumer had not gone out of his way to recruit only conservative Senate candidates. And several senators, encouraged and nourished by the blogosphere, such as Jon Tester and Jim Webb, were economic populists who didn't yelp about Wall Street reform. Along with Tester and Webb, newcomers such as Sherrod Brown in Ohio, Jeff Merkley in Oregon, and Amy Klobuchar and Al Franken in Minnesota all championed progressive causes, despite coming from red or purple states.

Lincoln survived her primary but was destroyed in the general election. An anonymous Obama aide took to the media to blast labor for flushing $10 million of its members' money "down the toilet," but the legislation they had bought was worth far more than that.

Elizabeth Warren kept pushing on her Consumer Financial Protection Bureau, demanding that it be run by a sole director rather than a commission, and strong independence. Warren deftly used the progressive media to pressure Dodd and other Senate negotiators. Each incremental report at The Huffington Post about a new plot to weaken the CFPB would lead to a flood of calls. Dodd, when he would see me in the hallway, began to roll his eyes, knowing I would be asking about the latest behind-the-scenes compromise that had yet to be written into the law. Each new story would elicit public pushback from Warren, labor and the blogosphere, and often get the compromise discarded. "He kept wanting time to go on so he'd have enough room to negotiate, and he kept not having room to negotiate. And then the music stopped and he had to put something on the floor," said one operative who worked closely on the bill, of Dodd.

In an roundabout way, Scott Brown deserves some credit for the CFPB. In January 2010, he won a special election to replace the late Ted Kennedy, and his win took the Democrats down to 59 senators. Voters are often mocked as irrational for their choices, and it would have been easy to do so in this case. Yet the White House did get the message.

Warren met with David Axelrod for the first time, by coincidence, the day after Brown's victory. Spinning to reporters, Axelrod had been putting the blame for the loss on Coakley, who, to be sure, deserved her share. But privately he also recognized that there was an anger in the population that the White House needed to understand and grapple with. The CFPB, he told Warren, was a clear way to do that. "We need to fight for this thing, need to show we're standing up for people and not just banks," he said.[166] The White House had always been publicly support-ive of the CFPB, but now it was committed on a political level, too. The White House also latched onto what became known as the Volcker Rule, a measure deeply hated by Wall Street, which bands financial institu-tions from gambling with government-insured money.

The next day, Thursday, the Boston Globe published an editorial sug-gesting Warren run for Senate against Brown in 2012. Warren encour-aged the rumors, which put pressure on Brown from the left, and he ended up voting for Dodd-Frank.[167]

As the bill moved to completion, Harry Reid saw a chance for a po-litical win-win. He put the bill on the floor, knowing it didn't have 60 votes, but from his perspective, there was no bad outcome. Either Re-publicans blocked Wall Street reform, which would make them look aw-ful, or they'd support it, which would be its own good thing. It was a tactic that had not been tried on the stimulus a year earlier, because Larry Summers and Rahm Emanuel were convinced that nothing over a certain dollar amount could pass. But what happened to Wall Street reform suggests their imaginations were too limited.

---

166   This comes from a source who was in the room. Geithner, contrary to his reputation as a bank shill, had been strongly supportive of the consumer agency from the beginning, though the feeling hadn't entirely been shared among Obama's top advisers.

167   The bill was weakened in small ways to win Brown's vote, and Brown, not the brightest bulb in the Senate, told me on the record he was doing it on behalf of specific banks in Massachusetts, even naming the banks. Democrat Russ Feingold of Wisconsin, meanwhile, voted against Dodd-Frank for its being too soft on the banks. He was right, but the bill would have been better had Dodd been forced to strength-en it to win Feingold's vote rather than weaken it to get Brown's. Feingold was upset in 2010 anyway.

As cloture vote after cloture vote[168] failed, Reid eventually grew impatient. He wanted to pull the bill off the floor and move on, said Chris Dodd, then chairman of the Banking Committee. "I and others were able to convince him that *no*, that we thought we could win the issue and we ought to keep it up," Dodd said.

That May, in an interview with my colleague Shahien Nasiripour, Warren put it in simpler terms: No more compromises. "My first choice is a strong consumer agency," she said. "My second choice is no agency at all and plenty of blood and teeth left on the floor."

She got her first choice.

Once the CFPB had been created, the question turned to who would run it. Geithner argued internally it absolutely could not be Elizabeth Warren, but his well-known animosity toward her had the counterintuitive effect of blunting his criticism.

Ben Nelson, a Democratic senator from Nebraska, had been made famous that year for the "Cornhusker Kickback," a concession he won in the ACA that was so egregiously unfair to the rest of the country that he had to publicly distance himself from it. The concession he wanted for his vote on Dodd-Frank was a pledge that Warren wouldn't run the CFPB. The night before the final vote, he made that fairly clear to reporters in the Capitol hallway, including me: "You don't know who's going to be head of the consumer protection bureau. You can't just send a rogue agency out on its own."

Emanuel saw the news and called Harry Reid. "We don't like her either," Emanuel told the majority leader. That was only partly true, as Axelrod and Valerie Jarrett were pushing for Warren internally, against Emanuel and Geithner. Though Reid had been a patron of Warren's, there wasn't much he could do, as the White House controls appointments. He spread the word that it wouldn't be Warren, and Nelson got on board.[169] "We wanted her to be the person who led the consumer [bureau] and I had a little pushback from my own caucus," Reid said, "mainly one senator whose name I won't announce, but with that, I didn't feel I could push it at that time." I asked if Rahm Emanuel had relayed the White

---

168   Cloture is required to break a filibuster, and 60 votes were needed to invoke cloture, as Democrats never eliminated the filibuster for legislation.

169   Nelson later denied to me he got any assurances "directly," whatever that's supposed to mean. "I've heard all the hallway rumors that you've heard. But I had no promise of that, didn't hold my vote out in anticipation of that, not with the White House," he told me. "Nobody from the White House told me anything like that, but I must say that I've heard from a lot of different sources, most of it coming from blogs, that somehow some assurances were made of that kind, but none were made to me directly."

House's concerns. "I do not remember that, but with Rahm," he said, "the first few words of any conversation was a bunch of swear words, so maybe we never got to the crux of the conversation."

Keeping Warren off the agency she had created, however, was a difficult position to hold publicly. Warren, after all, had come up with the idea for the agency and then had been its most vocal champion, both publicly and privately, as it ran through a sewage pipeline of bank lobbyists and came out clean on the other side.

Before the administration announced its decision, it invited first-term senators to the White House for a meet and greet. Among them were several allies of Warren, including Bernie Sanders and Jeff Merkley. Sanders pressed the point, asking Obama if he would name Warren to run the agency. Obama held up a glass of water. "That's the problem with you progressives," he said. "You see this as half-empty."

At the time, Democrats had yet to reform the filibuster for executive branch nominations,[170] and it was clear Warren didn't have 60 votes. But my colleague Nasiripour discovered something useful in the way the law was written: the president was entitled to name somebody to establish the agency while the Senate deliberated on a permanent director. Progressive groups led a pressure campaign to name Warren to that temporary spot, and Geithner was overruled. Warren's condition for accepting the job was that she would also be given the title of Senior Adviser to the President, so Geithner couldn't push her around.

Still, he set out to embarrass her early, leaking to the press that she was demanding a fancy new paint job in her office. Warren confronted him about the egregiously sexist attack and the leaks stopped. Geithner and his chief of staff, Mark Patterson,[171] under pressure from an embarrassed White House, both apologized to Warren, and she set up the agency without Geithner's interference.

Scott Brown, whose 2010 special election victory earlier had blown up Democrats' 60-vote supermajority, was up for reelection in 2012. His approval rating in Massachusetts was through the roof, and it looked like favorite son Mitt Romney would be running for president, making it a tough year to win back the seat.

Guy Cecil was in charge of recruiting candidates that year for the Democratic Senatorial Campaign Committee. He traveled multiple times to Massachusetts, but couldn't find anybody willing to take him on. "Scott Brown is unbeatable," he was told. "He's too good. None of the

---

170   That would come later, in significant part over a fight over Richard Cordray to run the CFPB, as well as NLRB and some D.C. Circuit Court of Appeals judgeships.

171   Patterson did corporate legal work after his time in the Treasury, but later returned to government service as counsel to Senate Minority Leader Schumer.

old guard wanted to run against him."

He turned his sights on Warren, part of a DSCC strategy that year to recruit the most progressive candidate they thought was electable in each state, a conscious policy he said they had not employed in previous cycles. "I'd go to Elizabeth's apartment on Friday nights and we'd have a beer," Cecil said. He knew she'd make a good candidate because of the questions she asked. *What is my job description as a candidate? What do I do? What decisions am I responsible for rather than my campaign manager?* Chuck Schumer, too, knew it was still Massachusetts, and in the right political environment, he could be beaten. So the man nicknamed Wall Street Chuck helped recruit Wall Street's number-one enemy to run for the Senate.[172]

During her last day at the White House, she sat down for an exit interview of sorts with Obama. She gave him the same advice she would later give Hillary Clinton ahead of her run for president, that he needed to understand how much anger was out there, and to surround himself with people who understood that, rather than with people from Wall Street and from the Rubin wing of the party. The housing and foreclosure crises were still ripping through the country, and she pressed him to take them seriously. He said that he wanted to hear more from her on what his approach to housing policy should be. "Get my email from Anita," he said, explaining that it was a complicated pseudonym.

As she left, she told his assistant, Anita Decker Breckenridge, what the president had said. *Well, just email me and I'll make sure he gets it,* she said, in what was likely a choreographed routine. Warren later emailed her some housing policy ideas, though nothing came of it.

---

172   I learned about this in a delicious way. One evening some HuffPost colleagues and I were having dinner with Sen. Jeff Merkley at Hunan Dynasty, Schumer's favorite Capitol Hill haunt. Schumer was there, as he is many nights, and came by the table to tell Merkley some good news, that Warren had finally committed to him that she'd run. He then looked, saw me, and, as if he were Jerry Seinfeld spotting Newman, said, "Oh. Hello, Grim," then added, futily, "That was off the record."

Thirteen

The Belt Tightens

If a historian was hunting for the moment Democrats gave up on their forward-looking economic agenda during Obama's first term, the last Thursday evening in May 2010 would be the best place to start.

It took FDR two congressional terms to blow his New Deal majority. Though Democrats still controlled Congress in 1937, deficit hawks, encouraged by Roosevelt himself, put the brakes on federal spending and curtailed efforts to end the Great Depression, bringing about what became known as the "recession within the Depression," or, just as accurately, the Roosevelt Recession. In 2010, Democrats had given theirs away before the second Memorial Day, and for the same reason — manufactured concerns about the deficit.

Late on that Thursday evening in May, Democrats were arguing on the House floor over the size of a jobs bill that was two days overdue for a vote. Obamacare had become law and the economy was no longer nosediving. But it wasn't recovering either. The injection of federal money from the too-small stimulus was wearing off. Millions more people were looking for jobs than there were job openings, and foreclosures continued to shatter families and neighborhoods. Since April 20, a BP-owned well in the Gulf of Mexico had been spewing oil into the water, with no sign of it stopping anytime soon. Things felt like they were coming apart.

The White House and congressional leaders were pushing for a new round of stimulus, and the question seemed to be not if, but how much, when word filtered through the lower chamber that the Senate had adjourned for the Memorial Day break. With no Senate, there could be no bill. "People were astounded — I mean *stunned*," freshman Rep. Gerry Connolly (D–Va.) told me.[173] "We're in the midst of this debate and trying to find a path to doing the right thing and they went out on recess? Without addressing these issues? Some of which have deadlines? I mean, there are going to be unemployed Americans who will not have their unemployment extended."

Connolly called it a signal to congressional leaders. "It may be a turning point," Connolly continued. "We only know that when we look back on something, really, but I think it's a growing and collective recognition that you're going to be held to a higher account if you're going to propose deficit spending for anything."

Off of the floor, Blue Dogs had claimed victory. Rep. Dutch Ruppersberger (D–Md.), who fought to shrink the size of the jobs bill, explained to me that the change in direction felt "really symbolic" and a sign that Democratic "party leadership is working with us to let this happen."

On June 1, several programs, including extended unemployment benefits, were set to expire. By the end of the week, 19,400 people would prematurely stop receiving checks, according to data from the Department of Labor. By the end of the following week, the number of premature unemployment exhaustions would climb to 323,400. The week after that, 903,000. By the end of the month, 1.2 million.

It was the third time that year that lawmakers had allowed extended unemployment benefits to lapse, and the second time they'd decided to leave town for recess fully knowing the lapse would cause panic and confusion among blameless layoff victims. But it was the first time that Republicans couldn't be blamed.

Small pieces of the package, much pared down, would eventually pass, too little too late. And at critical moments, it looked as if the hawks would feast on the entire spending bill, with House Majority Leader Steny Hoyer intervening at the last moment to bring whimpering Blue Dogs back into the kennel, but not before they'd trash the house. They were proud of their work. "The week we had talking about the need to pay for things that are not emergencies has paid off," said Jason Alt-

---

173   Connolly told me this for an article Arthur Delaney and I wrote for Huff-Post, and that Thursday in May can be precisely pinpointed as the day the party gave up on stimulating the economy, pivoting instead to attacking the deficit in the hopes of draining the tea party of energy. That failed. The story, published May 25, 2010, is headlined "Deficit Eclipses Jobs In Congress: 'Nickel-And-Diming The Most Fragile People.'"

mire, the Pennsylvanian who'd been elected with progressive and union energy, only to flip when in the House into one of the most conservative Democratic members of Congress.

That lobbying effort by Blue Dogs, to require any new spending to be offset by cuts or tax increases — known as PAYGO — lives on today, with Pelosi bringing it back in the first days of her new speakership in 2019.

Conservative Democrats in both the House and Senate argued that enough unemployment extensions had been granted and that the jobless should be warned there will be no more coming. That reasoning infuriated progressive Democrats. "So what would that do? If you're unemployed, what the fuck difference does that make to you? If you had a job, you'd take the job," Rep. George Miller (D-Calif.) told reporters before Friday's vote.

Connolly, president of the freshman class, said that members of Congress were feeling cross-cutting pressures, though he had no coherent response to it. "A year ago we were in the midst of the worst recession in 80 years and desperately trying to find ways to climb out of it," Connolly said. "We did the right thing and it's working. Now, a year and four months later, it's a very different situation." I noted to Connolly that unemployment had yet to come down. "Voters can hold seemingly contradictory views simultaneously," said Connolly. "That is to say, somebody can say, *I want you to fix the unemployment problem, but I want you to stop those drunken-sailor ways of yours. Get rid of that wasteful, overreaching spending you seem to love.* Voters can hold both views simultaneously, and it seems to me that politicians ignore that at their peril."

Hoyer met with Blue Dogs that Thursday morning and presented them with a new bill, which was trimmed by $50 billion. Blue Dogs wanted more but weren't sure what. "We went around the table and different members shared their perspectives, and each of them was a little different in terms of what they supported, how much they were willing to come up with new payfors,[174] whether they thought the answer was removing certain things and how much they wanted to remove," said Rep. Adam Schiff (D-Calif.),[175] one of the dozens of Blue Dogs who attended the Hoyer meeting. "I don't think there was a consensus among the members about the individual pieces so much as that there needed to be a greater degree to which whatever was in the package was paid for."

---

174   "Payfor" is congressional lingo that is sometimes also called an "offset." New spending must be "offset" with either new taxes or spending cuts. That's how you "pay for" a new piece of legislation, so Capitol Hill turned a payfor into a noun.

175   Schiff, later a hero of the online resistance for his probing of Russia's interference with the 2016 campaign, then became a top target of Republicans, who said he went too far in pushing conspiracy theories.

Leadership whipped throughout the day and met in the afternoon. House Whip Clyburn made it clear, said two people who were present at the meeting, that the package simply didn't have the votes and a new approach was needed. Several ideas were batted around. Hoyer asked Clyburn: *If we take out COBRA and FMAP, do we have the votes?* Clyburn said yes. Hoyer further suggested splitting the "Doc fix" (related to Medicare payments for doctors) and the rest of the package into two separate votes, making each vote an easier one in that the dollar figures would be lower. Taking out COBRA meant laid-off people would no longer get help with health insurance.

Cutting FMAP — federal dollars to help states pay for Medicaid — was a tough policy decision but an easier one politically, at least in the short term: home state elected officials such as state legislators and governors are often the most formidable opponents of a member of Congress. While reaping the political benefit of spending federal Medicaid dollars, state officials simultaneously criticize Congress for out-of-control, runaway spending. It's a game federal officials don't want to help their friends back home play. Unless, that is, they can get the state politicians to ask for the money, something they generally didn't do this time around. "We need to hear from both Democratic and Republican governors that they need this," said Ruppersberger.

It was well within the White House's power to pressure governors across the country to support the legislation, but it didn't happen. "It's obscene," Rep. Dave Obey (D-Wisc.) said of cutting COBRA. The cut would reduce deficit spending by less than $7 billion. Ethanol subsidies, which Blue Dogs support almost unanimously, come closer to $9 billion. Lurking beneath some Democrats' deficit concerns was the reactionary suspicion that unemployment benefits make people too lazy to look for work.

"We've had four straight months of job growth," Altmire said. "At some point you have to take a step back and look at the relative value of unemployment benefits versus people looking for jobs."

That was nonsense. The San Francisco Federal Reserve had done a study in April that found "extended unemployment insurance benefits have not been important factors in the increase in the duration of unemployment or in the elevated unemployment rate." And more progressive lawmakers such as Rep. Jim McDermott (D-Wash) opposed Altmire's approach, because it "doesn't seem very American" to "turn our backs" on constituents in need. The confusion on the Hill flowed directly from the White House. Senior White House adviser David Axelrod, in an interview that spring, explained to the New York Times that "it's my job to report what the public mood is." The public mood, said Axelrod, is

192

anti-spending and anti-deficit, and so the smart politics is to alleviate those concerns. "As a matter of policy and a matter of politics that we need to focus on this, and the president certainly agrees with that."

Obama had previewed the shift toward austerity in his January 2010 State of the Union address. "Starting in 2011, we are prepared to freeze government spending for three years," he said to applause. "Spending related to our national security, Medicare, Medicaid, and Social Security will not be affected. But all other discretionary government programs will. Like any cash-strapped family, we will work within a budget to invest in what we need and sacrifice what we don't. And if I have to enforce this discipline by veto, I will."

It was an odd political strategy because Axelrod knew that if it succeeded, it would be both bad policy and bad politics. He said as much when asked about the pressure from economic advisers to focus on stimulus and job creation. "I'm very much allied with the economic group, because even as a political matter it would be very shortsighted to take steps that would send us backward," he said in the same interview.

Axelrod's conflicted answers reflected a conflicted White House. His reference to the "economic group," though, is an insight into the internal struggle the administration was undergoing. While Axelrod was the one quoted in the Times, the push toward belt-tightening was driven by David Plouffe and Bill Daley, according to people on the Hill who worked with the White House. The "economic group," for all the ills that can be laid at their feet, were not pushing to slash the deficit. This was pure, albeit incompetent, politics, and Daley would later blame Trump's election on people's concerns about the deficit and big government.

In September 2011, the Washington Post ran a story about the government sending $120 million in checks to people who had died. Bill Daley hit the roof, as he later relayed to Brian Abrams for his book *Obama: An Oral History*.[176]

> I was enraged, and I remember Jack Lew, a good friend, was like, *You know, Bill, you don't understand. We send umpteenth billions of checks a month. It's not a big deal.* Well, it is a big deal to the average person. Something's wrong here. It's not working right....I know people say it's minor in the scheme of things, but the average person doesn't see the trillion-dollar thing. He lives in a much smaller world, and the Democrats dismiss that too easily. And therein lies the root of a piece of the Donald Trump thing. There is an aversion to big government. That's just inherent in our history, and when you ignore that, you do it at your own peril.

Obama, to relate to the imagined voters' "much smaller world," began using the bully pulpit to highlight deficit fears, by proposing an

176   This comes from an unpublished portion of the interview, provided to me by Abrams.

across-the-board spending freeze, creating a commission to reduce the deficit, and making it clear to progressive allies that the White House political team believed a deficit-reduction focus was important for the midterm elections. "He has demonstrated his willingness to cut spending in programs that he thinks are good programs that provide valuable services but that are not absolutely essential in a time when we have to tighten our belts, live within our means," White House press secretary Jay Carney told reporters in April 2011.

Plouffe and Daley were reading surveys that found independents softening toward Obama, and also expressing concern about the deficit. If Obama can tackle the deficit and work with Republicans, they reasoned, those independents would come around.

For progressives today, it's difficult to understand the fixation on the debt and deficit, but it goes back to the Democratic collapse in the 1980s, which is linked in their minds to being tarred as "tax-and-spend liberals." John Lawrence, Pelosi's longtime chief of staff, lived through it, retiring in 2013 after 38 years as a congressional staffer. "The debt and deficit spending, and growth in government, those are issues that Democrats really didn't pay sufficient attention to," he said, noting that his first boss, California Rep. George Miller developed the "pay as you go" idea in 1982 "primarily as a way of holding Republicans accountable for military spending and tax cuts, which they didn't have to pay for, but Democrats had to pay every time they wanted to increase domestic spending."

Eventually shorted to "PAYGO," Pelosi implemented it as speaker in 2007, but in the '80s, the party wasn't interested yet. "Democrats blew that off," he said. "It's not until the '90s that Democrats buy into the pay-as-you-go idea. By then it's way too late, and they've allowed Republicans to essentially establish themselves as the party of fiscal probity, even though they have absolutely no intention of actually governing that way."

The Obama political team's focus on the deficit — and Pelosi's before and since — raises the question: *Just who is this hypothetical midterm voter who leans Republican because of deficit concerns, but would vote Democratic if Congress trims a spending bill from, say, $250 billion down to $80 billion?* Most voters — and most reporters, for that matter — couldn't guess within a few hundred billion what the budget deficit is, and would struggle to put a dollar figure on the latest jobs-bill proposal. So how, then, could a voter cheer saving a few billion dollars by cutting off COBRA subsidies?

When I criticized the White House[177] at the time for its approach, ad-

177   In a July 2010 article in Huffington Post called "Mayberry Machiavellis: Obama Political Team Handcuffing Recovery."

ministration spokesman Matthew Vogel offered a statement that was telling, confirming that the administration did indeed consider the deficit one of the two greatest challenges it faced: "When President Obama took office, millions of people had already lost their jobs due to the recession and the deficit had ballooned. Over the last eighteen months, the economic team and the President's closest advisers have worked day and night to balance two of the greatest challenges our economy faces — putting Americans back to work and getting us back on a sustainable fiscal path. The Administration is united in its focus on getting the economy growing again, the most powerful driver of job creation and deficit reduction."

Were the argument not being made by such otherwise smart and savvy operators, it wouldn't even be worth grappling with. But as an idea, it survives to this day.

The focus on deficits has consequences. Without White House backing of more stimulus, the House of Representatives steadily hacked away at the jobs package that began as a several-hundred-billion dollar initiative and became a shell of itself. The refusal to get behind the jobs effort in Congress made it harder for Democrats to pin the delay on Republicans, muddling what could be a devastating message. By the summer of 2010, more than 1.7 million people, who'd been out of work for longer than six months, had been thrown off the rolls.

Yet Obama knew the history. Shortly after his inauguration, he met privately with House Republicans to hear their concerns, which boiled down to spending and the deficit. In response, Obama raised the specter of 1937, the year President Franklin Roosevelt cut spending, leading to a renewal of the economic collapse, according to several Republicans who were in the room. Pelosi knew the history too. "In the middle '30s they were concerned about what was happening so they tightened their belts in terms of spending," she told me back in February 2009, "and that caused a recession within the Depression, instead of keeping the momentum going."

In November 2010, Republicans made historic gains, seizing control of the House from Democrats. After a brief lame duck session, the window for the Obama administration's legislative agenda slammed shut. "It did not have to be as bad as it was," said Rahm Emanuel.[178] "You could argue there were things that were done that exacerbated what, no matter what, was going to be a challenging year. You could argue there were things you could have done that would have softened it a little, but nobody will ever know."

Still Plouffe and Daley plugged along, reaching out to Republican leaders to craft some sort of Grand Bargain[179] that would raise taxes and cut spending. Six months were wasted, ending with a debt ceiling debacle[180] that downgraded the nation's credit.

Plouffe's strategy to win over independents by cutting a Grand Bargain with Republicans was rooted in a misreading of polling data. The upside of having no genuine commitment to any particular policy or ideology — beyond winning elections — meant that once it became clear the sought-after "independent" voters were utterly unmoved by Obama's overtures to Republicans, Plouffe advised Obama to bag the whole thing. It also flowed by a misunderstanding of economics. Voters understand the debt and deficit as proxies for economic health. But the two are entirely unrelated, as Modern Monetary Theory[181] has explained.

Still, the mindset dies hard, and contributed to one of the biggest blunders of the eight years of the Obama administration. After winning reelection, the White House faced what came to be called a "fiscal cliff," in which a series of temporary policies all expired at midnight on December 31, 2012, including the Bush-era tax cuts. That meant that in order to repeal those tax cuts, all Congress had to do was nothing.

Reid and McConnell were deep in negotiations that would preserve the cuts for the middle class, but return many of the higher-end taxes closer to previous levels, and bring back the estate tax. Then the White House blew up the talks, pulled Reid out, and sent in Vice President Joe Biden to negotiate instead. McConnell quickly secured a much worse deal than he had already agreed to. "I wanted to go over the cliff," Reid said. "I thought that would have been the best thing to do because the conversation would not have been about raising taxes, which it became, it would have been about lowering taxes."

In other words, if the automatic tax hikes had taken effect, Republicans would be left to plead to reduce them. Instead, Democrats were

179   This was the D.C. term for a major deal that would include tax increases and cuts to Social Security, Medicare and Medicaid. The theory was that it would be wildly unpopular, but both parties would participate in it, so voters would have no way of punishing one entity over another. Credit where it's due: The tea party killed it.
180   Obama tried to use the debt ceiling as leverage to get Republicans to negotiate a Grand Bargain. Republicans tried to use it to get tax and spending cuts. Nothing happened and the Treasury nearly defaulted on its debt.
181   MMT is a reality-based description of how the economy works in a post-gold-standard world. A government like the United States, which has its own currency, spends money merely by authorizing it. The limitation to spending is not the deficit, but the resources — labor, materials, etc. — available to the economy. To understand MMT in practice, think of the Pentagon budget, which is never "paid for."

arguing for tax increases. "If we'd have gone over the cliff we'd have had resources to do a lot of good things in the country — infrastructure development — but it didn't work out that way."

Biden agreed to make permanent the bulk of the Bush tax cuts. I asked Reid how Biden defended his strategy. "It wasn't one that I agreed with," he replied politely, "so you'd have to ask some of his people."

The next four years in Congress were largely wasted ones, as divided government made sure nothing could get through. One of the few progressive advances came not in the elected branch of government, but in the Federal Reserve. Organizer Ady Barkan, one of the most creative thinkers in the progressive space, launched a project called Fed Up in 2012, which pulled together workers and progressive economists to pressure the Fed, led by Janet Yellen, to take a more reasonably and realistic look at the economy. The Fed's mandate is to encourage full employment and keep down inflation. But over time, it largely dropped the former, focusing only on the latter, as the two are often in conflict. A good way to keep inflation down is to make sure wages are low; one way to keep wages low is to make sure lots of people are unemployed, so employees can't pressure their bosses for raises. Any time the Fed saw wages start to tick up, it would raise interest rates, throwing people out of work and slowing the economy. It's a system that by design prevents regular people from getting ahead, allowing productivity gains to flow only to the top. Barkan made the case that the Fed needed to take seriously its mandate of full employment, and allow inflation to be a bit higher, recognizing that in a global economy, there was far more headroom for the dollar than the Fed thought. The group protested in the streets, most noticeably outside the Fed's annual gathering in Jackson Hole, Wyoming. Pressure like that had never been applied to the Fed before, and the board took notice. By 2014, Yellen put Fed Up on the official retreat agenda, and applauded the new thinking. Mainstream economists began to acknowledge that inflation was indeed being kept too low. Subsequent years have proven Barkan right, as wages have risen and inflation has stayed low. The pressure campaign and the developments since prepped the ground for Modern Monetary Theory — the idea that resources like labor are going to waste out of an irrational fear of deficits, tied to a misunderstanding of inflation — to begin to be taken more seriously.

In the Senate, though, for a time, gridlock was so tight that judicial and executive nominees couldn't even get through; Mitch McConnell simply refused to go along. Senate rules meant that without 60 votes, nominations couldn't get a final vote. The only option, Reid finally decided, was to change the rules. It took an enormous amount of cajoling, but he was able to convince his caucus to go along, with the caveat that the threshold of 60 would still apply to legislation and Supreme Court justices.

It finally happened in November 2013, with Republicans blocking a director for the CFPB, stalling on DC Circuit Court nominations, and jamming up so many nominees that the National Labor Relations Board couldn't get a quorum, meaning companies could run roughshod over labor laws. "We had over a hundred judges that Republicans wouldn't let us confirm," Reid said. "It had to be done....We had to do something."

When Republicans took over in 2017, they quickly got rid of the filibuster for Supreme Court nominees, and there was barely a peep in the press about it. Reid told me he thinks abolishing the filibuster entirely wouldn't be a disaster, and that he instructed one of his longtime aides, during the 2016 campaign, to draft a law review article outlining how and why it should be done.

The article was timed to land shortly after Hillary Clinton won the presidency and Democrats reclaimed the Senate, though neither event came to pass. The article ran anyway, though it was ignored by the press, given that Democrats were powerless to act on its recommendation.

The article was written by Reid aide and Senate veteran William Dauster, and titled, "The Senate in Transition, or How I Learned to Stop Worrying and Love the Nuclear Option." It was intended as a signal that Reid supported the idea of eliminating the filibuster. "The author thanks Senator Reid for his review and edits of drafts of this article," it noted.

"Hopefully it won't need to be done, but the way things are going, it probably will be done and we will wind up as Dauster indicated. But I'm not as convinced that it should happen immediately, but Bill's a legal scholar, he knows the Senate very well, and of course I was looking over his shoulder at everything he wrote," Reid told me, noting that it was written "under my direction." Abolishing the filibuster, he said, "wouldn't be good, but it wouldn't be the end of the world, because we'd still have a bicameral legislature, with six-year terms in the Senate, two-year terms in the House, and it would still be as the founding fathers envisioned it, a place where legislation would cool down."

With the filibuster reformed, Democrats started moving judges through, filled up the NLRB and other agencies, and appointed a permanent director to run the CFPB, Warren's deputy, Richard Cordray.

The judicial spigot was shut off, though, when Republicans took control of the Senate. Obama's Supreme Court nominee to replace the late Antonin Scalia, Merrick Garland, couldn't even get a meeting with a single Republican senator.

Nothing epitomized the dysfunction and malaise gripping Congress those two years better than a spring 2015 accidental battle over abortion rights. After a non-controversial human trafficking bill passed the Senate Judiciary Committee unanimously, Democrats realized that it included Hyde Amendment language, restricting the use of federal funds to pay for abortion services. It's complicated, but the compromise Congress has agreed to over the years is to approve Hyde language from appropriations bills, but not in other legislation; this broke the armistice. Inside Washington, Hyde is a red-line issue for abortion-rights groups (though it was included in the Affordable Care Act, too) and when it emerged that Hyde language slipped past the committee and onto the Senate floor, advocates erupted. Democrats demanded it be stripped out, arguing Republicans had hoodwinked them legislatively.

But Republicans controlled the Senate floor, and were thrilled to force Democrats to take vote after unpleasant vote on the issue, arguing that they hadn't hidden it during the negotiations.

That's when Minnesota Democrat Amy Klobuchar told colleagues in a private meeting that someone on her staff had indeed known the language was in there, but her aide had neglected to tell her. Her colleagues were stunned — not because of the screw-up, but because Klobuchar was blaming (and naming) a specific staffer, a huge break with cultural norms in the Senate. "I would never do that," Reid told me, recalling the incident.

The incident had added resonance because, among her colleagues, Klobuchar was known as one of the most difficult senators to work for. Staff cycled through at a rapid pace, and stories of her mistreatment of aides were legendary. Now, it seemed, the rest of the caucus was paying for her mismanagement, as a staffer had for some reason or other been too afraid to loop Klobuchar in on an important detail, and now the entire caucus was stuck.

One reason Reid wouldn't have had to call out a staffer was that his aides knew how badly he wanted to avoid the issue of abortion on the Senate floor. "I don't think my staff would do that," he said. "I could control what went on the floor to a large extent. I avoided battles on abortion, because there was never a winner in those debates. I went out of my way to avoid the issue. I had people like Barbara Boxer way on one side of the issue and [Ben] Nelson way on the other side of the issue. I never surprised either one of them, but I went out of my way and I think they both appreciated not to have to vote on those very vexatious issues very often."

Eventually, public opinion turned, and Republicans began to look like they were holding up a human-trafficking bill for no reason other than to humiliate Democrats, and an agreement was struck to move it through in a way that satisfied pro-choice groups.

All the while, the economy crawled forward. Stuck in the mud of austerity, job growth was stunted and wages stayed flat. As young people graduated from college underneath mountains of debt, they saw their futures fade before their eyes. Obama-era economic policies would produce a generation of socialists.

Fourteen

Senator Warren

Not long after Elizabeth Warren announced she'd be running for Senate in 2012 against Scott Brown, I went to Massachusetts to watch her campaign. But first I stopped at the encampment of Occupy Boston, which was then in full swing in the city's financial district. I wanted to know what the occupiers thought of Warren, fully aware that many of them eschewed electoral politics entirely. I was surprised to find about half the people I spoke with were fully in support of Warren's run, even as they condemned the idea of electoral politics as a viable path to change.

Later that week, at an event at a VFW hall in Brockton, somewhere in the middle of the state, she greeted people as they entered, gabbing amiably. I asked her how she was enjoying retail politics, and she said that she got a thrill from engaging with so many people. "I was born to do this," she said, quickly clarifying that she was referring to how much she enjoyed it, not that she was God's gift to glad-handing.

Moments into her speech, with my video camera running, she was interrupted by a tea party supporter who stood up and began berating her. He said he'd been unemployed since February 2010, objected to Warren's expressed affiliation with the frustrations of Occupy Wall Street, and argued that the tea party has been protesting Wall Street excess for longer than the nascent global movement camping out in downtowns across the country.

The crowd tried to shout the man down, but Warren told her supporters to let him speak. "No, no, it's alright. Let me say two things," she said. "I'm very sorry that you've been out of work. I'm also very sorry that the recent jobs bill that would've brought 22,000 jobs to Massachusetts did not pass in the Senate."

Warren went on to address his question about her association with Occupy Wall Street. "I've been protesting what's been going on on Wall Street for a very long time," she said, but added that the movement has its own independent agenda and will proceed along its own course.

"Yeah, so has the tea party," the man said, before losing his cool. "Well, if you're the intellectual creator of that so-called party," he said, "you're a socialist whore. I don't want anything to do with you." The crowd now shouted him down as he added that Warren's "boss," presumably referring to the president, was "foreign-born." He then attempted to storm out through a side door, but found it locked. "So, we are here to do work, and I think we have a reminder that we have a lot of work to do," she said as the heckler continued to struggle with the door, before awkwardly retreating out the back of the VFW hall instead.

That April, before President Obama released his "long form" birth certificate, 43 percent of Republicans, following the lead of reality TV star Donald Trump, believed that the president was either definitely or probably born in a foreign country, according to a Gallup survey. After he released the birth certificate, the number dropped, but still held at roughly one in four when polled in May.

A Republican tracker with a video camera was at the event, too, so after it ended, in order to conduct an interview, we ducked into the backseat of her car, parked in the VFW lot. With two of her aides in the front seats, the tracker shot footage of the car from just feet away.

Warren, in the darkness, reflected on the man's outburst, which she said was her first such encounter: "I actually felt sorry for the guy. I really genuinely did. He's been out of work now for a year and a half. And bless his heart, I mean, he thought somehow it would help to come here and yell names."

The assault stuck with Warren, and she continued to think about it throughout the night. I did, too, and I was conflicted about whether to report on it. It was an interesting exchange, and it foreshadowed the furor of the 2016 presidential campaign, a glimpse into the twisted rage that was transforming politics, rooted in economic anxiety and expressing itself as dangerous racism and misogyny. On the other hand, I didn't want to encourage copy cats and put her or other politicians at greater risk. Earlier that year, Gabby Giffords, one of the friendliest, warmest members of the House, had been shot in the head and nearly killed.

Warren emailed me later that evening to say she still wasn't upset with the man himself, but rather with those who attempt to channel his anger in a malevolent direction. "I was thinking more about the heckler. I'm not angry with him, but he didn't come up with the idea that his biggest problem was Occupy Wall Street," she said. "There's someone else pre-packaging that poison — and that's who makes me angry."

I ended up deciding to publish the video, and Warren later said she was glad that I did, even though that night she had hoped I wouldn't.[182]

She turned out to be a strong candidate, and began out-polling Brown. Cecil said that when he'd talk to the old guard in Boston, they remained unimpressed, "complaining that Warren should be up by more." Her campaign would be tested in April, when an article appeared in the Boston Herald that continues to resonate. It originated with a tip from a Native American Republican, who reached out to GOP operatives[183] and told them that Warren had previously claimed Native American status, a claim he found questionable.

As Warren had surged in her career, she started moving in circles that were further and further from her Oklahoma roots. At the same time, her aunts began passing away, leaving her feeling unmoored. It's not at all unusual for non-Native families in Oklahoma to grow up with stories about Native heritage, and Warren's was among them. In the 1980s, she began listing herself as Native American.

The Herald article, published in April 2012, noted that claims of Native American heritage were fairly common. "Both Hillary Clinton and Barack Obama claim to have Native American heritage, but we were never able to find evidence of that, and in both cases we traced their ancestry fairly thoroughly," Christopher Child, a genealogist at the New England Historic and Genealogical Society, told the Herald.

Internally, Warren's staff scrambled to find documentation to back up the stories told by Grandma Hannie, but came up empty. "I'm very proud of my heritage. I'm very proud of the stories my grandparents gave me," Warren responded, as pressure continued to mount. Her staff urged her to make clear to the public that she had not received any special treatment in the hiring process at any university. Though it was true — and an exhaustive Boston Globe examination in 2018 would find that it never came up in Harvard's decisionmaking — she refused, telling her aides she didn't want to appear as if she were undermining affirmative action, or implying that affirmative action was somehow wrong.

Because she genuinely believed the family lore, she was in a difficult position, and felt she couldn't simply apologize and move on without

182   Looking back, Warren's electoral career began with her being denounced as a "socialist whore," but seven years later, as she launched her bid for president, she was deemed not socialist enough for some on the left.

183   I learned this from the GOP operatives involved.

betraying her family. Her efforts to explain how prevalent the lore was in her family only backfired, coming off as tone-deaf, as when she relayed the story of her grandfather's photo that sat on her mantle. "My Aunt Bea has walked by that picture at least a thousand times," Warren told reporters, and "remarked that her father, my papaw, had high cheek-bones like all of the Indians do, because that's how she saw it. She said, *And your mother got those same great cheekbones and I didn't.* She thought this was the bad deal she had gotten in life."

Right-wing protesters stalked her at events, regularly breaking into whoops and chants and tomahawk chops. Despite it all, she beat Scott Brown on Election Day by eight points. Victory has a way of burying scandal, with the unwritten rule being that it will remain buried unless and until the politician seeks a higher position. But for now, she was on her way to becoming a senator, and I tagged along to watch her become official.

As she traversed the tunnel toward the basement of the Capitol, War-ren recalled the first time she had any experience with the Senate floor. It was 2002, and she had been working hard to oppose bankruptcy re-form proposals that were a top priority of banks and credit card com-panies — and for their leading senator, Joe Biden — looking to prevent consumers from shaking off steadily rising debt. When the bill came to the floor, she was certain that she had lost and turned off C-SPAN.

"I thought there's no point [watching], because I know what's going to happen," she said. "And the phone rings and there's this man shout-ing on the phone, and I just thought it was a prank call. And I started to hang up and — you know how you hear something? — I put it back to my ear and I said, *Senator Kennedy?* And he said, *We did it! We stopped that bill! Here, wait, let me put Dick Durbin on!* And he was in the Senate cloak-room, and that was my first connection ever to that real estate."

We ascended a staircase and Warren was directed by an attendant to an elevator marked "Senators Only." "Pretty cool," she said, when I asked how it felt to take the exclusive ride.

Though she had been lobbying the Senate on bankruptcy issues on and off since that first rodeo with Kennedy, being on the floor was a new experience. "That's the first time I've ever been on the Senate floor, literally the first time," said Warren of the dark blue carpeting she had threatened three years earlier to cover with "blood and teeth."

Senators get sworn in twice — once for real, and then once ceremo-nially in the Old Senate Chamber. She gathered with friends, family and supporters in the Kennedy Caucus Room before that ceremonial swear-ing in to take Kennedy's seat.

The Old Senate Chamber was used during most of the first half of the

19th century. Swathed in royal red carpeting and plush walls, the room earned the term "chamber" and hosted some of the greatest debates in American history. I noted that Sen. Daniel Webster[184] had delivered his famous "Liberty and Union" speech in the chamber Warren was about to enter. She would be taking Webster's seat, though not his desk.

"Daniel Webster's desk goes to the senator from New Hampshire, not the senator from Massachusetts," she noted, ever the professor, adding that she had heard it skipped over the border by dint of the great orator's last will. Webster, she noted, wasn't just a senator from Massachusetts but held Kennedy's seat, as did former President John Quincy Adams and the famous abolitionist Charles Sumner — who left actual blood on the Senate floor when he was brutally beaten within an inch of his life by a South Carolina congressman.

She and her husband, historian Bruce Mann, waited in line outside the old chamber, which is bathed in a plush red velvet. They watched as other women were sworn in. One of them was Heidi Heitkamp, a Democrat from North Dakota. Joe Biden, as vice president, was charged with emceeing the proceedings. "Spread your legs, you're gonna be frisked," Biden told the Heitkamp family. Warren was speechless, as was Heitkamp. Biden, through decades of saying idiotic and offensive things on the regular,[185] had effectively raised the bar on what could possibly be considered a gaffe. But even he seemed to sense he may have managed to clear it with that one. Apparently, when a photographer had told Heitkamp's husband to move one of his hands, Biden's mind had gone to a police pat-down, and his mind had gone, as usual, directly out of his mouth. "You say that to somebody in North Dakota, they think it's a frisk. *Drop your hands to your side*, y'know?" Biden added, trying to make the joke land. Warren and her husband looked at each other.

Biden turned to Heitkamp's husband, hoping for a bailout. "They think you're in trouble, right? You drop your hands to the side..." Her husband did his best to ignore him.[186] "Ahhh, I'm a little formal, I know," Biden concluded.

Biden was on better behavior swearing in Warren. Sen. Barbara Mikulski (D-Md.), the first woman elected without following a husband to the upper chamber, found Warren later on the Senate floor. She barely

---

184   The most famous line was, "Liberty and Union, now and forever, one and inseparable!" Delivered in 1830, it came 20 years before he advocated on behalf of the 1850 Compromise that included the Fugitive Slave Act, which, as noted in the prologue, produced the political realignment that brought out the Civil War.

185   In 2019, Biden promised to stop being a creep, saying that he understood "norms have changed."

186   C-SPAN caught most of this exchange. Google it.

Ryan Grim

came up to Warren's shoulder as the two embraced. Mikulski attached an official Senate pin to the lapel of the incoming senator's pantsuit. "Think of it," Mikulski said she told Warren, "like the Croix de Guerre for all the battles we women have fought."

"Congratulations," Mikulski said, with her eyes watering as she beat her hand against her heart. "You stand here now in the footsteps of so many women who for so long would have liked to have been here, should have been here, but didn't get the shot. You've got the chance. You have a band of sisters. And we're going to not only make history, we're going to change history."

First, though, she had to get a seat on the Banking Committee. Jeff Merkley was already there, and Ohio's Sherrod Brown was a senior member. Bank lobbyists made keeping her off the committee a high priority, but she had a friend in Reid, and Reid knew the progressive base wanted her on the panel. So he put her there. Republicans still held the House, so there wasn't much constructive that could get done, but she was able to play defense against what she saw as an Obama administration that still didn't understand that there was a class war going on, and that Democrats needed to be on the side of people rather than banks.

In July 2013, the White House invited a handful of progressive columnists and reporters for an off-record chat with a senior administration official. About a dozen of us gathered in the garden area behind the White House chief of staff's office, drinking the Sam Adams customarily offered up at such happy hours. The invite didn't specify it, but everyone there assumed the identity of the senior administration official would be Barack Obama, who had a habit of popping in on these types of things and bullshitting for 30 minutes to an hour, a way to flatter the press and hopefully earn some soft coverage, while also picking up some insight into what direction the press was headed on different topics.

Obama in private was identical to Obama in public, only with more profanity thrown in. Obama in private was also an opportunity for reporters to throw questions at him without feeling like we were performing for a national audience, though the downside was that his answers could only be used as leads. I threw two questions at him.[187] The one

187   The gathering was being hosted shortly after a Florida jury had acquitted George Zimmerman of murdering Trayvon Martin, and Obama talked about his disappointment in a way similar to how he did just days later in public, when he made a surprise visit to the podium. That Friday, he told the surprised press corps, most of which had not been at the earlier private gathering, "There are very few African American men in this country who have not had the experience of being followed when they are shopping at a department store. That includes me."
"There are probably very few African American men who have not had the experi-

that's relevant for this chapter was about the coming vacancy at the helm of the Federal Reserve. His pick for the next Fed Chair would be one of his most consequential political and economic decisions, and it was widely known that his former senior adviser Larry Summers was pining for the job. Indeed, Rahm Emanuel had promised it to him as part of his original job offer, but Emanuel was now Chicago Mayor Emanuel, so he wasn't around to cash that check.

Outside Washington, a major strike against Summers was his involvement in deregulating Wall Street in the 1990s as an adviser to President Clinton, and his push during 2009 and 2010 to keep the administration from doing anything to combat the foreclosure crisis, a fateful decision that we continue to live with today. His second strike was that he had been fired as Harvard president for being sexist and alienating

---

ence of walking across the street and hearing the locks click on the doors of cars. That happens to me — at least before I was a senator," he went on. Saying he didn't intend to exaggerate those experiences, Obama added that they "inform how the African American community interprets what happened one night in Florida. And it's inescapable for people to bring those experiences to bear. The African American community is also knowledgeable that there is a history of racial disparities in the application of our criminal laws, everything from the death penalty to enforcement of our drug laws. And that ends up having an impact in terms of how people interpret the case." Having said that, he ended with a note of optimism "As difficult and challenging as this whole episode has been for a lot of people, I don't want us to lose sight that things are getting better. Each successive generation seems to be making progress in changing attitudes when it comes to race. It doesn't mean we're in a post-racial society. It doesn't mean that racism is eliminated. But, you know, when I talk to Malia and Sasha and I listen to their friends and I see them interact, they're better than we are. They're better than we were on these issues. And that's true in every community that I've visited all across the country," he said, adding that "kids these days, I think, have more sense than we did back then and certainly more than our parents did or our grandparents did, and that along this long and difficult journey, we're becoming a more perfect union, not a perfect union, but a more perfect union."

He had made that same point, in similar language, in the White House garden, where I pressed him on it. Yes, I said, it's absolutely fair to say that in public racism is tolerated far less than it was even just a few years ago, and certainly less than decades ago. But, I added, for actual African Americans, things were getting worse, with the prison population, for instance, continuing to soar despite all the improvements in rhetoric. He said that he agreed with the point, and actually had been talking with his attorney general, Eric Holder, about an ambitious pivot toward criminal justice reform, which had so far not been a priority of the administration. An attempt was indeed later made, but he left office with the job far from finished.

professors. But inside the Beltway, the knock against him was that he was reputedly an erratic, volatile personality (not unrelated to his Harvard firing).

I asked Obama how important a steady temperament was to him as he thought about who to replace Ben Bernanke at the Federal Reserve. It was an obvious enough reference to Summers that he and the reporters chuckled. In his answer, he lauded Summers. He stopped short of explicitly saying that Summers was his top pick, but the impression was clear. He wanted Larry Summers. A few days later, Ezra Klein, who had been at the gathering, wrote a blog post saying that Summers was known to be Obama's first choice.

It was an alarming prospect. Completely setting aside Summers' work during the Clinton years, which alone should have been disqualifying, the role of the Fed chair requires somebody who can be calm in crisis — and who won't accidentally spark a crisis with flippant behavior. Summers had managed to get himself fired from Harvard for something he said *in prepared remarks.*[188] The gods of finance only knew what he could do to the global economy off the cuff.

At The Huffington Post, we made the decision between him and Janet Yellen (who was being pushed by labor and progressive groups) into a marquee battle. We put together a front page that went guns blazing at Summers.[189]

The next week, Obama ventured to Capitol Hill for private meetings with Democrats in both the House and Senate. The Democrats came out and told reporters he had made a strong defense of Summers, and particularly singled out The Huffington Post for making Summers "a progressive whipping boy." Rep. Gerry Connolly said Obama "felt that Larry had been badly treated by some on the left and in the press."

"Don't believe everything you read in The Huffington Post,"[190] Obama said in the room, according to Rep. Brad Sherman.

Staffers at the White House, however, were working at cross-purposes with their own boss. Summers had angered most of the people who had the opportunity to work with him, and some of those staffers worked privately with outside organizers who were waging a campaign against him.[191]

---

188   He made the argument, essentially, that men were smarter than women, which he didn't seem to realize he was refuting by example at the same moment.

189   HuffPost's front page splash, before it was neutered by a redesign, used to drive cable and newspaper coverage.

190   The New York Times had editorialized in favor of Yellen, and it gave me great satisfaction that he singled out HuffPost over the Times.

191   Idea for future historians: Look for White House emails on this. Call me in

Summers had been promised the job as Fed chair when Ben Bernanke stepped down and was furious at Bernanke's reappointment in 2010. The deal had been made to coax Summers into accepting a position as director of the National Economic Council, a step down from his previous service as Treasury Secretary. Yet it was Summers' tenure at the White House post in 2009 and 2010 that ultimately doomed the arrangement, as he frequently alienated members of his own party whom he would later need to win the Fed job.

For instance, Summers peeved progressives by squashing a transaction tax on financial industry trades that Obama reportedly supported. And Summers promised Oregon Senator Jeff Merkley, in exchange for supporting the second round of the Wall Street bailout, the administration would put $50 to $100 billion toward foreclosure relief and would lobby on behalf of cramdown — a law that would empower bankruptcy judges to reduce underwater mortgages and let people stay in their homes. Neither happened, and instead Summers later lobbied *against* Merkley's push for the Volcker Rule, and lobbied *against* cramdown. Privately, Summers argued that the foreclosure crisis should be allowed to work itself out, and that it had to crash all the way before it could take off again. The government, he said, shouldn't do more than "foam the runway."

It was an infuriating position to anybody who was in touch with the pain being felt by the people being destroyed by the crash. Merkley, not coincidentally, was the first senator to express public reservations about a Summers nomination, and the strategy to block him quickly zeroed in on the Senate Banking Committee.

Warren, Brown, and Merkley made three votes against Summers, but they needed two more to take him down, assuming that all Republicans would also oppose him (and anybody else Obama would nominate). Merkley took the lead in organizing the effort behind the scenes, with Warren working with outside groups and labor unions. Merkley worked hard on Jon Tester (Mont.), Heidi Heitkamp (N.D.) and Joe Manchin (W.Va.); all three of them held streaks of populism, with Tester's the most pronounced. He had been first elected in 2006 and ignored all of Washington's advice on how to win in Montana. He was unabashedly opposed to the Iraq War, promoted wind and other alternative energy, and ran as a populist dirt farmer.[192]

For Heitkamp, outside groups active in the effort deployed an unusual strategy. Heitkamp's voters back home were not particularly engaged

---

20 years and I'll tell you where to look.

192   He has largely served as a populist and was reelected in 2012 and again in 2018, though the party refuses to learn any lessons from him.

in a backroom contest between Yellen and Summers, unlike plugged-in, wealthy liberals in New York, Chicago and California. Much of Heit-kamp's fundraising base was made up of wealthy progressive women in those cities, and those women got organized. All of a sudden, Heit-kamp's phone was blowing up, with her donors letting her know how important it was to them that she not vote to confirm the erratic, sexist Summers, but instead get behind Yellen.

UltraViolet, an online women's group, and the National Organization for Women, played pivotal roles, identifying top donors and mobilizing women on the ground. Merkley continued to press his case over recess in August. When the Senate returned after Labor Day, he and Warren went in for the kill. Had Summers not opposed naming Warren to permanent-ly head the Consumer Financial Protection Bureau, she may not have been in the Senate at all. But that wasn't her or Summers' fate. "I don't think it's any secret that Larry was not my first choice," Warren said on MSNBC's "Morning Joe" the first Monday back from recess.

Merkley then spoke to Democratic senators on the committee during caucus meetings, and made Summers' affinity for Wall Street and prior support for deregulation the key element of his pitch. He homed in on Summers' backing for the Glass-Steagall repeal, which allowed banks to grow much larger and take on more risk. He also highlighted Summers' opposition to regulating derivatives in a battle with then-Commodity Futures Trading Commission head Brooksley Born. To make the point that Summers had not revised his approach, Merkley noted his intense behind-the-scenes opposition to the Volcker Rule, an attempt to rein-state some of Glass-Steagall's restrictions that was added to the Dodd-Frank Wall Street reform law by Merkley and Brown.

On a Friday in mid-September, he laid his cards on the table, telling the committee chairman, Tim Johnson of South Dakota, as well as Reid and the White House, that he had the five votes needed to sink the nomi-nation — which had still not been made publicly. That Sunday, Summers withdrew his name from consideration.

Andrea Helling, a spokeswoman for Tester, hinted that his tempera-ment, as well as Merkley and Warren's arguments, had been key. "Sen. Tester believes we need a consensus builder to lead the Federal Reserve," she told me. "He's concerned about Mr. Summers' history of helping to deregulate financial markets."

Heitkamp was also prepared to vote no, and organizers thought they would get Manchin, as well, which would have made six.

After the news broke, a top White House aide reached out to some of the women involved in the organizing with a note of genuine congrat-ulations. There's no telling what global financial calamity was avoided by the intervention of Warren and Merkley; Janet Yellen would become Fed chair.

Warren continued poking at the White House, vigilant for any Dodd–Frank backsliding and frustrated at the seemingly endless stream of bankers lining up to work in the administration — including high-profile trips through the revolving door such as Mary Jo White becoming Securities and Exchange Commission chair, and Citigroup's Stanley Fischer being named Federal Reserve vice chair. Blocking Summers from the Fed chairmanship hadn't sent a strong enough message, she realized, so she laid in wait for a Treasury nominee she could make an example of. That unlucky fellow was named Antonio Weiss.

Weiss was nominated in November 2014 to be Treasury undersecretary for domestic finance, shortly after Democrats lost the Senate.[193] His nomination came at the same time that Congress was trying to push through a partial Dodd–Frank rollback in the year-end spending bill, something that had become an annual tradition. "The battle was on for the soul of the Democratic Party," Politico declared, not for the first or last time.

Warren announced her opposition in an oped in The Huffington Post in mid-November, and the group CREDO Action sprang into...well, *action*. CREDO, a mobile phone company with progressive politics and a grassroots organizing arm, was run then by Becky Bond[194] and Murshed Zaheed, who launched a petition against Weiss, blasting a brutal message to their several million members.

One of those members, as it turned out, was Antonio Weiss' mom. Like her son, Weiss' mom identified politically as a progressive. Antonio Weiss had bought the Paris Review several years earlier to keep it from collapsing, and had been a proud supporter of Obama. On Wall Street, he was probably one of the more liberal people Obama could have found.

And so it was disorienting for Weiss to all of a sudden be caught in Warren's blender. His firm, Lazard, had specialized in what are known as inversions, where a large American company buys a smaller firm in a country with a lower tax rate, and legally moves its headquarters in a tax-avoidance scheme. Treasury Secretary Jack Lew had recently been blasting inversions, and was pushing policy to block them, making the optics of Weiss' nomination that much trickier.

Other outside progressive groups jumped into the fray, and progres-

---

193   The political terrain for Democrats was miserable. The economy hadn't fully recovered, and a sense of chaos was bred by 24/7 coverage of an Ebola outbreak and the conquest by ISIS of significant chunks of Iraq and Syria.

194   Bond would later help organize Sanders' field program, and then Beto O'Rourke's. Zaheed had most recently worked for Harry Reid.

sive media began pounding away, covering Warren's assault and digging into Weiss' record. West Virginia's Joe Manchin, who had joined Warren and Merkley in their war on Larry Summers, came out against Weiss, and Weiss' route through the Banking Committee became increasingly narrow.

On December 5, New York Sen. Kirsten Gillibrand went on MSNBC's "Morning Joe" and delivered what Weiss' supporters knew was the kill shot. She refused to say whether she would support Weiss, but added a word of praise for Warren. "I think Senator Warren's very clear," she said. "She believes that, as the person responsible for how consumers are affected, his background and his experience don't fit the requirements."

Heads exploded in New York and Washington. "The game in Washington had changed," Politico's finance reporter wrote in a Weiss eulogy. "Elizabeth Warren, sometimes disregarded by the White House as a largely irrelevant nuisance, could no longer be ignored. Bolstered by grassroots groups eager for any anti-Wall Street crusade and a vibrant progressive media that hung on her every word, Warren succeeded in knocking out Weiss' nomination."

Weiss pulled out and was offered the job of counselor, which didn't require confirmation, as a consolation prize. There he oversaw policy around the Puerto Rican debt crisis, and progressives regarded him broadly as an ally.

But Warren's point had been made: personnel was policy, and she was prepared to block anybody she found too close to Wall Street. The Obama administration, with two years left in office, was one intended audience for the message, but there was another as well. Hillary Clinton was already considered the presumptive Democratic nominee for president, and Warren's strategy was to influence Clinton by exerting power over her hiring. With a block of populists on the Banking Committee, the Senate was poised to do just that. Warren was the only woman in the Senate to decline to sign a letter, organized by Barbara Boxer, urging Clinton to run.

That same month, Clinton and Warren met at Clinton's home for a private conversation. The agenda was personnel, emails later published by Wikileaks revealed, with Warren pushing Clinton not to stock her campaign and her administration with Rubinites, or with Rubin himself. Clinton made no commitments, but said she understood the concern.

Warren declined to endorse Clinton, despite pressure to do so, but also continued to resist entreaties that she run herself. When it became clear that she had no intention to jump in, Bernie Sanders — believing that somebody needed to at least make the argument for the left in the primary — declared his bid.

The announcement was made at a Senate press conference and carried on C-SPAN, yet a million dollars came pouring in over the next 24 hours, the first indication that Sanders was much stronger than it was thought, and Clinton much weaker. Sanders, in March, had polled at 3 percent in a CNN survey — a poll that did not even include Trump on the Republican side. By 68-30, Democratic voters said they thought Clinton was the most electable candidate, and electability is particularly prized among the Democratic primary electorate, many of whom fancy themselves (against a long track record to the contrary) to be smart, strategic voters.

Warren faced pressure from her left, too, to get behind Sanders. But she never believed he had a chance to win — she would later say, and be pilloried for it, that the process was rigged against him — and her end game was to have significant control over Clinton's personnel decisions, to keep as many bankers out as possible. Endorsing Sanders could handicap that. The decision to stay neutral, though, would haunt her 2020 campaign, as many Sanders supporters would never forgive her.

"Pocahontas" continued to dog Warren, too. In 2016, Trump had made it his nickname for her, and back home, Howie Carr, a right-wing radio host, said he had swiped a pen with her DNA on it in 2012 and had it tested, but he didn't have enough saliva. He was determined to get a better sample, and Warren began looking over her shoulder at restaurants. Charles Johnson, a conservative provocateur, told me he was also working hard to get a DNA sample himself.

In February 2018, Warren tried to get ahead of it, and gave a surprise address to the National Congress of American Indians in Washington. "You won't find my family members on any rolls," and said, "and I'm not enrolled in a tribe. And I want to make something clear. I respect that distinction. I understand that tribal membership is determined by tribes — and only by tribes. I never used my family tree to get a break or get ahead. I never used it to advance my career."

She went on to defend her family's story. Whenever Trump attacked her, she would use the opportunity lift up the stories of Native Americans around the country and recenter the conversation on issues that mattered to them. It seemed she had settled on how she would handle the question in an upcoming presidential run, but something was still needling her — she was still looking over her shoulder at restaurants or events, wondering if there was a weirdo lurking nearby intent on absconding with her spit. Trump, at rallies, was offering a million dollars to charity if she'd take the test "and it shows you're an Indian."

Warren, with the exception, perhaps, of when it comes to drinking beer, is somebody who's comfortable in her skin, not ashamed of who she was or who she is. She didn't know if her parents' story was true, and she was as curious as anybody else. *Let's just get it all out there*, she decided. *Let's take the test.*

For years, as she faced political attacks over the issue, she had resisted enlisting her family in her defense. After all, if it was true that her family story held that there was Cherokee heritage, her family would be able to testify to that. And her three brothers were as Trump-country as they came, all working-class Oklahoma Republicans and veterans.

But with Trump relentlessly badgering Warren with the "Pocahontas" slur, they all agreed to go on camera for a video on the question. "It's offensive to me, not just as Betsy's cousin, but as a Native American," said Cherokee Nation citizen Ann Rowsey White in one of the opening scenes, referring to Warren by her childhood nickname. In the fateful scene, Warren gets on the phone with Stanford Professor Carlos Bustamante, a geneticist who had been an adviser to 23andMe and Ancestry.com. Getting the results, Warren appears intent on affirming her family's story. "Now, the president likes to call my mom a liar. What do the facts say?" she said.

"The facts suggest that you absolutely have a Native American ancestor in your pedigree," the professor replied.

Warren then clarified the story. "I'm not enrolled in a tribe, and only tribes determine tribal citizenship. I understand and respect that distinction. But my family history is my family history," she said. "My parents were real people. The love they shared, the struggles they endured, the family they built, the story they lived, will always be etched on my heart. And no one, not even the president of the United States, will ever take it away from me."

She dropped the video in October 2018, just weeks before the midterms. The initial reaction was positive, and it came along with heightened speculation that she was indeed running for president. A number of prominent Native Americans praised the announcement, including Deb Haaland and the Eastern Band of Cherokee Indians.

Then, enter: Cherokee Secretary of State Chuck Hoskin Jr., with a statement that changed everything.

> A DNA test is useless to determine tribal citizenship. Current DNA tests do not even distinguish whether a person's ancestors were indigenous to North or South America. Sovereign tribal nations set their own legal requirements for citizenship, and while DNA tests can be used to determine lineage, such as paternity to an individual, it is not evidence for tribal affiliation. Using a DNA test to lay claim to any connection to the Cherokee Nation or any tribal nation, even vaguely, is inappropriate and wrong. It makes a mockery out of DNA tests and its legitimate uses while also dishonoring legitimate tribal governments and their citizens, whose

ancestors are well documented and whose heritage is proven. Senator Warren is
undermining tribal interests with her continued claims of tribal heritage.

Trump took a victory lap on Twitter: "Thank you to the Cherokee
Nation for revealing that Elizabeth Warren, sometimes referred to as
Pocahontas, is a complete and total Fraud!"

NPR invited Hoskin on the air as his statement appeared in every article about the new video. The narrative quickly set in: Native Americans
were angry at Elizabeth Warren.

The next several months involved countless phone calls and meetings with tribal leaders, ending with Warren publicly apologizing for
confusing the question of heritage versus tribal citizenship. Immense
damage had been done, though, as it raised questions in primary voters' minds of whether Warren had what it took to beat Trump. It became definitional: Warren had botched the politics of the Pocahontas
response, therefore she was bad at politics. She announced for president
on New Year's Eve and on the campaign trail, it was common to meet
voters who preferred her as their top choice, but didn't think she could
win. In surveys, she remained mired in single digits for months.

Fifteen

Occupy Washington

There is an epidemiology to uprisings. Throughout history, revolutions and protest movements have drawn inspiration from each other. The status quo seems unchangeable until the moment it is changed, and then, all of a sudden, brand new possibilities open up.

In January 2011, tens of thousands of protesters flooded into Cairo's Tahrir Square, as the Arab Spring swept from Tunisia to across the Middle East. By February, Egypt's seemingly immovable dictator Hosni Mubarak had been overthrown, and unrest was spreading.

Back home, Washington was grappling with more mundane matters than freedom and tyranny — specifically, the debt ceiling, an arcane and arguably unconstitutional[195] glitch in the legislative process that requires Congress to not just appropriate federal spending, but also to authorize the government to sell treasury bonds to fund the spending not covered by taxes or other revenue.

Democrats had a chance during the lame duck to lift the debt ceiling when they still had the votes, or even eliminate it entirely. But Pelosi argued privately that leaving it in place would paradoxically give Democrats leverage to push through new spending programs. With Republicans in charge of the House, Pelosi argued, they would now be blamed for an inability to govern if they refused to raise the debt ceiling. And most of their tea party members would refuse to go along, so they would need to give Democrats something for helping out. Her reasoning was

---

195   Per the 14th Amendment, the federal government can't renege on debts.

sound — if she was dealing with reasonable opponents and an aggressive White House.

Instead, Obama saw the debt ceiling as an opportunity to strike a Grand Bargain with the new House Speaker, John Boehner, and offered to cut Social Security, Medicare and other spending to try to get there.

Very serious people, at the time, thought of a Grand Bargain in Washington as uncontroversial and nonpartisan, something above politics. Those fuzzy feelings were the product of hundreds of millions of dollars spent on anti-deficit-spending propaganda by billionaire Pete Peterson and corporate groups like Third Way. Peterson's organization, the Committee for a Responsible Federal Budget, was a powerhouse. His annual conference drew every big political name you could come up with. Peterson, between 2007 and 2011, spent some $500 million aimed at producing a consensus in Washington that cuts to safety net programs were essential. To put that in context, all corporations and unions together spent less than $20 billion lobbying, total, over that time period. All of them.

The debt ceiling loomed in early August, and the White House and Congress came up with a process dubbed as the Super Committee — 12 members, six from each party and six from each chamber. The bill they came up with could not be amended by either chamber, but instead would get an up or down vote. Austerity had extraordinary momentum behind it.

Then came Occupy Wall Street.

Nobody expected the Arab Spring would show up in the streets of the United States. It took a Canadian magazine to bring it over, but the foundation had been built more than a decade earlier. In the 1990s, the it magazine for lefties and anyone disaffected with mass consumer culture was called Adbusters. That decade saw the rise of a largely forgotten force that organized around skepticism of multinational corporations. Naomi Klein's book *No Logo* was the movement's bible, as students rallied against sweatshop labor and increasingly zeroed in on the exploitative nature of the U.S. corporate empire, enacted through multilateral institutions like the International Monetary Fund, World Bank and World Trade Organization.

Claire Sandberg, for instance, was a 16-year-old high school student when she first protested the IMF and World Bank on April 16, 2000, at an event known as A16. The night prior, she went to a protest at the Department of Justice against the prison-industrial complex, and was swept up in a mass arrest.

The attacks on 9/11 hit Pause on the anti-globalization movement. Ten years later, in the summer of 2011, *Adbusters* proposed an occupation of Wall Street, modeled after Tahrir Square, to protest the dominance of money in politics, and people like Sandberg, while continuing to work on other projects, were more than ready. Wall Street was chosen as the site to draw attention to the absence of prosecutions of bankers whose fraud had sparked the Great Recession.

Occupy dominated the news throughout the fall, and Sandberg spent much of her time at the Zuccotti Park encampment. Occupy's slogan "We are the 99 percent" put the focus on the country's super rich in a way that hadn't happened since the days of the robber barons. In the midst of it, Bank of America announced a new $5 monthly fee for debit cards. Amid outrage, it backed down and rescinded the fee, with Occupy getting the credit for the climb down.

The movement spread to cities and towns across the country, with encampments springing up in downtowns. In early November, a group of protesters set out from New York to Washington, calling themselves "Occupy the Highway," and aiming to hit the capital on November 22, the day the Super Committee was due to issue its legislation.

On November 21, it collapsed. "Super Committee Fail = Occupy Wall Street Win," celebrated Michael Glazer, an organizer of Occupy the Highway, in a statement that day. "The so-called Super Committee was a failure from the beginning. No one has the courage to stand up inside our corrupt political system and fight for regular Americans. So, we will continue to take a stand outside the system."

The willingness of that faction of protesters to even acknowledge the Super Committee was controversial inside Occupy, which considered direct interaction with the political system futile at best and corrupting at worst. But as Glazer emphasized, Occupy had blown up the Committee from the outside, by changing the political terrain to one hostile to austerity. Concerns over the deficit were replaced by a conversation about economic inequality, which helped set the stage for the 2012 presidential campaign, a matchup between the cartoon plutocrat Mitt Romney and Obama.

The Obama team credits their win with an ability to define Romney early as a one percenter whose wealth was built by syphoning money from the working class and leaving a trail of joblessness and misery behind. Obama was the guy who had saved Detroit, while Romney wanted to push it into bankruptcy. For that framing, he owes much to Occupy Wall Street. And if you get a Social Security check, or plan to one day, so do you.

For that simple accomplishment, it can be said to have won more battles in Washington than some longtime professional progressive institutions. But the legacy of that movement — or moment, perhaps —

stretches far beyond just that.

Occupy, and people involved with it, would go on to inspire and blend with radical resistance movements around the country. Many of them moved into environmental activism, and coupled it with a racial and economic justice analysis, while others — and sometimes the same people — became important figures in the Movement for Black Lives.

In August 2011, 1,252 people were arrested outside the White House, protesting the Keystone XL pipeline. In November, more than 10,000 people rallied again, encircling the White House.

A few months after the 2012 election, Obama flew to California for fundraisers. As he traveled from one billionaire's home to the next, his motorcade rolled past protesters, many of whom were holding posters demanding he block the Keystone XL Pipeline, with Obama's campaign logo supplanting the "o" in Keystone. "What do we want from our Presi-dent?" the protesters shouted.[196] "No pipeline for the 1 percent!"

The pipeline was planned to carry tar sands oil from Canada to the U.S., where it would be refined and exported. The first fundraiser had been at the home of Tom Steyer, a major donor whose top issue is the climate. Steyer came out of a private meeting with him worried about Obama's commitment. "He was extremely impressive in terms of understanding the issue," Steyer said.[197] "But he was saying, 'I need to put this in the context of a whole program that I'm trying to get to. This isn't the only thing I care about.'"

At a slightly larger private meeting that followed, Obama elaborated, citing a mortgage crisis that his own administration consciously chose not to address, and a stunted recovery that was the result of a too-meager stimulus, as reasons the public wasn't ready to address climate change. "The politics of this are tough," he said. "Because if you haven't seen a raise in a decade; if your house is still twenty-five thousand, thirty thousand dollars under water; if you're just happy that you've still got that factory job that is powered by cheap energy; if every time you go to fill up your old car because you can't afford to buy a new one, and you certainly can't afford to buy a Prius, you're spending forty bucks that you don't have, which means that you may not be able to save for retirement.... You may be concerned about the temperature of the planet, but it's probably not rising to your No. 1 concern."

The links to earlier movements were more than spiritual. In some cases, they were quite direct. Claire Sandberg, for being the victim of an illegal mass arrest at A16, was given an $18,000 settlement, which

196   The anecdote comes from a 2013 New Yorker article by Ryan Lizza, "The President and the Pipeline."
197   Ibid.

had been collectively negotiated. She used the money to co-found Frack Action, a group dedicated to banning fracking in New York, a fight that was ultimately, and improbably, won.

Organizing against Keystone continued, culminating in a mass demonstration outside the White House in 2014, the largest in decades, which included hundreds of arrests. That summer, on August 9, a police officer in Ferguson, Missouri, Darren Wilson, stopped 18-year-old Michael Brown and a friend for walking in the street rather than on the sidewalk. What happened in the next few moments became the subject of a grand jury inquiry, but regardless, it ended with Wilson shooting and killing Brown, leaving his body in the street for hours as a crowd grew.

The Movement for Black Lives that exploded from there adopted Occupy's radically decentralized power structure, which would shape the course — or courses — that it took over the next several years. No single leadership structure guides the direction of the movement, which has enabled experimentation and a diversification of tactics at a mass scale.

"Black Lives Matter is the true heir to Occupy because it uses militant protest, digital media, and fluid and opaque leadership structures to challenge state power," wrote Arun Gupta, a journalist who covered both movements closely, in an essay on Occupy's legacy. "The difference is Black Lives Matter began by targeting state force rather than its economic power. Ironically, by early 2012 some Occupy groups were squandering popular capital on *fuck the police* marches that drew only the hardcore. Black Lives Matter has gone the other way, from a cry against the routine killing of unarmed Blacks to connecting police violence to economic violence."

The Movement for Black Lives applied pressure on Washington to advance criminal justice reform at the state and federal levels; led to the adoption of body cameras across the country; and pushed the Department of Justice to more aggressively investigate police departments, forcing consent decrees on Ferguson, Cleveland, Baltimore, and more than two-dozen cities around the country.

In August 2015, a year after Brown was killed, two Black Lives Matter protesters took over the stage at a Bernie Sanders rally in Seattle, demanding his radical campaign focus more on racial justice and police violence.

At the annual Netroots Nation gathering that summer, protesters had similarly disrupted a speech by former Baltimore Mayor Martin O'Malley, who blundered in how he handled it, intoning that "all lives matter." The disruption at the Sanders rally had its own poignancy, in that the women were deploying tactics mainstreamed by Occupy, which had

221

itself mainstreamed the very ideas Sanders was running on. The broad frame of Occupy focused on the clash between the 1 percent and the 99 percent, echoing Sanders' inequality refrain over the years.

The protesters also called for an end to the dominance of money in politics, for Medicare for All, a job or income guarantee, and reform of Wall Street. After the Seattle rally, there was a receptive audience on Sanders' staff, working on the inside to urge him to meet the protesters where they were. Indeed, Claire Sandberg had by then joined the campaign, having decided that the only way to stave off apocalyptic climate change was to somehow radically shift the political terrain.

In early 2016, Sioux protesters on the Standing Rock Indian Reservation tried to draw national attention to the potential final leg of the Keystone XL pipeline, which was planned to be built adjacent to their land — which, on top of its climate change implications, threatened local water sources. Hundreds of indigenous people built encampments, joined by thousands of outside allies, and tense confrontations galvanized opposition to the pipeline. Remarkably, on November 6, 2016, just ahead of the election, Obama rejected the Keystone XL application, citing its climate impacts. It was a win that had seemed nothing short of impossible just a few years earlier.

Donald Trump campaigned on his support for the pipeline, and issued an executive order moving it forward four days after being inaugurated, but resistance went on. In early 2017, a former Sanders organizer, Alexandria Ocasio-Cortez, took time off from bartending to join protesters for several weeks at the frigid encampment. She came home and decided to run for Congress, making a Green New Deal a central part of her platform.

At her June 2018 victory party at a pool hall in the Bronx, activists got the crowd's attention by shouting, "Mic check!" — which would be returned by the people there: "Mic check!" It was a call and response that had long been part of radical gatherings, but became popularized at Zuccotti Park.

Now Occupy was heading to Washington. "It was right after I left Standing Rock that I knew I had to do something," Ocasio-Cortez would later tell reporters outside the Capitol.

Ocasio-Cortez represents a new wave of activists who came of age during the Obama administration, but are also a bridge back to the Occupy moment. Whereas the generation ahead of her was shaped by the Iraq War, torture, the expansion of mass surveillance and other easily identifiable atrocities, Obama appeared to be an ally. While the Occupy generation organized to push him left, those who came later focused energy elsewhere. The big effort on college campuses, for instance, was divestment from fossil fuels, a question that was separated from electoral politics and Washington, but flowed from the new generation's more intimate relationship with brands.

If the bible of the '90s was Klein's book *No Logo*, an updated version for the millennial generation, and those who came after them, would be *Good Logo*, or *Better Logo*.

Varshini Prakash was heavily involved in the divestment movement while at Amherst College, where she graduated in 2015. "Most of the climate movement was just so — honestly, kind of apolitical. And maybe that's because a lot of us were politicized under Obama," she told me. "At some level we were like, *We don't need to take control of the government, because the government is — there's this benevolent figure in the government who likes us and cares about the issues we care about, or at least says he does, and all we need to do is convince him of the right course of action.* And that proved to be untrue."

Obama, facing an economic crisis and with his legislative focus on health care, didn't want to be pushed on climate. His team polled the issue, and found that "clean energy" was more popular than addressing climate change, an ultimately unsurprising finding. Who's against clean energy? So the White House called in major green groups for messaging orders: Climate change wasn't to be talked about. "What was communicated in the presentation was: *This is what you talk about, and don't talk about climate change,*" said Betsy Taylor,[190] who was in the meeting. "I took away an absolutely clear understanding that we should focus on clean energy jobs and the potential of a clean energy economy rather than the threat of climate change."

The well-funded coalition that failed to pass climate change legislation was called Clean Energy Works, and the bill Pelosi muscled through the House, but watched die without a vote in the Senate, was the American Clean Energy and Security Act. "When I learned that, literally my blood boiled," Prakash said. "I'm like, *It's kind of the greatest existential crisis we're ever going to face as humanity, and we don't have that much time to do something about it.*"

The focus on "clean" rather than the urgency of the moment allowed fossil fuels to co-opt the conversation. *Coal might be bad, but what about "clean" coal?* Natural gas companies ran slick ad campaigns to make the fuel seem environmentally friendly and natural; fracking exploded, turning the U.S. into one of the globe's largest producers of fossil fuels. Republicans weren't forced to come up with a solution to climate change, because they could just point to their support for nuclear power, natural

---

190   From *The Guardian*'s 2012 report: "Revealed: the day Obama chose a strategy of silence on climate change"

gas and clean coal technology. Emissions continued rising, as did temperatures, as the clock kept ticking. "Climate change, to our frustration, was never an issue that rung a bell with voters, particularly in the throes of coming out of an economic crisis," said David Axelrod, explaining why the administration sidestepped a major threat to humanity.[199] "But now we're a decade down the road, and the road is surrounded by floods and fires in a way that is becoming more and more visible."

The 2009 United Nations Climate Change Conference was held in Copenhagen that December, and inside the White House, there was serious debate over whether Obama should go. The president wanted to, but Rahm Emanuel was advising him that it was too risky. Health care was on the rocks, the tea party movement was in full swing, and there was a chance the summit would be a failure. If it failed, Emanuel argued, it could infect the rest of the agenda. It was quintessential Rahm, worried that any failure in anything meant total failure in everything, so the smart move was to just do nothing. Obama ultimately overruled his chief of staff and went to the summit,[200] where a modest accord was struck.

Prakash's family came from southern India, and the changing climate there informed her urgent approach to the issue. In 2015 and in 2017, monsoon season was devastating. "There were apartment buildings that were just lifted up and taken away in the storm. And there were one million people in refugee camps," she said, adding that her family put up 15 refugees in their own home. "When people say it's 30 years down the road, it's like, *No, that's when we're just screwed.* That's when I'm switching my career paths to — I don't know — evacuation rescue teams."

Prakash is a co-founder of the group Sunrise Movement, put together by young people frustrated by the complacency of the large environmental groups. Big Green did not roll out the red carpet; Prakash said leaders of the major groups already in the space called some of their funders and pressured them not to back them, a not uncommon practice in the cutthroat progressive advocacy space.

After she and her friends in the divestment movement graduated in 2015, they emerged into a world that frightened them. Sanders was on the rise in the U.S.; Momentum in the U.K. and Podemos in Spain were all making noise; Brexit and Trump were pushing from the opposite di-

199   2019 interview with the New York Times
200   The NSA, meanwhile, spied on delegates at the summit, a story I broke in collaboration with Laura Poitras and a Danish daily news outlet, Information. It was my first experience reporting on documents leaked by Edward Snowden. Poitras and Glenn Greenwald, both of whom would later become my colleagues, were working with news outlets across the globe at the time.

rection. But very little outside Keystone XL was happening in the U.S. on climate. And time was running out. She sat down with Sara Blazevic, another student leader in the divestment movement, and gathered ultimately a dozen people, who were similarly freaked out.[201] They took a full year to analyze what the movement had done wrong, what it had done right, and what their new group could do differently to change the political calculus and give humanity some chance of acting before it was too late. The Bill McKibben group, 350.org, that had been leading the Keystone XL protests, incubated the nascent group, agreeing with their analysis that something had to give.

"We didn't just look in the climate movement," Prakash said. "We spent a lot of time with the civil rights movement, at some level the women's suffrage movement, looking at the way in which you actually shift popular opinion on these issues and what it takes." The language of Occupy was particularly resonant. "I was like seven years old, but that's where it all began," she said, explaining how it informed their decision to start "mapping the 99 percent and the one percent onto, for example, the fossil fuel industry, in the form of fossil fuel executives and lobbyists."

Sunrise Movement launched in July 2017, with eight people, all under the age of 26.[202] Their goal was that by the end of 2019, Democratic presidential candidates would be talking about the Green New Deal. "We were like, *What would it look like to basically create the next campaign for young people that would go viral, that would shift the political weather, that would fracture the walls that had been built up around us about what we could do and couldn't do in the fossil fuel divestment movement*," Prakash said.

Sunrise took the divestment logic to politics, pressing politicians to pledge to refuse money from fossil fuel lobbyists or executives, and were one of the few green groups to endorse and campaign for Ocasio-Cortez in her challenge to Joe Crowley. The whole time, they had circled November 13, the Tuesday after the general election, as the day they planned to occupy the office of Nancy Pelosi and demand she commit to a federal green job guarantee. On the Friday before the planned occupation, Evan Weber, the group's political director, had a thought: *Let's reach out to Ocasio-Cortez and see if she'll do something around it, maybe a tweet or a statement of support.*

He called Zack Exley, whose group, New Consensus, was helping build

201   Including Guido Girgenti, Becca Rast, and Jonathan Smucker, all three of whom would go on to work for the Jess King congressional campaign in Lancaster, Pa. Rast would later become national field director for the Sanders campaign.
202   Prakash, Stephen O'Hanlon, Cathy Kunkel, Victoria Fernandez, Sara Blazevic, Evan Weber, Dyanna Jaye, and Will Lawrence.

the policy infrastructure for the Green New Deal, and asked if he could connect them with somebody high up in her campaign. Exley asked him what the demand was for the action, and Weber told him it was leaning toward a green jobs guarantee.

That's useless, Exley pointed out. *Nancy Pelosi is for green jobs. She won't commit to a "guarantee," but that part will get lost in the press coverage.* Weber agreed, but with a big sprawling movement, it wasn't easy to get everybody aligned around a big new idea. Exley knew Ocasio-Cortez had run on the Green New Deal. What if she proposed that as a demand? Weber thought that would work.

Exley added Chakrabarti to the call, which he said was the way the distributed team communicated during the Sanders campaign. "The revolution would not have happened without 'add call,'" Exley said.

Chakrabarti agreed: a Green New Deal was a better ask.

He took the idea to Ocasio-Cortez. She didn't want to support the protest with a tweet, she told him. She wanted to join it. And she wanted to add a demand for a select committee on a Green New Deal.

Prakash said that when word from Ocasio-Cortez came back, "We were like, *Are you guys sure?*"

"That call that Evan made," she said, "was maybe the most important call of our lifetimes."

Book Two

The Rise of a Movement

Sixteen

Orientation

Alexandria Ocasio-Cortez was running late. It was mid-morning on a Tuesday in November 2018, one week after the election, and freshman orientation had already started. But that wasn't where she was headed.

It was okay that she was missing orientation, reasoned Corbin Trent, the Justice Democrats co-founder who had worked on her campaign and was now her spokesman. "If I were gonna be an asshole, I'd say she's providing *them* with an orientation," he offered, not inaccurately. Trent and Alexandra Rojas, stationed outside the Cannon House Office Building, both waited for Ocasio-Cortez on Capitol Hill. More than 200 climate activists, many of them high school and college students organized by the Sunrise Movement, had been broken into two groups, waiting in the building's basement for the signal to march on the office of incoming Speaker Nancy Pelosi.

But Ocasio-Cortez, who had offered to join the protest at the last minute, was nowhere to be found. "She's looking in the mirror, saying, *Come on, Alex, you can do this!*" Trent quipped. I had been planning to take the week off of my day job to work on the book you're reading, but Trent had called the night before to ask if I wanted to tag along on their adventure to Pelosi's office.

Trent was joking about the dialogue with the mirror, but there was truth to it. Ocasio-Cortez would later tell "60 Minutes" she was so nervous that morning she wanted to vomit. Those nerves were understandable. She was entering Congress as the youngest woman ever elected

229

and, at least in modern memory, there had never been a freshman who had joined a sit-in in the office of the chamber's Speaker. The massive freshman Democratic class — 67 strong, with 42 women, the largest class since Watergate — had been put up in a Washington hotel.

Chakrabarti, Rojas, and Trent had co-founded the organization Justice Democrats, which began as an effort to elect hundreds of new progressive Democrats and converted itself, in the last months of Ocasio-Cortez's challenge to Joe Crowley, into a weapon wielded solely on her behalf. Now Chakrabarti would become her chief of staff, and Trent her communications director. Rojas would go from co-director of JD to its sole head.

She climbed into a cab with Saikat Chakrabarti, and called Trent.

"We're at First and D," Trent told Ocasio-Cortez.

She looked up and saw a street sign, and signaled to the driver to let them out.

"Are you sure?" he asked. They weren't sure, but they stepped out anyway.

Washington is broken into quadrants, and they had exited at First and D Southwest, rather than Southeast — a long corrective walk in heels. She and Chakrabarti trudged up Capitol Hill, past the interminably long Rayburn House Office Building, built in the 1950s during the post-war boom, when Congress had outgrown its square footage, to finally arrive at Pelosi's building.

I told Ocasio-Cortez what she already knew, that she was going to be told that she's no longer simply an activist, that occupying the Speaker's office just isn't how things are done around here. What would she say to those people? "The way things are done has not been getting us any results for the last 12 years," she told me as we approached the building, referring back to 2006, the last time Democrats had swept into power in Congress. "So we have to find new methods."

I asked if she had any plans to get arrested in Pelosi's office. "I'm open to the possibility," she said, but concluded, with a grin that seemed to recognize the extent of her new status, that it was highly unlikely. We ascended the marble stairs to Cannon and pulled open the double doors, where security was waiting. Members of Congress have the privilege of bypassing the x-ray machines manned by the Capitol Police. Ocasio-Cortez wasn't sworn in yet, nor did the cops seem to recognize who she was, and, for one of the last times on the Capitol campus, she took off her stylish black coat and ran it, along with her handbag, through the metal detector.

We cleared through and headed down the hallway. "Hey!" shouted an officer.

"Somebody's coffee," he said, pointing to Ocasio-Cortez's cup. She sheepishly reclaimed it and tossed it in the nearest trash can.

Now the group had to find Pelosi's office, and, after wandering, they stopped to ask a young woman who appeared to be an intern — and who promptly pointed them in the entirely wrong direction. I decided to pierce the journalistic veil in the interests of efficiency. ("It's right up these stairs," I told them.) At the top of the staircase, we rounded a corner and were met with the crashing bulbs of a crush of reporters and a bank of television cameras. The secret hadn't held; the office was occupied.

Ocasio-Cortez planted her feet for an impromptu press conference as I shuffled off to the side. A CNN correspondent got in the first question: *Did you have a hard time finding your way here?* Hard time would be an understatement. How Rojas, Trent, Chakrabarti, and Ocasio-Cortez came together in a unique moment in time to put a kink in the course of history is a story of grit, persistence, idealism, faith, and no small amount of luck. And it started with Bernie Sanders.

Ocasio-Cortez may have been the youngest woman sworn in to Congress, but she was still significantly older than Alexandra Rojas, who had graduated high school only five years earlier, in 2013. By that spring, the shadow presidential campaign was already under way. Barack Obama had been reelected the year before, and Hillary Clinton was busy making preparations to succeed him, with one candidate after another announcing that they wouldn't challenge her.

The contest was far from Rojas' mind. With unimpressive grades, she focused more on how to get a college education without being swallowed by the student debt crisis. Her mother had emigrated to the United States from Colombia at age 9, while her Peruvian father had been born in the states. Her parents, living in working-class East Hartford, Connecticut, had children young and worked constantly, and Rojas and her siblings were largely raised by their grandparents.

In fifth grade, her father got a good job in Glastonbury, a wealthy, white, tony village that was seven miles but a world away from East Hartford. She had visited family in Peru regularly growing up, but that summer, when she went to Lima, the contrast was that much starker. "Lima is one of the most dangerous, dirtiest cities — and still beautiful. I love it," she said of a visit to her aunt's home. "When I showed up they had no roof. It was like a broken building and it just had a tarp over, like a literal tarp instead of a roof."

She also visited Cusco, where her family lived as subsistence farmers. She came home with almost nothing, having given everything she had to relatives.

"As a teen, I got super angry. Like, I couldn't go to the malls, couldn't go anywhere because I was just, like, *God, people are complaining about their lunch food*," she said, contrasting the upper-class life she was now a part of with what her family in South America, and her friends back in East Hartford, were living through. "In Colombia, my mom's side of the family is pretty much all dead because of a mix of the cartels, poverty, and just diseases over there. So I didn't really know it at the time, but it just pissed me off a lot. And I always paid attention to politics, but I never thought that I could get involved at all."

Social movements outside of electoral politics, though, were a way in. The first protest she went to in high school was for Black Lives Matter in the wake of a police shooting. As she thought about college, she learned that California allowed people who lived in the state for a year and a day to get in-state tuition. She saved money from her job at McDonald's and, before she'd even officially graduated, went west to plant her residency roots. She worked multiple minimum wage jobs to survive the next year, and enrolled in Orange Coast College, a public community college that is a top feeder to UC schools such as UCLA and Berkeley.

She became active in student government and organized against an effort to slash programs aimed at non-traditional students, such as one that offered classes at eight in the morning or after-work hours. But as the time to transfer drew near, California, to save itself money, tweaked its eligibility rules in a way that meant she could no longer get in-state tuition.

It was around that time, in May 2015, she was sitting in a coffee shop when her friend who had recruited her to student government, Lynn Hua, sent her a YouTube clip that would change her life. Rojas watched a granddad with wild hair and a rumpled suit, set against the backdrop of Lake Champlain, declare a revolution.

"Today, with your support and the support of millions of people throughout this country, we begin a political revolution to transform our country economically, politically, socially, and environmentally," Sanders said. "My fellow Americans: This country faces more serious problems today than at any time since the Great Depression and, if you include the planetary crisis of climate change, it may well be that the challenges we face now are direr than any time in our modern history."

This was not how politicians were expected to talk, Rojas knew. She gazed at the scholarship applications she'd been contemplating and decided to change course. "I listened to it and I just fell in love and I was just like, *Oh my God, I've got to do everything*," she recalled. "I started working with [Hua] and two other kids[203] just in our volunteer time, organizing all the

203   Cole Edwards and Kyle Machado, both of whom also have had rapid rises

community colleges, because they're a totally untapped resource of all these working-class people."

She began rallying community college students across Orange County behind the Sanders banner — and, in particular, students, with really diverse backgrounds who people usually ignore. "We did a lot of voter registration and hosting barnstorms before we knew that that's what they were," she said.

Bernie Sanders is famously cheap. It's part of his curmudgeonly grandfather thing, and, like the rest of his persona, it's real. Throughout his career, he resisted hiring any more campaign staff than absolutely necessary, and oftentimes less than that. Part of it was philosophical: Sanders for decades believed that staff were inherently corrupting of a politician, more likely to push him toward party orthodoxy and undermine the iconoclastic independence he had nurtured.

After the 2016 campaign, when he found himself at the center of a movement, he shed some of that philosophical reluctance — bringing on Matt Duss as a foreign policy adviser in his Senate office was a big step, as was hiring Ari Rabin-Havt as deputy chief of staff — but the penchant for parsimony remained.

Jeff Weaver, who left Sanders' office in 2009 to run a comic book store, came out of retirement, but few others joined the official campaign. Nobody who wanted a future career in Democratic Party politics was looking to join the Sanders campaign, as the Clintons had earned their reputation for score-settling and list-keeping. Even joining what was seen as a hopeless, hapless challenge to the Clintons was considered a betrayal; so for fundraising, Sanders turned to Revolution Messaging, a proudly leftist consulting firm that wasn't hunting for establishment business.

When Sanders first met with his digital fundraising team, they estimated they could raise about $15 million. That meant costs for staff and other overhead — like the digital organizing and field team — would need to be kept down. When his low-key Senate announcement — in the middle of the day, weeks before the Lake Champlain one — resulted in an eye-popping one million dollars in 24 hours, it became clear that more was possible. But Sanders and Weaver never believed it, convinced the small-dollar spigot would run dry at any moment. "When you're in a campaign, you don't know: is this huge fountain of small-dollar

---

in progressive politics. Machado joined Our Revolution. During the midterms, Edwards was Sanders' distributed organizing director, and in 2019 he was given that role for the presidential campaign.

money going to continue, or is it going to dissipate?" Claire Sandberg[204] explained. "There's a reticence to throw lots of staff and resources at things that are not proven."

One of Sanders' greatest assets has been the 40 to 50 years he spent outside the party establishment, offering the same, consistent critique of an economic and political system rigged for millionaires and billionaires. But those decades also left scars. Like a dog that was brought up in an abusive home, it was hard for Sanders to recognize that a new family was ready to take him in and love him.

Sandberg, however, could see it coming, and she wanted to be part of it. After her stunningly successful campaign to ban fracking in New York state, she sensed that climate politics were going to be held hostage by the presidential campaign. "Just looking at the landscape of what was going to be possible in the next year, it was clear to me that [Obama] wasn't going to do anything that was going to make Hillary Clinton look bad," she told me. "He wasn't going to go too far out in front of her and he already knew what he was doing on climate — Clean Power Plan, Paris, Keystone XL — and that anything else, he wasn't going to do, and that the best way to move the conversation on climate was going to be to influence Democratic primary."

Sandberg reached out to everybody she knew who might have some tangential connection to the small circle of Sanders advisers, and eventually connected with Zack Exley, who had been talking to the campaign about joining. The pair pitched themselves as a package deal, and Weaver bit. Exley was brought on as a senior adviser and Sandberg was made director of digital organizing. Their immediate task was to make good on the campaign's promise to host thousands of simultaneous watch parties on July 29 to demonstrate the campaign's breadth and depth of support. Exley and Sandberg quickly learned there'd be no cavalry coming to support the effort. "Bernie is a loner," Exley told me. "He does his own thing. But he also won't allow someone else to run an organization. He was scrutinizing every hire during the campaign and agonizing over it. The CFO was miserable; Bernie wouldn't approve anything."

---

204   Sandberg's early years of activism are covered in Book 1, Chapter 13. In 2017 she co-founded #AllOfUs with Waleed Shahid, who went on to become Ocasio-Cortez's first staffer. In 2019, she re-joined the Sanders campaign as its head of digital organizing. Her understanding of Sanders' potency as a candidate came from her feel for the energy of the moment. "People really thought that Martin O'Malley was going to be the kind of slightly more progressive choice, but it was clear to me early on that, having seen the speech, and knowing that he had the biggest email list of any senator, I thought, in a post-Occupy moment, no way that he's going to just get 5 percent," she reasoned.

It was fortuitous, because it pushed the digital team away from reliance on paid campaign staff and toward volunteers, of which there were thousands banging on the doors. Sandberg and Exley set about empowering thousands of people to host events, and built a volunteer help desk to handle thousands of incoming inquiries. That put them in conflict with the campaign leadership, which was nervous about the decentralized nature of the operation. Two days before the scheduled mass of events, a helpdesk volunteer sent a loosely organized answer to a volunteer host, who knew how to get ahold of Weaver, and forwarded it to him. Weaver forwarded it to Kenneth Pennington, the campaign's digital director, who oversaw the distributed operation at the time, as well as Sandberg, Exley, and a few others, saying that he was "very skeptical about any organizing program, the basis of which is folks should do whatever comes to mind."

On a call that night, Pennington explained that volunteers on the help desk had successfully responded to some 5,000 emails already, and some hiccups were inevitable. Sanders joined the call and when the team shared RSVP numbers — tens of thousands of people planning to attend more than 2,500 events — he was blown away. If that type of scale meant a few stray emails, so be it.

On July 29, more than one hundred thousand people gathered across the country to watch a sweating Sanders give a shortened version of his stump speech. "Bernie Sanders alone as president of these United States is not going to solve all these problems," Sanders said, the mirror version of the message that Donald Trump would later deliver. "The only way we take on the Koch brothers and take on the billionaire class, and people who have unbelievable money and power, the only way we can do that is when we put together a strong grassroots movement of millions and millions of people. And that is what I mean by political revolution, and that is what you are involved in today."

The Sanders campaign would revolutionize political campaigning in two different ways. The first has become synonymous with his campaign, the hundreds of thousands of donors who chipped in $27 at a time so that Sanders could take on the millionaires and the billionaires. Though it was done at eye-popping scale — more than $200 million was raised — it had descended directly from the Howard Dean campaign of 2003 and '04.

The second bequest the Deaniacs left for the Sanders campaign is less well understood, but no less important. In 2003, the Dean campaign pioneered the use of MeetUps to bring supporters together, though never quite connected the dots to make them more than a symbolic part of the operation. Exley had been a key player on the campaign, and wanted another shot at making the most of MeetUps, even if the once innovative platform of MeetUp.com had largely faded from politics.

The result would come to be called a barnstorm, and it has transformative potential for grassroots organizing for progressive candidates and has even been exported, by Sandberg, to Spain and the UK, where both Podemos and Momentum, respectively, implemented it with her guidance.

The barnstorm was pulled off in an appropriately anarchic way. Sanders' fundraising model was different than a typical high-dollar, super PAC–backed campaign, but otherwise the campaign was fairly traditional, with a focus on television ads and field staff dropped in the first four states: Iowa, New Hampshire, South Carolina, and Nevada. Jeff Weaver, the campaign manager, later said that if he had it to do over again he'd have spent more on TV.

Sandberg recalled a meeting with a leader of the field program, who didn't end up sticking around, as indicative of how traditional campaigners viewed what they were trying to do. "I remember him saying to us, *Listen, you guys, you're the dancing dog. Just be happy that the dog dances. Don't try to get it to do anything else*," she said. "He meant that the fact that you have this system where people on their own can go every week... with some friends and do a chalk-the-block-for-Bernie or do a honk-and-wave, a table at a farmer's market, is in and of itself an accomplishment, and that is the best that you can achieve, is having people where there are no staff basically just keep themselves busy with stuff that everybody knows is not actually valuable work."

Exley, with Becky Bond, who later joined the Sanders campaign, would go on to write a book about distributed organizing, which they called "big organizing." In essence, it requires trusting that a campaign's supporters can be more than dancing dogs, and can do big things for a campaign, unlocking an explosive amount of activism. To get people fired up enough to do big things, however, requires having either a bold and inspiring vision, or a horrifying alternative that pushes people to action. But it also meant getting the mechanics right. That's where the barnstorms came in. On one level, they're as old as organizing itself, and begin by assembling a group of supporters in a room and getting them fired up, then asking them to take action that will benefit the campaign.

Barnstorms intersect technology and face-to-face organizing. Email is a good way to raise money, and with a big enough list, it can effectively fill a room full of people for an event. But it's not very good at getting people to take any action beyond that, such as phone-banking or door-knocking.

One of the early versions of a Sanders barnstorm was supposed to be held in Massachusetts, with campaign staff planning to train volunteers to use VAN, the massive Democratic database of voters. It fell apart before it even began, as volunteers bickered with each other and the campaign couldn't explain what exactly it was trying to do. That was one of the first lessons, that the event needed to have a discrete, short-term goal, otherwise competing visions quickly descended into acrimony and chaos.

In October, Exley set out on a barnstorm tour of Tennessee with a new experiment: to see if the gatherings could be used to create an endless number of new events. He picked Tennessee because Corbin Trent, a new member of the digital team, had already done much of the organizing work there on his own.

In 2000, when Trent was 20, he inherited two fading manufacturing companies in Morristown, Tennessee, from his grandfather, B.C. Trent. "I ran the metalworking business into the ground," he said, citing his decision to upgrade equipment and, against objections, computerize the factory. "Maybe the old fuckers knew what they were doing."

The woodworking business lasted longer. But the company, which made component parts for other furniture makers — they'd make the curved back of a bar stool, for instance — suffered as its buyers went out of business or out of the country one by one. Trent understood that he was witnessing the knock-on effect of NAFTA, the free trade deal implemented in 1995 under Bill Clinton, and CAFTA, the 2005 version that extended the regime further south.

The woodworking firm went under in 2007 and Trent went to culinary school. But the life of a high-end chef means catering to rich people, and seeing it up close was too much. He was cooking at Restaurant North in tony Armonk, New York, a four-time James Beard-nominated restaurant where lunch tabs would routinely run into the five figures.

The lunch that did it for him cost roughly $18,000, which in itself wasn't out of the ordinary. It was the wine they ordered, a bottle of Romanée-Conti, priced at around $10,000, grown by a grandfather and a grandson on a small plot of land in France.[205] Trent had been reading about the wine, known as one of the best and most expensive in the world, and felt privileged just to be able to pour it. When the diners left, he noticed unfinished glasses and a bottle that was still half full. He did what any sensible person would do: poured the wine back in the bottle, corked it, and quit. "I decided right there I'm not spending my time, talent or energy making these people's lives any better," he said.

---

205   The winery is situated in a region of France that is trademarked, like Bordeaux. In French, it's known as an *appellation d'origine contrôlée* — abbreviated internationally as AOC.

Ryan Grim

So Trent moved back to Tennessee and launched a successful food truck, Crazy Good Burgers. That became a second truck, and when that one burned down, he pulled off an internet fundraiser to get it going again. Then came a third truck.

When Sanders jumped into the race, Trent dropped everything, selling the food truck business and organizing Tennesseans for Bernie. He reached out to Zack Exley — by guessing at every iteration of his email — asking if it was possible to get Sanders to come to northeast Tennessee if he could promise 5,000 people would show up. The answer was, *No, it was not*, but Exley was intrigued at the organizing under way, and they stayed in touch.

Exley put Trent to work, first compiling a 50-state guide to voter registration, then doing calls with state Sanders chapters to help them with organizing logistics. Eventually, Trent was brought on officially as staff.

"You have to remember in the very beginning, it was very hard for the Bernie campaign to hire pros," Bond said, "because it was just very clear that you'd be totally blackballed, not just from a White House or a federal agency job, but from any of the Democratic-aligned institutions. Even vendors who weren't employed by the Clinton campaign didn't want to work for the Bernie campaign, because they were worried about not getting business in the future. The professionals that joined were really true believers, like me and Zack, and then we really had to fill out the ranks from the super volunteers who'd never worked in politics before."

Again, it came with an upside, as folks like Corbin Trent were willing to try things that campaign veterans would have laughed off the whiteboard. At each event, Trent and Exley tried to figure out why the barnstorms just weren't clicking. Toward the end of each gathering, they would ask who there was willing to host an event at their house — a phone bank, for instance — and often 10 to 20 percent of the crowd would volunteer.

The first part of the experiment had proved a success — events were being created. But the crucial second part wasn't there. The campaign would email people to nudge them to go to the events that had been planned, but almost nobody would show up.

Throughout October, as Iowa and New Hampshire elections were fast approaching, Trent and Exley continued iterating at barnstorms. A new VAN training was organized in Nashville in November to teach hundreds of volunteers how to use the sophisticated software to create VAN accounts, to "cut turf" — sorting out what doors to knock on or what numbers to call — and build lists of voters. At the end of it, Trent asked Exley what the goal of the gathering had been. Exley told him it was to

238

get the volunteers hosting phone banks and making calls. "How did this help us get to that?" Trent asked, to which there was no good answer, so it was back to the drawing board.

The digital team had found no clear way to convert the mass of volunteers into actual voter contacts — the type of thing needed to win an election. The email list was mostly dedicated to fundraising, and the times they had used it to try to recruit phone bank hosts had mostly been duds. Now that they had a way of finding hosts, they couldn't get the guests to show up. Exley worried somebody in the campaign would compare their budget to their productivity in terms of voter contacts and shut the whole thing down.

They gathered for a retreat in Seattle in the middle of December to sort it out, and Sandberg suggested connecting the hosts and attendees right there at the event. Previous efforts had failed, including in Little Rock that fall. One of them, the most intuitive, had sorted people by neighborhood. "That turned out to be complicated because the way people live their lives is they might want to volunteer near where they work, or where their kids go to school, or a cool neighborhood I can hang out in, or where they think the people who will attend would be cooler," Becky Bond told me.

The logistics were daunting. Hundreds of people showed up at the barnstorms; how could they organize dozens of events in real time? They experimented with different approaches, but the one that landed was this: after people were asked who would host an event, they'd be told to come to the front or stand off to the side. Now they were trapped, and their commitment was real. Then the audience would be told, *Look, these people have committed to hosting an event — you have to commit to go and bring something.*

The first attempt was made by Trent at a barnstorm in Asheville, North Carolina, in January. There were still kinks to work out. They tried name tags and big signs people would hold up, before hitting on an altar call and a simple sheet of paper for folks to sign. "We did all this complicated, convoluted shit, when the answer is actually just a piece of paper with the host's name and with blocks for people to sign up," Trent said.

The volunteer hosts would be lined up and given one or two sentences to sell their event to the audience, without being allowed to hold the mic. Then the audience would be told to find the host of the event they planned to attend and sort out details. It was chaos, and a massive sorting would begin, but people would plan to meet, say, next Saturday at 2:00. One person would offer to bring chips, and another would bring dip. "Tammy is gonna host an event. You get people to walk up to Tammy. There's a sort of social contract made between them. Now they're ditching out on Tammy [if they don't show up]. That social contract became super powerful," Trent explained. "You looked someone in the eye and told them you were bringing dip. If you don't show up, there's chips and no dip. So you go, whether you want to or not."

In Orange County, Rojas attended a watch party on July 29 and began organizing her own events through the summer and fall. As barnstorms started getting off the ground, Exley asked a volunteer-turned-staffer from Orange County, Ceci Hall, to organize a dozen in California. She knew Rojas and the rest of the OCC crew from Millennials for Bernie and asked them if they'd do one. "We were like, *Oh my God, this is so crazy*," said Rojas. "*National Bernie staff coming down!*"

Believing the potential of the Sanders campaign lay in energizing and registering young people, Exley flew out to Orange County in early November. "The people that [typically] stood out at barnstorms were the people who fit the profile, more often than not, of the classic MoveOn/ Indivisible member — a 53-year-old white woman to be precise. But when I got to Santa Ana, there was this really well-organized group of college students, none of whom, or maybe one of whom, were white," Exley recalled. "It was these student leaders who took their student leadership skills and built something."

Rojas and Exley stayed in touch. "I just kept bugging the shit out of the campaign," she told me. "I was like, *I'll intern, I'll do whatever*."

When campaign leadership told him he could hire some interns, he knew who to give the spots to: Rojas, Lynn Hua, Cole Edwards, and Kyle Machado. The catch was they had to move to Burlington. "They were all working-class people with no money in the bank; it was really hard for them to go," said Exley. The four of them piled into Cole Edwards' white Nissan Murano, with luggage on the roof and hanging off the back.

Rojas didn't last long as an intern; she finagled her way onto the digital team, where she helped her new boss Sandberg with the texts-for-Bernie program and handled logistics for the barnstorms. "We started seeing a lot of the results coming in from these barnstorms, and it's like, *holy fuck, we're creating* way *more voter contact events through this way than we are any other way*," she said. Rojas and Lynn Hua expanded the barnstorming model to allow volunteers to run them. The campaign hosted roughly 1,000 barnstorms by the end of it, and some 650 were run by volunteers.[206] "Both of them were instrumental in turning barnstorms into something hundreds of volunteers could do," said Ceci Hall of Rojas and Hua.

The final innovation that made it all workable came from Chakrabarti, himself an unusual figure on the Sanders team. After graduating from

---

206   The stat comes from *Rules for Revolutionaries,* by Exley and Bond.

Harvard in 2007 with a computer science degree, Chakrabarti briefly worked for a hedge fund, then became the founding engineer for Stripe — the fifth employee of a payment processor now valued at some $20 billion. When the Sanders campaign launched, he queried his network to find a connection, and like all the others, that turned out to be super-connector Zack Exley. Exley brought him on board.[207]

Both Bond and Exley, friends since 2000, had tech backgrounds that allowed them to work smoothly with engineers. Bond had run the political organizing arm of an unusual progressive phone company, San Francisco–based CREDO, and Exley had run the political organizing arm of the global IT consultancy firm ThoughtWorks, where he worked with Aaron Swartz, a legendary programmer and activist.

"Zack and I, we both came out of digital and tech even though we really focus on organizing," Bond said. "We both realized that Saikat" — pronounced shoy-cot — "couldn't just contribute as a software development developer. Saikat started off doing a bunch of tech stuff, but slowly we pulled him in and made sure that a bunch of his portfolio was actually helping us both do and manage the organizing work." Chakrabarti put together a process that easily allowed organizers to snap a photo of the handwritten sheets, and upload that to the campaign website, where other volunteers would enter it in so that events could be facilitated and tracked.

The plane was finally ready to take off — but the campaign was at the beginning of the end. "We only built the runway, like, right before we ran out of it," said Sandberg. "We didn't even hire most of our distributed team until January 2016, and we'd only hit a million calls, out of the 85 million that we ended up making, by Iowa."

Sanders stunned the political world by effectively tying Clinton in Iowa in late January. As the result of a handful of literal coin tosses, Clinton emerged the winner, taking 23 delegates to Sanders' 21. All six Iowa superdelegates also went for her. But Clinton didn't have just a 29–21 lead. Before any votes had been counted, the Associated Press had

---

207   Throughout 2017 and 2018, documentary filmmaker Rachel Lears followed a handful of Justice Democrat candidates, Alexandria Ocasio-Cortez among them. In the film that resulted, Knock Down the House, there's a scene of a campaign rally in April in the Bronx. Zack Exley, Corbin Trent, and Chakrabarti are sitting against the wall, as Ocasio-Cortez pumps up the crowd of about a hundred. It's a barnstorm. "Who's willing to lead an event and have a couple friends over, or any one of the things we talked about?" Ocasio-Cortez asks. "Raise your hand." About 10 hands go up. "Now, if you just raised your hand, I want you to stand up," she says. The volunteers, as they rise, appear to realize they've been hooked. "Got 'em," she quips.

interviewed superdelegates and found her with commitments from 359 of them, to just eight for Sanders. That meant the press would report Clinton's overall delegate lead as something like 388 to 29, which looked insurmountable, making Sanders' unlikely bid appear that much more daunting.

In early February, Sanders crushed Clinton in New Hampshire, 60 to 38, winning the pledged delegate count 15-9. But adding in super-delegates, Sanders, even with such a lopsided win, carried the state by only 16-15. The Sanders campaign hadn't assigned anybody to the job of lobbying superdelegates until it hired Nick Brana[208] in October 2015, by which point Clinton had locked most of them up. Clinton carried the Nevada caucuses by five points on February 19. Days later, she blew him out in South Carolina, winning by nearly 50 points and posting a monster delegate lead. After the first four contests, the race moved to Super Tuesday in March. "All of the people from those states kind of fanned out to the other states with the expectation that it would be like New Hampshire or Iowa, in California, when volunteers had already hosted hundreds or thousands of events," Sandberg said.

That set up a conflict between the traditional campaign, which was running headlong into the radical distributed experiment that was now under way. In some states, the field team worked collaboratively with the distributed team — often because Sandberg had hired that state's director — but in others they effectively kicked the Sandberg-Exley-Bond operation out. In one state, the campaign shut down a volunteer-organized phone bank because the campaign was having a ribbon-cutting on its first official field office, and didn't want competition.

While Sanders continued winning key states, like Colorado, Wisconsin, Indiana, and a big upset in Michigan, the deficit was too much to make up, even as he battled through June and into the convention. And by April 2016, it was becoming apparent that the primary was no longer winnable, with a stake driven into it by a bad loss in New York. The only path Sanders had to the nomination was to convince Clinton-backing superdelegates to switch sides, as unlikely an event as is conceivable. Exley, Rojas, Trent, and Chakrabarti figured a way to channel the energy that had gone into the Sanders campaign. They teamed up with Isra Allison, and the notion they hit on was to run Bernie-style populists everywhere around the country. And they really meant everywhere — even

---

208   That hopeless job led to a role coordinating with the party for the convention. "I was on a DNC call with state chairs and DNC members and person after person in the party leadership, their biggest concern leading up to the convention was how the Bernie delegates were going to make a negative impression on the corporate sponsors," he said.

in Republican districts.

The underlying rationale was that many of Sanders' big ideas, like Medicare for All, actually polled well among Republicans, and that candidates who adopted that message could win voters in either party's primary. They called the new organization Brand New Congress: they wanted 435 brand new members.

Sandberg, for her part, stayed until the bitter end, turning off the campaign lights, and then joining a new group, Our Revolution, that Sanders set up to carry the political revolution forward. Sandberg's condition for joining was simple: Jeff Weaver could not run it. Weaver was in sync with Sanders when it came to the political revolution, but the question of how to wage it was different. The activists who were set to run Our Revolution wanted a distributed, bottom-up organization, while Weaver favored a more traditional model for an outside group — funded by billionaires and focusing heavily on TV.

Sanders promised that Weaver wouldn't head it, and made his former body man — the staffer who follows a politician around, making sure he has everything he needs — Shannon Jackson, the executive director.

His parsimony hadn't let up. On a conference call, Sanders asked how many people the group was by then employing. Jackson knew that whatever figure he gave Sanders would cause an aneurysm, so he lowballed it a bit. "Thirteen," Jackson fibbed, hoping to move on. His instinct was right. *What on earth*, Sanders demanded, *are 13 people doing all day?*

If Sanders thought Our Revolution was too big, he wouldn't have to worry for long. Jane Sanders decided to install Weaver as president, pushing to make OR a 501(c)4 which could take unlimited, dark money contributions, which would also mean it couldn't work directly with campaigns. It was the opposite of what the OR staffers thought they had signed up for.

Kenneth Pennington and Sandberg gave Jane Sanders an ultimatum: Weaver or us. Sanders went with Weaver, and a majority of Our Revolution went for the door. The group planned to leave quietly, not wanting to damage Bernie's reputation, but Weaver worried they were going to go to the press with the story, so he leaked it first. Sandberg hit back. "It's about both the fundraising and the spending: Jeff would like to take big money from rich people including billionaires and spend it on ads," Sandberg told Politico. "That's the opposite of what this campaign and this movement are supposed to be about, and after being very firm and raising alarm the staff felt that we had no choice but to quit."[209]

While Our Revolution splintered, Brand New Congress struggled to

---

209   Several of those who left, including Pennington and Hector Sigala, later joined Beto O'Rourke, as did Becky Bond and Zack Malitz. Malitz and Bond went

get its concept off the ground. After the November 2016 election, Cenk Uygur, the founder and head of the progressive news network The Young Turks,[210] reached out and said he wanted to find a way to support the group's efforts — but the thing about running Republican candidates seemed silly. Uygur told the outfit that TYT viewers would no doubt support the Democratic challengers, but they'd have no interest in getting bogged down in Republican primaries. Out of that conversation, Brand New Congress agreed to carve out a separate group, called Justice Democrats, that Uygur could support.

Young Turks fans came through with $2 and a half million in small donor contributions, which not only funded the operation, but built a list of activists Justice Dems could call on down the road for volunteer support or money for candidates. For months, though, the two groups were effectively one, with JD simply branded separately, and the money raised was legally transferred to Brand New Congress.

Uygur had been on to something with his theory on Republican primaries. Recruiting viable Bernie-style candidates to run in those races was proving close to impossible. "It was a ridiculous idea," Trent acknowledged to me, in the characteristic straight talk that would later make him well-liked by Capitol Hill reporters when he became Ocasio-Cortez's communications director.

Rojas, Chakrabarti, and Trent brought the matter to a head over the summer of 2017. The result was a full split, with Justice Democrats breaking away from BNC and becoming a genuinely independent organization. Sandberg, meanwhile, had spent much of the winter and spring after the 2016 election, like many other people, getting arrested on Capitol Hill, and pressuring Democrats to stiffen their resolve. She and Waleed Shahid founded a group called All Of Us, and their visit to Sen. Tom Carper's office on December 1 was typical of the genre, with about a dozen activists occupying his lobby until he came out to speak. When he did, they issued a list of demands, which included his opposing Trump every step of the way, and also stepping aside as head of the Committee on Environment and Public Works to make way for Jeff Merkley, a progressive senator.

"Thank you for those demands. I do not commit," Carper told them. "Donald Trump is gonna be our president, at least for a while. We should try to work with him. Where we can work with his administration, we

---

on to run O'Rourke's field operation in his Texas Senate run, further innovating barnstorms to allow volunteer-run offices to launch door-knocking canvasses. Sandberg, with an assurance from Sanders that Weaver would not be running the 2020 campaign, is back on board his presidential campaign.

210   I'm an on-air contributor to the network.

will. Where we don't agree with him, we'll fight like hell." They were promptly arrested.

Getting arrested day after day gets old fast, however, and Shahid reached out to Justice Democrats about folding his organization into theirs. Sandberg went to Spain and brought the barnstorming model. Her next stop was the UK to advise the Corbyn camp on how to get the most out of the energy behind Britain's version of Sanders.

That same month, Ocasio-Cortez cobbled together the money to travel to the Standing Rock Indian Reservation in North Dakota and join the protest against the Keystone XL Pipeline. The Young Turks, which Ocasio-Cortez watched frequently, had covered the protests closely. Before she left, her younger brother Gabriel got her permission to submit her name to Brand New Congress as a potential primary challenger to Crowley. In frigid temperatures, after watching the commitment of the indigenous protesters battling a pipeline company that seemed ripped from the pages of Howard Zinn, she resolved to ramp up her own commitment to the political revolution. When she returned to the Bronx, she got a call from Isra Allison, a top official at Brand New Congress. A few more video calls led to a dinner in the Bronx with Zack Exley and Saikat Chakrabarti. She was in.

Seventeen

Uncorked

On the morning of November 9, 2016, millions of Americans woke up in a fog. In New Holland, Pennsylvania, Annie Weaver, a teacher, stopped at the Wawa on her way to school and couldn't look anybody in the eye.

Brandi Calvert, a real estate agent in Wichita, Kansas, got out of bed only because she had to take her own boy to school. Before heading out, she told him what had happened, but he refused to believe her.

"I had to tell him that Donald Trump won the election, and I just remember feeling like the words coming out of my mouth were not real life," she said. "Even my 11-year-old was floored and couldn't believe it."

I walked my own daughter to school that morning in Washington, D.C., and went inside for her kindergarten biweekly open house. A third-grader had drawn the assignment of reading the day's news over the PA system, and he began with a brief history of the expansion of voting rights. He then ventured into more recent events: "In 2008, Barack Obama was the first African American elected president. This year, in 2016, Hillary Clinton was the first female president — nominee. In a surprising election, she was defeated by Donald Trump," he said. "Stop by Room 308 to see our timeline. Have a great day."

My daughter, with no propaganda on my part, had very much been "rooting for the girl to win" and found Trump to be a miscreant and a bully. She stood unusually silent, as her teacher, clad in black jeans and an olive green hijab, turned her face to hide her tears. There was nothing to say that day — nothing that could be said — to make right the raw fact that, after a hate-filled, vitriolic campaign, enough people in the United States had voted for Donald Trump to make him our 45th president.

Back in Wichita, Calvert drove home. "I did what a large portion of Americans did that morning," she recalled. "I went home and I called my mom, and sat on the phone, and went through the emotions of crying and being angry — and disbelief and surely it was a mistake and will be corrected. I'm still waiting for that to happen."

Up until the 2016 election, Calvert didn't really get involved in national politics. She dutifully voted in presidential cycles and had broadly liberal politics, but wasn't affiliated with either party. Since Calvert, then 36, was a little girl, she had admired Hillary Clinton, and was among the portion of the electorate who backed her enthusiastically, but she hadn't thrown herself into the effort to make her president. Like Weaver and millions of others, she felt a sense of personal responsibility — a sharp guilt — for what had happened on her watch.

As she reflected on what she could have done to help stop Trump, but hadn't, she heard about the Women's March in Washington and started looking into ways to make the trip happen. Then she had a better idea. "If I went to Washington it would be an incredible experience, but it wouldn't change anything here," she told me. "In Kansas, unfortunately and somewhat fortunately, we already know what America is in for under the Trump administration" — a reference to the conservative domination of state government. "So I thought maybe in this very dark situation, we could be ahead of the curve. I decided I was going to try to organize a Women's March by myself."

That spark in Calvert was just one of millions lit by the election of President Donald Trump. And the new political force Trump uncorked could become the most lasting legacy of his presidency.

That the American people are disengaged from politics is a commonly held belief, and one that has plenty of evidence over the years to back it up. Turnout for midterm and special elections has historically been anemic. Most people can't name their member of Congress, let alone who represents them in the state legislature. Supreme Court Justice pop quiz? Forget about it.

Broaden the definition of politics just slightly, however, and the American people are deeply involved, and deeply politically engaged. If politics is thought of as engaging with a local or national community toward a specific goal, no country on earth might possess a more engaged citizenry. It was, indeed, that very thing that blew away Alexis de Tocqueville in the 1830s when he traveled the United States and did the research that resulted in his defining treatise, *Democracy in America*.

"Americans of all ages, all stations in life, and all types of dispositions are forever forming associations," he wrote in one of his most famous passages. "They have not only commercial and manufacturing companies, in which all take part, but associations of a thousand other kinds, religious, moral, serious, futile, general or restricted, enormous or diminutive. The Americans make associations to give entertainments, to found seminaries, to build inns, to construct churches, to diffuse books, to send missionaries to the antipodes; in this manner they found hospitals, prisons, and schools."

An aristocrat, Tocqueville was stunned at the organizing capacity of everyday Americans. "I met with several kinds of associations in America of which I confess I had no previous notion," he wrote, "and I have often admired the extreme skill with which the inhabitants of the United States succeed in proposing a common object for the exertions of a great many men and in inducing them voluntarily to pursue it."[211]

In reporting on the resistance to Trump, I spoke, emailed, or texted with hundreds of women who were launched into activism by Trump's election, and a common thread that emerged was one that would not have surprised Tocqueville: they were already organizers — they just didn't think of themselves that way.

That was the case with Calvert. "I've always been very involved in [my son's] school, a small town school right outside of Wichita — did a lot of organizing for class field trips or parties, but nothing political up until the election," she said.

Lauren Park, for instance, would describe her pre-2017 community engagement as non-political. She fundraised for local schools and joined the board of an autism society after her son's diagnosis. For six years, she was on the board of the Boulder Valley Women's Health Center. Mindy Hogue Miller's sister, Ilyse Hogue, had been a longtime political activist, but Mindy, a physical therapist, had never considered herself particularly political. She volunteered for a variety of nonprofits, but was fine to leave the politics to Ilyse and the others who were at it full-time. Maria Gallagher was a college student at Northeastern in Boston and was heavily involved in mentoring. The night Trump won was the first time she protested. She reached out to some fellow mentors that she knew were more political than her, and joined them in a protest march

---

211   It was this same free association and organizing — the essence of democracy — that made none other than Karl Marx an admirer, in many ways, of the political system of the United States. He saw the war to abolish slavery as something of a revolution, and the radical period after the war, Reconstruction, was in many ways genuinely revolutionary.

through the city. Weaver, in New Holland, Pennsylvania, had long been active in her church, and had even done missionary work in Japan. But she, too, never saw any of that as political.

Gallagher, Hogue Miller, Park, Weaver, and Calvert, in working with local schools, as mentors, and with other community groups, are part of that civic body Tocqueville witnessed — a body that also includes the neighborhood book club, the potluck dinner, the friends of the local park, and the fundraiser for this or that cause (often, I discovered, related to autism). There's volunteer work, cures to be raced for, nonprofit boards to join, and awareness to be raised.

In authoritarian societies, these free associations are surveilled or suppressed, no matter how innocuous the cause, because power resides in the mere act of people organizing freely among themselves. That power quickly became evident in the weeks after Trump's election. Hogue Miller and Park's political activism went from fledgling to full bore. On the day after Trump's inauguration, they joined a local Women's March and helped found the Boulder chapter of Indivisible, working to organize citizen town halls with members of Congress; Park estimated the Boulder chapter was about 80 percent women. She joined another local women-only group that opened up membership to men after the first few months. She started going to town halls and protests, and started making calls and giving money for special elections.

Calvert, Hogue Miller and Park went deeper, even testifying before their respective state legislatures. Hogue transitioned from mostly disengaged from politics to seeing it take over her life. She would become instrumental in helping Democrats take control of the state Senate in 2018. The new majority leader, Sen. Steve Fenberg, would talk her into joining his staff as a top adviser, where she played a role in pushing through expansive legislation in 2019 to rein in fracking, over the fierce objections of the oil and gas lobby.

Gallagher and her mentor friends organized vans and buses for the Women's March in Washington. "When you're feeling hopeless and when you're feeling kind of lost, it's really powerful to be surrounded by people who feel like all of us are in it together, trying to fight for what's right," she said

At the town halls and protests, the breakdown was fairly equal along gender lines. But the organizing that takes part beforehand is more one-sided. That helps explain studies that have found roughly equal participation between men and women in the post-Trump political mobilization, because the studies define participation as simply attending an event. There are no extra points awarded for organizing it. "The meetings, the grunt work, the organization piece," Park said, "that's mostly women."

The first major post-Trump election to attract national attention came in Georgia, where Jon Ossoff ran to fill the seat vacated by Tom Price, who'd been named Health and Human Services secretary. The army behind Ossoff was so overwhelmingly female he began making references to the phenomenon on the trail. "This is a story about women in this community," Ossoff said after advancing to a runoff in April 2017.

At each polling location I visited in Georgia during the run-up to the initial vote, the activists manning the street corners were almost exclusively women. Many were getting actively involved in politics for the first time. That was the case with Sandy Rosenberg, who ferried me around the sprawling district that day. She had been a subscriber to my newsletter, and responded when I said I was looking for people who lived in that part of Georgia.[212] Several women had their teenage daughters with them, signaling that Trump may have stirred more than just one generation of women into action.

Larisa Pearlman, a local OB GYN, canvassed between her 24-hour shifts, going days with barely any sleep ahead of the primary. I had seen her early that April day at a polling location before running into her again at Ossoff's election night party. Later, Pearlman texted to ask me to connect her with my Latina sister in-law, who lives in the area, and her colleague, whom she'd met at the party. Pearlman needed Spanish speakers — a persistent deficit among a mobilization dominated by white people. The connection represented just one instance among thousands of this network growing and strengthening organically, with no leaders or paid organizers nearby. (During the weekend before the final runoff, Pearlman brought her husband out on the trail with her, and said he took to it well.)

Women like Pearlman, Park and Calvert are following in the footsteps of Phyllis Schlafly's army — with the shoe worn on the other foot. In 1972, Schlafly sparked a reactionary movement against the ratification of the Equal Rights Amendment. She tapped into cadres of conservative churchgoers who became radicalized in opposition to the counterculture, the sexual revolution, and the feminist movement of the late 1960s and early 1970s. In other words, Schlafly did not invent a new network, but merely activated one. It was not that these women had been previously disengaged; it was that they had been mostly disengaged *from national politics*. And this network of women's entry into the arena transformed the country.

There is no one defining characteristic of what became loosely known

---

212   If you've gotten this far in the book, you should sign up, too. It's free, so why not. You can find it at badnews.substack.com.

as "the resistance." It was more an upsurge of energy across the board than it was a movement that can be traced to a founding or a set of goals. The phrase that most often pops up in conversations with new members of the resistance is the need to "do something."

What exactly that "something" is has many potential allies, but for those who've been active in left politics for sometime, people like Calvert, an enthusiastic backer of Hillary Clinton over Bernie Sanders in the 2016 primary, can seem suspect. But in many cases, that skepticism is unwarranted.

During the primary and after, the Clinton campaign often referred to how Hillary ran on "the most progressive platform in American history." Sanders backers respond that it was his campaign that forced her to go there and, besides, she was unlikely to have stood by much of it. And they have evidence, citing, for instance, Terry McAuliffe's assurance at the Democratic convention that, whatever Clinton said during the campaign, she'd end up signing the Trans-Pacific Partnership[213] regardless.

That skepticism, however, makes a fundamental mistake by looking at the candidate Calvert supported, rather than at the supporter herself. Calvert is not Clinton. She has never spoken to an audience of Goldman Sachs bankers. She didn't vote to invade Iraq. And one reason Clinton could sign onto such a progressive platform was that her own supporters, like Calvert, were already for it. They were willing to vote for her as a moderate to help elect the first woman president, but they were much happier to support her as a progressive.

The suspicion trickled down to the candidates running in the various special elections, yet it was often misplaced. It was folks like Calvert (who was a leading organizer for leftist James Thompson in Kansas) and Naureen Akhter (later a lead organizer for Ocasio-Cortez) who, in the wake of the Women's March, threw themselves into the campaign of Jon Ossoff, for instance. Ossoff was derided by Republicans and leftists alike as a corporate Democratic stooge foisted on the district by the D.C. establishment. In reality, the DCCC made clear at the time to both reporters and to Ossoff's campaign that it found the district unwinnable and a waste of resources. Instead, small donors from across the country pumped tens of millions of dollars into the campaign — by the end, more than 400,000 people would give, shattering House records. Some 13,000 people volunteered for the campaign. People wanted to fight, whether the party did or not.

The race was broken into two parts. If a candidate got 50 percent in

213   This was a 12-country trade deal, modeled after NAFTA, the US was negotiating with Pacific Rim nations, part of a geopolitical strategy to counteract China and empower US corporations.

the first round, they'd win outright. Any less than that, and the top two would go to a runoff. The DCCC expected the top-two finishers would both be Republicans, and the party committee's main contribution to Ossoff's first round campaign was to push it to dramatically scale back its field operation and focus on television instead. The advice was ignored. It grates on Ossoff to this day that for some on the left, his campaign has become a symbol of failed milquetoast centrism. "The corporate Democrat thing irks me and is inaccurate," Ossoff told me.

The reputation stemmed from the 29-year-old political neophyte's reluctance to precisely identify his politics, defining himself more as anti-Trump than anything else. He shied away from touchstone progressive issues like Medicare for All, and the squishiness led to some ambivalence from Sanders himself. But for those whose analysis focuses entirely on corporate money as the undermining influence in politics, Ossoff's race complicates that picture, and needs a closer look, because it's difficult to imagine a Democratic majority in Congress that does not include districts like Georgia's Sixth. In suburban Atlanta, the district has working-class pockets, but is, on the whole, quite affluent. Driving through it, I thought how odd it was that a Democrat could even be competitive there. Internal polls of the district did indeed show a bare majority supported Medicare for All, but when the questioners drilled down, it was clear that people meant they supported allowing everyone the option of Medicare. Medicare as the *only* option polled extremely low. Now, it's fair to say that leaders should not be guided by polls, but House candidates in special elections aren't leaders, they're nobodies. It's the responsibility of the progressive movement to give those candidates the space to endorse Medicare for All, not the other way around. The movement can't simply rely on unique figures like Ocasio-Cortez to do the work for them.

Still, the advantage of embracing positions like Medicare for All can be that it excites the progressive base, goosing donations, organizing, and turnout. Ossoff, quite evidently, did not need that. He raised more than $20 million from small donors, more than can be reasonably spent in a short House race; volunteers knocked on more than a million doors, and around the country people made millions of calls. The energy was there, and Ossoff had no need for help from corporate PACs. "The last thing I gave two shits about was what PACs were gonna give me money. It wasn't a consideration," he said. Instead, the idea was to allow the grassroots energy to lift him over the top, without him getting in the way. It's a debatable strategy, but it isn't inherently corrupt.

It nearly worked. In the April runoff, Ossoff finished first with 48.1 percent of the vote — 1.9 points, or roughly 1,300 votes, shy of the 50 he needed for a knockout win. His general election opponent, Karen Handel, had been a notorious official at the Susan G. Komen Race for the Cure, where she had barred Planned Parenthood from sponsoring its eponymous contest. Ossoff ran roughly half his ads attacking her for the move, not the strategy that would be employed by a centrist or Blue Dog candidate, particularly in a state like Georgia, which in 2019 would move toward banning abortion outright. His platform was downright radical compared to the program Rahm Emanuel had encouraged Democrats to run on in 2006, and showed just how far progressives had pushed the party to the left — so far, that Ossoff now seemed conservative. In the runoff, he again pulled 48.1 percent, losing to Handel. But the district by then had a captain in every single precinct, and his list of 400,000 donors helped candidates across the country. In 2018, Lucy McBath ran for the seat, motivated into politics by the murder of her son, who was killed by a white man at a gas station who claimed her son and his friends were playing music too loud. Everytown for Gun Safety, the Michael Bloomberg-backed group she had joined in the wake of his death, poured millions into McBath's campaign, which, ideologically, closely resembled Ossoff's. On Election Day, she stunned Handel, tossing her out.

Ossoff's was just one of a spate of special elections where Democrats had been surprisingly competitive early. In Montana and in Kansas, Sanders and his group Our Revolution backed musician Rob Quist and civil rights attorney James Thompson, respectively. Both ran as unabashed progressive-populists in deeply red territory. Thompson fell 7 points short in a district vacated by Mike Pompeo, who had carried it by some 20 points. In Montana, where Trump carried the state by 20 points, Sanders spent the weekend before the election crisscrossing the state with Quist, who narrowed that Republican margin to six.

On the ground and across the country, Quist and Thompson had the strong support of people like Calvert and Akhter. In fact, if not for Calvert, there may have been no Thompson.

"The success of the Women's March in Wichita is one of the reasons we felt we had a chance to win here," Thompson told me. "Many volunteers told me they just had to 'do something.'" Calvert, said Thompson, became one of his strongest campaigners, and was just one of many women volunteering for the campaign who were brand new to politics. Thompson rode that energy and surprised the Kansas Democratic establishment by besting their preferred candidate in the primary, before briefly capturing the nation's attention with his unapologetically liberal campaign. Anybody who wrote off the Brandi Calverts of the world as unreliable allies in the progressive movement would have no way to explain what happened with Thompson and Quist.

For his part, Quist, with little help from national Democrats beyond Sanders, managed to raise more than $5 million for his campaign, much of it from small-dollar donors around the country.[214] Attention was focused on Thompson only late in the game, but activists pumped several hundred thousand dollars into his campaign in the final week, most of it through the Democratic grassroots site Daily Kos, which had its own battles with Sanders backers during the presidential primary.

The work the new activists were doing was intersectional, too. On the last Saturday in January, the first weekend of Trump's presidency, he implemented his promised Muslim ban.[215] Protesters flooded airports in New York, Boston, and Washington, D.C., in spontaneous bursts of outrage. Back in Wichita, Calvert called some friends and they all spread the word. Some 200 people protested at the Wichita Eisenhower National Airport. In Lancaster City, Pennsylvania, Annie Weaver, fresh off the Women's March in Washington, came out to a protest against the ban, where she was recruited into a burgeoning new group called Lancaster Stands Up.

The simple fact is that the Democratic Party is far more divided at the top than it is at the bottom, where there is broad agreement on a suite of issues considered radical among the elites. The alliance of Sanders, Daily Kos, and the women who made up the backbone of the resistance, getting behind candidates like Thompson and Quist, demonstrated how the Democratic Party's future is likely not to resemble its past.

The PTA mom Trump unleashed is more radical than you think. As Tocqueville saw them, the value of these free associations, these endless community groups, was in their distinction from the state. Nearly 200 years later, the American political system is responding in just the way Tocqueville would have predicted. The resistance didn't build a network of activists and organizers from scratch. It flipped the switch on the book club. A few days before the Women's March in Wichita, Calvert kicked her organizing into high gear, making sure the city was prepared, the speakers were lined up, and all the logistics were set.

Thousands of people flooded the streets of downtown Wichita. "Plan-

---

214   Once he did start to catch fire, the Quist campaign hired Washington consultants who promptly shut down his populist campaign and replaced it with utter mundanity. He lost.

215   Oddly, I was the first to obtain and publish Trump's Muslim ban, on January 25, for HuffPost. I say that partly by way of patting myself on the back, and partly as a symbol of just how slapdash and chaotic the early days of the administration were. I got my hands on it because a draft version had begun circulating among immigrant rights groups, who shared it with me.

ning a birthday party sure was a lot different than planning a Women's March for 4,000 people," she said, "but I at least had some type of structure and understanding of how to put it together."

Eighteen

Obama's Farewell Gift

After Trump's election, the first battle to foreshadow the coming clash between the grassroots and party leaders came when Keith Ellison announced his run to chair the Democratic National Committee. Ellison had been Sanders' most prominent backer in the House and Sanders immediately returned the favor with his own endorsement.

His bid started to look like a way for the party to heal the divisions from the primary by uniting behind Ellison. Sen. Charles Schumer, the incoming minority leader, endorsed him, as did Randi Weingarten, the head of the American Federation of Teachers and a prominent Clinton supporter. Elizabeth Warren jumped in early, too, and Ellison appeared well on his way. That's when the Obama White House kicked into gear and called reporters, including me, to make the case that Ellison was a poor choice for the DNC. They recruited Tom Perez, at the time a popular Labor Secretary, who had been considering a run for Maryland governor. Perez jumped into the race, and a dogfight for delegates began.

The DNC race was also the first time national reporters encountered South Bend, Indiana, Mayor Pete Buttigieg, who ran arguing that he would bring a needed Midwest voice to the party. I moderated a debate in Washington among the candidates, and beforehand I set up a way for them to signal their grassroots support by getting supporters to sign a petition backing them for DNC chair. Ellison won, with more than 9,000, but Mayor Pete finished second, racking up a surprising 5,789.

At the debate, I couldn't tell much about his politics, but it was clear he had political skill. After Ray Buckley, another DNC chair candidate, mentioned that he was gay, Buttigieg got my attention, and I gave him the floor. He slipped in the same personal information, but in a much more subtle way. "Let me tell you about my Thanksgiving Day," he said. "Thanksgiving morning, by the way, I spent in a deer blind with my boyfriend's father, so how's that for a 2017 experience? In the afternoon we were sitting around the coffee table," he went on, transitioning to a discussion of health care costs.

Had the Obama wing thrown its weight behind Buttigieg, history might have turned out differently, but by then they were committed to Perez, who made the case that Ellison was a poor choice because as a member of Congress, he couldn't devote his full energies to the position. Ellison responded by saying he would resign his seat if he won.

Puerto Rico, it turned out, would play a major role in the outcome of the contest. To help round up votes, Ellison called his friend Luis Gutiérrez, then one of the most high-profile Puerto Ricans in Congress, representing Chicago. Gutiérrez called one of his top allies in Puerto Rico, Senate minority leader Eduardo Bhatia, to game out getting the delegation on Ellison's side. "Here's our problem," Bhatia told him. "We just got kicked out."

Bhatia then told an incredulous Gutiérrez about a brazen coup that his opponents on the island had just pulled. Essentially, backers of Puerto Rican statehood had managed to replace all the Democrats on the DNC with a new group of politicians, many of whom are effectively Republicans. They did it by calling a secret meeting of the DNC on the island that was noticed with a business card size advertisement in *El Nuevo Día*. "They posted something in the newspaper, which fulfilled some fucking rule to have a meeting of the Democratic Party," Gutiérrez said. "Only the statehooders showed up."

Statehood on the mainland United States is assumed to be a progressive position, but on the island, the debate cuts across the political spectrum, with some on the left opposing it and some on the right supporting it. The two major parties in Puerto Rico tend to be organized around the issue, with conservatives and liberals in each. One party, the New Progressive Party, or NPP, is made up of statehooders — both Democrats and Republicans. The Popular Democratic Party, meanwhile, advocates for the status quo, and is a broadly centrist party that also includes both liberals and conservatives, and both Democrats and Republicans.

None of the Democrats from the Popular Democratic Party had been told of the meeting. The meeting was held in the office of Charlie Rodriguez; those who showed up declared a quorum and elected a full slate of delegates to the DNC, naming Charlie Rodriguez the new president of the Puerto Rico Democrats. Rodriguez at the time was backing Jenniffer González as Resident Commissioner, the non-voting congressional representative for the island. He had also been a backer and key fundraiser for the island's Republican former governor, Luis Fortuño.

"So Charlie Rodriguez makes a deal with Perez: *You have to support statehood; if you do, you get all the delegates*," Gutiérrez said. "Guess who now is a prominent statehooder?"

Perez didn't come out for statehood right away and, as Gutiérrez explained, the party had long taken a neutral position on the issue, believing there was no point inflaming one side or the other. The Puerto Rican delegation delivered all five of its votes to Perez, and he finished up 213.5 to 199 on the first ballot, which was shy of the 50 percent needed, so it went to a second ballot. With it clear Perez would win, delegates moved heavily his way, and he prevailed 235-198, with Ellison even losing a vote in the second round.

Had the Puerto Rican delegation gone for Ellison, instead, the second round may have gone differently, but either way, it was New York that made the key difference for Perez, and it showed that either Chuck Schumer lacks any real power in his home state or he didn't flex it for Ellison.

Of the state's 23 delegates, only five went for Ellison. Andrew Cuomo and Joe Crowley's political machines, meanwhile, teamed with Puerto Rico to install Perez as DNC chair. The votes of the New York and Puerto Rico delegations help explain events later that year that would have seemed otherwise unusual, including Perez's shock endorsement of Cuomo in the gubernatorial primary in May, and Perez's endorsement in June of Puerto Rican statehood.

Bhatia, meanwhile, challenged the seating of the delegates before the Credential Committee. The deck was stacked there, too. New York's Manuel Ortiz, governor Ricardo Rosselló's lobbyist, was a member of the committee, and *El Nuevo Día* later obtained emails showing he worked hand in hand with Rodriguez to squash the protest.

Perez, after basing much of his campaign on his willingness to make the DNC chair job full-time, quickly signed on to teach a course at Brown University, requiring him to be away for a significant chunk of each week. It wouldn't take long for him to become regarded as perhaps the least effective DNC chair in modern memory.

Nineteen

Two Nations, Indivisible

Around three in the afternoon on the first Monday of 2017, Bloomberg reporter Billy House tweeted a curious bit of news: House Republicans were considering moving the Office of Congressional Ethics under the oversight of the House Committee on Ethics.

That may sound like a trivial amount of chair-shuffling, but the aim of the move had real meaning. One of those offices has independence from the House Republican leadership, while the other doesn't. The independent one was being crushed, and there was still three weeks until Trump's inauguration.

That evening, Republicans gathered for a closed-door discussion and vote on the proposal, which had been put forward by Rep. Bob Goodlatte (R-Va.) as an amendment to the rules that would govern the lower chamber for the next two years. A handful of members argued in opposition, including the Republicans' No. 2 man, Kevin McCarthy of California, but the amendment won the secret vote handily, 119-74, and became part of the full rules package.

The measure was extraordinary. It would rename the OCE to become the Office of Congressional Complaint Review. It would bar the office from investigating any anonymous tips. It would block the body from moving forward on any investigation without full approval by members of Congress who oversee it, yet it would have no investigative ability to uncover evidence in order to obtain that approval. It would require the body to shut down an investigation on orders from those same members of Congress. And if the office learned of potential criminal activity, it would be barred from directly contacting law enforcement, a restriction of dubious constitutionality (and one devoid of ethics).

The debate over the move, as it often does, initially played out on Twitter, and given such a partisan time, it was unusually lopsided against it.

Leah Greenberg and Ezra Levin watched closely. Former congressional staffers, the pair had recently published a Google doc filled with suggested strategy for people searching for ways to resist Trump. They called it the Indivisible Guide, and it had become an overnight viral sensation. By January, organic Indivisible chapters were popping up everywhere.

As soon as Ivonne Wallace Fuentes, an associate history professor at Roanoke College, saw the news about the ethics office, she pulled the trigger on the Indivisible chapter she'd long been thinking of starting. Back in Washington, Greenberg and Levin noticed that it had been created and knew that Roanoke was in Goodlatte's district. "We got her on the phone and we were like, *Hey, just so you know, you're now the center of this national thing*," Greenberg recalled. Wallace Fuentes already knew. "They pulled together an impromptu protest at Goodlatte's office that made a bunch of local press," Greenberg said. "Then we got them connected to Rachel Maddow and that was kind of the moment when we went national."

That Monday night, the public erupted at the news that the GOP had secretly nuked its own independent ethics watchdog. Wallace Fuentes and thousands, maybe millions, of others flooded the phone lines in Congress. By morning, it was front-page news on major papers, and President-elect Trump, clearly observing the fury, jumped into the debate on Twitter, chastising House Republicans for boneheaded timing: "With all that Congress has to work on, do they really have to make the weakening of the Independent Ethics Watchdog, as unfair as it may be, their number one act and priority. Focus on tax reform, health care and so many other things of far greater importance!"

With a group of a dozen, Wallace Fuentes went to Goodlatte's office and Indivisible made sure the local press knew about it — and at least three reporters with cameras showed up. Wallace Fuentes recalled one suggestion from the Indivisible Guide: pictures or it didn't happen. So she and two other budding activists posted a video on Facebook outside his office.

Now under intense pressure, House Republicans reconvened on Tuesday, and this time voted to undo what they had done. Former Ethics Chairman Charlie Dent (R-Pa.) said he voted against the amendment

Monday night. "Calmer heads prevailed this morning," he said, adding that Republican leaders had made sure to note Trump's tweeted opposition in cajoling a reversal.[216]

Trump was credited for the GOP about-face, but it was a misreading of the moment, as he had merely reacted to the overwhelming public pressure. By the time he weighed in, condemnation had been swift and furious. "I could have told you last night when we left [before Trump's intervention] this would be undone," Rep. Mike Simpson (R-Idaho) told reporters Tuesday when asked how much influence Trump's tweets had.

The one-eighty was significant because it sent a strong signal that public opinion and public pressure still mattered, even two years away from the midterm elections, and with viral posts about fascism and authoritarianism making the rounds.

"Very soon after the election, there are two news items I remember vividly," said Levin. "One was some future Trump staffer or appointee talking positively about Japanese internment camps as a historical example for how we might deal with Muslims. And the other was a story about Chuck Schumer saying, *We lost, and when you lose, you've got to cut deals, and maybe we can work on infrastructure.* So there's this real vision for 2017 that could be: *We will have a Democratic minority that cuts deals with Trump in order to build roads and internment camps?* And it was shocking."

Levin and Greenberg had both worked on the Hill for progressive Democrats — Levin for Texan Lloyd Doggett and Greenberg for Tom Perriello,[217] but by 2016 both were now working at nonprofits (Greenberg combating human trafficking and Levin working on poverty) when Trump was elected. Something about the nonprofit work felt off in the face of a threat as existential as Trump. "The typical technocratic policy advocacy work that is done in D.C. became less — much less attractive to us, in fact, not just less attractive, but dangerous in the context of the Trump administration," Levin said. "It provides a cover of bipartisanship to an authoritarian or wannabe authoritarian administration. And that position in November was actually somewhat radical."

---

216   This comes from a story in The Huffington Post I wrote with then-colleague Matt Fuller.

217   Perriello was elected in 2008 in rural Virginia, flipping a Republican district by running as an unapologetic progressive. He voted for the ACA, climate change legislation and the rest of the Democratic agenda. In the 2010 wave, he lost his seat, but by a much closer margin than Blue Dog Democrats in similarly conservative districts. He went to the State Department, and Greenberg went with him. In 2017, he ran for Virginia governor, with Greenberg again working with him, but lost a close primary to Ralph Northam.

Despite losing the popular vote for the White House and getting fewer overall votes for Senate seats than did Democratic candidates, Republicans were on the verge of controlling all three branches of government, and had telegraphed their intention to ram through the most aggressive agenda possible — beginning with repealing the Affordable Care Act, followed by a tax cut for corporations and the super-rich, all aimed at reshaping the structure of government and society. The ethics faceplant suggested less may be possible than Republicans thought. "That was really the first sign for the GOP of what was about to hit," Greenberg told me.

It was also important because the presidential election was characterized by a series of moments that defied political gravity, and had people questioning whether Trump was somehow invincible. Remarks by Trump, whether public or privately recorded, that would have ruined any other candidate simply ran off his back — or, in some cases, even gave him a boost. The disorienting campaign has led to speculation that nothing was the same in American politics. But that Tuesday showed that public opinion — people — still mattered.

The ethics office had been established in the wake of the investigation into former lobbyist Jack Abramoff, which was driven most publicly by Sen. John McCain. I asked McCain if he agreed with my take that its preservation meant public opinion still mattered. "I think it still does, especially with the low approval rating Congress has already," he said, adding he was glad to see House Republicans reverse themselves.

On Wednesday, Rachel Maddow covered the fight, bringing Ezra Levin on air at the top of the show and playing the clip of Wallace Fuentes at Goodlatte's office.

At the time, it was not obvious that a significant pushback against Trump would be generated. Elected Democrats in Washington were in full retreat and talking about compromising with Trump, and the professional progressive infrastructure was shell shocked. In her introduction to her segment with Levin, Maddow made the case to her millions of viewers that resistance was not futile. In fact, it was one of the first uses of the word resistance to describe what was about to come. Maddow played the clip of the protest at Goodlatte's Roanoke office. "All right, guys, we just came from visiting Congressman Goodlatte's office," said Wallace Fuentes. "We had 12 people, we delivered New Year's cards. It was easy, it was fun." Coming out of the clip, Maddow offered a short instruction to viewers: "Read *Indivisible*. It really works. *Indivisible*."

Wallace Fuentes' mother happened to be watching, and was startled to see her daughter's face on Maddow.[218] Her first reaction, she later told

---

218   I was an MSNBC contributor for three years, ending in 2016, and still occa-

her, was "deep dread." She had lived through the civil war in Guatemala, and associated dissident political activity with torture and repression. Then she moved past her fear. *Maybe we're not in Guatemala*, she decided. "In this country," she told her daughter, "we can do this."

The appearance on Maddow's show was game changing. "I think Maddow's role in identifying the movement early and providing it exposure to the broader world is under-appreciated," said Levin. "She saw exactly what was happening on the ground, and in her coverage she didn't center me or Leah or the people in D.C., but the people who were actually leading it across the country. And that was incredibly pivotal. Her coverage educated folks about something real that they personally could be part of in their own backyards. To this day I still get people who tell me, 'I saw you on Maddow back in January 2017 and we started our group the next day.'"

Indivisible wasn't quite an organization by the time of that segment, which was why Levin was introduced as an "author" of a guide rather than a founder of a group. Whatever it was, it started in Austin over that Thanksgiving. Levin and Greenberg, who are husband and wife, were visiting family and out with a college friend who was enraged by Trump's election and eager to "do something." The friend was running a Facebook group dedicated to resisting Trump that had 3,000 members, which they called Dumbledore's Army. "They were showing up for protests and they were sending postcards to Paul Ryan and they were calling the electors" — the folks in the Electoral College, which pre-resisters briefly thought might thwart Trump — "and they kind of all felt like they were throwing stuff at a wall," Levin told me.

Over drinks at an Austin bar, Levin and Greenberg explained how tea party protesters had shaken up Congress in 2009 and 2010, spelling out exactly what works on a member of Congress — and, importantly, what doesn't work (like sending postcards to Paul Ryan). Their friend was transfixed; this was precisely what she and her group needed to know. At the time, countless guides to resisting fascism were floating around, but none was practically oriented for people looking to do something on a daily or near-daily basis.

Levin and Greenberg put their thoughts down into a Google doc and shared it with smart folks back in Washington, refining the guide along the way. "We got some feedback that it was dark and that we should make it more optimistic," Greenberg said. People were like, *What about Michelle Obama? Like, when they go low we go high?* And we were like, *No.*"

When it came time to publish the document, only two former Hill staffers, Angel Padilla and Jeremy Haile, put their names on it with Levin

---

sionally appear on the network.

and Greenberg. The answer to why can be found in the very advice it of-fered. Half of the problem for activists, the document explained, was the Democratic Party, which could not be assumed part of the resistance, but needed to be pushed and prodded into action. That wasn't something a typical Democratic staffer would want to be associated with.

They let it fly on December 14, making the document public. Levin tweeted it out. "He had like 500 followers," recalled Greenberg.

The recommendations were straightforward. "Trump is neither pop-ular nor does he have wide congressional margins. We can fight this. The guide is pretty simple," Levin tweeted. "You get a few people together locally, focus like hell on your members of Congress, & never give an inch."

None of the DC hands they had shared it with early had a sense of how explosive it would be. "We didn't really get any feedback that indi-cated that people were going to have the emotional reaction that they did to it," Greenberg said. "There were tons of Google Docs in this moment and we thought this would just add to the library," Levin added.

In Google Docs, when another person is viewing a shared file, they show up as an odd-looking, colored animal labeled "armadillo" or "hip-popotamus" or whatever. Quickly, it looked as if somebody had opened the cages at the zoo. First 10, then 20, then 50, then 99 other people were reading and downloading the document. Soon emails and tweets started coming in, people complaining the document was overloaded and they couldn't download it. They realized that the page stopped counting at 99, and there was no telling how many people were reading it.

"We had understood this to be a relatively cynical, rear-guard strat-egy for protecting as much as you could in a sort of dark, terrible mo-ment," Greenberg said. "But actually it was sort of this experience of power, a re-empowerment for people: *Oh, there's actually something that I can do.*"

Levin and Greenberg had an early feel for how grassroots Democrats were responding to the moment. So too did Stephanie Hansen. The spe-cial election season kicked off in December 2016. Delaware Democrats had nominated Hansen to run in a February special for a state Senate seat that would decide control of the chamber. The Republican nominee, a retired cop from New York, had run in 2014 and lost by just 2 points.

As Hansen campaigned door to door, she had a front-row seat to the historic awakening that Levin and Greenberg had been channeling. "What I saw on the ground, beginning in December, was that the Dem-ocrats in the community were very depressed, very sad," she told me. "There was a lot of anguish, from December 21 till right about the in-auguration."

Naureen Akhter, a young mom in New York City, was also shaken into action by Trump's election, and her first phone-banking ever was for Democrat Jon Ossoff in an April 2017 special election in Georgia's 6th Congressional District. The Democratic Congressional Campaign Committee, the party's organ in charge of winning elections, hadn't wanted to compete there — worried that a Democrat had little chance of winning, even though Trump had won the district by a mere 1.5 points. But grassroots donors, driven by the need to "do something," poured millions into the race, effectively nudging the party in.

Akhter was disappointed when Ossoff fell just short of 50 percent in the first round of voting and lost in a runoff, but she still wanted to join her local Democratic Party. It proved difficult, as details of the when and where of the party's meetings remained closely guarded, and party officials never let her know when they were happening, despite promising to do so over email. She finally found an event being put together by a local state senator. She went and learned that he had been a member of the Independent Democratic Conference, a group of Democrats who caucused with Republicans. (The IDC was formally dissolved in 2018.) None of it was inspiring.

By chance, she stumbled upon a different candidate's campaign event: Alexandria Ocasio-Cortez, running in the Bronx and Queens. Akhter decided that if she couldn't join the party, she would beat it. She became one of Ocasio-Cortez's top volunteers and eventually her director of organizing.

Around the country, I heard stories similar to Akhter's — local parties that were content with the way things were run, and weren't interested in all these new folks showing up. But as far as I could tell, that was the exception. The rule was that the new folks were embraced, and revitalized local organizations.

The biggest problem they had was space.

Party meetings that had once been sleepy affairs, dominated by Robert's Rules of Order and a handful of graying activists, have become standing room only. The overflowing crowds sent stunned party regulars scrambling to find new venues, while the surge in interest, and the coinciding fundraising boost, enabled local chapters to hire staff and build infrastructure in previously unthinkable ways. "I'm as busy this year as I was at any time last year in the heat of a huge election," Mark Fraley, chairman of the Monroe County Democratic Party in Indiana, told me in February 2017. Fraley said he received 65 emails in a single weekend from people requesting to become precinct chairs, a thankless job that normally requires begging and pleading to get someone to fill. The county party restructured and added five deputy chairs to channel all the energy, and created six new committees. "What's very different is that it's made the party younger," he said. "Young people never really wanted to have as much of a meaningful part in the Democratic Party infrastructure. Now that doesn't seem true anymore." Groups like Swing Left, Flippable, and The Sister District Project, all formed after the election, routed people to swing districts where they could be most effective, and Justice Democrats launched an initiative to primary corporate-controlled Democrats. But the swelling ranks of county-level meetings indicated that the grassroots movement under way was poised to do more than just pop-up some outside groups; it was swamping the Democratic Party itself.

My HuffPost colleague Amanda Terkel and I interviewed dozens of activists and local party organizers in 24 states that February — red, blue, and purple — and found a strikingly similar pattern.[219] Trump became liberals' greatest organizer, with one extraordinary move after another drawing public outrage. By then, his Muslim ban was on hold, his popularity was plummeting, national security adviser Mike Flynn had been fired, Obamacare repeal was looking less likely and Labor Department nominee Andy Puzder had been defeated.[220] The wins gave the new activists confidence that their work meant something.

Back in Delaware, volunteers and small donations flooded in from across the country, and, on February 25, Hansen trounced her opponent by 16 points.[221] When I talked to her nearly two years later, just ahead of the election, she told me that the energy she still felt on the ground had, if anything, only increased since then. She still saw bumps of small dollars come in, she said, and can tell by her ActBlue fundraising page when Trump has done something particularly horrific or offensive.

---

219   The story was headlined, "The Movement Resisting Donald Trump Has A Name: The (Local) Democratic Party."

220   I played a role in Puzder's rejection when I broke the news for The Huffington Post in early February that he had employed an undocumented household worker. The irony was that there were several much better reasons for him to go down — spousal abuse, for instance, and a string of wage theft violations at his fast-food franchise — but the undocumented worker played into GOP suspicions that he was soft on immigration, so they tossed him overboard. As Politico wrote after he withdrew a few days later, "It was mainly the potency of the immigration issue that weighed Puzder down when The Huffington Post reported that he'd employed an undocumented worker for several years (and didn't bother to pay back taxes until after he was nominated)."

221   We sent Paul Blumenthal to cover the election and his dispatch that night was read by more than one million people by the end of the next day. That's when I knew the resistance, or whatever it was, was real.

All of that enthusiasm was starting to get noticed in Washington, and not always in a pleasant way. Before President Trump appeared before cameras to bestow his Supreme Court rose on Judge Neil Gorsuch, protesters were already gathering outside the Brooklyn apartment of Senate Minority Leader Chuck Schumer, demanding he take a firm stand against whichever man Trump nominated.

Later that evening, he did just that, announcing that Gorsuch would need 60 votes to get through the Senate, which amounted to a declaration that Democrats planned to filibuster. The move came not long after he had chided Sen. Jeff Merkley (D-Ore.) for suggesting that he would filibuster Trump's pick no matter who it was. Whether Schumer's decision was specifically driven by the thousands outside his Park Slope building, who had been organized by the Working Families Party, or the crowds who had gathered at JFK airport, or the millions who had marched across the country the week before is impossible to know for certain.

All of a sudden, elected Democrats started asking how those bullhorns worked. The night after the Schumer protest, Democrats, led by the Senate minority leader and House Minority Leader Nancy Pelosi, held an impromptu rally on the steps of the Supreme Court. With the audio faltering, Pelosi led the assembled politicians in a rendition of "This Land Is Your Land," with Sen. Cory Booker of New Jersey even trying his hand at, yes, a bullhorn.

Democrats couldn't have looked any more awkward if they tried, and Trump didn't miss the opportunity to mock them on Twitter. But the next morning, the organized resistance continued, with Senate Democrats boycotting two votes scheduled for Trump nominees who had either lied, misled the committee or withheld information about their financial backgrounds. Later that day, they used a rare parliamentary maneuver to force a delay on a vote on the nomination of Sen. Jeff Sessions for attorney general.

The obstruction, defiance and stiff opposition came after a week of progressive outrage at Democratic elected officials, who activists believed were too quick to cave and normalize Trump's presidency. Progressive activists, of course, had been criticizing elected Democrats for being too weak for decades. But this time the charge was landing, and it was changing the way the party positioned itself against Trump.

Protests broke out everywhere, from Pittsburgh to Dayton, Ohio, to Palmer, Alaska. And Democrats were well aware that the base wanted action. Some pleaded for reason. "Some are day one, literally, *why-haven't-you-impeached-him-yet* type people," said Dick Durbin, the Senate's number two Democrat. Adam Schiff said at the time he wasn't sure where it would go. "The more radical the administration is, the more radicalized our base becomes, which just feeds the Breitbart crowd, and who knows where that ends," he said.

Kamala Harris, elected to the Senate in 2016, felt some of it, too. In fall 2017, it was clear that she was making moves toward a White House run, and a handful of stories were published by writers sympathetic to Bernie Sanders, criticizing Harris for being too tough on poor and minority defendants as a prosecutor, and not tough enough on wealthy, well-connected white ones. As the pile-on grew, Harris reached out directly to Sanders to ask if he could do anything to tamp it down, people familiar with the entreaty told me. Sanders told Harris he didn't have control over what his supporters or sympathizers were saying. He advised her not to hit back, suggesting it would blow over soon enough. For old-school Democrats like Harris, who understood power as top-down and centralized, it seemed absurd to suggest Sanders couldn't control his supporters. To Sanders' supporters, it would be equally ludicrous to suggest that he could.

Marco Rubio, the Republican from Florida, fresh off his loss to Trump in the primary, said that Democratic senators were griping to him about how much the base wanted to fight. "Many Democratic colleagues tell me they have heavy pressure from left-wing radicals to oppose everything even before they know what it is," Rubio tweeted in early February. McCain assumed it would backfire. "They're still not over the shock," McCain told me. "I mean, people weren't just measuring the drapes, they picked out their offices and they were hiring assistants. I just don't think they've recovered yet to put together a cohesive plan. So what's the easiest thing to do? Block everything...Many times, when we were in the minority, we were very frustrated and the government shutdown is a classic example of everybody got frustrated — *So by God, we'll shut down the government.*"

Yet it was precisely the energy of that base that, two years later, took back the House and saved Democrats from sinking deeper into the Senate minority.

That energy would soon be turned on the party establishment itself. "We put out an endorsement guide that explicitly said primaries are a good thing," said Ezra Levin. "We care about the direction of the party and we wouldn't be down a thousand seats across the country if the Democratic Party were performing well."

Twenty

Dead Enders

Annie Weaver, 52, had spent the fall watching the oafish Donald Trump stumble toward Election Day with a mix of horror and amusement. She was confident that the country at large, and particularly her community, would reject the man. *"We're such a Christian community, a community that looks out for each other*, I thought, who values character way more than I guess a lot of people did," said Weaver, referring to her Amish Country community in Southeastern Pennsylvania.

Sitting in church that weekend, she felt betrayed. The values being professed by the congregation were a lie. Looking around at her long-time friends and fellow parishioners, she wondered, *How did you vote for him?* After a lifetime of ministry, she left her church. Weaver also looked inward, asking how she could have done so little in the face of a threat so grave. As soon as she learned about the Women's March in Washington, D.C., she vowed to go. On January 21, Weaver carried a sign listing her motivations to march, first among them the children she teaches. She made a New Year's resolution to herself that this next election would be different.

She became a foot soldier, and then a lieutenant, in a grassroots army that blended electoral politics with community organizing — a strategy that paid surprising dividends both on the ground and at the ballot box. Local progressives have flipped myriad seats in deeply red strongholds, beat back a prison privatization effort, and seriously checked police brutality for the first time in Lancaster City's history. And while Weaver couldn't name her district's congressional candidates in 2016, in the following cycle she became an intimate participant in one of the most innovative Democratic House campaigns in the country — Jess King's race in Pennsylvania's Amish Country.

King, a Mennonite, was born and raised in Leola, where Weaver's husband worked in the Styrofoam cup factory. Her family found refuge in Lancaster around 12 generations ago, and for many there, little has changed: the Amish still ride in horse and buggies and eschew modern conveniences like electricity.

Lancaster County, Pennsylvania, is what might be called Trump Country. The region, rural and deeply religious, went solidly for Republicans in 2016, as it had consistently in years past. Weaver had always been afraid to talk politics in New Holland, finding few like-minded souls. But Trump's win galvanized a dormant streak of progressive values. As Weaver managed her own internal crisis, concerned local faith leaders, small-business owners, social workers, teachers, and students called an emergency meeting in nearby Lancaster City to think through how to react to the impending Trump presidency.

King helped the group reserve meeting space in the historic building where she ran her nonprofit. Several hundred people showed up for the meeting, a staggering turnout for the area. The next month, 400 people showed up — some 600 the month after. The congregants decided to formalize the energy into a new civic group called Lancaster Stands Up. They began meeting regularly to organize around assaults like the Muslim ban and the attempt to repeal the Affordable Care Act. They also began targeting the local elections coming up that November.

Weaver first encountered LSU after she saw on Facebook that it had organized a gathering in Lancaster Square to protest the Muslim ban. Two thousand people packed the square, making it one of the largest protests in Lancaster City history. LSU collected her contact information at the event. They also went the extra step — LSU organizer Julia Berkman-Hill called Weaver personally to get her more involved.

Weaver began going door to door in Lancaster City on behalf of a variety of causes that LSU had made its own. She rallied in defense of the Affordable Care Act and canvassed for a slate of Democratic candidates running for the Manheim Township school board.

In June 2017, King launched her bid for Congress and had to leave LSU, which legally must remain independent from the campaign. She planned to focus a populist-progressive campaign on canvassing and harnessing grassroots enthusiasm. If suburban Republicans came along, attracted by the promise of Medicare For All or tuition-free public college, then great, but they would not be King's target.

Lancaster Stands Up voted to endorse King, as did a local immigrant rights group with a broad grassroots network, Make the Road PA. Justice Democrats got behind her as well. King then sought to secure the endorsement, or at least the neutrality, of the major players in Democratic Party circles. Her campaign reached out to EMILY's List,[222] which was founded to elect pro-choice women to Congress. EMILY's List sent King a questionnaire, which she filled out and returned, affirming her strong support for reproductive freedom. That was October, by which point her campaign had broken the $100,000 mark, a sign of viability she had hoped would show EMILY's List that she was serious. "We followed up a few times after and did not hear back," said King's spokesperson, Guido Girgenti.

It turned out the Democratic Party had other ideas — or, at least, it had an old idea. As was happening in races across the country, party leaders in Washington and in the Pennsylvania district rallied, instead, around a candidate who, in 2016, had raised more money than a Democrat ever had in the district and suffered a humiliating loss anyway.

Christina Hartman, from the Democratic Party's perspective, did everything right during the previous election cycle. She worked hard, racking up endorsements from one end of the district to the other. She followed the strategic advice of the most sagacious political hands in Pennsylvania, targeting suburban Republicans and independents who'd previously voted for candidates like Mitt Romney, but were now presumed gettable.

"For every one of those blue-collar Democrats [Donald Trump] picks up, he will lose to Hillary [Clinton] two socially moderate Republicans and independents in suburban Cleveland, suburban Columbus, suburban Cincinnati, suburban Philadelphia, suburban Pittsburgh, places like that," Ed Rendell, the state's former governor and titular leader of the state party, had predicted to the New York Times.

Hartman, with the energetic support of the Democratic Congressional Campaign Committee and EMILY's List, used her fundraising prowess to go heavy on television ads to drive her moderate message, confident that the well-funded Clinton ground game would bring her backers to the polls.

It did not.

Hartman was swamped by Republican Lloyd Smucker by 34,000 votes, badly underperforming even Clinton, who lost the district by about 21,000 votes. Trump and Smucker had indeed picked up some blue-collar Democrats, but not enough Republicans switched over to make up for the loss.

---

222   It stands for Early Money Is Like Yeast.

After spending $1.15 million in 2016, she had finished with 42.9 percent of the vote. In 2014, a terrible year for Democrats, a little-known Democrat spent just $152,000 to win almost the same share, 42.2 percent of the vote.

In July, Hartman announced she would make another run at it in 2018. She quickly found the support of the state's Democratic establishment, led by Rendell. Along with Rendell came failed 2016 Senate candidate Katie McGinty; Attorney General Josh Shapiro; Auditor General Eugene DePasquale; Treasurer Joe Torsella; and Reps. Dwight Evans and Brendan Boyle of Philadelphia, and Matt Cartwright from Lackawanna. The simultaneous announcement of endorsements from the top elected officials in the party is a way to send a signal that the party has chosen its candidate. Another signal came in September, when Rep. Joe Crowley of New York, the House Democratic Caucus chair, gave money to Hartman through his leadership PAC. EMILY's List followed suit, endorsing Hartman in December without extending a courtesy call to King's campaign, Girgenti said.

The rapid consolidation around Hartman wasn't a slight to King — it was just how the party does business. "I had no idea about King when I decided to back Hartman," one member of Congress told me. "I got behind her basically because we simply needed a good candidate and I had supported her in 2016. In a seat like that, which isn't a Tier 1 race but could be viable in a wave year, we're typically just looking for someone who could be good. Compared to what we've always had in PA-16, Christina is good."

The decision stung, King said.

In mid-October, the DCCC hosted a candidate week in Washington, bringing in Democrats running for the House from around the country for trainings and networking. Hartman was invited; King was not. As part of the candidate gathering, an off-the-record happy hour with national reporters was hosted by the DCCC in the "Wasserman room" at the Democratic National Headquarters.

In his farewell address, President Obama offered practical advice for those frustrated by his successor: "If you're disappointed by your elected officials, grab a clipboard, get some signatures, and run for office yourself."

Yet across the country, the DCCC, its allied groups, or leaders within the Democratic Party worked hard *against* some of these congressional candidates — publicly backing their more established opponents. Winning the support of Washington heavyweights, including the DCCC — implicit or explicit — is critical for endorsements back home and a boost to fundraising. In general, it can give a candidate a tremendous advantage over opponents in a Democratic primary.

The way to win party support is to pass the phone test.

In order to establish whether a person is worthy of official backing, DCCC operatives will "rolodex" a candidate. On the most basic level, it involves candidates being asked to pull out their smartphones, scroll through their contacts lists, and add up the amount of money their contacts could raise or contribute to their campaigns. If the candidates' contacts aren't good for at least $250,000, or in some cases much more, they fail the test, and party support goes elsewhere.

That emphasis on fundraising can lead the party to make the kinds of decisions that leave ground-level activists furious. James Thompson, who lost a close special election in Kansas and ran again for the Wichita seat in 2018, said the DCCC was specific about why it wanted candidates to raise money. "They want you to spend a certain amount of money on consultants, and it's their list of consultants you have to choose from," he said. Those consultants tend to be DCCC veterans, who, before leaving for the private sector, hired their replacements, who then dole out contracts.

But the party also decided to examine whether a candidate was backed by a local Indivisible group or other activist chapters when evaluating potential lawmakers. That was a significant change and suggested a tantalizing future for the party. The *Citizens United* decision[223] may have opened the floodgates to unlimited spending by the wealthy, but its paradoxical long-term result could be the creation of a two-party system — in which one is fueled by millions of small dollars and the other is backed by a handful of billionaires. That, ironically, could produce a level playing field. And it is not an outcome the DCCC is necessarily opposed to as an institution, though the consultant factions that make a living off the current system would need to be overcome.

The contrast between King and Hartman was evident in the results of a questionnaire distributed as part of the LSU endorsement process. When asked, for instance, about her position on a controversial pipeline opposed by community members, King responded, "Fracked gas pipelines threaten our land and water just so a few oil and gas executives can get a little richer. I stand in opposition to the construction of the Atlantic Sunrise pipeline." Hartman wouldn't take a position.

Weaver probably voted for Hartman in 2016, but she can't be sure. In 2018, Hartman's approach felt lacking. Weaver and her fellow LSU-ers voted overwhelmingly to endorse their former comrade. The King campaign played to win, but along the way, it had a broader impact —

---

223   A 2010 Supreme Court ruling that struck down wide swaths of the campaign finance regulatory regime.

advancing progressive issues and aiding like-minded local candidates.

In November 2017, Democrats picked up seats across the state, but the party did particularly well near King's district. In Lancaster City, Democrats swept the council, winning all four seats with a historically diverse slate of relatively progressive candidates. The city, which is 30 percent Puerto Rican and host to many displaced by Hurricane Maria, also elected a Puerto Rican member of the school board, Salina Almanzar, only the second in the city's history.

In Manheim Township, a historically conservative area where Weaver canvassed for LSU, Democrats won all six school board seats. Dianne Bates, a progressive millennial, won her Borough Council race in arch-conservative Millersville. Elizabethtown hadn't had a Democrat on the town council since the 1970s, but last fall they elected an IBEW member, Bill Troutman.

The energy built around electoral organizing was soon channeled in a new direction when LSU organizer Michelle Hines noticed an item about the local prison in the paper. The county, it appeared, was preparing to outsource its prisoner re-entry program to the for-profit prison company GEO Group. For the last decade, a coalition of nonprofits had worked to find housing and jobs for inmates released from prison. But they would be shut out of the new profit-driven approach — depriving parolees of a wide array of support.

LSU reached out to Have A Heart for Persons in the Criminal Justice System, one of the key groups involved in prisoner re-entry. It was an unusual meeting of minds. "Their approach is they meet with the commissioners and judges and prison board, and organize people involved, and lobby them," Hines said. "Our approach is to kind of blow things up. We decided to blend those approaches."

In November, that "social base" was effectively rallied into a standing-room-only crowd, which bombarded the Lancaster County prison board with objections. "The profit motive works wonders when it's focused on mattresses, farm machinery, and investments," Franz Herr, a volunteer with the coalition, told the board. "It oversteps its moral bounds when it becomes a tool for extracting profit from the servitude of human beings." Facing unexpected pushback, the board shelved the plan.

To Jonathan Smucker, a co-founder of the group, the win represented more than a single victory. "There's a process of showing people that when we build our capacity to throw down in numbers and apply pressure, it can win, it can change things," Smucker said. It shows people that action isn't futile." (In classic Lancaster fashion, yes, Jonathan and GOP Rep. Lloyd Smucker are related.)

"One of the nuts we're trying to crack here," added Smucker, was "how do you build political power in an area like this, where people of color's participation is not ornamental or tokenistic, but where people of color, like, actually have a voice within that — but where the organization, if it's district-wide, is going to be majority-white at the same time? That's a hard thing to do."

Lancaster's segregated culture has given LSU ample opportunities to try, one of them arising this past June, when a video of police violence in Lancaster City went viral. The incident happened after two local police officers gave contradictory orders to a young black man sitting on a curb — one told him to stick his legs straight out, the second told him to cross his ankles. When he complied with the latter, the former tased him without warning, all of it caught by a bystander on video.

LSU organized an emergency demonstration the next day on the steps of the old courthouse. The victim, Sean Williams, 27, watched from the side, amazed by the support pouring in from around the globe as well as recognition from the mayor and local prosecutor. The issue of police brutality was hardly solved, but for the first time, it had been publicly checked. "We're making sure that we're elevating issues that don't just matter to people in more affluent parts of town," Smucker said. "And I think that any time a group does that, there's some initial skepticism, which I think is deserved. But I think when you are not afraid of walking on eggshells when you have some humility, and when you stick with it and you keep showing up, people take notice after a while. And I think that's part of what happened with these two fights."

While most campaigns outsource their policy, communications, digital, and even field programs to Washington-based consultants, King did it in-house with local staff. Becca Rast, King's campaign manager, first organized her high school to march against the Iraq War, in 2006, with help from Smucker, who at the time was the national field organizer for the War Resisters League. Rast's teenage co-organizer, Nick Martin, was the King campaign's field director.

Smucker had been politically active since he was a high school student in the 1990s. He was one of the leading forces behind the anti-globalization protest known as A16 in 2000, was deeply involved with Occupy Wall Street, and authored the influential book *Hegemony How-To: A Roadmap for Radicals*. Rast and Smucker married and moved to Oakland, where Rast was a top organizer for 350.org, the cutting-edge environmental group that made opposing the Keystone XL pipeline a top priority.

But eventually, they felt the pull of home. "I just really, deeply believe that the Democratic Party and progressive movements have written off places like this in the country and it's a huge mistake," she said.

As for Martin, he came back too after years of social justice work, in-cluding organizing against mountaintop removal in West Virginia. Back in Lancaster, he was a leading organizer with Lancaster Against Pipe-lines before becoming the regional field director for the Bernie Sanders campaign.

Rast, Smucker, and Martin were among the co-founders of Lancaster Stands Up. Leaders of both the King campaign and LSU separately ar-gued that the way to break through in a place like Lancaster was to lead with strong, progressive values, but not get bogged down in lefty jargon. Both in Washington and around Pennsylvania, party operatives took no-tice, and the DCCC was intrigued. "It has been very interesting to see," Rast said, "this genuine, *Wow, you guys are really working hard and trying something new. We don't necessarily believe that you can win*, but there is a respect-the-trade kind of dynamic going on."

Asked if the national party had counseled them before redistricting, Rast explained: "When we were in the old district [which leaned less Re-publican], they did give me some input and advice. At this point, they're just fine with what we're doing. They literally, they will say, 'Well, our consultants wouldn't work hard for you, so it makes sense that you're doing the strategy that you're doing,' because they know that we'd be a low priority because we're R+14" — meaning the district leans 14 points toward Republicans.

Early in 2018, Weaver felt ready to organize back in New Holland, and urged LSU to let her canvass there in the hopes of starting a branch — New Holland Stands Up. Berkman-Hill of LSU agreed: she knew of several other New Hollanders who'd shown a similar interest. By March, Weaver and a handful of locals were ready to host their own town hall, and blanketed the town of 5,000 with fliers. If nobody answered a door, she'd leave one behind — an act rooted in faith that some tiny sliver of the population will pick it up, read it, and that it will matter.

When Weaver left a flier in Zak Gregg's screen door, he wasn't home. But it was rescued from the elements by Gregg's roommate, who left it on a table inside their row house. When Gregg got home from his wood-working job with Premier Custom-Built Cabinetry, he ignored it at first. But eventually, some text at the bottom of the leaflet caught his eye. *Where's Lloyd?* It was a reference to the area's congressional represen-tative and King's opponent, Republican Lloyd Smucker, who, the flier explained, refused to hold town halls.

The event, per the flier, was being supported by Lancaster Stands Up, Keystone Progress, and Our Revolution. The last group sounded familiar to Gregg, 20, who voted for Sanders in the Pennsylvania primary and was heartbroken by his loss. When a Google search confirmed that Bernie's political revolution had come to New Holland, he broke down in tears.

Gregg was not in a good place. Growing up nearby in a hard-edged, conservative, evangelical home, he questioned, at around age 14 or 15, the worldview with which he'd been raised. It started with a person he called his "first real friend."

"We connected over video games and about some of the books that we were reading, and we had French class together," Gregg recalled. "And then one day I just kinda figured it out. I'm like, *Oh, she's gay.* And I had been raised to think that gay people are evil and shouldn't even be considered human. And now I'm faced with, *Well, I know [her], I care about her, she's my friend, but I'm supposed to think that she's bad?* And it took a while, but I eventually got to the point where I'm, like, *my thinking is just wrong. I can't keep thinking this way.* And then that just kind of led to everything else. Like, *Oh, maybe immigrants aren't the problem. Oh, maybe inner-city folk aren't the problem. Maybe it's the system that surrounds it.*"

Alone in New Holland — bored and alienated at his cabinet-making job, struggling to understand his place in the world — he could escape his old way of thinking but hadn't found a new community. "I was depressed and I had horrible, suicidal thoughts," Gregg recalled. Like many young people before him who broke away from strictly religious and troubled homes, he found himself mired in crisis. Through his tears, he studied the flier Weaver had left. Then he read up on Rep. Lloyd Smucker. Nearly all of his political contributions, Gregg found, were coming from corporate PACs. He resolved to go to the April 10 town hall.

Some 50 people showed up that night — a startling turnout for a town of 5,000. Gregg marveled at the number of people in the room, calling it a community with the power to fight back. He took the microphone, laying out in detail how much corporate PAC money Smucker was taking, running through his top donors. As a teacher, Weaver said, she was impressed. "He had done his homework." As someone hoping the area could be turned around, she was deeply moved to see this son of Lancaster County taking action. "As soon as he stood up and started speaking, I wanted to cry," Weaver said.

Weaver talked Gregg into block-walking with her. The two made an odd political couple, the Clinton-backing resistance mom and the young Berner, but their diversity was a source of comfort. Weaver said that when Gregg and other young Sanders backers showed up to the town hall and saw older people like her there, it motivated them to know that they weren't alone. "If they'd have passed me by on the street, they'd have said, 'There goes a Trump supporter,'" said Weaver. ("That's true," Gregg confirmed.)

Gregg's ability to coax Trump supporters his way took Weaver aback. Most of Gregg's family and coworkers had been Trump supporters, and he had no problem understanding their mindset, knowing which buttons to press to provoke a shift of perspective. It helps that he looks the part, complete with the facial hair fashion often seen on the pilot of a horse and buggy — a thick beard that loops like a helmet strap. No mustache. "Poverty in New Holland has grown substantially in the last eight years," he told me. "How are people supposed to get by? And it's like, I don't blame people who voted for Trump. Most of the people that I work with at Premier, they voted for Trump, and they're like, *I cannot vote for somebody who's going to keep the status quo, because our health care is terrible and our wages aren't getting any better.* So it's like, might as well throw the first stone."

His best way in was the issue of corporate money. King took none, while Smucker was awash in it. No matter how many doors Weaver and Gregg knocked on, they'd been unable to find anybody who thought it a good thing for corporate wealth to finance politicians.

Gradually, Gregg opened up to Weaver, Berkman-Hill, and others about his childhood and the dark thoughts he'd been having. They pushed him to get help and were there on many late nights when he needed somebody to talk to. He started therapy and channeled the darkness into his canvassing. "He is amazing at persuading people because he's very empathetic," Berkman-Hill said, "and he knows what it's like to not feel like anyone is listening to you."

Gregg helped organize another town hall in New Holland, this one on a Sunday in August for the King campaign. He waited until after the event to approach King. "You don't understand how important it is to me that you are running this campaign, and that you are creating a community that wants to help each other in their own town," he said. "That's the reason I'm still here and in my own town."

As far as Washington was concerned, when the Pennsylvania Supreme Court redrew congressional lines earlier in 2018, ruling that Republicans had unconstitutionally gerrymandered the state, the path to victory for the Democratic nominee in King's district went from narrow to nearly foreclosed — and Lancaster became pointless. The state as a whole became much more favorable to Democrats, but that was accomplished in part by taking blue areas out of King's district and spreading them elsewhere. Reading, a Democratic town where King had been organizing, was replaced by a stretch of rural countryside packed with traditionally conservative voters. The county where Weaver teaches, Chester, was cut out of King's district, but her hometown in Lancaster County remained squarely in the new district.

One night in February, both King and Hartman were scheduled to appear before the Lancaster Democratic Party to make a closing argument for the endorsement. There was no sign of Hartman until just before the meeting began, when she strode forward, face streaming with tears, and announced that she was withdrawing from the race. King was stunned.

But Hartman wasn't finished running. Days later, she announced she was planting her stakes in the congressional district just to the west, one that was more favorable to Democrats.

Some King supporters believed, not without justification, that an additional motivation for the hopscotch was at play: Hartman wanted to avoid a brewing upset in the primary. In the fourth quarter of 2017, King reported raising more money than Hartman. And it had been Hartman's fundraising prowess that had earned her the party's backing in the first place. King did it again in the first quarter of 2018. It was one thing to amass more grassroots support — that could be overcome by bombing the airwaves with ads. But to raise more money, too? Something was off.

It turned out that the party's indifference to King worked to her advantage. King didn't yet have a viral ad like Randy Bryce in Wisconsin or the loud support of any national progressive figures. Instead, she got a boost from an unlikely source: tech workers organizing around opposition to some of the practices of their own companies.

Hartman's move, meanwhile, symbolized the opposing model of politics. Rather than being driven by community investment, her campaign grew so few real roots that it could literally box itself up and move to a different part of the state. Hartman, in her statement explaining it, said that the new voters were similar enough to the old ones. "I've always put the hardworking families of central Pennsylvania first — and in that way, nothing has changed," Hartman said. "The old PA-16 and the new PA-10 are very similar — they're filled with men, women, and children who deserve a stronger voice working for them in Washington." Without a network of volunteers or community support, Hartman had to rely primarily on paid canvassers to gather signatures to get on the ballot in her new district. The petitions were challenged, and nearly all of them appeared to be invalid. Hartman dropped out of the race before she could be disqualified.

After winning the 2008 election, Barack Obama largely shut down his grassroots network of activists, and the party fell into a steep decline. But King, who took her daughter to three Obama rallies back in 2008, hadn't forgotten how effective his methods were. "We've taken real inspiration from the way Obama campaigned in a place like this," King told me after an event in Lancaster City, "and across the country, to not write off places based on their PVI scores, but to actually talk to people, to be for things, to train volunteers to get involved so that you're scaling up through people and not just being kind of a traditional establishment candidate, raising money, buying TV ads."

The day after the New Holland event that Gregg helped organize, King reflected in her office on how the strategic decision to run a field-driven campaign had yielded unanticipated benefits. "This is a place that he has found community and connections and it's like, these aren't the things that you forecast when you're thinking about running a grass-roots, field-driven campaign. It's totally insane," she said, shaking her head and recalling her exchange with Gregg. "One life at a time."

The campaign ran something they called Jess Camp, consciously patterned after Camp Obama, a training ground for organizers. "I just have this vision, or this picture, of the muscle of civic engagement being exercised and strengthened as they go through that," King said. The flexing of that muscle has the potential to redefine what's possible for Democrats. For years, the party treated its members as cattle to milk for donations and then herd to the polls come Election Day. One email sent out by House Majority PAC in 2018, a super PAC linked with the DCCC, was instructive. The group, run by Ali Lapp, a Rahm Emanuel deputy on the 2006 campaign, sent a survey to its members. Its money question, after asking if the voter wanted to see Democrats take over the House: "Do you know the best thing you can do is donate to organizations such as House Majority PAC?"

As her million-dollar fundraising haul suggested, King didn't overlook the importance of a war chest, but she didn't tell supporters that giving was the most important thing they could do. Tapping voters for money is like fracking. *Dig enough holes and you can squeeze out what you want, but the toxic approach leaves a poisoned land behind.* The DCCC and its super PAC deal with that problem by buying new emails to replace the ones they churn through, until every hole's been drilled. But that's not a sustainable approach.

King treated supporters like a renewable resource instead, training volunteers in organizing and then giving them genuine responsibility. She said new volunteers had rarely gained that type of experience with other campaigns. "When I do block walks, canvasses with people and ask if anybody's done this before, the most common answer — well, most people haven't done it before — the people who say *yes*, the place where they did it was with Obama," she said. "There are very few people that say, *Yeah, I got totally involved in the Clinton campaign*, because there just wasn't a field [program]. It was more of the traditional, DCCC, establishment campaign — and I know people canvassed and worked hard, but it wasn't quite the same."

King's campaign was designed to be a vehicle for the stifled ambitions of the talented, motivated people who hadn't left Lancaster County, and those who had returned after some time away. (Nick Martin, the field director, told me they used an "if you build it, they will come" model.)

The misery of modern life, paradoxically, was a benefit to King's campaign. People were finally starting to talk about "bullshit jobs" — the title of Occupy activist David Graeber's book that zeroed in on the soul-crushing monotony that has made up so much of our professional lives.

Rast said that particularly among retirees, who may be adrift after a life in the workforce, the campaign seemed like more than just a volunteer opportunity. In a world devoid of meaning, King's campaign gave supporters a way to find purpose in their lives. "Every church that I was involved in, I was children's ministry, I was youth leader, I was praise team," Annie Weaver said. "Having left the church was really hard on me. And what I guess I've kind of discovered through all of this, is that this just kinda has become my new ministry."

Weaver does not have a bullshit job — but teachers in Pennsylvania have been treated like shit, suffering daily indignities at the hands of a tea party-dominated state legislature that has done its best to undermine public schools and smear teachers as the real problem at the heart of an American education crisis.

Gregg, he said, enjoys making cabinets — for himself or for a friend, but not all day, everyday for the latest kitchen redesign in the latest McMansion carved into fading farmland.

Out on the campaign trail, Weaver also got to know a New Holland man whose wife is a local minister. He knew that Weaver had been divorced from her church since the election, and invited her over for a Bible study. After praying on it, she accepted the invitation.

She loved it, and on a Thursday night in September, she went back again. "It's a Mennonite church," she told me laughing. "I didn't see that one coming."

That month, Gregg quit his job at Premier and started working full-time as a canvasser for Lancaster Stands Up.

"I like to think that we're helping each other in a lot of ways," Weaver said, "more than just what this was intended for."

Twenty-One

Mrs. Hayes

Jahana Hayes had no chance. She launched her campaign just 12 days before Connecticut's convention for the 5th Congressional District race on May 14, with no infrastructure or real funding. But the biggest problem was that Hayes, a teacher, had no political experience.

By November, she'd become one of a group of insurgent women of color who stormed into Congress with backgrounds far different than the types of candidates recruited by the DCCC. But first she, like the rest of them, had to get past the Democratic Party, before they could come to Washington and rescue it.

Her first obstacle was the local Democratic convention. Each district in Connecticut holds one, and the winner gets the endorsement of the party, which comes with infrastructure, publicity, and favored status on the primary ballot. The endorsed candidate nearly always became the nominee, so Hayes knew she had to make a strong showing. Outside of the convention was a scene, however, not typical of Connecticut political events. A middle school drumline, known as the Berkeley Knights Drill Team and Drum Corp, was banging away out front.

The Berkeley Heights housing project, where Hayes had grown up, sat four miles from Crosby High School, where the convention was being held. It felt like a world away, but the Berkeley Knights had crossed that bridge because one of their own was in the race. Hayes got in line with them. "I knew all the steps and everybody's like, *How do you know that?* I was like, *Because they haven't changed it.* It was born in the projects just to give us something to do," she told me.

Hayes had been a student at Crosby High, but a pregnancy derailed her, sending her to a separate school for expectant moms. "I always wanted to be a teacher, but when that happened, I was like, *Well, I guess I screwed that one up*," she said of that moment 28 years earlier. From there, it had been an odyssey of low-wage jobs, community college, then her first teaching job, then graduate school and ever-increasing recognition for her teaching ability.

Her bid picked up momentum almost as soon as she launched it. She had been named 2016 National Teacher of the Year — which came complete with a White House visit — and that earned her the attention she needed to get her calls returned; delegations to the convention agreed to hear out her last-minute pitch. Local unions got excited, with firefighters, United Auto Workers, and others getting behind her. People close to Chris Murphy, who had previously represented the district but now served in the Senate, helped her campaign take off.

Were Hayes to somehow come out on top, she would become the first black candidate ever nominated by Connecticut Democrats. She would be the only black person serving in the U.S. House[224] or Senate from all of New England. She would also become one of only a few black members of Congress serving a district in which white people made up a majority of the voting population.

Hayes faced off against Mary Glassman, a well-known, well-financed candidate who was largely expected to walk away with the nomination to replace the outgoing Elizabeth Esty unchallenged. Glassman, who worked for a local education agency, had run for lieutenant governor in 2006 and 2010 — losing the general election the first time, and then losing the primary on her second attempt. Glassman was also the former first selectman of Simsbury, a mayor-like position for a wealthy enclave on the outskirts of Hartford. She raised $100,000 out of the gate, hoping to clear the field. By all accounts, she was a fine candidate, the type that Democrats would typically settle for. She had put in her time with a couple failed statewide bids, so it was her turn.

But 2018 was different. The convention began with a drawing of straws to determine the speaking order among Hayes, Glassman and Manny Sanchez. Hayes won the draw and the privilege of going last, a victory soon interrupted by her first realization that this affair might not be on the up and up. Glassman supporters protested, arguing that in fact Glassman should be able to go last, despite not having won that right. The chair eventually ruled for Hayes, but it struck her as an unusual back and forth.

224   Ayanna Pressley would also break this barrier in 2018.

After the first tally, no candidate had a majority — a victory for Hayes in itself — though Glassman held a lead. Sanchez, winning about one-fifth of the vote, dropped out, pitting Hayes against Glassman in a new round of voting. Eyes locked on the screen on stage tallying the votes of the delegates, as it delivered the most astonishing news: Hayes had won an outright majority[225]. Her backers, along with the former students who'd come to witness this next stage of her improbable journey, exploded in celebration. A girl who had grown up in the nearby projects had crossed the tracks and would now become the first black woman endorsed by the overwhelmingly white, wealthy Democratic Party in the district. It was the kind of only-in-America story that made liberals beam with price.

Hayes was stunned. *Could this really be happening?*

Not quite. Pretty soon, a different kind of American story began to play out. With the votes in, Tom McDonough, the convention chair for Connecticut's 5th District, asked from the stage whether any delegates planned to switch candidates. Vote switching is not unusual, according to local operatives familiar with Connecticut politics. But even as no delegates came forward to make a change, the period to switch candidates stayed open as people jockeyed on the floor.

Chris D'Orso, who served on the Board of Aldermen for Waterbury and as a delegate to the convention, had been involved in local Connecticut politics for more than twenty years.[226] He'd never seen anything like what he saw that night when it came to the vote-switching period after Hayes emerged with the majority. He described it as "all hell breaking loose" with people scrambling, resulting in "audible yells" from frustrated delegates in the room. "It wasn't just Jahana's delegates who were mad," he said. "Tons of people were seriously confused why this voting period was still open. It almost seemed like it went on just long enough for [the] New Britain [delegation] to make that last change."

Manny Sanchez, after dropping out, spent the rest of the evening watching from the back. "Initially, it seemed like it was a split," he said of the New Britain delegation. "I stayed out of that process, told them to vote their conscience."

Their consciences were apparently conflicted. The head of the New Britain delegation, Bill Shortell, made three separate trips to the stage to announce switches in the agonizingly protracted period after the vote. When he walked away the last time, enough delegates had changed their votes to put Glassman over the top, with a count of 173-167. "Things

---

225   Local news reports put at 172-168, though accounts differ slightly.

226   This account is partially drawn from a story I wrote with Rachel Cohen on the convention at The Intercept.

happened on the floor," Sanchez summed up, "and votes changed."

At that point, Glassman's supporters began calling for the vote to be gaveled. And it was — quickly. McDonough declared that Glassman had won the official endorsement of the Democratic Party.

D'Orso, who ended up voting for Hayes, put it like this: "I can't say if they were doing something on purpose, but you don't have to be a conspiracy theorist to walk away and say, *What just happened?*'"

Shortell described the situation as "very sensitive," "very delicate," and one he was "not too inclined to talk about." He later told the local press that "the switchers made up their own mind." After the gavel came down, Hayes' supporters fumed about what they saw as a racist injustice.

Hayes calmed the group down, a real-life rendition of the iconic "Saturday Night Live" segment that aired after Donald Trump's 2016 presidential victory, with mournful white liberals coming face to face with the meaning of the election results. She told me that her life had prepared her for what happened. "They were very upset," she confirmed of her backers. "I was like, 'Guys, you don't live this long in this community, in this skin with no —'" she broke off. "They were more upset than me."

"I was like, *You know, this was amazing that we even got this close*," she added. That night, she challenged her supporters to buck up, knowing that she'd have to raise an awful lot of money if she wanted to continue the race.

In Connecticut, any candidate who wins the votes of at least 15 percent of the delegates earns a place on the ballot, but the party endorsee almost always wins the primary. Winning at the convention gives the candidate a favored status at the top of the ballot and a special designation that indicates she is the favorite of the party. News coverage mistakenly referred to Glassman as the nominee, and the party publicly congratulated her, signaling support to primary voters, who tend to be well-informed, particularly in an upscale district like Connecticut's 5th. In the wake of the convention, Hayes asked her political friends what came next, and they all told her the same thing: *Raise a mountain of money; with enough of it, you can defeat Glassman (again) in the August primary.*

The day after the convention she called on her supporters to make 1,000 contributions of $10 each in 24 hours to show that her campaign had real grassroots support. She told me she hit the $10,000 mark easily. Our story in The Intercept raised her another $34,000, I was later told.

The emphasis on money, Hayes told me, was frustrating, but also a driver of her decision to plow forward into the primary. She didn't want to let the system win that easily. "You have to go through the first hurdle of getting through party insiders, and then the next hurdle is money," she said. "So, this whole process unfairly eliminates somebody like me before we can even get to the voters. So I just [said], *I'm all in and I'll figure it out.* You know, I'm old — I'm no stranger to obstacles."

The local press covered the convention outcome as Democrats going with "experience over enthusiasm," but Hayes thought she could use her lack of political experience as evidence that she wasn't corrupted by the process. In a district dominated by the health insurance industry, she came out as a supporter of Medicare for All, along with other touchstone progressive issues such as free public college and a $15 minimum wage.

Hayes had a persuasive way of arriving at strongly progressive political positions by linking them to her own life experiences. Her stance on college flowed from the lifesaving role education played for her. On Medicare for All, she referenced a trip abroad she'd taken. "When I was teacher of the year, I traveled to some really poor countries in Africa with the U.S. State Department," she said. "There are places around the world that are still struggling with this issue. But in a country like the United States of America, the fact that there are people who go without health care is a tragedy, right? Something like that, I feel, is just basic."

And she said that some people who hear about her teen motherhood may assume she opposes abortion rights, but that couldn't be further from the truth. "Government has no place in that decision," she said.

Sanchez, who is half-black and half-Puerto Rican, would also have broken barriers had he run and win. His third-place showing at the Waterbury convention gave him the opportunity to have his name on the ballot, but he worried that if he moved forward, he and Hayes would split the non-Glassman vote in August — and they would both lose. "It's definitely something I'm considering. I don't take it lightly," he said of a three-way battle. I told him we were writing about what had happened to Hayes at the convention, which meant she'd be getting national attention, and I checked in with him on a daily basis until he told me he had decided to drop out.

It was a major boost to Hayes, who now could go head-to-head with Glassman.

He added that Hayes' near-win came as no shock to him. "Having met her, having seen her in action, it didn't surprise me at all," he said. This was all unfolding as Democrats across Connecticut were furious at gubernatorial nominee Ned Lamont, who had signaled he'd run with a nonwhite candidate for lieutenant governor, but ended up picking a white woman the day after Hayes' defeat.

The same day, a bit to the south in Pennsylvania, Democrats went to the polls for their own primaries. In two predominantly white districts, they too had a chance to nominate impressive black candidates who'd have been viable in the general election against Republican incumbents: Greg Edwards in the Lehigh Valley and Shavonnia Corbin-Johnson in Harrisburg. Both lost close races without the support of the party.

It was also unfolding in the context of a surge of labor unrest coming from teachers across the country. It had started in Mingo County, West Virginia, when then-state Senator Richard Ojeda brought together local mine workers and teachers frustrated at their low pay and poor working conditions. The mine workers, Ojeda told me, encouraged the teachers to strike, even though it was illegal to do so in the state, and promised to stand by them if they did. The county's teachers went for it. That wild-cat strike, juiced by an Ojeda speech on the Senate floor that went viral, spread to other counties, and soon the entire state was on strike, besieging the state capitol building. Teachers in Oklahoma and then Arizona would follow their lead, all winning major concessions and triggering strikes that continued through 2018 and into 2019.

Hayes was part of that uprising and picked up national attention, earning an endorsement from Kamala Harris. She also suffered bizarre setbacks, with the local chapter of Our Revolution, the organization that sprang from the Sanders campaign, endorsing Glassman. OR's anarchic spirit would allow pretty much anybody to set up a local chapter, and I interviewed the young man who launched the one that endorsed Glassman, despite her not supporting any of OR's suite of issues. He seemed like a moderate young Democratic Party activist, the type of kid who joined the College Democrats, and said that the process had been followed properly and hoped it would help heal divisions between the left and center in the party.

The U.S. Chamber of Commerce, which almost never endorses Democrats, also backed Glassman, making her perhaps unique in political history in having both Bernie's group and the Chamber on the same side. Just before the election, MoveOn jumped into the race — on the side of Glassman. I had asked MoveOn earlier if it was following the race. They hadn't been, so they polled their membership and were surprised when the vote came back for Glassman. Internally, its leadership debated whether to withhold an endorsement or honor the process and endorse a candidate, Glassman, that nobody on the MoveOn staff wanted to endorse. It's often joked that a liberal is somebody who won't take their own side in an argument, and the quip bore out in this case, as the liberal outfit decided to endorse Glassman.

On Election Day, Hayes trailed in the polls, but told a reporter for The Intercept[227] she was confident because they were probably missing

227   Story was written by Eoin Higgins.

her voters. "I'm relying on first-time voters, voters who have been dis-engaged," said Hayes outside of the Torrington Armory. "I'm trying to start a conversation."

Hayes thumped Glassman by 24 points. MoveOn looked deeper into its endorsement process and discovered that Glassman's campaign had directed its supporters to vote in the straw poll, which was an explicit violation of the ground rules. (MoveOn made a rare public apology to Hayes.) She won the general election by 12 points and on the day of the swearing-in, was seated just to the right of Ocasio-Cortez, where she took selfies and told the freshman from the Bronx the wild story of her convention victory-turned-loss-turned-victory.

Twenty-Two

Primaries Matter

Sarah Smith lost badly, but sometimes that's not what matters. Her race helped push Congress to vote to end a war.

In 2015, the United States began providing logistical support to Saudi Arabia, in addition to tens of billions of dollars in arms sales, as the Gulf state waged war in Yemen. The bombing campaign and mercenary ground troops produced a humanitarian catastrophe of biblical proportions, with cholera and starvation rampant. Progressives in Congress were working to stop it, but they had nowhere near a majority, and D.C.'s liberal think apparatus was uninterested in pushing the issue. Rank-and-file House Democrats often took foreign policy cues from Rep. Adam Smith, who represents Washington, one of the major weapons-producing states. As the top Democrat on the Armed Services Committee, he wielded influence over the Pentagon and its billions in spending power. Relatively hawkish, Smith had been a longtime supporter of the Saudi regime, reluctant to force an end to the war.

In 2017, Rep. Ro Khanna (D-Calif.) and Sanders, in the Senate, launched an effort to invoke the War Powers Act[228] to stop the conflict. The resolution is "privileged," meaning the leaders of the respective chambers can't keep it off the floor. According to people involved with the effort to pass the resolution, the starkest change in Adam Smith's

---

228   Enacted in 1973 in response to the Vietnam War, which Congress had never declared, it gives privileged status to a resolution — meaning leadership can't block a vote — to end a conflict.

approach came in the wake of the June 26 primary victory by Ocasio-Cortez in New York, who shocked the political world by unseating Crowley.

That appeared to focus Smith's mind on his own primary election, scheduled for August 7. Washington state uses a top-two system, meaning that all candidates run in the same primary, and if the top-two finishers are from the same party, both of those candidates advance to the general election. Polls showed that Sarah Smith, backed by the Justice Democrats and endorsed by Ocasio-Cortez, was in striking distance of finishing second.

Ocasio-Cortez's upset victory had confused many veteran politicians, who sensed that things were changing, and nothing could be taken for granted. Throw in two people named Smith on the ballot, and things could go terribly wrong for one of them. When the primary came around, Adam Smith was the top vote-getter, and Sarah Smith looked like she might finish third — the media even called her race — until her vote count began creeping up toward the top Republican challenger.

Ocasio-Cortez followed the returns closely. "Sarah Smith is actually looking like she's going to the general," she texted me. "Media called her race too early!" She added that she had launched her campaign together with Smith as part of the original Justice Democrats cohort and helped as much as she could.

She made it into the general election. Sarah Smith said she could sense Adam Smith becoming less hawkish in real time. "I went after him about Yemen every time I got an opportunity to, and I kept hammering him," recalled Sarah Smith. "When Ro [Khanna] was leading the charge, I started talking about how Ro is a junior congressman in his first term and he is *leading* on this, where Adam has failed for years, and I talked about how we didn't just get involved in Yemen. And then Alex [Ocasio-Cortez] won and people started noticing my campaign and me talking about getting us out of Yemen, and they started to become very interested. And all of a sudden, Adam started to change his tune."

Adam Smith rejected this characterization entirely. "I was actually on the Yemen stuff before I even knew she existed," he told me. "It's not just about Yemen, it's about Saudi Arabia more broadly, the authoritarian crackdown, obviously the murder of Khashoggi. They are becoming more and more lawless in the way they're acting and not just in Yemen, but elsewhere.... I'm happy to push our administration and Congress to do more on that issue."

Because I cover the politics of the Arab Gulf, and Gulf influence on Washington, I knew Jamal Khashoggi, and had actually had lunch with him six weeks before a Saudi death squad dismembered him inside a

Saudi consulate in Istanbul.[229] Smith is absolutely right that his murder played a major role in shifting public opinion and, in particular, congressional opinion toward Saudi Arabia, but Smith's shift began while Khashoggi was alive.

His opposition to U.S. involvement in Yemen became decidedly more forceful as Sarah Smith's candidacy became more potent. In 2016, Adam Smith was just one of 16 Democrats to vote against defunding Saudi Arabia's use of cluster bombs. On July 26, 2018, Smith trumpeted his success for winning restrictions on war activity in Yemen in a defense appropriations bill passed by the House. It wasn't terribly strong, however. The bill, also backed by Khanna, prohibited the U.S. military from providing in-flight refueling to Saudi and other coalition aircraft involved in the Yemen war, unless the secretary of state could certify that "the governments of Saudi Arabia and the UAE are taking certain actions related to the civil war in Yemen."

On September 6, one month after Sarah Smith clinched a primary win, Adam Smith announced that he was introducing a War Powers Resolution, with Khanna and Mark Pocan (D-Wis.), to end the Yemen war. Given his perch on the Armed Services Committee and influence on matters of foreign policy, Adam Smith's public push for the resolution signaled to rank and-file Democrats that it was an issue worth supporting, and the party broke en masse in favor of the resolution. Both Hoyer and Rep. Eliot Engel (D-N.Y.), another leading hawk who happened to chair the House Foreign Affairs Committee, endorsed the Yemen resolution in late September. That led to what's called a "jailbreak" on Capitol Hill, in which a surge of members all switched their positions at the same time.

Adam Smith won the general election easily, beating Sarah Smith 68-32. One week after Election Day, House Republicans beat back the resolution. One month later, it came up again, and this time it barely failed as five Democrats voted with Republicans against it.

That same morning, Smith sat down with the trade reporters to offer his pessimistic take on the resolution. His anger at how Saudi Arabia and the UAE carried out the war — "the closing of ports, the cutting off

---

229   He disappeared inside the consulate on a Tuesday, and I spent much of that week asking lawmakers, White House officials, and Saudi officials if they knew of his whereabouts, and whether he was being held against his will. On Friday, October 5, I wrote a story for The Intercept quoting senators such as Chris Murphy demanding his release, and threatening consequences if he didn't turn up soon. On Saturday, we learned that he had been butchered. At lunch, he had said that he wanted to start writing columns for The Intercept, on top of his column with the Washington Post.

of aid and food, a relentless bombing campaign, and the civilian devastation that's resulted from that is largest humanitarian crisis in the world" — was undiminished, but he was no longer enthusiastic about the War Powers Resolution.

He noted that U.S. presidents have almost unfettered control over the military, and that Congress would have to completely defund the military operation to block the president's actions. "It's not so much that the War Powers Resolution is going to make the administration go, *Oh, shit, well, we really wanted to do this, but since you hit us with this, we won't,*" Smith explained. "It's that it will put public pressure on them to change what they are doing — and we've already seen they've stopped the refueling."[230]

When Smith referenced the resolution that he and Khanna had introduced, he characterized it as solely Khanna's resolution. "The War Powers Resolution thing," Smith told the reporters, before groaning. "There's no way in the world you can write these stories that's going to come out in a way that's positive for me, but I'll say it anyway: The War Powers Resolution is only so useful."

I asked him where he would rank the War Powers Resolution as an effective tool to nudge Saudi Arabia in the right direction, and he demurred. "Look, I mean, we cannot dictate to Saudi Arabia their foreign policy, so we shouldn't have illusions about that," he said. "We have to figure out where can we nudge and prod and push them in a direction that is better. So I think it's a mistake to look at it as if there's something we can do that would, just like that, change the way they interact. My great hope for that region is that the Sunni and the Shia and the Persians and the Arabs can find some sort of peaceful resolution to their current disputes."

Sarah Smith said Rep. Smith excelled at sounding dovish while at the same time helping to perpetuate war. "He'll talk about, *Oh, I'm so progressive, I'm working with Ro very closely on this. It's abhorrent what we're doing in Yemen,*" she said of her former opponent, "but if you push him on any other bill beyond that, he won't talk about it — radio silence — or he'll have a million excuses. He is the excuse king."

After Democrats took control of the House, the resolution passed, with Smith voting yes.

---

230   This was in a briefing with reporters who cover the weapons industry, as reporting by *Breaking Defense.*

Twenty-Three

The Zeal of the Converted

The night of Ocasio-Cortez's primary victory, the first name she listed in her victory speech, as the next in line for a startling upset, was Ayanna Pressley.

Ocasio-Cortez is a deeply loyal person, and Pressley, backed by Justice Democrats, had campaigned with her. Pressley, already elected as an at-large city councilwoman in Boston, was the more powerful of the two before Ocasio-Cortez won, and now the Bronx victor wanted to return the favor. Pressley was facing a September primary against 10-time incumbent Michael Capuano. Pressley's position gave her a number of advantages, but the dynamics were different in her race.

Capuano, like Crowley, was an entrenched white incumbent in an increasingly diverse district. But Capuano wasn't angling for House Speaker and, while he did take corporate PAC money, he had a much more progressive record than Crowley. And while Ocasio-Cortez had been working the bar and fitting in activism when possible, Pressley had been a full-time politician, which came with disadvantages. Pressley had been an outspoken supporter of Clinton and, in that role, had regularly trashed Sanders publicly along with one of his signature items, Medicare for All. She had also taken substantial amounts of corporate money throughout her career, and even had the backing of lobbyists and elite donor class figures in her congressional bid.

Pressley's record was laid bare in an August 18 article in The Intercept with just over two weeks to go before the election. The handful of people who made up Justice Democrats had spent the last year trying to recruit hundreds of candidates, and had little time for the kind of vetting that more established groups conduct. It was the type of approach that enabled them to scale quickly, but could also come with surprises, like this one. The leaders of the group were livid, but Alexandra Rojas was particularly infuriated, feeling betrayed. She wanted to publicly rescind the endorsement, a move that may have tanked the campaign, but one that would send a message about what JD was willing to tolerate.

Others in the group suggested phoning Pressley to hear her defense, and to get a renewed commitment that whatever her previous politics, she was a comrade in the political revolution now. The call was tense, but Pressley made her case and promised that she believed fully in the progressive vision being laid out by JD. She also pledged to issue a new statement vowing to refuse corporate PAC money after the primary.

Rojas was surprised I had learned of that moment, and she hesitated to talk about it. "Yeah," she finally said. "We did that — or, I did that. And it was really tough.'"

"My philosophy is we have to hold them accountable every step of the way. It doesn't matter if it's a week before your primary: if you take corporate money, that's a litmus test for us. Based on what we found and what they said, we felt like that statement was sufficient, and they proved that their donations were clean — for the congressional."[231]

Polls had Pressley losing by double digits going into primary day, but the no-corporate-money pledge turned advantageous. Aside from her race and gender, it distinguished her from Capuano, forced her to hunt for small donors around the city, and those small donors were some of her best ambassadors on the ground. In neighborhoods where she got a disproportionate number of small donations, she handily beat Capuano. And while Capuano's money came mostly from the wealthier areas of

---

231   Rojas said the group took into account that Pressley's background was different than a typical organizer, and that the revolution needed converts, too. "I don't think it's smart for the progressive movement to just always be shame, shame, shame, when someone fucks up once, or even has a whole history of fucking up. Like, it's very clear: Ayanna is a bad-ass legislator. She spent a ton of time on the Hill, went to city council and before that she had activist roots. And then she ran for Congress. She's got an interesting history that's not like a Rashida and not like an Alexandria, but she's here now, and I want her to stay, and I think she wants to as well," Rojas said. "So it's as a new area that we're navigating to have these progressive leaders like Ayanna who are sort of new to this movement space, but they're ready to fight, and that's because of the work that we've done as a movement to push them to be there. So she was one of the few we had to do that for, and some didn't work out, and some did."

north Boston, Pressley got contributions from all over the city, including in the poorer neighborhoods. That likely accounted for the error in the polling, as pollsters assumed people in those neighborhoods would turn out at a much lower rate than they did.[232] She ended up blowing out Capuano by 18 points.

The night of her victory, Ocasio-Cortez told me she became convinced that her win wasn't a fluke, but part of something bigger. She hit the road in support of a slew of insurgent candidates, including Cori Bush in St. Louis, who was taking on Lacy Clay, the scion of a local dynasty, whose father had co-founded the Congressional Black Caucus. She also rallied for Abdul El-Sayed's run for Michigan governor, and Brent Welder, the Justice Democrat-backed candidate in Kansas City, Kansas. Bernie Sanders joined her in Michigan and Kansas, and in Kansas she felt her first blowback. EMILY's List had previously backed a candidate in the race who dropped out amid allegations she had sexually harassed a subordinate. So the outfit recruited a new woman to run, Sharice Davids, who ran on her exciting profile: a Native American lesbian and mixed-martial arts fighter who'd served in the Obama administration. Democrats who assumed Ocasio-Cortez's victory had been all about identity politics were stunned that she would support the white guy over Davids, but Welder was running on the same platform as Ocasio-Cortez, while Davids was running a standard Democratic campaign.

Davids ended up narrowly winning the primary, with a roughly $700,000 infusion from EMILY's List's super PAC, one of its largest investments in a 2018 primary. Welder won solidly in the district's heavily black precincts, but Davids was carried to victory by white liberals in the suburbs.

Bush and El Sayed lost, too. Centrist elements began testing the strength of Ocasio-Cortez, who had become an overnight sensation after her June victory, yet instead of sliding out of the news cycle, had only grown bigger since. Joe Lieberman emerged in the pages of the Wall Street Journal to urge Joe Crowley to challenge her in the general election.

The Working Families Party had assumed Ocasio-Cortez had no chance of beating Crowley, and was already in a brawl with Gov. Andrew Cuomo, so endorsed Crowley in the race, not looking to pick too many fights. That meant that even though he lost the Democratic primary, he occupied the WFP ballot line — and refused to give it up.[233] Crowley's

---

232   The data were analyzed by Bobby Constantino and a team of researchers, and covered in The Intercept in Nov. 2018.
233   The WFP asked him to get off the line, but he refused, claiming it couldn't realistically be done. That was a lie, but the national media bought it. Nobody no-

allies in Queens and the Bronx pushed him to make a serious run. He was waiting, it seemed, to see if Ocasio-Cortez would flame out or do something that disqualified herself in the eyes of voters, in which case he'd reluctantly accede to the groundswell of popular demand for a white knight to ride in November.

Ocasio-Cortez was convinced he'd mount a last-minute bid. "We were hearing very concrete things on the ground," she told me. "For me, the only time when I felt a little better was in the September 13th primary, when we took out like half of the Queens machine. And we took out a really major player in the Bronx down ballot, and we replaced them all with a sweep of progressive candidates. That, and Ayanna's win in Massachusetts — those were two moments where I was like, this is not a fluke. This was not an accident. This is a movement. And we worked hard in those two areas to make that happen because we didn't want to just be a fluke or be alone, or be vulnerable in that way."

While still feeling vulnerable, she commissioned an intensive survey of the district to find out if the arguments being thrown against her had been sticking. The poll was conducted in mid-September by Lake Research Partners[234] and found Ocasio-Cortez with a 48-17 approval rating among all voters in the district; Crowley, who'd been serving in elected office since 1999, was a nobody. One quarter of people had never heard of him, and another quarter had no opinion. He registered a slightly higher unfavorable rating — at 19 percent — than Ocasio-Cortez.

The survey also tested three knocks against her — that she was too inexperienced, spent too much time outside the district, and had been focused on issues that didn't really matter to constituents. All three arguments were overwhelmingly rejected. One question asked:

> Since winning her primary, Alexandria Ocasio-Cortez has spent more time running around the country promoting an unrealistic socialist agenda than she has in her own district listening to voters. She hasn't even been elected to Congress yet, and she's already trying to build a national profile and pursue her own personal ambitions. The voters of our need a representative whose top priority is to help them, not increase their own celebrity.

By a 50-42 margin, voters in the district said the criticism gave them no doubts. The poll didn't mince words, and also asked about Ocasio-Cortez's most visible mistake, when she'd buckled in an interview and said she wasn't an expert on Israel/Palestine. It asked:

---

ticed later that Cynthia Nixon had no trouble getting off the WFP line after she lost the Democratic primary.

234   The Celinda Lake-owned firm that EMILY's List bars candidates from working with. I obtained a copy of the private poll.

> Alexandria Ocasio-Cortez is wrong on foreign policy, especially when it comes to American-Israeli relations. She has stated publicly her belief that the state of Israel is engaging in an illegal occupation of Palestine, and this past summer, she wrongly accused Israeli defense troops of engaging in a massacre even though they were defending Israeli territory. Ocasio-Cortez has even admitted that she's "not an expert" on the issue. Ocasio-Cortez's ill-informed views don't belong in Congress.

Even given the framing of the question, 46 percent said it left them with no doubts about her, while 44 percent said it did. Her team had been telling her that her fears of a Crowley surprise were unfounded, and the survey helped put her at ease.

As she continued taking flak from both the center and the right, it became apparent that this would be the new normal. At a campaign strategy meeting, Corbin Trent noted that it had been much simpler when all they had to do was take on Joe Crowley. Ocasio-Cortez cut in to say that while they might be playing at a higher level, the same insight should still guide them. "They've got money," she reminded her team. "We've got people."

Twenty-Four

The Year of the Woman

Among the responses of millions of women shaken by the election of Donald Trump, Rose McGowan's was perhaps the most historically consequential. Trump had been credibly accused during the campaign of sexually assaulting or harassing 17 different women. On October 28, less than two weeks before Election Day, I obtained and posted video of Trump grabbing, forcibly kissing, and humiliating an Australian actress on stage at a corporate conference because she had declined earlier to introduce him to the crowd. It was grotesque behavior, and it followed the "Access Hollywood" recording in which Trump made his infamous "grab them by the pussy" boast. It was one thing to hear him talk about doing it. It was another to watch him do it[235] on stage in front of thousands. But bigger news would break that day: at the last conceivable moment, FBI Director James Comey had reopened his investigation[236]

235   You can watch for yourself and decide. Google the article's headline, "Video Shows Donald Trump Sexually Humiliating Woman Before Large Audience."
236   On May 9, 2017, James Comey learned he was fired through cable news. Trump had made the decision on the advice of his senior counselor, his son-in-law Jared Kushner, who told him that Democrats would support the decision, because they despised Comey, holding him responsible for Trump's win and Clinton's loss. The advice was laughably wrong. Democrats, by this point, were obsessed with the notion that Russian President Vladimir Putin had orchestrated Trump's victory, and had done so while colluding with the Trump campaign. It was the only way to explain such an anomalous election result, and Comey was the law enforcement figure

303

into Clinton's email habits.

Clinton's polling numbers dove. And when, on the weekend before the election, Comey cleared her, that announcement, too, sent her tumbling further, as the short investigation seemed rigged to those skeptical of Clinton.

As we would later learn, Trump and his lawyer Michael Cohen had been paying off adult-film actress Stormy Daniels to keep Trump's affair with her quiet, keeping the focus on Clinton's emails in the waning days of the campaign.

For McGowan, that the country could elect Trump despite all the evidence of his sexual predation — his first wife, Ivana, charged him with rape in a memoir — reminded her too much of Hollywood, where men she knew to be rapists, and whom the whole town knew to be rapists, dominated the industry.

She resolved to do something about it, though she wasn't sure what. As one step, she made a donation online to UltraViolet, a women's group that had called out both Democrats and Republicans in the past over sexual misconduct. In March 2017, the group saw her donation come in, and reached out to set up a phone call.

When McGowan connected with the group's executive director, Shaunna Thomas, she said she admired how UltraViolet refused to let partisanship get in the way of holding predators to account, which made it something of an anomaly among liberal women's groups.

McGowan considered writing about Hollywood and rape culture. *Having rapists (and others who defended and protected them) create the films that the country watched*, she reasoned, *must have something to do with the country's endemic rape culture.* She had experienced it herself, she said, at the hands of one of the most powerful figures in Hollywood. She wasn't sure she wanted to name her assailant but McGowan told Thomas, who had grown up in Beverly Hills, that she probably knew who she was talking

Democrats believed would uncover the truth of the conspiracy. They reacted with fury to his firing. Kushner, though, was right in one isolated case. Back at her home in Chappaqua, Hillary Clinton was celebrating the news. She had spent the winter and spring poring over survey and turnout data, calling friends and former aides relentlessly, analyzing and re-analyzing. It was, her friends believed, both part of her grieving process, but also holding her back from moving on. When she learned that Comey had been fired by Trump, she was ecstatic. Comey had finally gotten what he had coming. "In the immediate aftermath, people weren't sure how to respond," her 2016 spokesman Brian Fallon recalled. "There were people who started buying into Trump's rationale." Clinton was ultimately dissuaded by advisers from issuing a statement applauding the move.

about.

Thomas had an inkling, but asked if McGowan wanted to give her a hint.

"He recently hired Malia Obama as an intern," McGowan said.

"That's who I thought it was," Thomas told her.

Later, Thomas was reminded of another conversation she'd had with a Hollywood actress about rape in the industry. It was with Ashley Judd at Democratic operative David Brock's house on the night of the White House Correspondents Association dinner in 2015.[237] Judd hadn't told Thomas who specifically she was talking about.

On April 18, after her call with McGowan, Jodi Kantor from the New York Times reached out. Thomas had been a source for her before, and they were on good terms. The board of the New York Times had been thrilled with the paper's coverage of Bill O'Reilly's sexual misconduct, Kantor told her, and thought it was a place the paper could make a mark by devoting more resources. She wondered if Shaunna had any suggestions of other men to look into.

"Oh, that's easy," Thomas said. "Harvey Weinstein. Talk to Rose McGowan and Ashley Judd."

On May 8, 2017, she connected Kantor and McGowan. "Rose, lovely to e-meet you," Kantor wrote in a familiar opening line that belied the history-making moment unfolding. "We are interested in doing some investigation into harassment of women in Hollywood, and I'd appreciate hearing your perspective. Not looking for quotes at this point — just a deeper understanding of the truth — so perhaps we can start by talking discreetly."

The resulting article, published in October 2017, along with a story published shortly afterward by Ronan Farrow[238] in The New Yorker, would rate among the most culturally consequential pieces of journalism published in generations. When actress and activist Alyssa Milano took to Twitter and asked millions to follow her lead and share stories of their assaults and harassment, the #MeToo movement was born.

It was inextricably linked to the election of Trump, but it began to

---

237   I was at that after-party, too, and spoke with Judd the same night, getting into an argument with her about the virtues of the 12-Step program as it applied to opioid addiction. She's a deep believer in it, and I was working on a story with Jason Cherkis on how the program was killing those addicted to opioids. The story, finally published in January 2016, was called "Dying to be Free." If you or anyone you know is struggling with opioid addiction, read it.

238   McGowan later said she was talking to both Kantor and Farrow to keep pressure on them so the story wouldn't drop. NBC News famously refused to run it, so Farrow took it to The New Yorker.

target misogyny and a culture of impunity for abuse wherever it could be found. In electoral politics, that meant that male-dominated political power structures were no longer getting a pass.

2018 would come to be known as the Year of the Woman, and though there had been several before it, this one lived up to its name. Nobody was better positioned to channel this energy than EMILY's List, yet the year would be a complicated one for the group, as two related, overlapping but also distinct forces battered down Washington. Women from the far left to the center-right rose up in gale force strength against Trump, but at the same time a grassroots insurgency — often led by women — targeted a Democratic Party establishment that had been so feckless as to allow Trump to rise. EMILY's List enthusiastically allied with the former force, but was either indifferent or hostile to the latter.

That left EMILY's List in difficult spots all over the country. One of the first to face them came in Chicago, where the group tried desperately to stay out of the first serious Democratic primary of the cycle. The incumbent could not have been a more blatant beneficiary of patriarchy had he appeared in a comic book. Much like his father, Bill Lipinski, incumbent Dan Lipinski owes his career to the boys' club of the Illinois machine. In 1975, Mayor Richard Daley, one of the longest-serving city bosses in American history, named the elder Lipinski the Democratic committeeman for Chicago's 23rd Ward, one of the more powerful elements of the city's machine. (More than 40 years later, in his 80s, he was in the same party position.)

That same year, 1975, Bill Lipinski was elected to the city council, serving as an alderman for the ward. "Elected," here, is a term used loosely, as the seat was essentially handed to him by the machine. After Harold Washington's mayoral win in 1983, Lipinski played a leading role in the Council Wars, pulling every lever to jam him up. In 1992, new congressional lines had been drawn by the statewide party, and lo and behold, Lipinski had been dealt a winning hand. With a bevy of votes from the 23rd ward, he waltzed into the House in 1992 — dubbed the Year of the Woman, incidentally — where he proceeded to build a career as a broadly conservative legislator — loudly anti-choice, right wing on foreign affairs, a leading Blue Dog in the chamber.

In 2004, as he had every prior cycle, he advanced past his primary easily. But then he made a surprise announcement: Lipinski would retire (and soon turn to a life of lobbying), but he had instructed the 23rd ward Democrats to place his son, Dan Lipinski, then a University of Tennessee professor, on the ballot. This was not political advice that the committee, which Lipinski still ran, could refuse. With no primary, and no serious general election opposition, Professor Dan Lipinski coasted into Congress, where he carried on his father's tradition of representing this blue district in as conservative a fashion as he could, while facing no electoral opposition.

After the 2010 Census, Lipinski won a new redistricting, effectively making his district more conservative by carving as many liberal enclaves out of his district as he could. Rep. Luis Gutiérrez, a fellow Illinois Democrat, watched it happen: "All of a sudden, one day I woke up and I saw the 2011 map that I was going to run in 2012 under, and I said, *Whoa! What happened to Bucktown? Wicker Park? What happened to all my inner-city folks?* All of a sudden I have cul-de-sacs, I have Brookfield Zoo, I have southern suburbs — doesn't sound like part of a Hispanic congressional district, right?"

Instead of becoming more progressive as his party shifted left, Lipinski had moved his own district to the right. As the Democratic Party realigned on immigrant rights, LGBT issues and reproductive freedom, Lipinski's retrograde views stood out within the caucus, particularly after the 2010 tea party wave swept out many like-minded Democrats who served in red districts. A serious primary challenge to Lipinski was just a matter of time — after all, that's why he redrew his own district — and it finally came in the form of Marie Newman, a small business owner and local activist.

The coalition that got behind Newman was remarkably broad, with one foot in the establishment and one foot out: Daily Kos, Kirsten Gillibrand, and Gloria Steinem backed Newman early, followed by an organized coalition of five progressive groups, led by NARAL Pro-Choice America, and joined by the Human Rights Campaign, MoveOn, the Progressive Change Campaign Committee, and Democracy for America in late November 2017, for the election set for March 21.

Even Gutiérrez and Jan Schakowsky, both fellow members of the Illinois congressional delegation, took the extraordinary step of endorsing Newman. (Gutiérrez retired in 2018, replaced by Chuy Garcia.) Two groups, however, were noticeably absent from the effort, despite pleading from the organizations involved: Planned Parenthood and EMILY's List. For the former, the decision was not easy. Planned Parenthood's first priority was keeping clinics up and running. If it didn't, people could die, as nearby women would be left without access to quality health care. The party machine, with control over money flows, could not be challenged lightly.

EMILY's List, however, had no such problems. It runs no clinics and has long been purely a Washington-based political operation, with a mission to elect pro-choice Democratic women. Yet it is institutionally reluctant to challenge incumbent Democrats, even ones with anti-choice records being primaried by pro-choice women, and internally the group's leaders were not convinced the race was winnable.

It was the first major non-decision the group would make of the cycle that would put it at odds with the resurgent progressive movement — even as the explosion of women running for office, organizing Indivisible groups and marching in the street put the group squarely in the center of the media narrative. A June 2018 Time magazine profile of EMILY's List called its headquarters "the national nerve center for this year's groundswell," noting that the group and its Super PAC had spent nearly $20 million early in the cycle, to go along with more than $500 million over the past three decades.

"We've been practicing 33 years for this moment," EMILY's List President Stephanie Schriock told Time. But 2018 would turn out to be a far more complicated political moment than EMILY's List was built for. While a record number of women won House seats against Republicans, and many with EMILY's List support, the group's reluctance to get in the trenches with leftist women challenging establishment men left it merely observing, and sometimes battling, this new movement. They weren't alone in missing the energy. In January 2018, Time magazine ran a cover story on women running for House seats that included photos of 48 women on the cover. Not pictured: Alexandria Ocasio-Cortez.

In Chicago, the Service Employees International Union finally forced EMILY's List's hand. As part of a conversation with a local newspaper, Newman and Lipinski clashed over the minimum wage, with Lipinski rejecting the notion of a $15 an hour minimum. That, it turned out, was too much for the SEIU, whose brand was closely linked with the Fight for 15.[239] The local teachers' union, too, got behind Newman, a bold break from the party machine. That, in turn, made the neutrality of Planned Parenthood and EMILY's List simply absurd. On February 2, six weeks before the election, and after months of pressure to get involved, they finally announced support.

In the final few weeks of the campaign, a group of local billionaires also got into the race, funneling one million dollars through the dark-money group No Labels. Mark Penn crafted the campaign strategy, per internal emails I obtained, and No Labels blasted TV with negative ads against Newman.

On election night, Newman fell just 2,000 votes short and Lipinski survived 51-49 — likely for the last time. Backers of the Newman cam-

---

239   It wasn't the comment that was too much for the SEIU, I later learned. At The Intercept, we ran a story with the headline "Union-Backed Democratic Congressman Rejects $15/hr Minimum Wage." A source involved in the internal discussion later told me it was that headline that pushed them to endorse Newman.

paign came away sure they would have won had EMILY's List gotten in earlier, or if No Labels hadn't dropped a million dollars in the final weeks.[240]

It was the first underground battle of the 2018 cycle between progressive groups and EMILY's List, but many more would come, as the group lined up almost exclusively behind the more conservative, business-friendly candidate in race after race, even when other pro-choice women had run in the primary. If a progressive woman ran against an establishment-backed man, the group was likely to simply sit it out.

The group was founded to right a glaring wrong: the massive under-representation of women in elected office. In 1985, it pioneered the bundling of small dollars to create a new power center that could compete with the male establishment. At the same time, it was built by political insiders, some of them lobbyists. That doesn't mean they built EMILY's List to further the interests of corporate clients, but it does mean the organization's DNA was somewhat conflicted from the beginning — insurgent and anti-establishment, yet of and funded by elements of the establishment. The outfit rightly rejected the outcome that it saw in Washington, with barely any women serving in the House or Senate. But the group was reluctant to embrace any type of agenda that would challenge the system that had produced that outcome.

The solution, to leave the system in place but swap in women when it didn't harm the Democratic Party, has been met with limited, but not trivial, success. By 2018, there were just 23 women in the Senate, and 87 in the House.

EMILY's List's first success came quickly, when the group landed Barbara Mikulski in the Senate in 1986 — the first woman elected on her own, without following a husband. In 1991, Professor Anita Hill came forward after her former boss, Clarence Thomas, was nominated to the Supreme Court, and described his repeated sexual harassment of her. Though Judiciary Committee Chairman Joe Biden played a key role in that, his undermining of her was largely behind the scenes, while Republicans, and their allies on the radio and the press, trashed her in the open. The 1992 election became the first of several to come to be dubbed "The Year of the Woman," and it ushered in four new women to the Senate — doubling the total — and women in the House rose from 30 to 48.

The fight for gender equality stalled out, with the numbers falling when Republicans took over Congress and staying flat the next 12 years. The 2006 blue wave, the next chance to bring women into Congress, was a flop. The House saw 53 new members of the House; just 10 were wom-

240   In 2019, she announced a rematch with Lipinski.

en. Eight of the 10 new senators elected were men.

EMILY's List followed that performance by going all in for Hillary Clinton the next year, her first run for the presidency. The primary campaign against Barack Obama pitted the group against young people, who went overwhelmingly for Obama, and black voters generally. When she fell short, magazine pieces started popping up about the organization's woes.

Four years later, the group had a chance to repair its relationship with the progressive community. By that cycle, the progressive movement had built up the digital and organizing capacity that had been rolled out first in the Dean campaign, and looked to flex some muscle in two open primaries. EMILY's List would play a key role in both.

The two races were in Albuquerque and San Diego. Both pitted progressives against big-money-backed centrists. In Albuquerque, the liberal energy was behind Eric Griego, a New Mexico state senator with a strongly progressive record. Running to his right was Michelle Lujan Grisham, a protegé of former Gov. Bill Richardson. Lujan Grisham had run in 2008 but lost the primary to Martin Heinrich. In 2012, Heinrich, a progressive, rose to become a U.S. senator, creating the opening in the House.

Meanwhile, in San Diego, support on the left was behind Lori Saldaña, while the corporate wing of the party rallied around Scott Peters.

The problem, organizers of the progressive effort quickly realized, might be EMILY's List. The group had endorsed both Lujan Grisham and Saldaña, following their model of supporting pro-choice female Democrats. In this case, that dictate aligned them with progressives in the case of Saldaña, and put them up against the liberal coalition in the case of Lujan Grisham.

Leaders of the coalition backing both Saldaña and Griego reached out to EMILY's List in an attempt to deconflict.[241] The progressive leaders told EMILY's List they fully understood that it was well within its rights to endorse both women, and that they weren't suggesting it do otherwise. But if it planned to spend big money on just one race, could the group please spend it in San Diego on Saldaña, so that they were not working at cross purposes? After all, many of EMILY's List's donors also funded the progressive groups, meaning their money would literally be spent on both sides of the New Mexico race.

It was a moment of reckoning for EMILY's List, a relatively low-

---

241   This is a military term that has become widely used thanks to the air war over Syria. Russian and American jets stay in communication so that they don't accidentally go up against each other, which is a process that falls short of cooperation, aka "deconfliction."

stakes decision with high-stakes implications. Did it consider itself part of this burgeoning progressive movement? Or did it have its own agenda? Looking at the two races, it was also clear which woman had more clout. Lujan Grisham hailed from a New Mexico political dynasty, and Richardson, a Clinton cabinet official, was still a major Washington player. Saldaña, on the other hand, was a relative nobody — an organizer, a community college professor, and a member of the General Assembly.

EMILY's List made its decision. The group would indeed spend money on only one race — but it would pick New Mexico, going to war with Griego and the groups backing him, while leaving Saldaña on her own. Thus, in the pages of history, EMILY's List can claim to have backed a woman of color in New Mexico — a noble pursuit, given the dearth of such representation in Congress — but on the ground, Lujan Grisham won, ironically, by contorting Griego into the browner candidate.

She did it with a mugshot. As a young man, Griego, like George W. Bush and Beto O'Rourke, had gotten a DUI in Texas. Lujan Grisham got ahold of his mugshot and plastered it on TV. Though Lujan Grisham scans as Latina in Washington, back in New Mexico it's more complicated, with camps divided between families — like the Lujan Grishams, who proudly trace their origin to Spain, and those like Griego's, who are more associated with Mexico. "Identifying with your European ancestors, there's some caché there," Griego told me of New Mexico's politics. "The Lujans in particular [fit] in this old school New Mexico camp of, *We're Spanish, we're not* — they use the word *Hispanic*, but they don't really identify as indigenous or Mexican. They identify as Spanish, really."

In the primary, it can be advantageous to win over racist voters to claim Spanish rather than Mexican heritage, and Lujan Grisham used the photo to suggest Griego was too much of the latter. "She was a county commissioner; she used her county law enforcement connections to get a copy of the photo," Griego told me. "If you look at the ad and you understand New Mexico and Albuquerque politics, it was a way to basically really dog-whistle that I was the brown, crime guy."

While Latinos populated about two-thirds of the district, at the time they made up only about 40 percent of the voters, so it was crucial to win the white vote. "She very much tried to nurture the most — she really didn't play up the Hispanic thing at all, and actually overperformed with white voters," he said. "They were able to buy two to three weeks — almost solely based on EMILY's List money — two to three weeks essentially of attack ads, which really, our tracking polls showed, made all the difference in the world. We lost women in droves."

Griego took responsibility for the DUI in the first place, but was bothered that the photo appeared to have been doctored. "I don't ever remember being that tanned as the picture that they ran in the ad," he said. "I mean, it was also January when I got popped in Dallas, so it was very cold and so I hadn't had sun in a while, so it should have been a much lighter version of me. But the picture that they ran in the ad was a very brown version of me. At the end of the end of the day — a 20-year-old DUI and some unpaid traffic tickets — they ran this really effective ad that made me out to be just kind of a thug, even though I was a state senator and I'd been a city councilman."

In San Diego, the woman on the wrong end of the EMILY's List decision had a unique perspective from which to analyze it: she lectured at San Diego State in the country's oldest women's studies program. She noticed that EMILY's List hadn't offered a full-throated endorsement — she wasn't on the list itself, but a separate category of people the group generally supported but wasn't doing much for specifically. It was a pattern she recognized from her study of how patriarchal institutions grappled with an influx of women. "It's not always just patriarchal institutions doing this; that is just how institutions defend themselves against interlopers, or what they perceive as interlopers," she told me. "What you see is the dominant group maybe doesn't exclude them, but creates new kind of levels."

Saldaña cited the examples of accounting and medicine, which added new levels — CPA certified rather than licensed, and physician's assistant or nurse practitioner, respectively — that in many ways were functionally equivalent to a more senior role, but were largely held by women, while men retained the higher status and pay.

In Saldaña's case, the new rung was being created for progressive candidates with grassroots support but without big money backing. While in Washington for a candidate training, she said, she met with the group's finance director, who cited her low fundraising as a reason they couldn't offer full support. The chicken-and-egg answer was frustrating, but more so was the example he gave her. He noted that Christie Vilsack, the wife of Agriculture Secretary Tom Vilsack, had held a fundraiser the night before and raised gobs of money. Saldaña needed to do the same. "I felt like comparing the wife of a Cabinet member's campaign against my campaign is really not an effective comparison," she recalled.

"I felt that they were very elitist," she continued. "They didn't do any events for me. They didn't do any national appeals for me. They didn't do a lot of these things that they did for other candidates that were on the full EMILY's List."

On Election Day, Lujan Grisham beat Griego by just over 2,000 votes. Saldaña lost to Scott Peters by significantly less than that.

Instead of electing two progressives — one man and one woman, both Hispanic — the party had elected two conservatives — one man and one woman, only one of them Hispanic, the other white.

Elections swung on just a few votes can still have lasting consequences. Peters went on to become the chair of the New Democrat Coalition in the House, the Wall Street wing of the party, and consistently organizes against progressives in the party.

Lujan Grisham, after racking up a conservative record in Congress, ran for governor of New Mexico in 2018, and was invited to speak at the 2018 EMILY's List gala. In a year when Democratic primary voters were pining for female candidates, Lujan Grisham won the nomination, and in the heavily Democratic state, won the general election, too.

After the primary victory, she spiked the football in the faces of progressives. In an interview with the Albuquerque Journal, she unloaded on the left. "There are plenty of Democrats in Congress who don't reflect my priorities or values," she said. "I won't join the progressive caucus because I think they have looked to minimize national security and productive, smart defense investments. That's made me very nervous."

Lujan Grisham, who had been a co-owner of Delta Consulting, a firm that managed the state's high-risk health insurance pool, also came down hard against Medicare for All. But she was the Democratic nominee.

Because Heinrich, a progressive, beat Lujan Grisham in 2008, he became senator in 2012 and strengthened the Democratic caucus' progressive wing. But because Lujan Grisham and Peters won their close primaries in 2012, nearly a decade later they're both prominent leaders in the party, pushing it to the right. Lujan Grisham is now talked about as a presidential contender as Democrats go searching for credible Hispanic women who can run — ignoring the reality that she won her first federal office on the back of white votes by painting her opponent as too brown.

By 2018, Griego was political director for the Working Families Party in New Mexico, and oversaw several stunning insurgent upsets of conservative Democrats in state legislative primaries. But he was stumped on what to do about Lujan Grisham after she won the gubernatorial primary. "She's put progressives in a really, really tough spot, because we have nowhere else to go," he said. "She's a Hispanic woman and it's almost like, if you're a good progressive, you'll get behind her."

Meanwhile, there was a three-way Democratic primary to replace Lujan Grisham in Congress. The candidate with the backing of the most progressive groups was Antoinette Sedillo Lopez, but the liberal community was split between her and Deb Haaland, who stood to be the first Native American woman in Congress. Though she had a mixed record, she ran on a thoroughly progressive platform. Rounding out the primary was Damon Martinez, an Army vet and former prosecutor, running as the pro-business moderate in the race.

The dark money group No Labels dumped a million dollars into the race on behalf of Martinez, funding by billionaires. EMILY's List again faced a decision, but this time chose not to play favorites between Sedillo Lopez and Haaland. The group dove into the race with attack ads against Martinez, hoping that one or the other women would win. Haaland won.

Elsewhere around the country, however, EMILY's List was picking favorites. Nowhere did the group have more trouble than New York state.

By February 2018, it was becoming clear to EMILY's List that there were far, far more women running than they could ever have anticipated, and they needed more capacity. What they also needed, but never got, was a smoother endorsement process. As it was, all endorsements had to go through what was called a "choice council," which consisted of head honcho Schriock as well as other board members, senior leaders, and founders. Scheduling all those people was a nightmare, which made moving with any quickness impossible.

Compounding that problem was a basic lack of staff commensurate with the surge of women running. Fortunately, though, money was not a problem. To lighten some of the congressional load, EMILY's List turned to a veteran campaign consultant, Angela Kouters, who had a long career in Democratic politics, including a top position in the 2006 midterms at the DCCC with Rahm Emanuel. When she arrived in February, she was assigned New York, where she worked with Karen Defilippi, the group's Northeast political adviser. Defilippi had gotten her start with Hillary Clinton's 2008 presidential campaign, but Kouters knew next to nothing about New York state politics. The file she was handed didn't help, and so she spent her first few weeks on Google, reading news clippings.

From there, she had to decide where EMILY's List should plow resources. Don't worry about New York 14, she was told early. That was the seat held by Joe Crowley, who was pro-choice, so there was no need to look at the primary challenge being waged by the obscure Alexandria Ocasio-Cortez.

One of the races on the group's radar was for the congressional seat representing Syracuse. Juanita Perez Williams, in November 2017, had lost a race for mayor in a landslide to an independent candidate, even managing to lose her own neighborhood precinct by two to one. In some lines of work, a failure so complete, in such an otherwise favorable climate, might earn somebody a demotion, a period of probation, or a rethinking of whether the person's skill set fits within their envisioned career path. But this is Democratic Party politics, where consequences are for the people, not the politicians. The performance earned her a call from EMILY's List's Karen Defilippi, as well as an invitation to the headquarters of the Democratic Congressional Campaign Committee.

Within just a few days of the loss, Perez Williams was in Washington, D.C., sitting down with top-tier Democratic operatives who saw, in her impressive bio — a Latina, a prosecutor, and a veteran — the makings of a promising 2018 congressional candidate.

She was flattered, she told them, but she declined the entreaties to take on popular Republican incumbent John Katko — though she made sure to let the public know that she'd been recruited by national Democrats. "They all came together and were calling me, telling me I could do this," Perez Williams told syracuse.com in an interview in January. "While I'm very humbled to be asked, I'm going to sit this one out and support the designee."

With Perez Williams out of the race, a field of three was gradually winnowed down to one, as local officials, county Democratic parties, and Indivisible chapters all rallied around Dana Balter, a local professor of public policy.[242] In Syracuse, Balter became the consensus choice. Perez Williams herself got behind her, giving $250 at a fundraiser on the Thursday before Easter.

But national Democrats weren't finished with Syracuse. All of a sudden, local party officials began hearing rumors that Perez Williams was getting in after all. By then, The Intercept had become the news outlet most closely covering Democratic primaries, and a Syracuse party chair reached out to let me know what he was hearing. I asked Meredith Kelly, a spokeswoman for the DCCC, if the rumors were true, and she responded with a statement that neatly distilled how the party thinks about candidates. "Juanita is a Latina, an accomplished veteran and prosecutor, and has deep roots and support in the Syracuse region, and she has every right to run for Congress," Kelly, who went on to work for Kirsten Gillibrand's 2020 presidential campaign, told me in a statement.

Nobody, of course, was questioning her right to run for Congress, rather the wisdom of the decision so late in the primary. Had she announced in January and run an energetic campaign, she may have cleared the field. But in the meantime, the local community had become deeply invested in Balter.

Just days after her donation to Balter, Perez Williams decided to exercise her right to run. Perez Williams explained to an exasperated local progressive movement that Balter simply hadn't raised enough money

---

242   Balter was herself a founder of a local Indivisible chapter, and one of the most difficult challenges the movement faced in 2018 was losing its local leaders to campaigns for office.

or gotten enough attention nationally, so she decided to jump in to try and save the party.

But now she had a new problem: New York requires a candidate to gather 1,250 signatures of Democrats registered in the district, and adds all sorts of arcane layers onto the process to make it difficult for challengers to get on the ballot. The New York Democratic Party advertises itself as the oldest in the nation, and its petition-gathering laws are one way among many that it builds moats around incumbents.

The petitions are only a problem for campaigns without a big team of volunteers and a chest full of money, as a consulting industry has built up around the law, and turn-key operations will get a candidate the signatures needed, for a price. Perez Williams told the local press she was running an all-volunteer canvassing operation, but that was a lie. A local resident sent me a photo of a flier offering $15 per hour to canvassers. I called the number and the woman who answered the phone confirmed that it was indeed a paid operation to get Perez Williams on the ballot. The DCCC, it turned out, funded the operation.

Four Democratic county chairs from the district, all of which had been kept in the dark about the DCCC maneuvering, released a unified statement blasting the party for its intervention. Ian Phillips, the Cayuga County chair, complained to the DCCC's Tim Persico. Persico hadn't coordinated with the local officials, he told Phillips, because he was too busy. "I've always been a defender, even when I read your long piece" on the DCCC putting its thumb on the scales, Phillips told me. "I just want to burn it down. These guys are terrible. They're wrecking races all across the country."

New York law professor Zephyr Teachout, who ran for state attorney general in 2018, told me that Persico's problem was fundamental. "Structurally, they're going to be idiots because there's no way they can bring in the talent to do it right," she said. "Their strategy is stupid in the first place and bad for democracy, but then it's *really* stupid because they have 26-year-olds sitting around who don't know anything about the real world deciding which candidates should win."

In the spring, Perez Williams flew down to Washington for the EMILY's List annual gala, where she posed for a red-carpet photo. "A woman's place is in the House!" she posted on Facebook, along with the pic of herself celebrating with the pro-choice organization. Facebook, though, was not typically a place Perez Williams had gone to hail the virtues of abortion rights. When taking into account state-level races, EMILY's List can wind up playing in hundreds, perhaps thousands of primaries. Vetting that many candidates from Washington is hard.

Vetting them on the ground was much easier. Though she had secured the endorsement of EMILY's List for her 2017 Syracuse mayoral run, she was widely known back home as a zealous crusader on behalf of the unborn, frequently engaging in flame wars with other Democrats on social media. Her belief that abortion was against God's law and ought to be banned was well-known around town, and she made no effort to conceal it.

When Ireland effectively banned abortion in August 2016, she celebrated the news on Facebook. In another post, she expressed hope for Hillary Clinton to come around to her "pro-life" perspective. Her activism — described in her own words as "pro-life advocacy" — extended to the real world, too. In January 2016, she posted about having just attended the March for Life in Washington, the most high-profile event put together by the movement working to criminalize abortion.

It's impossible for a national organization to know everything about every candidate they endorse. Her invite to the gala was a strong hint she was about to get the EMILY's List nod, and an EMILY's List source told me that the decision was close to being made when Aída Chávez and I reported for The Intercept about her true feelings on abortion rights.

Her Facebook posts had been flagged for us by local Democrats, which pointed toward an inherent flaw in the national approach and a benefit to organizing locally and trusting grassroots organizations. While a national group can't be expected to know about every angry post a candidate put up on social media, the people who fought with her in the threads sure as hell remember it. They didn't have to do expensive opposition research to learn about Perez Williams — because they already knew her.

We posted our story days after the gala, and Perez Williams was quickly bound for Washington again, this time with some explaining to do. She was ushered into a conference room with Schriock; Judy Lichtman, a co-founder; research director Jenna Kruse; and New York staffer Kouters. Lichtman, now in her 70s, had argued six cases before the Supreme Court, and is a dynamic force. "She's the sweetest 70-year-old grandmother, but she will end you in a heartbeat if you ever cross EMILY's List," said one staffer admiringly.

Her matronly presence in the meeting gave it a feeling of substance, as Kruse walked Perez Williams through her Facebook posts, asking her to explain her thinking and, most importantly, how she would vote on the issue. Perez Williams insisted that despite her personal beliefs, she would always vote to uphold abortion rights. The personal-political distinction is one that reproductive rights advocates have grown familiar with, and while it's less than ideal, voting is what matters to the women being affected by the laws. But her participation in so much political advocacy against abortion rights — action that went beyond merely holding personal beliefs — gave the group pause.

Judy Lichtman pressed the issue, telling Perez Williams the stories of Blanche Lincoln and Mary Landrieu — both strong Democratic senators who had the backing of EMILY's List, but crossed the group on a critical 2002 abortion vote. The world's sweetest grandmother then added: "If you fuck us over, we will end you."

They didn't have to. Dana Balter ended her with a string of brutal campaign commercials highlighting Perez Williams' anti-choice position. Kouters, who had come on late, asked the DCCC why they had recruited such a flawed candidate. Nobody wanted responsibility. The DCCC told Kouters that actually EMILY's List had recruited her. Either way, she didn't end up getting the EMILY's List endorsement this time around. Yet as primary season in New York heated up, the focus on Perez Williams began to look awfully strange in comparison to the broader contest playing out across the state.

From Long Island to Upstate New York, women at state and federal levels engaged in a struggle against the oldest and most patriarchal machine in U.S. politics. In something of a break from the norms of campaigning, most of those women ran in unison, cross-endorsing one another in a collective show of solidarity. Cross-endorsements tend to be rare because when a candidate endorses another candidate, she automatically angers any of her would-be supporters who might also support the opponent of the candidate. In other words, if Cynthia Nixon endorsed Ocasio-Cortez, allies and supporters of Joe Crowley inclined to back Nixon might think twice. Yet, with few exceptions, the women did it anyway.

That type of solidarity had been the exclusive province of bosses in Albany. Up until then, New York was governed by a system known around the state as "three men in a room": the governor, Senate leader, and head of the Assembly. To prevent voters in one party or another from exerting influence over those men, they ensured power was split between the parties. The balancing mechanism employed by the bosses was the IDC — or the Independent Democratic Conference. This was a group of eight Democrats in the state Senate, organized partly by Governor Andrew Cuomo, who caucused with Republicans. Along with other Democrats who caucused with Republicans outside of the IDC, they effectively handed power in the chamber to the GOP.

Jessica Ramos, who successfully challenged an IDC member in 2018, said she witnessed it first hand as an activist. "You knew that your only hope was to convince the governor to take pity on you and actually want to work on your issue and figure out how to get it through the Republicans," she said told me. "That was the main reason he created the IDC, was to create that [power] center for himself."

The insurgent assault on the IDC and the related male-dominated machinery of New York politics was launched and carried to completion without EMILY's List lifting a finger. That the group sat out the most consequential female-led uprising of the 2018 cycle was not an oversight, but the logical conclusion of the political strategy the group adopted at its founding — not to challenge the system or the establishment itself, but rather to slot individual women into it — and leaned into as it grew. Since the New York machine was led by men who claimed to support abortion rights, and was funded by many of the same donors who backed EMILY's List, the group looked elsewhere for fights.

It was, ultimately, Trump who blew up the IDC. His election woke up Democratic voters across the state, and they organized themselves into Indivisible groups or otherwise became intimately engaged with local politics in a new way. When they researched their own representatives, many learned they had been voting for Democrats who allied themselves in Albany with Republicans — with a party now led by the racist, sexist, xenophobic creature in the White House. That could no longer be tolerated.

The newly fired-up local activists organized primary challenges to all of them, most being led by women like Jessica Ramos, Rachel May, and Alessandra Biaggi. Cynthia Nixon, who challenged Cuomo for governor, made the IDC the centerpiece of her campaign: Ocasio-Cortez, challenging Crowley, made his endorsement of a local IDC state senator a prominent part of hers.

In Rochester, the Democratic establishment got behind a top boss in the State Assembly, Joseph Morelle, who ran for the House seat that opened up after Louise Slaughter's unexpected death. He was being challenged by a pro-choice female investigative journalist named Rachel Barnhart, whose regular presence on local TV news gave her high name recognition. But EMILY's List was indifferent to Barnhart, a posture that persisted despite a sharp turn in the race, when Morelle's prior role in dismissing rape allegations against a top Democratic Assembly staffer emerged.

Barnhart's opponent may have been pro-choice, but his career had also been enabled by his longtime support of disgraced party boss Sheldon Silver, who had a track record of ignoring claims of sexual assault and harassment in the Assembly. In 2001, Silver dismissed the claims of Elizabeth Crothers, a then-24-year-old staffer who accused Silver's chief counsel of rape. Morelle supported him: "I absolutely don't believe a word of it."

Crothers ultimately declined to press charges, and instead filed an internal complaint in the hopes of at least getting Silver's counsel, J. Michael Boxley, fired. That didn't happen, and two years later, Boxley was arrested and charged with raping another young aide, and walked out of the legislature in handcuffs. He ultimately pled guilty only to sexual misconduct, but at his sentencing, admitted: "On that evening, I had sexual intercourse and there was not consent." (Despite that admission, he was sentenced to only six years of probation, no prison time.)

Silver's grip on the Assembly took years to shake loose, despite a half-million-dollar settlement paid in compensation for his mishandling of the Boxley affair. In 2012, under fire for his mismanagement of a different sexual harassment case, Morelle continued to defend Silver. As the New York Times reported then:

> Assemblyman Joseph D. Morelle, the chairman of the Democratic Party in Monroe County, said, "People in our conference not only have great affection for Shelly [Silver], there's a lot of respect for his skills as a leader, as a speaker, and as an attorney." Mr. Morelle, who is close to Mr. [Andrew] Cuomo, has been seen as a potential successor to Mr. Silver, but laughed off the suggestion on Thursday, adding, "He remains strongly supported."

It took a few more years for the law to catch up with Silver, but Morelle stood by him to the end. In 2015, Silver was arrested for corruption, launching a legal odyssey that resulted in two separate convictions.

Crothers, who now lives in Washington, D.C., traveled to Rochester for a campaign event with Barnhart, endorsing her and condemning Morelle for dismissing her rape allegations in 2001. Silver, she said, apologized to her after the second victim came forward, but Morelle hadn't until she re-emerged.

The Barnhart campaign's own polling showed Morelle at 35 percent, Barnhart at 20 percent, and a handful of other candidates in the single digits. With Morelle holding a tight grip on in-state fundraising, Barnhart pinned her hopes on EMILY's List to put her over the top in a now-winnable contest.

Barnhart approached EMILY's List armed with her poll results and a pragmatic pitch: the seat was clearly vulnerable since Slaughter had nearly lost in 2014. Morelle's long career made him easy to paint as a corrupt politician. But according to Barnhart, EMILY's List wasn't convinced. They told her that she needed to use one of their approved consultants to conduct a new poll. Without it, they said, there would be no endorsement. Barnhart reached out to the consultant, who priced the survey at $25,000. (An EMILY's List spokesperson said that the group simply wanted the most accurate data.)

The poll, Barnhart told EMILY's List, had been vouched for by Celinda Lake, arguably the most prominent female pollster in the game. She couldn't have known it, but that only hurt her case: EMILY's List won't work with Lake.

In Texas, Lillian Salerno discovered that during her Dallas primary. The group, she said, told her that if she used Celinda Lake as a pollster rather than one of their preferred consultants, there would be no endorsement. Salerno threatened to tell the press she was being strong-armed, doing a little strong-arming of her own. EMILY's List caved and endorsed her. It wasn't enough, as she lost her primary; Lake declined to comment on the rift.[243]

In district after district, the outfit aligned itself against progressive candidates. In perhaps the most awkward case, it took on Laura Moser, a leading figure in the resistance, in Houston. The primary was crowded, and a former Goldman Sachs analyst named Alex Triantaphyllis told people on the campaign trail he was recruited by the DCCC, even though he wasn't officially endorsed. Moser, a writer and mom who had launched Daily Action, which enabled hundreds of thousands of newly energized activists to take a single piece of political action per day, had a large grassroots operation. Lizzie Pannill Fletcher, a corporate attorney, had the backing of EMILY's List thanks to a top donor in Houston. The DCCC wanted Moser destroyed, believing she was too liberal to win in the district. Just ahead of the primary, the party took the extraordinary step of releasing a book of opposition research on Moser, highlighting articles she'd written at the beginning of her career, and alluding to some sort of corrupt relationship with her husband's consulting firm, Revolution Messaging, which had worked for Bernie Sanders' 2016 campaign.[244] It was a staggeringly audacious charge, given that the DCCC's standard operating procedure was to favor consultants with ties to its own leaders. The DCCC had previously shared the oppo, at least, with the Fletcher campaign.[245]

It backfired. Progressives rallied around Moser, who had ranked third in the polls, and pushed her to second in the primary, which put her in a runoff against Fletcher. The DCCC had sunk Triantaphyllis, turning its own recruit into collateral damage. But it was worth it for the party

---

243   EMILY's List President Stephanie Schriock has long been critical of Lake privately, blaming her for Martha Coakley's Senate special election loss in Massachusetts in 2010. Coakley also lost a 2014 race for governor, so it's a bit tough to hang Scott Brown on Celinda Lake.

244   Arun Chaudhary was also a videographer on the 2008 Obama campaign and went on to work in the White House.

245   I know this because the Fletcher campaign shared the oppo with me. I used bits of it, but ignored the rest, considering the charges strained.

committee, as Moser lost the runoff, and Fletcher went on to win the general election, joining the New Democrat Coalition as a freshman.

The most difficult EMILY's List decision to explain, though, came on Long Island. When Liuba Grechen Shirley decided to seek the Democratic nomination to run for Congress against the GOP's Long Island mainstay, Peter King, she faced all the usual structural barriers that make it difficult to dislodge incumbents. But she also had to deal with a more immediate hurdle, one invisible to most men running for office: child care. Who would watch Grechen Shirley's kids while she knocked on doors, gathered signatures, called donors and voters, choked down rubber chicken at endless luncheons, and put in the round-the-clock hours it takes to beat an entrenched incumbent like King?

Federal law was unclear on whether she could use campaign money to pay for child care — though it was entirely clear to Grechen Shirley that without child care, there could be no campaign. So she took the issue to the Federal Election Commission. And she won.

Women's groups celebrated the opinion as a significant step forward for feminism. EMILY's List trumpeted Grechen Shirley's landmark win: "This is an important first step in leveling the playing field! Congress is still 80 percent men, and if we want to break down barriers for those who want to run, we need to ensure moms have access to affordable child care." Her Democratic rival for the nomination, DuWayne Gregory, however, knocked her for even suggesting the possibility that child care could be part of a campaign, calling it "a very slippery slope." It would seem like the easiest endorsement call that could possibly be put at the doorstep of EMILY's List. But Gregory had a lot of friends.

In 2014, when Cuomo was challenged by Zephyr Teachout — who also did not have the support of EMILY's List — he created something called the "Women's Equality Party." New York at the time allowed "fusion voting," which meant two or more parties could nominate the same candidate and tally their votes together. Cuomo's new Women's Equality Party endorsed Cuomo.

The "party" once again backed Cuomo in 2018, this time against Nixon. Why did the WEP support Cuomo over his female, pro-choice opponent with a strong record of LGBTQ advocacy? Asked to explain, Susan Zimet, chair of the WEP, was explicit about the cronyism involved. She told the New York Times: "Yes, Cynthia is woman, and yes she represents a lot of our values, but we have a governor who literally created the party." She was equally dispassionate about the party's backing of Grechen Shirley's opponent, Gregory. "I see that Liuba is running a pretty remarkable campaign; I admire her," she said. "But DuWayne came as a recommendation through our state committee person."

As it turned out, Rich Schaffer, head of the Suffolk County Democratic Party, which exerted power over the district, was a political ally of Republican Rep. Pete King — despite serving in different parties. Gregory was Schaffer's handpicked candidate not because he was a threat to King but, rather, because he wasn't. His candidacy served to prevent any potentially emerging opposition, like Grechen Shirley's. Indeed, it had worked just fine in 2016, when Gregory had been the Democratic nominee and was trounced by King.

Over the course of several weeks in June, I reached out repeatedly[246] to EMILY's List asking about the group's decision not to endorse Grechen Shirley and other women running in New York. "At EMILY's List, we are thrilled by the number of women stepping up to run across the country, including in many important races in New York," said Christina Reynolds, the EMILY's List spokeswoman who'd been a deputy of Rahm Emanuel's during his 2006 chairmanship of the DCCC. "Given the volume of women running, the endorsement process is still ongoing and we are closely monitoring the great women candidates running in competitive New York primaries."

Finally, on the Friday before Election Day — too late to include in mailers, and certainly too late to be of use for fundraising purposes in the primary — they officially endorsed Grechen Shirley.

Congressional primary day was a debacle for EMILY's List, but a tremendous day for other women. Erin Collier, the lone woman running in a crowded field in Upstate New York, lost badly. Balter, trailing Perez Williams in the polls, beat her handily. On Long Island, Grechen Shirley knocked out Gregory. Joe Morelle won with 46 percent, yet Barnhart, having barely spent a dime, drew 20 percent. Carolyn Maloney, a longtime incumbent and the only other woman the group endorsed for the House, barely fended off a challenge from Suraj Patel. And in the Bronx and Queens, Ocasio-Cortez thumped Crowley by 15 points.

Instead of viewing the election calamity as the natural outgrowth of their strategy that prioritized men already in power over women challenging them, as long as those men were pro-choice and Democratic, EMILY's List scapegoated its lead staffer responsible for New York. The Friday after the New York primary, Angela Kouters was fired. That afternoon, she posted a quote on Twitter that had been put into heavy rotation by the Clinton campaign during the 2016 presidential primary, but this time turned it on EMILY's List: "There is a special place in hell for women who don't help other women."

She added: "As a survivor of childhood abuse, poverty, sexual assault,

---

246   This was for a story on the group's New York strategy, published on June 26, 2018.

political sabotage, and so much else, you've just awoken a sleeping giant. Hell is going to feel like a spa by the time I'm done."

The group's strategy, with Kouters gone, remained identical. As the primaries moved to the state-level contests, EMILY's List continued to stay out of races that pitted women against the IDC men. But it did get involved in the attorney general's race. Cuomo's nemesis, Teachout, was running for AG. To have one of the country's sharpest legal minds with subpoena power and jurisdiction over Trump's business empire was either an intoxicating or frightening possibility, depending on your perspective. But she would also have jurisdiction over Albany corruption, and had promised to go after it. Cuomo pulled every lever he had to stop her.

Tish James, a longtime progressive housing rights activist, and the city's public advocate, also got into the race. Cuomo told James that if she refused the support of the Working Families Party, which was where she had gotten her start — but which was also the party backing the primary challenges against the IDC and Cuomo — he'd support her publicly and financially. She took the deal.

Teachout was strongest upstate, but that strength was undercut when Rep. Sean Patrick Maloney, also from upstate and an ally of Cuomo's, jumped into the race, with no apparent path to victory. With Maloney splitting the upstate vote, that gave James the inside track in a three-way race. Though both women were progressive and pro-choice — and Teachout was running while pregnant — EMILY's List jumped in on the side of Cuomo's candidate, James. It couldn't endorse Cuomo (the group only backs women) but did get behind Kathy Hochul, Cuomo's running mate.

On Election Day, the IDC was annihilated, with six of the eight going down. Rachel May, Jessica Ramos, and Alessandra Biaggi all won. Julia Salazar, with Ocasio-Cortez's help, beat her incumbent opponent, Marty Dilan, an ally of the IDC. In a Jackson Heights state Assembly race, Catalina Cruz, a Dreamer who was previously undocumented, knocked off a machine incumbent.

Ocasio-Cortez told me the focus on the IDC helped her demonstrate a distinction between herself and Crowley, who had endorsed a local IDC member. Biaggi said after the election that Nixon's relentless hammering of the IDC was critical to the takeover, and it didn't hurt that Cuomo spent his $30 million attacking her rather than defending the IDC. "The moment that Cynthia got into the race, it helped my campaign, because she started talking about the IDC almost incessantly," said Biaggi, who beat the IDC's leader.[247] "Every day, *the IDC, the IDC, the IDC*, and for peo-

---

247   She said this on CNN.

ple who didn't know what it was, it gave them the education about what had been going on."

In January, when the new members were sworn in, Democrats — finally — fully controlled the state legislature, and progressives were driving the agenda. As its first act, the new body passed into law the Reproductive Health Act, a sweeping defense of reproductive freedom that Cuomo had long claimed to support, but the IDC had bottled up.

On January 22, 2019, Cuomo signed the bill. EMILY's List was silent.

Twenty-Five

Betomania

By 2004, Beto O'Rourke had tried his hand at punk rock and at the 9-to-5 life in New York City, and was now back in his hometown of El Paso, just across the border from Juarez. His father had been a well-known judge in the county, a position in Texas that is as political as it is powerful. There was an election coming for an El Paso city council seat, and O'Rourke, given his name recognition, had a reasonable chance of at least being taken seriously.

And so he set out going door to door to win votes. But he quickly realized he hadn't answered one thing: *Why should people vote for him?*

The first door he knocked on, he offered a vague pitch for a better community. "I was a brand new candidate with no money, and I said, 'My name is Beto and I'm here to tell you I want to run to represent you on city council, and I want more jobs, and greener grass in the parks, and better streetlights, and the first person says, 'If you want my vote, you're going to make sure that we save Resler Canyon, because the developers are gonna ruin this beautiful arroyo and all this wildlife,'" O'Rourke told me.[248]

Resler Canyon was just that, an arroyo that city sprawl threatened to close in on. "Second door I knock on, I do the same pitch. I get the same answer. Third door I knock on, I say, 'My name is Beto O'Rourke, and I'm here to save Resler Canyon.'"

It's quintessential Beto: charming, honest, self-effacing, and funny

248   This was an interview I did with O'Rourke at a SXSW event in March 2018.

— yet at the same time leaves you wondering just a little about what you heard. Did he just confess to that great political sin of sticking a finger in the air and heading where the wind is blowing? Then again, if that's what nearly all politicians do, should we be grateful for the transparency? And beyond saving Resler Canyon and greener grass in the parks, what does he stand for?

O'Rourke, in his longshot 2018 challenge to Republican Senator Ted Cruz in Texas, did no polling of the public, but did his own version of focus groups. By traveling to deeply conservative areas and taking questions until each audience was exhausted, he got a priceless feel for what was on the minds of voters. He didn't skip polling for a lack of campaign funds. His small-dollar operation pulled in so much money — more than $80 million by the end — that calling it a record doesn't do it justice. He raised more, for instance, than Jeb Bush did for his entire 2016 presidential campaign.

After spending 2018 as a progressive rising star, he infamously instagrammed a dental visit, embarked on a soul-searching tour of the country he documented with Medium diary entries, launched a presidential bid, raised more than $6 million in his first 24 hours, then positioned himself as a unifying, pragmatic, next-generation candidate.

Perhaps unsurprisingly, it all started with weed.

In the latter half of the 2000s, a bloody drug-cartel war was raging just across the border from El Paso in Juarez, Mexico. The intractable conflict claimed tens of thousands of lives and produced a climate of fear in the region. Most politicians were calling for an ever-more militarized response, which only fed the conflict. O'Rourke, then on the city council, introduced a resolution that took a different approach. Given that the war was being driven by demand for an illegal product, perhaps the United States should consider legalizing and regulating that product. His focus was on marijuana, but he also called for "an honest, open national debate on ending the prohibition of narcotics."

O'Rourke's resolution passed 8-0 and was headed to the mayor's desk for his signature when the local congressman, Rep. Silvestre Reyes, a conservative Democrat and former border patrol guard, sent a letter, along with other Texas congressmen, to the mayor, calling on him to veto it. The mayor complied, and Reyes then lobbied each council member personally, making veiled threats that the city would lose federal money if the veto was overridden.

Four members of the council switched their votes and supported the veto; three of them publicly cited the funding threat as the reason for backing down.

Reyes told me at the time that he got involved because other members of Congress approached him to ask what on earth was going on in his city. "[T]he publicity that was generated last week...made it seem that the resolution was calling on Congress to legalize drugs," Reyes said.

"That was the perception up here," added Reyes, then chairman of the House intelligence committee, "and a number of members brought it to my attention and asked me directly, *What gives with your city council? Why are they wanting to legalize drugs?* So, I told them, essentially, *please let the mayor's veto stand and put this behind us. We've got huge issues that are facing us as a Congress. We've got a stimulus package, where I'm working hard to get money going directly to the city to fund projects that'll put people to work.*"

Reyes feared that other members of Congress would use the publicity against El Paso in the funding fight. He cited his long-running battle in Congress against the notion that El Paso was running out of water. Whenever he tried to get federal funds for El Paso's base, Fort Bliss, or other projects, his colleagues would raise the water issue, he said: *Why invest government funds in facilities in an area that's going to run out of water?* "So that's the concern," he said. "Anytime you have negative percep- tions, you open the door for others to use that as leverage to get more money in their districts and not in mine. I'm up here representing the district and I can tell people based on my experience what helps me and what doesn't."

Reyes' interview with me was his first public confirmation that he had been tying his lobbying efforts to threats of stripping funding from the city. O'Rourke told me later[249] that after reading Reyes' comments in an article I wrote in The Huffington Post, he was so livid he vowed to primary Reyes. He launched that challenge in 2011 and his upset of Reyes was itself historic, as it marked the first time a member of Congress had lost his job for being too tough on the war on drugs. That reoriented political incentives in Washington, as all of a sudden Democrats had to think twice about their rhetoric.

After his election, O'Rourke had a hard time finding his footing. During freshman orientation, one presentation from the Democratic Congressional Campaign Committee felt particularly ominous. It came on November 16, 2012, barely a week after the election, and it was all about fundraising. The amount of time that members of Congress in both parties spend fundraising is widely known to take up an obscene portion of a typical day — whether it's "call time" spent on the phone

---

249   By sheer coincidence, my friend Jeff Hild was hired as his legislative direc- tor, and I met O'Rourke at Hild's apartment shortly after he arrived in Washington, which is when he told me about his reaction to Reyes' remarks in my story. I had no clue until then the story had pushed him to run.

with potential donors, or in person at fundraisers in Washington or back home. Seeing it spelled out in black and white, however, can be a jarring experience for a new member.

O'Rourke and the other freshmen were shown a PowerPoint presentation[250] laying out the dreary existence awaiting these new backbenchers. The daily schedule prescribed by the Democratic leadership contemplated a nine or 10-hour day while in Washington. Of that, four hours were to be spent in "call time" and another hour was blocked off for "strategic outreach," which included fundraisers and press work.

An hour was walled off to "recharge," and three to four hours were designated for the actual work of being a member of Congress: hearings, votes, and meetings with constituents. If the constituents were donors, all the better. The presentation assured members that their fundraising would be closely monitored; the Federal Election Commission requires members to file quarterly reports.

Even members in safe districts, they were told, were expected to keep up the torrid fundraising pace, so that they could contribute to the defense of vulnerable colleagues.

Years later, I mentioned "call time" to O'Rourke and he immediately recalled that miserable orientation. He assumed that this was just how it would have to be done. He was reassured, though, that some of the fundraising targets would be hit easily. After he'd won his primary, after all, checks began pouring in from corporate PACs around the country, eager to ingratiate themselves with the incoming member of Congress. *He hadn't solicited any of them*, he reasoned, *so what harm could there be in cashing the checks?*

He soon discovered that was wishful thinking. "It's not going to change who you are in any fundamental way," O'Rourke explained. "Perhaps you're not on the defense committee, and you couldn't care less what's in the defense bill, but you know that there's a $10,000 check coming from Boeing. Why piss those guys off? Why not just vote their way, if it's no skin off your back and you don't understand the issue very well to begin with?"

It's a matter of priorities. Most members of Congress have a handful of issues they care deeply about — what he called "issues one through ten" — and on the rest, they're ambivalent. It's on the rest where the calculus is easily made that the smarter move is just to vote with the money. El Paso is home to Fort Bliss and more than 30,000 enlisted members of the U.S. Army, so O'Rourke fought to get on the Armed Services Committee shortly before the election. But he was already develop-

---

250   I obtained a copy of the PowerPoint presentation and published parts of it in The Huffington Post. O'Rourke was not the source.

ing a reputation as somebody who wasn't enthusiastic about fundraising, so the party leadership kept him off. *They didn't appoint you to that committee your first session in Congress because they just didn't think you were going to make the money off of it,* he was told. *That's like a wasted seat for us.*

During that same orientation when the DCCC let freshman lawmakers in on the realities of their coming service, another group called No Labels gave a presentation. Mark Pocan, elected in the same year as O'Rourke, remembered the presentation vividly.[251] The group was forming its own caucus in Congress. "The moment we were sworn in, we were given lapel pins to brand us as the Problem Solvers Caucus, which was sponsored by No Labels," the Wisconsin representative recalled.

O'Rourke, too, had long been intrigued by the hopeful prospect of bipartisanship. (His first Facebook Live video to go viral, in fact, was his long car ride from Texas to Washington with GOP Rep Will Hurd, who represented the district adjacent to O'Rourke, stretching 800 miles from El Paso to San Antonio.) A bipartisan caucus dedicated to solving problems sounded good. His legislative director warned him it could be useless or worse, but, like Pocan, he went to one of the first meetings. To his credit, he came back from it shaking his head and never did join.

To his discredit, he joined the New Democrat Coalition, the Wall Street-friendly wing of the party. On a personal and stylistic level, the move made sense, as it fit O'Rourke's desire for common ground — the Obama refrain of *no blue states or red states, only the United States.* And O'Rourke grew up deeply privileged, with a powerful father and education at an elite boarding school in Virginia. (He was born Robert O'Rourke to his Irish-American family, but was nicknamed Beto at birth — "Beto" being a common shortening of "Robert" or "Roberto" in El Paso.)

On the question of the substance, though, membership in the New Democrat Coalition clashes with O'Rourke's progressive political instincts — the type that led to a call for the legalization of all narcotics in 2009, for instance. In Congress, O'Rourke was a strong progressive on LGBTQ equality, women's rights, foreign policy, immigration, and drug policy. Yet when it came to fiscal and economic policy, he drifted decidedly moderate, if not conservative. He was fixated on the debt and deficit, routinely making references to it in his speeches and public comments. The ACA was passed before he came to Congress, but he was critical of it as going too far. He often voted against the Democratic Party and with Republicans[252] on banking issues.

---

251   This was from a blog he published in The Huffington Post.

252   See David Sirota in The Guardian for the most thorough rundown. Sirota would later go on to work for the Sanders campaign, but produced his reporting long before that.

There was no political need for O'Rourke to vote that way, as his district was solidly Democratic, and over time his economic politics began drifting closer to his social politics. He became a strong defender of the ACA after voicing skepticism, and by 2018 was publicly backing single payer.[253]

His left-wing instincts are real, which make him all the more confounding as a politician. At the height of the 2014 migration crisis at the border, I interviewed him about the U.S. role in destabilizing Central America, and he dove into the history of the Dulles brothers,[254] the CIA's overthrow of Jacobo Arbenz, and its history of support for dirty wars.

And then there was his early refusal to take PAC money. But, again, complicating the picture was his refusal to take *any* PAC money. Not all corporations are the same, but a blanket refusal of all corporate PAC money made sense. And some labor money comes with strings attached that could arguably[255] be detrimental to the public. But all of it? It's a policy reminiscent, again, of Obama, who for most of his first term would only criticize "Washington" rather than "Republicans."

And then there's Israel. In July 2014, while O'Rourke was still a freshman, Israel launched a bombing campaign and then ground invasion of Gaza, after Hamas militants kidnapped and murdered three Israeli teenagers. A United Nations report would later find evidence of Israeli war crimes against civilians in the barrage that followed, which killed more than a thousand people, many of them children. O'Rourke told me at the time he thought of his three small children as he saw images of young ones pulled from the rubble of Israeli shellings in densely populated areas.

I could tell that his emotional reaction was a genuine one, and he was determined not to let the slaughter happen in his name. Before adjourning for the summer recess, the House rushed through an aid package to support the Israeli Iron Dome missile interceptor system. The timing of the vote was purely symbolic — the money wasn't needed at the moment, but Congress wanted to rush it to show full-throated support of Israel at the height of the war, even as nations around the world condemned its assault.

---

253   In the 2020 campaign, he backed off it, saying he preferred the Medicare for America Act, which allows employer-provided insurance to remain in place.

254   He had clearly read, at minimum, Stephen Kinzer's The Brothers: John Foster Dulles, Allen Dulles, and Their Secret World War. If you haven't read it, put this one down and go get it.

255   The Communications Workers of America, for instance, are terrible on net neutrality. A lot of building trades are bad on pipeline construction. And then there are police unions.

O'Rourke cast one of just eight votes against the money, and the response from the pro-Israel lobby was swift, furious and well-coordinated, hitting him everywhere from The New Yorker to his local paper. Responding to the uproar, he held a series of meetings with pro-Israel groups and local Jewish leaders, agreeing to visit Israel on AIPAC's dime the next year, and the lobby expressed hope that O'Rourke would come around and oppose the Iran nuclear deal Obama had been negotiating.

The threat from the Israel lobby to unseat O'Rourke never materialized. The following March, Israel's Prime Minister Benjamin Netanyahu visited Washington and addressed Congress at the invitation of the House Speaker John Boehner — not the president, as was the custom — and O'Rourke was one of 58 Democrats to boycott the speech.

That spring, he took the trip to Israel he had promised. When he returned, he was asked at a town hall if he'd have voted differently knowing then what he knew now. No, he said, "I think our unequivocal support at times has been damaging to Israel."

In the summer, the Iran deal was finalized and O'Rourke pledged his support, declaring it "an impressive diplomatic achievement that has the potential to peacefully resolve one of the most intractable problems facing our country and the world." Like the rest of Congress, he continued broadly supporting foreign aid for Israel, but the unrelenting pressure campaign from the lobby had failed. On the campaign trail in 2019, he slammed Netanyahu again.

O'Rourke easily won reelection in 2016. When he'd first entered office, he had planned to serve only four terms, and this would be his third. Instead of running for one more reelection in 2018 and then stepping down, O'Rourke decided to go out with a bang: he would take on Senator Ted Cruz. Cruz in 2016 had finished second in the GOP primary for president, and was savaged throughout by Trump, who accused his father of having a role in the assassination of JFK, called his wife ugly, and planted a story in the National Enquirer accusing Cruz of multiple affairs. Cruz responded by calling Trump a "sniveling coward," among a bevy of other insults. At the Republican convention, Cruz spoke but refused to endorse Trump, and was drowned out by boos.

He would, of course, later endorse Trump and become a major booster of the sniveling coward.

When I traveled to Texas during the Senate campaign, I didn't meet a single person who had a positive impression of Ted Cruz, even though I met plenty who planned to vote for him because he was a Republican. If Cruz was dark and unlikeable, O'Rourke would contrast with him as sunny and likable. That meant swearing off negative campaigning, a decision that was broadly questioned by journalists and national campaign operatives. The O'Rourke side insisted that people knew enough about Ted Cruz already, and that extra 30-second ads hammering wouldn't hurt him, especially because so many people already disliked him but planned on backing him anyway. If that was the case, what was the value in them disliking him slightly more? If O'Rourke wins the Democratic nomination, a similar question will face him.

O'Rourke did break from that pledge occasionally. "He's dishonest. That's why the president called him 'Lyin' Ted,' and it's why the nickname stuck, because it's true," O'Rourke said of Cruz at their final debate.

O'Rourke's ground game, though, was what made his Texas run different. After the exodus from Our Revolution, some of Sanders' best organizers were seeking their next thing, and O'Rourke's Senate run looked like it. Zack Malitz and Becky Bond reached out and made their pitch to David Wysong, O'Rourke's longtime Capitol Hill chief of staff. They had seen his initial explosive fundraising success and knew that it represented real energy that could be tapped. They told him about the distributed organizing model they had built on the Sanders campaign (despite upper management's skepticism of it) and argued that if it were fully integrated into a campaign from the beginning, it could be exponentially more successful. Wysong knew that O'Rourke wanted to run a different kind of campaign — one without consultants or pollsters. Beto just wanted to travel around the state and hold town halls, talking to as many Texans as possible, both in person and through Facebook Live. If Malitz and Bond could channel the support into a volunteer field program, that sounded like the exact sort of thing O'Rourke would be into.

Wysong liked it, took it to Beto, and Beto signed off. Kenneth Pennington and Hector Sigala, who'd been senior figures on Bernie's digital team, also joined, and were given total freedom to execute the distributed organizing model, going beyond what they had tried in 2016. They allowed supporters to set up "pop up" campaign offices that would be local hubs for volunteers, and more than 700 popped up.

Text messages flew from volunteers' phones with hurricane force, likely setting records (and annoying countless people, too). The campaign publicly posted a heat map that showed the real-time activity of its volunteers, up against its targets, an unheard of level of transparency. On the Sunday before the election, the campaign knocked on 340 doors per minute, and hit roughly half a million that weekend.[256] The Cruz

---

[256] Stat comes from Justin Miller, writing in the Texas Observer in December 2018, "How Beto Built His Texas-Sized Grassroots Machine." Michael Whitney's October 2018 report in The Intercept, "How Beto O'Rourke Raised a Stunning $38 Million in Just Three Months" is also essential reading into the mechanics of the distributed

team saw its lead slipping away, and while O'Rourke ended up losing, it was much closer than polls had suggested. Claire McCaskill, in Missouri, lost by six points, while O'Rourke lost by 2.6 percentage points.

Relying on volunteers can bias a campaign toward white people, however, who have the time or means to volunteer. "A volunteer program will not get you a huge base of black and brown volunteers because they don't have the time and money to do that," said Cristina Tzintzun, head of the Latino organizing group Jolt Texas. The October 9 voter registration deadline meant a lot of the energy in the last month couldn't bring in new voters. "That was really unfortunate."[257]

The campaign supplemented the volunteer operation with a massive paid field staff at the end of the campaign, which was able to go into the neighborhoods that had been overlooked, if perhaps too late. But it showed what was possible with a marriage of distributed organizing and a massively well-resourced campaign, which was the model O'Rourke brought into his 2020 presidential campaign by turning over the reins to Becky Bond.

But it didn't last long. O'Rourke backtracked on his pledge not to take money from fossil-fuel executives, and walked back his commitment to Medicare for All. Still, he launched his campaign in mid-March with an explosive burst of volunteer-driven text-messaging, raising some $6 million in 24 hours. It was a sign that there was still something there, and if O'Rourke could keep those supporters engaged, he had a chance to run a new kind of campaign. A few days after his launch, he tapped Jen O'Malley Dillon[258], Obama's 2012 deputy campaign manager and the former executive director of the DNC. Alarm bells among progressive organizers immediately went off. "She's one of the hardest working people," said one former OFA official, "and definitely has strong opinions about the things she cares about. You wouldn't want to get between her and her role. She definitely thinks of herself as field. It's hard to imagine how those two will work together." The arrangement lasted barely a month. In mid-April, both Bond and Zack Malitz quit.

---

campaign.

257   Interview with Justin Miller.

258   She came from Precision Strategies, which does a heavy amount of corporate consulting.

Twenty-Six

AOC

Blanca Cortez and Sergio Ocasio-Roman met when they were both young. Sergio, who lived in the Bronx, was visiting family on the island of Puerto Rico. Soon enough, the two were hitched, and Blanca, who spoke only Spanish, moved to the mainland, where they settled into a small Bronx apartment in a working-class neighborhood called Parkchester.

He set up an architecture firm, Kirschenbaum Ocasio-Roman, in 1986. Three years later, they had a baby girl, Alexandria, followed by a boy, Gabriel. When Alexandria was two, the family bought a three-bedroom home in Yorktown Heights, a suburb in Westchester County, about 40 minutes north, planning to move there when the kids were ready for school, which they did when Alexandria was five.

That move, and the life her family made in Yorktown, has been the subject of intense scrutiny by the conservative media. That was no surprise, and so when, at The Intercept, we first wrote about her race, we pulled her property records and scrutinized the timeline. The records matched the story she had told us. Her campaign website was strictly accurate, but left pieces of the story out in what looks to be an effort to link herself as closely as possible to the district she was running to represent. "She ended up attending public school 40 minutes north in Yorktown, and much of her life was defined by the 40-minute commute between school and her family in the Bronx," the site read during the campaign.

Knowing her full story, it's clear that by "her family" she means her sprawling extended family in the Bronx that she visited on weekends, and by "commute" she's referring to the drive from Westchester to the Bronx. A reader first coming to that sentence might assume something different, that she was living with her family in the Bronx and commuting to school. But then a second thought might occur: *Well, she couldn't legally be going to a public school in Yorktown if she lived in the Bronx.*

Using a statement that is strictly, precisely accurate yet obscures a broader truth is a common move in politics, and Ocasio-Cortez has deployed it on other occasions. When her congressional office accidentally published a Green New Deal FAQ that was embarrassingly unedited — it erroneously included a line saying that anybody "unwilling to work" would be financially taken care of — she went on Twitter to explain. "There are multiple doctored GND resolutions and FAQs floating around," she wrote. "There's also draft versions floating out there." Both of those claims were strictly true, but only one — the draft version floating out there — was relevant to the screw-up. Including the (true) statement that some doctored versions also existed could only be included to mislead.

The campaign site has since been changed, and became more explicit about the circumstances. "She ended up attending public school in Yorktown, 40 minutes north of her birthplace," according to the revised text. "As a result, much of her early life was spent in transit between her tight-knit extended family in the Bronx & her daily student life." But — and this is what makes it more complicated than the conservative media would care to admit — when it came to her experience growing up, the notion that Ocasio-Cortez came up in the Bronx was not necessarily untrue.

Even though she's a Boricua born in the Bronx and I'm a white guy born in Allentown, Pennsylvania and raised on the Eastern Shore of Maryland, I immediately connected with her story and understood what she meant. Growing up in a poor, rural area, my family was poor even relative to the rest of the community. The local public school district was ranked near the bottom of the state, below many Baltimore schools, which were at the time notoriously bad.

My mother, Cindy Quinn, raised my brother and me while working low-wage jobs — at an adult daycare center, then as activity coordinator at a nursing home, and for a time she also worked a night-shift at a halfway house. We were on food stamps and free lunch, and our house was constantly falling apart, a danger to everybody living in it. Our washing machine often wouldn't drain, which meant that I had to use a hose to empty it. Without a shopvac, that meant syphoning the water out. If you've never syphoned dirty water out of a washing machine, it requires precisely timing the removal of the hose from your mouth so that the sludge spills into the grass, rather than serving you a laundry slurpee. To this day, the notion of poverty conjures up the taste of dirty laundry water.

All of that is true, yet it's not the whole truth. My parents split for good when I was five and every other weekend I would visit my father, George Grim, in Allentown, Pennsylvania, where I'd been born. He wasn't rich, but as a school psychologist for the Allentown School District, he led a comfortable life. The house was not dangerous; it was well-painted; it had a TV; things worked; when something was gone, we could go to the store and get more of it.

Also, and I think more importantly, both my parents went to college, as did all four of my grandparents. That created an impression in me that I was going to college. It simply wasn't a question. And seeing real middle-class life in Allentown gave me a different perspective on the life I was living on the Eastern Shore.

Ocasio-Cortez has often talked about that phenomenon, about how she "grew up between two worlds," opening her eyes to the role bad luck — not lack of merit — played in people's circumstances. "I was born in a place where your zip code determines your destiny," she said at the beginning of her viral campaign video.

Her story also rings true in the way she focuses on her family, and specifically her mother. Experiencing poverty personally is of course a crushing experience. But in some ways, psychologically, it's harder to see a loved one experience it, particularly a mother. For a son or daughter, that someone as loving and hardworking as one's mother is suffering in poverty can be a traumatizing indictment of the world they live in. Nothing could be clearer evidence that a system is wrong and broken than the suffering it inflicts on a mother. An entire genre of hip-hop has grown up around the homage to a struggling mother. "My mom scrubbed toilets so I could live here," Ocasio-Cortez said of Westchester after the conservative press came after her. In the documentary on the campaign, she adds, "she would clean a woman's home in exchange for SAT lessons for me."

There's nothing simple about the experience of poverty, a trauma that manifests in people in many different ways. It is also that rare experience that people work hard to obscure in real time, yet almost universally tend to exaggerate later in life. There's deep shame in being poor, yet great pride in having been poor, a contradiction that was best put into words by Dolly Parton, in her song "In The Good Old Days (When Times Were Bad)."

The chorus goes: "No amount of money could buy from me/The memories that I have of then/No amount of money could pay me/To go back and live through it again."

In school, Alexandria went by Sandy, and like Alexandra Rojas in Connecticut, she stuck out. Yet Sandy was a good student. At Yorktown High School, she won second place in a science competition, for which MIT's Lincoln Laboratory named an asteroid after her — 23238 Ocasio-Cortez. She graduated in 2007 and attended Boston University. In January 2008, while home for winter break, she registered to vote as a Democrat. A fierce primary between Obama and Hillary Clinton was underway, and Ocasio-Cortez, then 18, was all in for Obama. She phone-banked in between classes and tried to absentee-vote in primary, but her application couldn't get processed in time, so she took an overnight Chinatown bus to make it home in time to cast her ballot.

Though she is perceived as a bomb-throwing radical who leapt from behind the bar and into Congress, while at BU, she interned for Sen. Ted Kennedy, the type of move made by people who have a real interest in politics. It was there that she met and began dating Riley Roberts, and the two have been together ever since.

While she was in college, Sergio Ocasio-Roman was battling cancer. "My father knew my soul better than anyone on this planet," she said.[259] "He really made me believe that I had true power in this world."

She was in an economics class when she got a call from her mother saying he had taken a turn for the worse. She raced to a cab and caught the first flight home, making it in time to say goodbye. "Make me proud," he told her.

Losing her father as she was just trying to figure out how to make her way in the world was a crushing blow, both spiritually and financially. The burden fell to her mother, who was still raising Gabriel at home. "When my father died, she was left a single mother of two, and again she had to start over," she wrote in an Instagram post after she was sworn in to Congress. "After he passed we almost lost our home."

Her mom juggled odd jobs — cleaning houses, driving a school bus, answering phones — to stay afloat. Sergio had died without a will, so the estate wound up in the local surrogate court, where lawyers prey on families in desperate situations. People from the bank would pull up to the house and take pictures, as the family scraped to avoid foreclosure. It wasn't until 2012 that the court finally cleared the estate. Ocasio-Cortez had graduated by then, and was living in the Bronx apartment where she had been born, and where Sergio had run his business.

At 21, she started bartending and waitressing at Coffee Bar and Flats

---

259   Quoted in the documentary Knock Down the House.

Fix to help out at home and cover the expenses of the apartment. The now-defunct Coffee Bar had a reputation for hiring models and actors, and had the same owner as Flats Fix, a taqueria and bar.

In summer 2012, she launched Brook Avenue Press, which strived to publish children's books that portrayed the Bronx in a positive light, as well as education curriculum for local schools. In 2012, Sen. Kirsten Gillibrand invited Ocasio-Cortez to a press conference, where she and others stood behind Gillibrand and other politicians as they unveiled a tax break for people who started new businesses.[260]

Her book publishing company was housed in the Sunshine Bronx Business Incubator, which was also featured at the Gillibrand press conference. The incubator also launched GAGEis, Inc., and named Ocasio-Cortez "lead educational strategist," a credential that remains attached to her pre-Congress life. Whatever GAGEis hoped to accomplish, it flopped, and the incubator itself went belly up too.

By this point in her life, the proper way to understand Ocasio-Cortez was as a bartender. This was not something she was doing in the summer between semesters. It wasn't something she did on the side. It was her job, and she was starting to wonder, and to worry, whether it was her career, her life.

She recalled that time in her poignant Instagram post after being sworn in. "It wasn't long ago that we felt our lives were over; that there were only so many do-overs until it was just too late, or too much to take, or we were too spiritually spent," she said of her mother and herself. "I was scrubbing tables + scooping candle wax after restaurant shifts & falling asleep on the subway ride home. I once got pickpocketed, & everything I earned that day was stolen. That day I locked myself in a room and cried deep: I had nothing left to give, or to be. And that's when I started over. I honestly thought as a 28 year old waitress I was too late; that the train of my fulfilled potential had left the station."

Yet she never let her light go fully out. Sandy's co-workers could tell there was something different about her. "She wasn't like the other girls," one barback at Coffee Bar and Flats Fix told me, who bonded with her as a fellow Puerto Rican. "She wasn't just a pretty face trying to get tips. She was always working toward something."

The life of a server, particularly a female one, includes enduring constant indignities. Coffee Bar, the one known for hiring models, actors

260   When Gillibrand later endorsed Crowley in the primary, Ocasio-Cortez tweeted an article about the event at her. After Ocasio-Cortez won, Gillibrand sent the campaign a check for $5,000 from her political action committee. The campaign sent it back. The two offices work closely together, though: Gillibrand's team did constituent service for Ocasio-Cortez's office at the start of her congressional tenure.

and other attractive waitstaff, was a prime source of them. One afternoon in 2015, a manager told the crew to line up against a wall and he would rank them by looks, with the most attractive getting the best section.[261] She quit on the spot, storming out. After much pleading, she eventually returned to both jobs, but with a promise the "contest" wouldn't be repeated.

In 2016, she got caught up in the enthusiasm of the Sanders campaign, following the coverage of The Young Turks and other alternative news outlets, such as The Intercept. It was after the presidential election that her brother submitted her name to Brand New Congress — and she set out on a road trip through Flint, Michigan, bound for Standing Rock.

At Standing Rock she decided to get serious about her run for Congress. The protest encampment was a challenging place to be at any time, but in December 2016, it was brutally cold, and the private, militarized police working on behalf of the pipeline companies had ramped up their use of violence. Seeing the grit and the sacrifice on display would have been enough to put anybody's circumstances in perspective. If the people here could fight this hard for their land, surely she could mount a bid for Congress. Something new had to be done, as neither political party was up to the challenge of the moment. "I saw a fossil fuel corporation that had literally militarized itself against American people," she later told an interviewer during her campaign, "and I saw that our incumbents in both parties were defending them and were silent. And I just felt like we're at a point where we can't afford to be silent anymore, and we can't afford to sit out a political process that we may have grown very cynical over."

The day she got home, she got the call from Isra Allison, one of the group's founders, that Brand New Congress wanted to nominate her to run. Chakrabarti flew out to New York to meet her, inviting Exley, too. They ate at a sparsely filled Thai restaurant in Manhattan, and Exley remembers being deeply impressed.

Exley first emerged into the national spotlight in 1998 when he built the first viral political parody site. He bought the domain name GWBush.com and put up items about Bush's cocaine use and otherwise skewered him. Bush's lawyers tried to get it taken down, and Bush himself called Exley a "garbage man."

Exley's roots in left-wing activism made him unusual as a campaign operative. Having a foot in both worlds gave him an understanding of what, and how, messages from the left could be sold to a broader public, and which elements instantly turned people off. Exley was relieved to

261   A former bartender colleague of hers first told me this story, and Ocasio-Cortez confirmed it happened.

342

find that Ocasio-Cortez was, for lack of a better word, *normal:* "She was obviously a normal person. That might be a loaded term, but she was not a subcultural lefty or subcultural person of any weird little fringe subculture. She was a person who could communicate with anyone and make a connection with anyone."

By this point she'd been living in the Bronx for six years, and whether you consider her childhood stomping grounds as there or Yorktown, the Bronx was home now. And so on May 10, 2017, she filed her paperwork — with Knoxville, Tennessee, listed as the location of her campaign committee, home of BNC — to run for Congress. Her primary opponent would be Jose Serrano in New York's 15th District.

The filing was a mistake, and even before she amended it, there's public evidence that she was campaigning against Crowley the entire time. On June 7, for instance, she participated in an "Ask Me Anything" chat with a Bernie Sanders-community subreddit and repeatedly referenced Crowley. "Brand New Congress is a post-partisan movement, which means that I am already working with GOP candidates like Robb Ryerse[262] in Arkansas and Danny Ell[y]son in Georgia to clean up our political system," she wrote to one redditor. "We know that we are all acting in good faith and service to our nation and are willing to prioritize our similarities first and settle our differences later, instead of the other way around."

Hints of the Green New Deal are peppered throughout that chat, too. "I believe we need to invest in roads and building out the infrastructure needed to switch to a renewable economy by 2028. I also believe we need to do this through PUBLIC corporations like the Tennessee Valley Authority in order to create the most jobs possible with the highest standard of living for the Americans working on these audacious projects."

Serrano, as it happened, had attended the 2012 press conference with Gillibrand. Brand New Congress was new to all of this, as was Ocasio-Cortez, and she didn't live in Serrano's district, nor did she intend to challenge him. It took two months to file amendment paperwork, but it was delivered on July 17, again with a Knoxville address, this time targeting the right district: New York's 14th, the home of Joseph Crowley, longtime King of Queens.

As 2017 wore on, it became increasingly clear that BNC wouldn't have anywhere near its 435 primary challengers, and JD wouldn't run races against every Democrat, nor did they have the capacity to do so even if they had the candidates. Ocasio-Cortez, for instance, got little help from either outfit as she mounted her part-time bid. The two groups split up

---

262   He lost badly but took over Brand New Congress in 2019, and met Ocasio-Cortez in Washington that year, coincidentally in the offices of The Intercept.

for good, with JD going with the Democrats and BNC left without much of a mandate.

Waleed Shahid, who went with JD, surveyed the primary landscape. The original plan, to spark a mass movement, wasn't working, he argued. They needed to pick a few races and put all their chips in. He landed on New York's 14th District as one with the right politics and demographics for a potential upset. Joe Crowley had been in office for decades as the district had transformed underneath him. He was being bandied about as the next House Speaker, so taking him down would leave a mark.

His district had changed, and Crowley was now out of touch. Indeed, the Queens native had long worried that changes to the area he represented could leave him politically vulnerable, and in the previous redistricting battle he had come out on the losing end of a classic New York politics knife fight. Like most grudge matches in the state, it went back generations. Congressional redistricting after the 2010 cycle was drawn by the state legislature, with Assembly Leader Sheldon Silver, a Democrat, playing the decisive role. In 2000, the Queens machine backed a coup against the iron-fisted Silver, led by Assemblyman Michael Bragman, a close friend of Crowley's. The coup failed, and Crowley and Silver were still enemies in 2011 as Silver was in charge of remapping the state's congressional boundaries. Crowley hired lobbyist Brian Meara,[263] a close ally of Silver's, to buy his way out of trouble, but failed. Silver stuck him with a chunk of the Bronx, meaning the King of Queens had a new realm to worry about. Nobody challenged him in 2012, 2014, or 2016, but in 2018 his free ride ended.

Ocasio-Cortez intellectually understood that she was the right woman at the right moment[264]. "He can't get challenged by any down ballot incumbent," she said during the campaign. "Anybody who wants to keep their job in New York City would never dream of challenging Joe Crowley. It has to come from outside of Queens. It has to come from someone who's new on the political scene that they don't see coming, that they can't offer a job or pressure in another way. And it has to be somebody who represents our community in more ways than one. Basically, an insurgent, outside grassroots candidate who's a woman of color from the Bronx."

Shahid made the pitch, and the others went for it. That's how Shahid, in September 2017, became her first on-the-ground staffer.

Heading into the campaign with 30,000-foot optimism, what he saw

---

263   This was reported by Maggie Haberman in Politico in 2011. Meara would later turn on Silver and help send him to federal prison for corruption.

264   She said this in the winter of 2018, before making it onto the ballot, as captured in the documentary Knock Down the House.

on the ground left him heartbroken. Ocasio-Cortez was still working four days a week at two bars, and he had to schedule calls with her while she rode the bus to work and back. *This just isn't possible*, Shahid thought.

Up until February 2018, Ocasio-Cortez was still working shifts that kept her off the campaign trail from as early as eight in the morning until 11 or 12 at night. So to squeeze a few more hours of campaigning into a week, she used her time on the bus to hit the phones. The set-aside phone time meant suffering a longer commute from the Bronx, because it required ditching the subway, but it was worth it.[265] "I switched," she told me. "I used to take the train, but then I started to take the express bus, which would take a little bit longer, but I could make phone calls and send emails and stuff on the ride. I used to take the six [train] down to Union Square, and then I started taking the VXM6." When she could make it to events, she would electrify those who showed up. Often several dozen black and brown working-class people would show up — most had been Sanders supporters and either hadn't heard of Crowley or had and wanted him gone. For Shahid, off to the side, watching this charismatic candidate connect with her audience wasn't exhilarating; it was painful. "Who's going to tell them she can't win?" he thought. "Who's going to tell them this is impossible?"

And then he'd realize he needed to speak, because often Ocasio-Cortez would end her speeches at supposed fundraisers without asking for funds. Consultants drill into candidates that they *must* ask, that they can't leave it to anybody else — that people are giving to *you*, not to a staffer. It's hard for anybody to ask for money, but it's particularly hard for working-class people, who have never wanted to admit they need help.

Her first month in the campaign she raised about $1,500, thanks to two contributions of $500 each and two for $225. In July she bagged roughly $2,000. She hit just over $1,500 in August, and then September 1 shows her first maximum contribution of $2,700, from Saikat Chakrabarti. Around that time, he was becoming increasingly convinced that Ocasio-Cortez could win and that she was JD's best shot at upending the status quo. He agonized, because he wanted to leave JD and work for Ocasio-Cortez full time, but didn't want to abandon the candidates they had recruited and made promises to.

She raised another $800 that month. October was also a tough month, and just $400 came in. It wasn't hard for Crowley to ignore this operation. She raised just under $3,000 in November, and about $7,000 in December.

---

265   Shahid first told me this anecdote, and Ocasio-Cortez confirmed it: "I used to take the six down to Union Square, and then I started taking the VXM6."

When Exley and Chakrabarti had recruited her over that Thai dinner, they had told her that a movement of hundreds of candidates to replace the entire Congress would create national attention, energy, and money. She wouldn't have to do "call time" — dialing for dollars that all candidates dread. But by now it was clear the national movement wasn't happening, and Shahid and Ocasio-Cortez battled over "call time."

The way Justice Democrats is set up allows them to give a candidate $5,500 worth of help, in either cash or in-kind contributions. Super PACs can give unlimited help, but can't coordinate. That means that, legally speaking, Ocasio-Cortez needed to raise enough money to pay Shahid's salary, or he'd be forced to leave.

One afternoon, he pulled up the shared spreadsheet and saw she hadn't entered anything from her scheduled call time. "I texted," explained the millennial insurgent to her millennial campaign aide. "That's not how it works," said a flabbergasted Shahid.

To shut him up, she sent him a screenshot of a text conversation that ended with a voter promising to give $200. Crowley by that point in the cycle had several million dollars in cash on hand. In December, after one of their many fights over fundraising, Ocasio-Cortez took to Twitter to vent:

Consultants: "Why don't more working class people/women/people of color run for office?"

Consultants: "If you're going to run you need to raise at least $200k through your network or don't even bother."

Consultants: "Such a mystery."

That month, Shahid made the case that the group should pick a single candidate and go all in, and he recommended Ocasio-Cortez. "I think we should focus entirely on Ocasio as our sole OG. She needs a lot of help," he wrote in a memo. "She doesn't have a lot of connections in the district in terms of either volunteers or political leads or potential donors who would donate $500 or more. It's a real problem. She doesn't have a lot of leadership of doing things inside her district that gained her respect over the years unlike someone like Jess King."

The group debated the idea, and would eventually adopt it, but not yet. Naomi Burton, a filmmaker and member of Detroit's Democratic Socialists of America chapter, noticed in March that Ocasio-Cortez didn't have a campaign video. Burton DM'd the 28-year-old challenger on Twitter and offered to produce it. The campaign had something like $6,000 in the bank and spent effectively everything they had on it. One month later, Burton and Nick Hayes, on behalf of their working-class media production company, came to the Bronx to shoot the video, which

Ocasio-Cortez scripted.

Fortunately for Ocasio-Cortez, her path to victory didn't require an extraordinary amount of money, or even that many votes. The Queens Democratic Party — aka the Queens machine, of which Crowley was the head — maintained its political dominance through the ballot — not the ballot box, but access *to* the ballot itself. Getting on it was extraordinarily difficult. The sheer number of signatures required — 1,250 — wasn't the daunting part. But if any mistakes were found, the entire page of signatures could be ruled invalid. Every signer had to be a registered voter in the district, and the canvassers had to be registered to vote in the district, too. The machine appointed all the local judges and any challenges made by the machine went before those judges. The petition deadline was only two months before the primary, so a court challenge could effectively keep them off the campaign trail for much of that time.

Ocasio-Cortez's plan was simple: Get enough signatures that a court challenge was unlikely, then get just enough votes in a low-turnout election to win. "The default setting for the race was that Crowley was going to get almost no votes — that's how they structure it in these primaries," Exley said. The congressional primary was set for late June, while the state-level races — governor, state senator, et al. — were scheduled for September, diluting interest. The machine theory was that in a low-turnout affair, the die-hard voters (mostly elderly) cast ballots, and they tend to share a personal connection to or an affinity for the incumbent. It's a structure that has been extraordinarily effective at protecting incumbents, but has an obvious weak spot: if a challenger could generate just enough votes, they could knock somebody out without needing millions of dollars. "There were two questions," said Exley. "Can we turn out some number of votes? And then the other question was, could Crowley turn out a bunch of *additional* votes?" In other words, could the machine still hit on all cylinders?

The petition drive was organized by mom and food blogger Naureen Akhter, who had previously tried to volunteer for the local Democratic Party but was ignored. Sometimes alone, sometimes with a handful of volunteers, they scoured the district in a five-week-long sprint, not stopping until the last moment. The campaign turned in more than 5,000 signatures. "Here we are, April 12, 2018, and we're on the ballot," Ocasio-Cortez told the camera crew following her,[266] after dropping them off. "Unless he sues us."

In a decision he likely regrets to this day, Crowley did not sue, and the sprint to June 26 was on. It would have been a bad look for a man looking to maintain enough progressive cred to become Speaker, which

---

266   This scene is captured in Knock Down the House.

may have influenced his decision. "If he were running against an older white man, he'd probably have sued," Akhter guessed.

The next day, April 13, I got a text from a friend, Matt Stoller,[267] who had been a source of good story ideas for years. Through late-2017 and early-2018, I was covering various insurgent challenges being waged around the country, but hadn't paid particular attention to Ocasio-Cortez. "Hey, do you know anything about Alexandria Ocasio-Cortez and her challenge to Crowley in Queens?" Stoller texted.

"That would be wild," I replied. "Imma reach out."

The first thing reporters tend to do when looking into a candidate — even ones who hate the influence of big money on politics — is check FEC records to see how much they've raised. If there's nothing in the bank, a campaign typically doesn't have a serious chance of winning. Ocasio-Cortez "raised 60k in the 4th quarter, not half bad. I bet she did a lot better in Q1," I texted Stoller. "Headline writes itself: Joe Crowley is Running for Speaker. But he Might Lose his Primary First."

For the life of me, I have no clue where I got that fundraising figure, and it was wildly off. She had raised slightly more than $10,000 for all three months. Which raises an amusing possibility: Did I make the most important editorial decision of my career based on a huge math error?

It doesn't matter now. I called around to a few sources who know New York politics well, and they all said effectively the same thing: *Alex is great, but she can't win. The Queens machine is just too strong.* When I reached out to the campaign, Daniel Bonthius, a volunteer who was doing press work, called back — an immediate sign of just how bare-bones the campaign still was. I asked him to run through the case for why she had a chance. In a perfect world, maybe a candidate's perceived viability shouldn't be the main criterion for coverage. But in our world, in which news resources are scarce, an outlet that spends too much time covering failed candidates blows its own credibility. Readers stop paying attention, and meanwhile good stories elsewhere go uncovered.

There's also the matter of *access* to consider. The Intercept brands itself for "fearless, adversarial journalism," and that is, indeed, the aspiration. Yet it was becoming increasingly clear that Crowley was headed for the speakership — if not in 2019, then probably by 2021, with deep support in the progressive caucus as well as among New Democrats and

267   I first encountered Stoller in 2008 when he was blogging for, I believe, MyDD, and was planning to attack something I had written at Politico. To his credit, he reached out to me first, and I explained my side, and the piece wasn't as bad as it would have been otherwise. We've been friends since, and he went on to work for firebrand progressive Alan Grayson in the House, then Bernie Sanders in the Senate, landing later at Open Markets Institute, which focuses on monopoly politics.

Blue Dogs. He was, far and away, the most well-liked member of Congress in either party.

In covering the Hill, there's no need to be liked by powerful members of Congress or their staff, but to be completely iced out can — at least theoretically — make your job harder. Later that summer, when I was covering Kerri Harris' insurgent challenge against Tom Carper, the Delaware senator's spokeswoman was quite direct: "The caucus sees what you're doing. You're no different than the Free Beacon,[268] and you're going to be treated the same way."

It's possible to push through those threats, but it's absurd to pretend they don't exist, or are meaningless. But Bonthius laid out the case, and he made sense. Plus, *even if she doesn't win*, I reasoned, *Crowley is destined for bigger things, and as-yet was largely unheard of nationally, so this would be an opportunity to introduce the public to a potential future House Speaker.* I decided that if we were going to cover the race, we might as well do it all the way, and we began on a near-daily basis.

Aída Chávez, The Intercept's congressional reporter, was in the Bronx by April 18, spending the day with Ocasio-Cortez not long after she'd turned in her petition signatures.[269] At one point, Chávez mentioned to Ocasio-Cortez that she worked out of the Capitol on a daily basis. "Oh, wow," Ocasio-Cortez replied, her eyes widening.

By late April, Chakrabarti couldn't wait anymore. Shahid, Ocasio-Cortez's first aide, had left the campaign in March to work for Cynthia Nixon's gubernatorial bid, but they finally took up his suggestion to focus almost exclusively on Ocasio-Cortez. Chakrabarti, Rojas, and Trent all left Knoxville for New York. Trent handled press for her, Rojas managed the field program, and Chakrabarti joined her campaign full-time. "It was a chip-pushing in moment. If that didn't work, our whole thing was done," Trent said. "Justice Dems just went all-in and just diverted it all to her." The group had a list of about 330,000 members and pounded away to fundraise for Ocasio-Cortez and find people willing to canvass and phone-bank. "We stopped raising money for anybody else, including ourselves," Trent said.

That, as Chakrabarti had feared, led to some deeply bruised feelings among the other candidates JD had recruited and trained. There would be no national movement. "We abandoned them — promised the world

268   The Carper campaign was particularly angry that Glenn Greenwald and I had written about the senator's admission that he had hit his wife and given her a black eye in the 1980s. The Free Beacon is, broadly speaking, a dark-money funded vehicle for right-wing opposition research.

269   We sent a photographer, too, a fortuitous decision, as the wires had almost no photos of Ocasio-Cortez available the night she won.

and delivered shit," Trent acknowledged, though he agreed with the difficult decision. "This thing, while it's amazing, was a complete and utter failure for the original idea. I'm not saying it wasn't an insane idea, but that was the idea we were selling people. This is utter, abysmal failure."

Perhaps the most relevant variable in Ocasio-Cortez's electoral success was that the drop-off voters — folks who typically vote in presidential years, but not in midterms — didn't just vote, they got involved. Chakrabarti hadn't realized how successful his organization's efforts were to convert the email list into activists until he arrived in the district.

Justice Democrats might not have built exactly the movement it had foreseen, but there was indeed something of a movement afoot. A number of the JD candidates and their teams were in touch throughout 2017, swapping campaign innovations. A critical one was developed by the field team behind Jess King in Pennsylvania, and shared with the Ocasio-Cortez crew. It was, like all such innovations, simple in hindsight: they used voter files to find local residents on social media, rather than at their physical residences. Then they would target them with digital ads. Now the voter knew who Jess King was, and had a sense that there was something substantial behind her, because her name was popping up in their feeds. Having made a potential voter aware of the campaign, they would then follow up by sending a canvasser to knock on the voter's door. The combination of the digital ad and the door knock added up to more than the sum of its parts, as the voter was much more receptive to King's message than they would have been with just a cold call.

Chávez and I published our first story in May, a broad profile of the race, headlined "A Primary Against the Machine: A Bronx Activist Looks to Dethrone Joseph Crowley, the King of Queens."

It laid out the case for a potential upset, noting that she had more than 8,000 individual donors already, which suggested the 5,000 signatures she and her team collected were no fluke. With low turnout, a vote total in the high-four-figures might be enough. "For many readers in Washington, it was the first they had heard of Alexandria Ocasio-Cortez," Politico Magazine later wrote.

Ocasio-Cortez told the Washington Post the story was a "game changer." Donations came in and other news outlets began covering the race, which had its own feedback effect.

One week later, the Means of Production video went viral. "This race is about people versus money. We've got people; they've got money. It's time we acknowledge that not all Democrats are the same, that a Democrat who takes corporate money, profits off foreclosure, doesn't live here, doesn't send his kids to our schools, doesn't drink our water or breathe our air, cannot possibly represent us," she said in the ad, whose power lied in its sophisticated approach to the intersection of class and identity. She leaned into the Hispanic pronunciation of her name, which gave pop to her demand that "it's time for one of us." But she left room for viewers to interpret the message not as "one of us brown people" but "one of us working-class people."

Just running as a progressive wasn't enough. "In the very beginning, I was running with a very strong progressive base and a very strong progressive coalition," she said. "But that alone was not enough to take me over the top. And it was when I really leaned in on this broader message and crafted a progressive message that was rooted in my life story that we were able to really capture a much wider electorate, even though my progressive message was still the same. And so I think it's important that we don't ignore the power of identity, because it is very powerful."

One week after the video launch, she sat for an interview with Jeremy Scahill for his podcast Intercepted, and then for a video interview with Glenn Greenwald. I had lunch with an official from MoveOn, Karthik Ganapathy, and asked if his organization was following the race. They weren't, but would survey its membership in the district. To their surprise, their activists overwhelmingly preferred Ocasio-Cortez. They still could have stayed out of the race, since going up against the potential incoming speaker came with significant risk, but they went for it, and endorsed her.

Crowley didn't help himself on the campaign trail. At one gathering with Queens millennials, meant to be outreach to the cohort of the community turning on him, he stood before a group of about two dozen and made his case for why he should be returned to Congress for a 10th term. In his view, it was "destiny."

"I was born for this role," Crowley boasted at a May 20 meet-and-greet. His opponent was trying to make the campaign "about race" — a strategy he called "unnecessarily divisive" at a time when the party needed to be "fighting Republicans, not other Democrats."

"I can't help that I was born white," Crowley lamented.

Even though it was a small event that was supposed to be filled with Crowley supporters, the comments were leaked. One attendee reached out to the Ocasio-Cortez campaign and repeated what Crowley had said. Daniel Bonthius,[270] still doing volunteer press work, shared the tip with me, explaining that he didn't know what to do with it other than forward it on. I told him I'd need to speak with the person, even if it was off the record, and he connected us.

The original source stayed off the record, but named others who were

---

270   Bonthius, then a volunteer, now her congressional scheduler, gave me permission to name him. "That was my first leak," he said.

there. One of those who heard Crowley's speech, Nick Haby, a member of the Lesbian & Gay Democratic Club of Queens, surprised me by immediately agreeing to speak on the record when I called him, confirming everything, and sending me to other people who were present. Haby had previously been a Crowley supporter, but he soured on him after watching the off-putting speech, which incidentally followed Crowley's endorsement of New York State Senator Jose Peralta, a member of the renegade IDC.[271] Haby knew he was likely facing serious repercussions from the machine, but didn't want to hide behind anonymity, what with Trump creating hysteria around fake news.

Vijay Chaudhuri, a spokesperson for the Crowley campaign, told me to talk to Andy Aujla, the host, who, he said, would refute that Crowley had said that it wasn't his fault he was born white. But when I talked to Aujla, he said that while he didn't hear Crowley opine on the political implications of his whiteness that particular evening, he had heard an iteration of that remark before: "I have heard him say at other places, 'I can't help the color of my skin or anything like that, but I am very diverse, I support very diverse people,' or something to that extent."

Haby told me that the club might have been willing to endorse Ocasio-Cortez, but she hadn't shown up or filled out their questionnaire. She explained that with limited resources, she had mostly ignored the Democratic clubs, which had long been outposts of the machine, particularly after one experience where a club rushed to endorse Crowley before she arrived at a meeting. "It's never been our strategy to court a system led by Crowley, which is what these Dems club are as long as he is their chairman," she said. "Instead we work with activist groups across intersectional issues (BLM, DSA issue caucuses, etc.) to get stuff done." When I told her an LGDCQ Club member had gone on record about a Crowley fundraiser, she revised her take slightly: "I do think that I perhaps overstated how strong this machine was in its loyalty to Crowley. When I started everyone told me it was a done deal. As I've gone further, I've seen that his support isn't as strong as people say it is."

One problem Ocasio-Cortez had to overcome, paradoxically, was Crowley's low profile. Cuomo and the IDC were the focus of local activist ire, and Crowley, away in Washington doing whatever it was he did, wasn't a priority. But Crowley's endorsement of IDC member Peralta had been extremely helpful in drawing a distinction between him and Ocasio-Cortez, and connecting him to a local fight, to progressive reformers who were sympathetic to her but more interested in ousting Cuomo. "That's how we ended up getting Indivisible and TrueBlue/NoIDC en-

271   That was the caucus that split with Democrats and aligned with Republicans.

dorsements," she said.

In early June, The Intercept's Lee Fang published an investigation into how Crowley's inner circle had enriched itself under his reign as king of Queens, particularly by exploiting their control of the surrogate's court, also known in Queens as the widows and orphans court. It was the same exploitation Ocasio-Cortez had witnessed at the Westchester version. Crowley's cronies had previously even run a foreclosure mill, taking money from major banks to carry out evictions. Ocasio-Cortez, in her ad, had accused Crowley of "profiting off of foreclosures." Helping fend off foreclosure is a key element of constituent work some congressional offices engage in and, in years past, would have been the work of a city machine, which looked out for residents in exchange for acquiescence to a little graft. Crowley's machine, instead, was carrying out the foreclosures.

Panicked, Crowley publicized an endorsement he had long ago received from Rep. Ro Khanna, before there had been a competitive race. Khanna was elected in 2016 and quickly became a Justice Democrat, then was named a co-chair of the 2020 Sanders campaign. He was mercilessly pummeled online for the endorsement nonetheless. Active on Twitter, and responsive to criticism from the left, Khanna rethought his endorsement. After several hours of awkwardly explaining himself, he announced that he was *also* offering an endorsement of Ocasio-Cortez. "If we'd have scripted the whole thing, we couldn't have done it better," Corbin Trent later told me. As absurd as a "dual endorsement" may be, the way the drama unfolded in real time put a brighter spotlight on the race than a simple endorsement could ever have. Khanna wound up being the only member of Congress to endorse her.

That summer, news broke that Trump had been systematically separating children from their parents and caging them at the border. On June 13, Crowley, along, strangely, with his friend John Cusack, and other members of Congress, planned to commit civil disobedience at the office of Customs and Border Patrol with other members of Congress, to get arrested as a protest to Trump's cruel detention policy. But the police ignored the members of Congress, refusing to arrest them. So they marched to the White House, in the hopes that Secret Service would be more obliging. But it was a brutally hot day, and a profusely sweating Crowley wobbled and fainted while walking up 15th Street. It made headlines back home, and felt like a win for Crowley.

Crowley's private polling had him up by 30 points, but in such a low-turnout environment, it didn't feel safe with the surging energy around Ocasio-Cortez. "The campaign just grew exponentially" in those last several weeks, recalled Naureen Akhtar, who had tried to join the

Democratic Party and been unable to find her way in. Crowley started blanketing the airwaves with TV ads, filling mailboxes with glossy fliers and robocalling Democratic voters. He also agreed to a debate.

On the day of the debate, Friday, June 15, she was in her apartment with Riley Roberts, her boyfriend who was also a key campaign volunteer. *Take up space*, she told herself, pushing her arms out as far as possible, aware of how stark the physical contrast would be on stage. *I can do this. I am experienced enough to do this. I am knowledgeable enough to do this. I am prepared enough to do this. I am mature enough to do this. I am brave enough to do this.*[272]

Neither side delivered a knockout blow, and Ocasio-Cortez more than held her own. In some significant ways, the debate was held on the challenger's political turf. Rather than her call to abolish ICE becoming a liability, Trump's caging of children made Crowley's refusal to call for its abolition a problem. *Crowley had referred to ICE as fascist — why*, she wondered, *was it controversial to shut down a fascist agency?*

Each candidate was offered the opportunity to ask one another a question. Ocasio-Cortez asked Crowley if he would step down as chair of the Queens County Democratic Party, an implicit challenge to his dual role as boss of the Queens machine and an elected member of Congress. He declined, going on to awkwardly name the people of color he had helped place in office. Crowley, meanwhile, pledged to Ocasio-Cortez that he would support her in the general election if she beat him in the primary and asked if she would do the same.

Both his question and her answer were revealing. Ocasio-Cortez explained that her support of him wasn't up to her — that she was part of a movement, and she was happy to take his request back to the people who made up that movement. They would decide democratically whether to endorse him. It was as radical an expression of the process of democratic socialism as has ever been allowed on NY1, New York City's local news channel. Crowley's request, however, said even more than that. The winner of the primary in Queens and the Bronx automatically wins the general election — there was no serious Republican opposition — so Crowley didn't need Ocasio-Cortez's endorsement to win in November. Why, then, did he ask about it?

Simple: It was about Crowley's race for Speaker of the House. Even as he faced an existential threat to his political career, his focus remained upward. But Ocasio-Cortez had been screwing that plan up by revealing how little support Crowley had among national progressive groups. She had drawn endorsements from a host of them in the run-up to the vote, including MoveOn and Democracy for America, which joined the local

272   The scene is captured in the documentary Knock Down The House.

Indivisible group, Our Revolution, Democratic Socialists of America, and, of course, Justice Democrats. So Crowley didn't need Ocasio-Cortez for his general election in the district; he needed her in his presumed upcoming bid for Speaker of the House, hoping that he could point to her endorsement and say, *Yes, we faced off in a primary, we debated, but we came away allies.*

The pair was scheduled for a second debate on Monday, this one hosted by Ocasio-Cortez's neighborhood newspaper, the Parkchester Times. Before it started, she spotted Crowley's spokeswoman, Lauren French, in the venue, and assumed that Crowley had shown up. Instead, he was in Queens at a community meeting. Citing a scheduling conflict, he sent a surrogate instead, Annabel Palma, a former city council member.

In Washington, the conventional understanding of Crowley's loss was that he had been caught sleeping. Exhibit A was found in the fact that he skipped the Bronx debate. That misses that, for one, he had just debated Ocasio-Cortez on television — so it's not as if he was ignoring her — and it also misunderstands *why* he skipped the debate. Crowley believed, tactically, that he potentially had more to lose by showing up. That it blew up in his face does not change the fact that he thought skipping was the smarter move. It was a poor political decision, but not one made because he considered her a lightweight. On the contrary, he had a genuine sense of the threat, and responded by trying to minimize it.

After she won, the New York Times would catch hell for not having run a single dispatch about the race, even as The Intercept covered it on a virtually daily basis. But an editorial that ran in the Times that Tuesday had a seismic impact on the race. "When asking New Yorkers for their vote, most candidates would begin by showing up," began the broadside. "Not Representative Joseph Crowley." And it ended with just as much of a bang. "Mr. Crowley is far from the first candidate to decline to debate a challenger he is heavily favored to beat," the *Times* editorial board noted. "But his seat is not his entitlement. He'd better hope that voters don't react to his snubs by sending someone else to do the job."

The overlap between New Yorkers who vote in Democratic primaries and New Yorkers who read the New York Times was awfully heavy, and there's no telling how many people read that editorial and cast a protest vote against Crowley, hoping to send him a message while never thinking that he might actually lose.

Crowley continued stepping on rakes. That week, he planned a fundraiser in Washington with the city's top Republican lobbying firm, the BGR Group, founded by Haley Barbour[273] and other GOP veterans. The K

---

273   Barbour, if you recall from Chapter 3, had unsuccessfully challenged, in 1982, Democratic Mississippi segregationist Sen. John Stennis.

Street invitation was promptly leaked to me by a lobbyist. Lee Fang reported the story the same day the *Times* editorial landed. Now, one week before the primary, we had begun to characterize Ocasio-Cortez's effort as "a surprisingly strong challenge."

In the final weeks, a flood of small dollars from across the country poured in, as people began to believe she could actually pull this off, with Khanna's unusual dual endorsement having triggered a tsunami of money. The cash was immediately pumped into paid canvassers, who buttressed the sidewalk-weary volunteers who'd been pounding on doors for months. "It felt like the cavalry had arrived," Akhter recalled.

With troops on the ground the weekend before the election, Ocasio-Cortez pulled something extraordinarily: she left. She flew to Tornillo, Texas, and took part in a demonstration outside a temporary detention facility holding children who were seeking asylum. Her call to abolish ICE intersected with the moment in a way nobody could have predicted, as the country was hitting a moral rock bottom. When she returned, she sent an email to supporters that was reflective of the authentic, vulnerable approach to politics for which she would become famous. Having read thousands of political-fundraising emails, I can say the tone of this one was markedly different.

As it became reasonable to think victory was possible, she began to feel the weight of a movement on her shoulders and was terrified about letting people down. "With so many people in our district struggling to pay rent, being pushed out of their homes, fighting stagnant wages, and trying to get their kids the education they deserve, we can't afford to lose this one," she wrote to supporters. "There are so many people counting on us, and I know we won't let them down." She signed off, as she had throughout the campaign: "Pa'lante, Alexandria."

That same weekend, Crowley aide Lauren French met a friend for drinks, and the friend, intrigued at the online enthusiasm for Ocasio-Cortez, asked if the insurgent had a chance of toppling French's boss. "She'll get 10 percent and get a job with The Young Turks," French quipped. On Election Day, social media came alive with accounts of machine-driven shenanigans at the polls. An insurgency hardened by the 2016 primary and years of machine dominance in the city saw another rigging underway. Turnout was extremely light. I'd have to sit at a polling place sometimes for 30 minutes before a voter arrived. Across the Bronx, I interviewed about a dozen voters — strikingly, all of them voted for Ocasio-Cortez.[274]

---

274   I did hear of one particularly vile Crowley voter that day. Frantzy Luzincourt, a 19-year-old African-American student at CUNY, experienced some of that bigotry first hand as he manned a polling station at Philip J. Abinanti Elementary

As the sun was setting, canvassers reconvened in the Bronx and swapped stories about what they'd seen. With no exit polling, anecdotes were all they had — but they were adding up to something that warranted optimism.

The volunteers had fanned out across the district, focusing particularly on areas in Queens and the Bronx where an influx of young people had been changing the character, complexion, and politics of the neighborhoods. Whether the volunteer had been in Astoria, Sunnyside, or Woodside, all gentrifying neighborhoods in Queens that the campaign targeted heavily, they shared the same story: Turnout, while it was certainly low on an absolute scale, seemed higher than usual, and the people turning out were young, they were diverse, and they were pumped for Ocasio-Cortez.

Many of the voters appeared, to the canvassers, like stereotypical young Bernie Sanders supporters. According to a precinct-by-precinct analysis[275] of the results, Ocasio-Cortez's success can be attributed, in large part, to the strategy of mobilizing so-called "drop-off voters" — folks who voted in the 2016 presidential campaign but rarely voted in midterms. The drop-off voters didn't drop off, and the analysis undercuts the prevalent media narrative, which suggested she only won because she was Hispanic and got the votes of Hispanics. In fact, Crowley — Irish-American and from Queens — was presumed to perform better there than Ocasio-Cortez, who was expected to carry her home borough. The analysis, having mapped out votes across the district, found the exact opposite of the pundits' conclusion: Crowley was crushed almost everywhere, but he did better in the Bronx than in Queens.[276]

Gentrifiers, even among gentrifiers, remain an unpopular demographic, and so it can be uncomfortable to acknowledge the role they played in her win. (Though Trent, ever the straight talker, had no such compunction: "It was the gentrifiers," he said.) But while the economic resources possessed by gentrifiers often exacerbate the financial pres-

---

School in the Bronx. A woman with powder-white hair and sunglasses, who Luzincourt guessed was in her 70s or 80s, was blunt with him. "I wouldn't vote for that fuckin' spic if you paid me," she told Luzincourt about an hour before I interviewed him. He also relayed details of the encounter to fellow volunteers, who confirmed he had shared the story in real time.

275   Conducted by Steven Romalewski, director of the Mapping Service at the City University of New York's Center for Urban Research.

276   "You can also see that most of her votes...were not predominantly Hispanic, so they're a more mixed population, and are areas where — this is kind of a term of art — are in the process of being gentrified, where newer people are moving in," said Romalewski.

sures felt by long-term residents, after the global financial crisis and Great Recession, crushing student debt and soaring rent means that many of these new residents of Queens and the Bronx are decidedly downwardly mobile, and have political interests that align closely with longtime residents.

I arrived early at her victory party to set up. To signal the race's importance, I had organized a panel to cover the returns live.[277] The first numbers to come in looked surprisingly good for Ocasio-Cortez, but many election nights that year, and in years prior, had begun with promise but ended in defeat. Yet the next round of numbers expanded her lead. The next update even more. Pretty soon, more than half the precincts were in, and she still had a big lead, one that just kept growing.

In the car on the way to the billiard hall hosting her party, Ocasio-Cortez wouldn't let anyone look at their phones, even as the clock struck 9:00 and numbers began coming in. She couldn't look. As they approached, though, she saw something startling — reporters sprinting to get into her party. She stepped out of the car. On the sidewalk, she and Riley paused for a long embrace. "Whatever happens, I love you," he told her.

Just moments after she entered, the crowd exploded in celebration as the chyron flashed her victory. She cupped her hands to her mouth. "Oh my God," she said, then, instantly composing herself, gave a brief interview to the NY1 reporter next to her. Without hesitation and with nothing prepared, and no expectation that she was going to win, she stepped onto a bar stool and delivered a barnburning speech to a crowd that was small — maybe 50-75 people — but melting down.

"This victory tonight belongs to each and every single person in this room," she declared, gesturing around the small, tightly packed bar. "Every person out here this evening changed America tonight. And what I wanna make very, very clear, is that this is not an end; this is the beginning. This is a beginning because the message we sent the world tonight is that it's not okay to put donors before your community."

"And what you have shown is that this nation is never beyond remedy, it is never too broken to fix," she said. "We will be here and we are going to rock the world in the next two years."

"Rock it!" shouted Trent.

"Because every person in this room is going to D.C. with me," Ocasio-Cortez continued. "We have to dedicate ourselves each and every single day to this fight, cuz I can't do it alone. So not only do I need to

277   Briahna Gray from The Intercept; Emma Vigeland from TYT, who had done early dispatches on her race; Virgil Texas and Will Menaker from the podcast Chapo Trap House.

get elected, but we've got a whole bunch more primaries to go. And when we get to November, we should be electing a caucus of people on these beliefs and on this change. So I'mma tell you right now — Imma tell you right now — we've got Ayanna Pressley in Massachusetts, we got Cori Bush in Missouri, we got Chardo Richardson in Florida, we got a whole bunch of more races."

Rebecca Katz, a Cynthia Nixon aide, found Trent after the speech and marveled at the lack of reporters at such an historic event. "They're on the sidewalk," he explained. Trent, in the glow of victory, had no plans to allow the media, which had ignored the campaign, to have any part of the celebration. "They didn't RSVP," he told her, "so I'm not letting them in."

Earlier that evening, Ocasio-Cortez had faced the same challenge, stopped by security at the door. But she made her way inside

Twenty-Seven

Which Side Are You On?

Cynthia Nixon's campaign wasn't going badly. After announcing her bid for New York governor in March 2018, the actress and longtime activist generated enough buzz to make a credible run. To beat Andrew Cuomo, she'd have to pitch the political equivalent of a perfect game, but the anti-establishment mood meant that it wasn't impossible. As April turned to May, her campaign was being taken increasingly seriously, particularly by Cuomo, who was waging a behind-the-scenes war to ensure no one who ever wanted to work in Democratic politics got anywhere near her. On the first Saturday in May, it fell apart.

At the New York City Cannabis Parade, Nixon appeared on stage to call for the legalization of marijuana and an end to the racist drug war. Afterward, she stopped for an interview with Mona Zhang, a freelance writer who covers cannabis and the industry. There, she elaborated on her proposal. "Now that cannabis is exploding as an industry, we have to make sure that those communities that have been harmed and devastated by marijuana arrests get the first shot at this industry," she said. "We [must] prioritize them in terms of licenses. It's a form of reparations."

Now, I can make the argument that what she said is defensible. Reparations, indeed, are deserved by victims of the drug war, and there is a sense of justice in making sure that those who were harmed by a wrong can be the beneficiaries of an effort that later tries to right it. There's also an injustice in the way that the industry has been growing, with the financial gain going largely to white business owners, while black vic-

361

tims of the war on drugs remain in prison or saddled with records. All of that is true. But the comment was politically tone-deaf, and was quickly caricatured by the New York media as, *Sorry for slavery — here's some weed*. It surely meant that Nixon wouldn't be pitching that perfect game, and if there was a moment that her campaign went from a longshot to no shot, that may have been it.

It wasn't an off-the-cuff gaffe. The reparations argument had come from her close adviser, Caroline Murray.

Murray had connections — she had previously dated and was long-time friends with Nixon's wife Christine Marinoni, who had a progressive political background and suggested Murray play a leading role in Nixon's campaign. Nixon, too, had been friends with Murray for years, and eagerly brought her on. Marinoni, too, became a senior figure in the campaign. Campaign staff and consultants, after all, were not easy to come by, as Cuomo made clear that anybody who so much as appeared in the same room as Nixon could consider their career in New York politics over.

The reparations calamity was just the most visible manifestation of Murray's influence, Nixon staffers said. Even though she wasn't the official campaign manager, everything seemed to run through her, they complained — particularly the field program, and nothing ever seemed to get done. Fundraising languished (though, again, Cuomo had put a kink in that hose) and at least one high-level staffer quit.

Senior staff tried multiple avenues to pressure Nixon to do something about Murray, but no luck. Rebecca Katz, one top adviser, met with Nixon one-on-one before July 4 and urged her to cut Murray loose, warning, to no avail, that she'd become a toxic presence. Outside groups tried too, including officials at the Working Families Party, which was backing Nixon; and the Alliance for Quality Education, where Nixon's wife had worked. New York City Mayor Bill de Blasio didn't endorse either Cuomo or Nixon, but his enmity for Cuomo was no secret, and his staff worked closely with the Nixon campaign. (Katz had previously worked for de Blasio.) They, too, urged the campaign to cut ties with Murray and failed.

In August, the staff doubled effectively overnight. They had previously wanted to form a union, but there hadn't been enough people to make one work. With its larger size, the workers were itching to organize. The staff of Randy Bryce, running in Paul Ryan's Wisconsin district, had been the first to unionize, followed later by workers for Jess King, running in Pennsylvania's Amish Country. It didn't take long to get consent from rank-and-file workers, and the staff circulated a survey to find out what people felt was the most pressing issue. It wasn't close: dealing with Caroline Murray was the top concern.

The organized staff came to the campaign's leadership with its demand to be recognized, and in the negotiations over a contract, let it be known that the main issue was Murray. After about a week of negotiations, Murray relented, and left the campaign. What some of the most influential people in New York had been unable to do, a union had achieved with relative quickness.

If you assume that Murray deserved to be thrown overboard, that achievement alone would have been a marked success, an example of how workers, organized together, can make an enterprise more just, more efficient, effective and powerful. The negotiations between the Nixon camp and its staff served as a warning sign to future Democratic campaigns that will be grappling with their own unions. In early August, staffers submitted a 35-page document to campaign manager Hayley Prim with their list of demands, which included limiting hours and expanding paid days off during the get-out-the-vote period. That staff, most of which had been hired in late July or August, was asking for three paid days off in September, in addition to taking off Labor Day and a day each weekend before Election Day, typically the most active days of canvassing for a campaign. The primary was set for September 13, which meant just five or six days of work in the crucial final two weeks.

The biggest ask, though, was for a severance agreement in which staff would be paid for a set amount of time after the campaign ended. At this point, a decent number of the staffers had only been on board for a few weeks, and with just six weeks left, they asked for a large chunk of the remaining budget to be set aside as a cash payout to themselves. This is where it got tricky: the candidate, her top aides and her rank-and-file staffers were all committed progressives, all joined in a project to overthrow the Cuomo machine. All were supportive of the idea that workers deserve economic security. But the money in the campaign coffers had been donated to help Nixon win her election. How would small donors feel if the $27 they kicked in went not to a worker's salary, not to an ad, not to pizza for volunteers, but as part of a large severance package for people who had worked on the campaign for one month? At what point does the demand cross an ethical line?

The union made repeated threats to strike or to go to the press about the state of the negotiations, noting that if it did so, the resulting publicity would create a disaster for the campaign, which put them in a tremendously powerful bargaining position. There was also a lengthy back and forth on maternity leave — the union asked for 20 weeks — that was debated purely on principle, as nobody was pregnant or due to give birth by September 13.

After the Murray situation had been resolved, management hoped the rest of the talks would run smoothly, but the major demands remained and would have cost the campaign well into the six figures, perhaps the entire amount in the campaign treasury. Decisions about spending were put off as the negotiations went on.

The agreement was finally signed on August 22, which meant the campaign and its workers ate up three of the last six negotiating workplace rules for an enterprise that was due to end in less than one month. The concession made on severance — each staffer, no matter how long they'd been on the campaign, would get two weeks pay after the campaign ended — which took an unexpected six figures away from a planned media buy.

With the contract in place, things picked up noticeably with different elements of the campaign finally coordinating. Yet the limits put on how much staffers could work, particularly on weekends and evenings, crimped activity down the stretch. The debate was held on August 29, and prep staff had been cut way down to meet union rules. Senior staff were instructed not to call union members in the evening in advance of the debate, so policy people were cut out of evening debate prep.

In other campaigns that had unionized, such as Randy Bryce in Wisconsin and Jess King in Pennsylvania, working hours hadn't been a significant issue; because campaigns, by their nature, don't take breaks between 5 p.m. and 9 a.m. the next morning. They are grueling affairs and, unless the candidate is a billionaire, typically cash-strapped. Weekends, early-mornings, and late-evening events are routine, because that's often when voters are off-work and available.

On Election Day, Nixon lost 66-34.

Both the senior staff and union members wondered what might have been possible with an efficient campaign from the start. Had she gotten to 40 percent, it's likely her running mate, Jumaane Williams (who lost by six points) might've been pulled across the finish line in the lieutenant governor's race. Ultimately, given how badly she was outspent, she never had a shot, and people in her campaign and outside it determined in their autopsy that her profile probably made winning impossible. Though she was able to win white liberals and did well with millennials and young people of all color, she scanned simply as a rich white lady — an image sharpened by the role she played on "Sex and the City." Most if not all of Nixon's voters also went for Jumaane Williams, but Williams romped in Brooklyn, including in the black and brown precincts, while Nixon had been beaten badly there.

In the race for attorney general, Congressman Sean Patrick Maloney played the role of spoiler against Zephyr Teachout, and syphoned off votes in Upstate New York. Letitia James, the public advocate, came out on top. Teachout, Nixon, Williams, and Ocasio-Cortez had all cross-endorsed one another, but only Williams and Ocasio-Cortez benefited.[278] That left New York progressives to conclude that in the future, insurgent candidates need to win black and brown working-class neighborhoods, and to do so they ought to be black or brown themselves.

---

278   "Get your coat, we're going to the Bronx," adviser Rebeca Katz told Nixon as the returns came in on the night of June 26, as it appeared Ocasio-Cortez was headed for an upset victory. I interviewed Nixon at the victory party, and even though she'd been running for months, it still felt surreal to be talking to Miranda.

Twenty-Eight

Brett

On Thursday, July 5, 2018, the Trump White House leaked its short list of potential nominees to replace the outgoing Supreme Court swing vote, Justice Anthony Kennedy: The three finalists had been pared down to Brett Kavanaugh, Amy Coney Barrett, and Raymond Kethledge.

In Palo Alto, California, Christine Blasey Ford scrambled upon seeing the news. A professor of psychology at Palo Alto University, Blasey Ford had long been watching the rise of Kavanaugh with dread. In high school, he and a drunken friend, Mark Judge, had sexually assaulted her at a small gathering, and Blasey Ford felt as if she would have been raped had she not managed to escape. She had to do something before Kavanaugh graduated from the short list to nominee status. Over that July 4 weekend, she shared her plans with a few friends, and on July 6, she called the Washington Post tipline. She also called the office of her member of Congress, Anna Eshoo, drafting a letter to her as well.

Blasey Ford first spoke with a staffer at Eshoo's office, then met with Eshoo on July 20, by which time Kavanaugh had been nominated. They spoke for about an hour and a half, and "she wished me to move this to another place," Eshoo later told KCBS Radio. That other place was into the hands of Sen. Dianne Feinstein, the top Democrat on the Senate Judiciary Committee. "She knew she wanted the information to get into the appropriate hands," Eshoo said.

Eshoo suggested she put the allegations on paper in a letter to Feinstein, and her staff hand-delivered it to Feinstein's staff on July 30. A letter like that has a special significance on Capitol Hill, particularly one that has been seen by two separate offices. It represents the latent threat of a leak, and one with a time stamp on it. Her letter included a request: "As a constituent, I expect that you will maintain this as confidential until we have further opportunity to speak." That line would end up being used repeatedly by Feinstein as she claimed that, in fact, Blasey Ford never wanted to come forward, and was only forced out by the media. But that argument ignored that Blasey Ford had already taken repeated steps to come forward, had already told friends she planned to do so, had already come forward to two congressional offices and reached out to the press, and was only asking for confidentiality until she and Feinstein spoke.

Throughout August, Feinstein's staff and Blasey Ford spoke multiple times. Clues to how those conversations went later emerged in reporting by The New Yorker's Ronan Farrow and Jane Mayer. The pair reported that "Feinstein's staff initially conveyed to other Democratic members' offices that the incident was too distant in the past to merit public discussion, and that Feinstein had 'taken care of it.'" They added, based on sources close to the California lawmaker, that "Feinstein also acted out of a sense that Democrats would be better off focussing on legal, rather than personal, issues in their questioning of Kavanaugh."

Some Democrats, indeed, would be better off with that focus. One of them was Feinstein. Because of California's unusual top-two primary system, she was facing progressive Democrat Kevin de León. That meant Feinstein was leaning on conservative Democrats and Republicans to help lift her over de León. The only way Feinstein could lose was if something wild happened that threw the race into chaos and infuriated conservative voters — who didn't love Feinstein, but preferred her to de León. For Feinstein, a quiet confirmation process focusing on "legal, rather than personal, issues" was the safest bet. The same was true for Senate Democrats running in states that Trump won, where their path to victory was to keep turnout low among Trump supporters. A furious debate over allegations of sexual assault just ahead of the election would have the opposite effect. Chuck Schumer, meanwhile, repeatedly told outside allies that a furious stand against Kavanaugh would enrage Trump supporters and only disappoint progressive voters. "We have no power," he explained repeatedly.

Blasey Ford's primary concern when she reached out to Congress was not the electoral fate of Feinstein or Sen. Joe Donnelly in Indiana. Still, after hearing out Feinstein's staff, and watching Senate Democrats' inability to dent Kavanaugh throughout August, Blasey Ford agreed that the smartest decision at that point was to remain silent.

As far as Senate Democratic leadership was concerned, the summer had been quiet around Kavanaugh, and that was just fine. The baseline for recess protests in the minds of lawmakers remains the summer of 2009, when tea party agitators flooded Democratic town halls, blasting away at their member of Congress, decrying death panels, and demanding opposition to this socialist stalking horse. The town halls dominated the news and penetrated the political consciousness in Washington. In February 2017, during the first week of recess, a similar onslaught, but from the other direction, took over the news cycle, as Indivisible and other progressive groups rallied at town halls or at congressional offices. Many held mock town halls with cardboard cutouts of their legislator if he or she refused to show, and the novelty of the stunt drew local coverage.

The energy continued into the summer of that year, with furious protests against the repeal of the Affordable Care Act. Demonstrators mobbed members of Congress back in their districts and swarmed the Capitol, with John McCain, Lisa Murkowski, and Susan Collins driving a stake into the repeal at the end of July. Then in September, sitting in the Senate barber shop, Lindsey Graham and former Sen. Rick Santorum of Pennsylvania, neither of which knew anything about health care policy,[279] cooked up a nonsensical plan to repeal Obamacare and replace it with block grants. That restarted furious protests, until enough senators announced publicly that, no, they wouldn't vote for that either.

It was in that context of protest that Democratic leaders viewed the quiet recess in 2018 as evidence that the country was not opposed to Kavanaugh, and that Democrats could quietly let him move through. That overlooked a few basic elements, notably that Senate Republicans held essentially zero public events all summer, specifically to avoid protests about Kavanaugh. Hundreds of events were held around the country, but they got no coverage, because there was no lawmaker there, and the cutout thing had lost its novelty to the press.

Take an August rally in Denver, Colorado, targeting Republican Cory

---

279   As Graham said at the time: "So, this idea came about from a conversation at a barber shop. Rick Santorum — I was getting my haircut and he says, you know, you've got an opt-out bill — opt out of Obamacare if you don't like it, take the money and do state-controlled systems. Why don't you do what we did with welfare reform in '96, which is basically take the same amount of money and block grant it?...I've been doing it for about a month. I thought everybody else knew what the hell they were talking about, but apparently not," Graham clarified, adding he had assumed "these really smart people will figure it out." I ran his comments in a story accurately headlined: "Lindsey Graham on Obamacare Repeal: I Had No Idea What I Was Doing."

Gardner: Several hundred protesters rallied in Civic Center Park and local reporters were on hand, earning a two-minute segment on that night's local CBS broadcast. Called "Unite for Justice," it was one of dozens held that day around the country. The news segment, however, ended with a remarkable statement. "A pro-life rally was scheduled to run in opposition to the protest, but no one attended," the anchor said.[280]

The "pro-life movement" is often thought of as vibrant and powerful, and in politics, perception can be more important than reality. But in reality, the movement consists of a few thousand diehards who show up every year for the March For Life, padding out their numbers by busing in high school kids. That non-movement was similarly inactive on behalf of Kavanaugh, despite a more than $30 million budget[281] from conservative groups that even included money to hire protesters to show up at offices like that of West Virginia's Joe Manchin. By a 2-1 margin, the public has consistently said it wants *Roe v. Wade* upheld. But Democratic leaders who came of age in the reactionary era of Phyllis Schlafly suddenly lose their ability to read survey data when it comes to lady parts. Even as women were powering the resistance to Trump, Schumer became agitated with women's groups pushing for Senate Democrats to fight.

An outside progressive group that had been set up to fight Kavanaugh, called Demand Justice, even cut ads against Heidi Heitkamp, Manchin, and Donnelly. At the time, all three were likely *yes* votes. They showed the ads to Schumer and warned that they planned to spend seven figures on them — a fortune in North Dakota and West Virginia — if Democrats didn't use the confirmation hearings to challenge Kavanaugh in a serious way. The ads called the Democratic senators hypocrites for their Obamacare rhetoric, chiding them for claiming to protect it even while voting to confirm a Supreme Court Justice who very well might vote to overturn it. Schumer was furious.

Kavanaugh's confirmation hearings kicked off more than a month after Blasey Ford's letter had been delivered to Feinstein, and two months after she had reached out to Eshoo's office. They began with fireworks, with Sen. Kamala Harris, Feinstein's California colleague, interrupting Chairman Chuck Grassley to question the legitimacy of the hearings, given that Democrats had just the night before been dumped tens of thousands of documents from Kavanaugh's time in the Bush administration. New Jersey Senator Cory Booker would later publicly release some of those documents, claiming he was willing to take whatever con-

280   My Intercept colleague Aída Chávez covered this remarkable segment, and the lack of grassroots energy nationwide on behalf of Kavanaugh.
281   NARAL Pro-Choice America did the math, cited in the article by Chávez.

sequences may come, though it turned out that they were already public, so there were none. If it were designed to be a show to demonstrate to the Democratic base that the party's senators were in full fight mode, it was effective. Though it did nothing to slow Kavanaugh's confirmation.

His four days of testimony wrapped up on Friday, September 7, and he was cruising toward confirmation. That afternoon, however, the Capitol Hill rumor mill cranked up, and word of a letter containing explosive allegations began its circulation. Oftentimes reporters are the mosquitos that carry the rumor from office to office in attempts to confirm it. Several Democrats on the Senate Judiciary Committee learned about it this way.

The rumors swirled throughout the weekend and eventually got to me. I was on the bus in the morning when I got a call about it. I was a logical choice for a call like that, as I'd gotten a reputation as a reporter willing to publish stories that were true and important that might cause me problems with sources, or otherwise be the subject of controversy. Earlier that year, I was the first Washington reporter to break the news of White House Staff Secretary Rob Porter's abuse of ex-wives, complete with a photo of the damage he'd done to the eye of his first wife.

It wasn't because I was the first reporter to learn about it. Porter was a key source for the White House press corps, and his presence in virtually every important meeting made him critical to those beat reporters. Bob Woodward's book *Fear* appears to have benefited greatly from Porter. The most reliable, talkative, and well-placed diplomatic source in Washington was UAE Ambassador Yousef Al Otaiba. In 2017, a story I wrote exposed his underground lifestyle, which involved sex trafficking and other forms of exploitation.

The source on the phone, however, didn't have many details, had not read the letter itself, and had heard multiple versions of the story, so couldn't confidently relay it.

I started making calls and managed to learn a new detail — that the woman was now being represented by Debra Katz, a prominent #Me-Too-movement attorney and Democratic partisan. I also learned that the woman had been in touch with both Feinstein and Eshoo.

From there, I tried a reporting trick that is useful when the time to investigate a tip is truncated: the bluff. I emailed Katz and asked if she had time to talk, but got an auto-reply, explaining she was out for the Jewish holiday. So I called her law firm's front desk and said that I knew Katz was out that day, but needed to speak to one of the attorneys who was handling the case of the woman who had reached out to Anna Eshoo and Dianne Feinstein with allegations regarding Brett Kavanaugh. People working the phones at the front desk are typically the best to try this move on, because they're not paid to interact with the press or obfuscate or deny. They're there to answer phones and direct callers to the right place.

"Sure, that would be Joseph Abboud," she told me, and patched me through.

I told Abboud why I was calling and he said he would talk to other lawyers at the firm and get back to me if they decided to comment. With that, I knew something serious existed, though I still didn't even know the name of the woman. I called Eshoo's office and the front desk there sent me to her spokeswoman, Emma Crisci, who told me that I was asking about a constituent matter, and therefore they couldn't comment. It was, in its own way, another confirmation that the matter was real.

My colleague at The Intercept, Jim Risen, it turned out, had known Debra Katz as a source for years. I briefed on the situation and he called several times a day trying to get to her, but she never answered or called him back. Feinstein's office was the same. The normally responsive press staff didn't answer phone calls or respond to emails. I called around elsewhere on the Judiciary Committee and learned that word of the letter had seeped out to some of them, and that at least one Democrat had pressed Feinstein to share the letter, or allow it to be viewed, and had been rebuffed. That Democrat was Feinstein's California colleague Kamala Harris.

Whether the allegations in the letter were true or not — or, indeed, what the precise allegations were — was its own story, and I didn't have it. But the fact that Feinstein was battling with fellow Democrats on the committee over the issue was a separate story. And that one I had.

By now it was Wednesday, and the Senate would return for its first vote of the week at 5:30 p.m.. A Senate vote meant that senators would stream out of their offices and through the Capitol to the floor of the upper chamber. Reporters would then congregate in the basement and near a bank of elevators off the Senate floor, ready for a few minutes to hit them up for comments. The reporters stay glued to their phones, and I knew if I timed the story right, every relevant senator would be peppered with questions about it.

It's common when working on a sensitive story that a source or a subject will make a plea — based on nothing more than a reporter's conscience — that this or that detail should be withheld. Sometimes the request is made that the story be held completely, with a rationale given for how publishing could be damaging. Those requests are not always honored, but they're always taken seriously if offered in what seems to be good faith. At no time over the course of those three days did anyone from the law firm representing Blasey Ford or in Feinstein's office or elsewhere ask us to hold or kill our story, or suggest that Blasey Ford had decided she wanted to remain anonymous.

We published our story at 5:24 p.m., and it quickly made the rounds among Capitol Hill's reporters. Feinstein largely ducked questions but her response made clear it was something serious. That evening, her committee colleagues demanded a private meeting and implored her to move on the allegations. She relented, and that night turned the letter over to the FBI to include in Kavanaugh's background file. That move assured it would leak fully, because now the White House and everyone on the Judiciary Committee had access to it. There's no evidence that she reached out to Blasey Ford to ask her consent to do so, yet Feinstein would use Blasey Ford's August reticence to come forward to justify her decision to sit on the letter.

Feinstein's decision to sit on the letter made the new strategy Democrats settled on appear disingenuous. *There should be no vote*, Democrats argued, *until the allegations could be fully investigated by the FBI.* It would have been an entirely reasonable request had it been made in a timely way, but after holding it back through the hearings, it appeared like Democrats were throwing up anything they could at the last minute to derail Kavanaugh. That wasn't the truth — I'm quite certain that Feinstein would have preferred to take that letter to the grave. But for a rightly cynical public, it was a reasonable conclusion.

McConnell and the Trump administration relished the fight, agreeing with Feinstein that it would be big trouble for Democrats in states like Indiana, Missouri, and North Dakota, and might even save the House for them. Yet what was good for Senate Republicans was not necessarily fortuitous for Kavanaugh's confirmation chances. Kavanaugh was flailing, and a friend floated the possibility that Blasey Ford had actually been assaulted by a different boy. That boy had been at Kavanaugh's private school on a scholarship, and was now a teacher in North Carolina. It was an utterly absurd theory, and it was shot down immediately by both the teacher and Blasey Ford.

On Sunday night, September 23, The New Yorker published a new allegation, this one made by Deborah Ramirez, in a story written by Ronan Farrow and Jane Mayer. As soon as I saw the headline, I knew it was unlikely to be fatal to Kavanaugh: "Senate Democrats Investigate a New Allegation of Sexual Misconduct, from Brett Kavanaugh's College Years." Making Senate Democrats the subject of the headline suggested the magazine was less than confident in its story — or, like me, was short on details — and the New York Times would later claim that the paper had investigated the incident but didn't run a story on it. Ramirez alleged that when she was extremely drunk in college, Kavanaugh had exposed himself to her at a small party. Other people remembered hearing about the incident, and the evidence was convincing, but not airtight, and Republicans used the vagaries in it to throw dust in front of the first allegation.

Then Michael Avenatti struck. Avenatti was a pivotal character in the early years of the Trump administration. As a lawyer for adult film star Stormy Daniels, who was paid hush money to cover up an affair with Trump, he helped send Trump lawyer Michael Cohen to prison and rattled Trump in any number of ways. But in the Kavanaugh affair he overshot. He released an affidavit from a client who insinuated that Kavanaugh had taken part in gang rapes. Under questioning from journalists, she told conflicting accounts, and backed away from pointing the finger squarely at Kavanaugh, saying only that she'd seen him waiting in line outside a room where she believed an assault was going on. Republicans seized on the flimsiest of the allegations, preferring to focus on them instead of Blasey Ford's, and used them to discredit everything. It's my own opinion, having watched the politics unfold close up, that Avenatti's intervention was a major, perhaps decisive boost for Kavanaugh.

On September 26, Kavanaugh released his calendar from his senior year, and written right there on it was a gathering just like the one Ford had described, with many of the same people: *Go to Timmy's for Skis w/ Judge, Tom, PJ, Bernie, Squi.* "Skis" was a reference to brewskies, or beers, and it flew in the face of Kavanaugh's absurd claim that he'd never been at a gathering like the one Ford had described. "Judge" was Mark Judge, who Blasey Ford said was Kavanaugh's accomplice in the assault.

The next day, September 27, the Senate Judiciary Committee heard from both Blasey Ford and Kavanaugh. Blasey Ford came off as extraordinarily credible. She was asked why it was she could remember details of the attack so vividly, but not remember where exactly the gathering was. *How could she be so sure it was Brett Kavanaugh?* "The way that I'm sure I'm talking to you right now — it's just basic memory functions, and also just the level of norepinephrine and epinephrine in the brain that sort of, as you know, that neurotransmitter encodes memories into the hippocampus, so that trauma-related experience is locked there, so other memories just drift."

Asked what her strongest memory was, she replied, "Indelible in the hippocampus is the laughter. The uproarious laughter between the two. They're having fun at my expense."

After she finished, the committee adjourned, and Democrats held what's known on Capitol Hill as a "caucus lunch." Normally held on Tuesdays in the Senate's LBJ room, caucus lunches were started by Lyndon Johnson as part of his effort to turn the position of majority leader (which had always been largely ceremonial) into one with real power. That meant organizing the caucus, and a weekly lunch was a way to get them all in the same room.

As the Democratic caucus gathered, the mood was upbeat; the morning had been emotionally tormenting, but Kavanaugh appeared to be dead. Fox News guests were declaring her testimony profoundly moving and credible.

Schumer stood up in front of his colleagues and shared his analysis of how Blasey Ford's testimony had played in the press. *There was no way,* he said, *that Kavanaugh could survive.* That meant that the smartest Democratic move at this moment was to not get in the way. *Don't do anything,* he told Judiciary Committee members, *that could screw this up and give Republicans some way to paint Kavanaugh as the victim. Stand down,* he said.

Kavanaugh's performance was the opposite, and as he shouted and cried through his prepared remarks, attacking Democrats and a broad left-wing conspiracy, it seemed clear that he had disqualified himself. Certainly a man with this fiery partisan temperament, who would later have to apologize for things he said *in his prepared remarks,* couldn't be confirmed. "This whole two-week effort has been a calculated and orchestrated political hit," Kavanaugh exclaimed, flipping pages angrily, "fueled with apparent pent-up anger about President Trump and the 2016 election, fear that has been unfairly stoked about my judicial record, revenge on behalf of the Clintons and millions of dollars in money from outside left-wing opposition groups."

"This is a circus," he continued. "The consequences will extend long past my nomination. The consequences will be with us for decades. This grotesque and coordinated character assassination will dissuade confident and good people of all political persuasions from serving our country. And as we all know in the United States political system of the early 2000s, what goes around comes around!"

It was an embarrassing meltdown, the opposite of judicial temperament. As the hearing went on, however, it became increasingly clear that Republicans were determined to fight to the bitter end. They had one ace up their sleeve they knew they could rely on, and that was Susan Collins. The Maine Republican was something of an honorary member of the Bush family, and she had known Kavanaugh for years. She got her start in politics as a congressional aide to Rep.-turned-Sen. William Cohen. Collins was close to George H.W. Bush, who has long maintained a presence in Maine. At the end of the first Bush administration, Collins was appointed New England regional director of the Small Business Administration. In 1996, she was elected to the Senate to replace her mentor, Cohen.

Kavanaugh himself had effectively married into the Bush family. He served as an attorney for George W. Bush's campaign, playing a major role in the legal battle between Bush and Al Gore. He then served in the Bush White House, and had a position of intimate influence, regularly attending Oval Office meetings.

Bush nominated Kavanaugh to the D.C. Circuit Court of Appeals in 2003 and Democrats put up a serious fight, arguing that he was far too partisan to be within striking distance of the Supreme Court. The push-back dragged out the confirmation process for three years, and he wasn't confirmed until 2006. Bush stuck by him throughout it, and Kavanaugh refused to withdraw.

There is a certain type of professional climber in Washington who subsumes that most intimate of relationships, marriage, to their own ambition. The right marriage can mean everything in a rise toward the top, and Kavanaugh, on that front, did well by himself. In 2004, while his nomination languished, Kavanaugh married Ashley Estes, who had been George W. Bush's personal secretary dating back to his days as Texas governor. They had met in the Oval Office, and the Bushes attended the wedding.

George W. Bush called Collins repeatedly throughout the process, and while she pretended publicly to remain undecided, McConnell never worried about her vote. More worrisome were folks like Jeff Flake. Flirting with a presidential bid, and having sworn off reelection, he was the wild card.

On June 26, Ana Maria Archila,[282] co-director of the Center for Popular Democracy, cast her vote for Alexandria Ocasio-Cortez at her polling place in Queens and then took a train to Washington, where she was organizing mass civil disobedience against Trump's policy of imprisoning children seeking asylum in the U.S. ("Alexandria was supposed to come because she was gonna lose," Archila said.) After Kavanaugh was nominated to the Supreme Court, Archila stayed in Washington off-and-on to challenge him.

By that Friday, she was done, and planned to return home on a train in time to pick up her kids up from school. But a friend and colleague of hers, Daniel Altschuler, was headed for the Hart building in the morning, and so she went by to say hello. Hart is just blocks from Union Station, so, with luggage in tow, she trudged back one more time to the Senate office building that had been the scene of so many occupations and arrests over the past year.

Maria Gallagher had signed a petition being circulated by the group UltraViolet calling for an investigation into Blasey Ford's allegations

---

282   Archila appeared in Book 1, Chapter 8, for her work on immigrant rights.

— the type of action typically derided as "slacktivism." But petitions have several purposes. One, of course, is on the surface: in this case, *investigate the allegations.* Beyond that, outfits are seeking new donors and activists, using petitions to find them. Following up on the petition signing, UltraViolet sent a new email to Gallagher and others, signed by Shaunna Thomas, urging people to protest at the Capitol. Those people who RSVP'ed received a follow-up email from Melissa Byrne, also on behalf of UltraViolet. It included Byrne's phone number, giving Gallagher added comfort that she'd be meeting up with real people.

Just 23, Gallagher worked at a financial services firm, but had been deeply moved by the courage of Blasey Ford to come forward. The first time she came to Hart, she dropped off coffee and went to work. On this day, though, she would stay at least for the morning, but she had no plans to do anything more than hold a sign in the background. When she showed up, she texted Byrne, who told her to find a friend and go stake out Jeff Flake's office. She found Archila's friend: "She grabbed my friend and my friend grabbed me and I was thinking, like, Oh, *I'm just going to drop them off — it's 9:00, the [committee] meeting starts at 9:30. We're not going to see him. We never see these people."*

UltraViolet had put Flake on its target list per the advice of Faiz Shakir, who was at the time the political director of the ACLU.[283] With that decision, the same scrappy women's group that had connected Rose McGowan and Jodi Kantor, helping spark the #MeToo movement, had just set in motion another historic event.

When the trio got to Flake's office, they saw a few reporters outside, including CNN's Suzanne Malveaux, and realized Flake was likely still inside, so Archila decided to stay for awhile. It was the first time Archila and Gallagher had met, but they hit it off, and Archila was stunned at how she had arrived at Hart. "She fucking came because she got an email," Archila said. "I was like, who does that? Well, *she* does that. She's amazing, she's the person of my dreams." Outside Flake's office, they realized they also had a shared experience: both had been sexually assaulted, and both had told nobody. Archila had first shared her experience inside Flake's office, to his staffers, that week, though Gallagher's was still fully private.

As they waited, Flake announced his decision. His agonizing was over and he announced he would be voting *yes* on Kavanaugh at the hearing that was just minutes away. His office blasted out a statement that landed in the phones of the reporters outside his door. They read it aloud. "Archila and Gallagher gasped," Malveaux recalled, "becoming very

---

283   He was previously a top aide to Harry Reid, knew the Senate well, and would become Bernie Sanders' campaign manager for the 2020 cycle.

emotional." Flake's *yes* vote was the final dagger in the heart of the opposition.

The next moment has become iconic in part because of its rawness and authenticity. Despite all the planning and strategy that goes into protest, all of the pretense had been shorn from it by the way it unfolded. "If we hadn't seen the press release, we wouldn't have been so angry," Archila said.

"We spotted Flake darting from his office with a few staffers and heading down the hall," Malveaux recalled.[284] "We took off after him, as did the women. We caught up with him just as he was getting into the elevator. The doors were closing, and Archila literally and figuratively put her foot down — causing the doors to open."

Malveaux began to get out a question, but Archila spoke over her. "On Monday, I stood in front of your office with Ady Barkan, and I told the story of my sexual assault," she said, referencing Barkan, an activist and colleague of hers who is dying of ALS and had his own viral exchange with Flake during the fight over the tax cut. "I told it because —"

"I need to go, I need to go to the hearing," Flake cut in, helplessly pressing the Close Door button.

"I recognized in Dr. Ford's story that she is telling the truth," Archila went on. "What you are doing is allowing someone who actually violated a woman to sit on the Supreme Court. This is not tolerable. You have children in your family. Think about them. I have two children. I cannot imagine that for the next 50 years they will have to have someone in the Supreme Court who has been accused of violating a young girl. What are you doing, sir?"

Flake continued jamming his thumb at the elevator button, as the door screeched with impatience. Gallagher, as though something inside her had just burst, exploded into what had been just a two-way exchange. "I was sexually assaulted and nobody believed me," she told Flake, with an unmistakable rawness. Flake's demeanor changed. He took his hand off the button, stuffed both hands in his pockets, and bowed his head.

"I didn't tell anyone, and you're telling all women that they don't matter, that they should just stay quiet because if they tell you what happened to them you are going to ignore them. That's what happened to me, and that's what you are telling all women in America, that they don't matter. They should just keep it to themselves because if they have told the truth, you're just going to help that man to power anyway.

---

284   Malveaux wrote about being present for this historic moment for CNN in an essay, "The elevator moment: when to speak up, when to stay quiet, and the power of both."

That's what you're telling all of these women."

Gallagher grew angrier still. "That's what you're telling me right now. Look at me when I'm talking to you. You are telling me that my assault doesn't matter, that what happened to me doesn't, and that you're going to let people who do these things into power. That's what you're telling me when you vote for him. Don't look away from me," she demanded, as he looked up at her in anguish. "Look at me and tell me that it doesn't matter what happened to me, that you will let people like that go into the highest court of the land and tell everyone what they can do to their bodies."

The reporters asked if Flake wanted to respond. He did not. "Do you think that Brett is telling the truth?" Archila asked. "Do you think that he's able to hold the pain of this country and repair it? That is the work of justice. The way that justice works is you recognize harm, you take responsibility for it, and then you begin to repair it."

Reporters asked again, "Senator, do you care to respond?"

"Do you think that he's telling the truth?"

Flake was noticeably reluctant to say he believed Kavanaugh. "You have power when so many women are powerless," Gallagher reminded him.

"I need to go to the hearing," Flake answered. "I just issued a statement. I'll be saying more as well. There have been a lot of questions here."

By the time Flake arrived at the hearing, something had changed. In a dramatic announcement, he said that, despite his statement moments earlier, he was no longer willing to vote yes unless the FBI was allowed to conduct its investigation into the allegations. "It immediately felt to me like a trap," Archila said. "He basically saved the Republicans from doing something really stupid, walked them back from the cliff a little bit, gave cover to everyone."

The Kavanaugh scandal was crushing Republicans in suburban swing districts, with college-educated women repulsed and flipping in increasingly greater numbers to Democrats. Evangelical white women, however, concentrated in states like Indiana, Missouri, Florida and Georgia, were getting fired up, angry at Democrats and the fake news media for smearing a good man's name.

In other words, by digging in on Kavanaugh, Republicans had thrown away any shot at saving the House in order to make sure they didn't lose the Senate. Another goal may have been to prove that protests in Washington against the breaking of norms didn't matter. It was important for McConnell to show that the direct-action pressure campaign didn't work, because the long-term Republican plan to hold power relies on structuring rules that let a minority of the country rule over the majority — whether it's through gerrymandering, voter suppression, right-wing dominance of the courts or the undemocratic Senate itself. Making public protest feel futile is essential to that project.

When Susan Collins finally took to the Senate floor to announce her decision, there was no hint that it was ever close for her. She bought fully into the bizarre theory that Blasey Ford simply forgot who had attempted to rape her, and that it certainly wasn't Kavanaugh. She launched into a full-throated defense of Kavanaugh and a dissection of Blasey Ford's allegations. As she spoke, a fundraising page set up by Ady Barkan, which was collecting money for Collins' future Democratic challenger in 2020, crashed. As it struggled to come back online, the money poured in, first two million, then three million, then four million dollars.

Collins calmly laid out her arguments for Kavanaugh's fitness for a lifetime appointment to the Supreme Court. She believed he would maintain protections for Americans with pre-existing conditions seeking medical care; that he would not hesitate to vote against the favor of Trump should the situation arise; that he would support same-sex marriage and access to contraceptives; that he would honor the precedent set in *Roe v. Wade* "as a constitutional tenet that has to be followed." Of course, if all of those things were true, conservatives would not have enthusiastically embraced Kavanaugh as their man for the Supreme Court.

The Maine senator lauded the organizations that supported Kavanaugh throughout his judicial career, including the American Bar Association. It became clear as Collins made this point that she had not yet seen the letter from the ABA to the Senate Judiciary Committee released that morning, announcing a plan by the group's standing committee to reopen its evaluation of Kavanaugh.

When the subject turned to Blasey Ford, Collins was careful to make clear that she did indeed believe Blasey Ford was sexually assaulted. She just didn't think it was by Kavanaugh. She went out of her way to break down each point in Blasey Ford's testimony that did not "meet a standard of more likely than not," conflating a Senate confirmation process for a lifetime appointment to the Supreme Court with a civil trial.

Collins took pains to point out that Leland Keyser, Blasey Ford's friend whom she had placed at the party where her alleged assault occurred, said she didn't know Kavanaugh. The senator asked *Why, if Blasey Ford left the party early without saying goodbye to anyone, no one called the next day to ask why she left, or if she was OK.* "It is when passions are most inflamed when fairness is most in jeopardy," Collins argued, citing due process concerns. In the end, Collins absurdly suggested that she hoped Kavanaugh's nomination would restore Americans' faith in the Supreme

Court, easing partisan tensions and decreasing the number of 5-4 decisions the court handed down.

While the outrage over Kavanaugh bolstered the median House Democratic candidate looking to flip a suburban district, a separate class of candidates paid a price. In rural areas, where Trump voters had either been open to siding with the Democrat, or considered sitting the election out, the battle struck a partisan chord. Canvassers in rural districts across the country saw it at the doors they knocked on, and the antipathy toward Democrats blended with Trump's fearmongering about a migrant caravan racing the southern border, creating the impression of a hostile takeover of white America by feminists and foreigners.

In Lancaster County, Pennsylvania, conversations were harder for people knocking doors for Jess King. In 2014, the previous midterm, King's district had fewer Republicans, but when its map was redrawn in 2018, it became even redder. Still, in 2014, Republican Joe Pitts had won the seat with 101,000 votes; the Democrat garnered only 74,000. This time around, inside even more hostile terrain, King drew 114,000 votes — a stunning number for Lancaster and York Counties, and well more than enough to win in a good number of districts around the country. Yet conservative turnout was so explosive that her opponent, Lloyd Smucker, reeled in 164,000 voters out. More than 100,000 people who had sat out the midterms in 2014 came out; tons of those went for King, but tons more stuck with Trump.

Candidates and their supporters noticed the same trend across the country — in Richard Ojeda's West Virginia district, voters went home to Trump, and he lost by nine points; in Iowa, a fired-up GOP base blunted J.D. Scholten's momentum against white nationalist Steve King; in rural Virginia, legendary investigative reporter Leslie Cockburn, running as a Democrat, saw opposition to her solidify.

In some states Trump won, however, Democratic senators never wavered and didn't pay a price. Tammy Baldwin (Wisconsin), Sherrod Brown (Ohio), Bob Casey (Pennsylvania), and Debbie Stabenow (Michigan) all cast confident votes against Kavanaugh and won easily. Jon Tester voted for Kavanaugh and survived a close race in Montana. Bill Nelson voted against him in Florida and was polling well ahead of Rick Scott, but a badly designed ballot in Broward County appeared to have cost him the election.[285] Heidi Heitkamp voted against Kavanaugh and leaned into her opposition, raising millions from around the country. She lost by 11 points. Claire McCaskill in Missouri and Joe Donnelly in

---

285   He lost by 12,000 votes, and 34,000 people in Broward, which went 2-1 for Nelson, left the Senate race blank. It was tucked underneath the form's instructions, and was easy to miss.

Indiana each lost by six.

Joe Manchin, in West Virginia, announced his support of Kavanaugh just moments after Collins did, at which point his vote was meaningless. Senate insiders were convinced that if Collins had voted *no*, Manchin would have too. He won by three and a half percentage points, less than the margin the Libertarian peeled off, 4.2 percent.

Democrats, though, flipped Arizona, as Flake hadn't run for reelection, as well as Nevada, where Harry Reid's machine powered Jacky Rosen over the finish line. That left Republicans with a 53–47 advantage in the Senate. In the House, though, Kavanaugh likely cost Republicans a decent number of seats: at least 12 races were decided by five points or less.

For Mitch McConnell, that was all beside the point. McConnell easily could have dropped Kavanaugh for the next Federalist Society–vetted, prep-school graduate and the tilt of the Supreme Court would have been no different. McConnell is famous for his ability never to display or betray any emotion, but as the protests around the Capitol campus heated up and began influencing the public debate, he grew visibly irate on the Senate floor. Pushing Kavanaugh through, by that point, had a single purpose. It was to look those protesters in the eye and say, in as clear a voice as possible: *No, you don't matter.*

Twenty-Nine

The Green Dream

Wednesday, November 28, 2018, could very well have been the day that the Democratic Party nominated Joe Crowley to be House Speaker. Nancy Pelosi had spent the weeks since the election fending off a rebellion from her right while trying to nail down the votes of the incoming freshman class who had campaigned on the need for "new leadership" in Washington, some of them specifically calling for Pelosi's head.

Crowley had long been viewed as the Democrat most likely to take Pelosi's spot when she retired or was pushed aside. Throughout 2018, his operation seeded stories in the D.C. press about his ambitions, while he publicly insisted he wouldn't challenge Pelosi directly if she ran again for the gavel. The rebellion against Pelosi, without Crowley in the conversation as a potential alternative, failed for a lack of an alternative. "You can't beat somebody with nobody," Pelosi's allies noted repeatedly, deploying what was an accurate, if not exactly inspiring, campaign slogan.

Elections for caucus leaders began on a Wednesday morning, and in a twist of narrative fate, Joe Crowley, still chair of the caucus, oversaw the proceedings.

Staff was barred from the private session, resulting in something of an intimate atmosphere inside the main auditorium at the Capitol Visitors Center. After 10 long years, Democrats would finally retake control of the House. They had flipped 40 seats on Election Day, and another 23 new freshmen were replacing Democrats who had retired or passed away. Jahana Hayes, 2016's National Teacher of the Year, who upset the Democratic establishment candidate in a primary, was one such new member, as were Rashida Tlaib and Ilhan Omar, who were replacing John Conyers and Keith Ellison, respectively.

The dean of each region — the longest-serving member — introduced each new freshman to a round of thunderous applause. Then Eliot Engel, who represents parts of the Bronx and Westchester County, took the stage to introduce the new members of Congress from New York, each to an explosion of enthusiasm. Except for one. At the mention of Alexandria Ocasio-Cortez, the caucus offered polite golf claps.

After the caucus acquainted itself with its new members, Crowley moved to the election for his own leadership position, chair of the caucus. In a Washington Post story the day after her primary win, Ocasio-Cortez was asked if she'd support Nancy Pelosi for Speaker. She said she thought it was time for "new leadership" but added she didn't know who the alternatives were: "I mean, is Barbara Lee running? Call me when she does!"

I posted her suggestion on Twitter, and it went viral. With a Barbara Lee for Speaker campaign picking up steam on social media, Lee announced not that she'd be challenging Pelosi, her longtime Bay Area ally, but that she would run for Crowley's vacated position. Linda Sanchez, a Los Angeles Democrat who had beaten Lee in a leadership race in 2016, later said she was jumping in, too.

Three weeks before the election, citing personal issues, Sanchez unexpectedly dropped out. The issue was that her husband was being indicted for embezzlement in Connecticut. That same day, Hakeem Jeffries announced his own run. A fresh face in his 40s, the Brooklyn lawmaker spent much of 2018 on cable as an effective Democratic Party messenger.

Congress is like a high school in many ways; one being that it is saturated with rumors. Shortly after Jeffries entered the race, the talk among Democrats turned toward the role of Pelosi in his decision to run. Some of Pelosi's opponents in the caucus had been hoping Jeffries would make a bid for Speaker. They had been counting on Crowley as their credible alternative to Pelosi, and Jeffries, a protegé of Crowley's, was a natural Plan B to fill that role. A number of members of Congress who supported Lee, as well as some who backed Jeffries, were convinced that Pelosi had recruited Jeffries to run against Lee — not necessarily to undermine her Bay Area ally, but to prevent Jeffries from running for Speaker. In other words, *Don't come after me, go after her*.

In either event, Jeffries' bid was a boon to the trio of septuagenarians in the top three leadership positions, as it offered a release valve to reduce the pressure in finding younger faces among the brass. Concern that Pelosi was behind Jeffries mounted as the race tightened. With her vaunted whip operation, it was assumed that if Pelosi wanted Lee to win, she had the tools to make it happen. Perhaps she was distracted by her own challenge, or maybe she was losing her touch, but she didn't lift a finger to help Lee.

Headed into the auditorium that morning, both Lee and Jeffries believed they had the commitments they'd needed to win. Lee was so sure she had the votes that her camp told the coalition of progressive groups — including MoveOn, NARAL, Color of Change, and Democracy for America — that were supporting her on the outside not to swamp House Democrats with calls. What she didn't know was that Crowley had been doing more than emceeing the proceedings. In the runup to the vote, he told a number of House Democrats that Lee had cut a check to Ocasio-Cortez, painting her as part of the insurgency that those in the room considered a viable threat.[286]

A kernel of truth in the charge: Lee's campaign did indeed cut a $1,000 check to the campaign of Ocasio-Cortez, but did so on July 10, two weeks *after* she beat Crowley. Since then, Steny Hoyer, Raúl Grijalva, and Maxine Waters, as well as the PAC for the Congressional Progressive Caucus, had all given money to Ocasio-Cortez's campaign committee. It's not an unusual phenomenon — a way to welcome an incoming colleague — but Crowley's disingenuous framing linked Lee to the growing insurgent movement, despite her decades of experience in Congress.

Lee took the stage with some 30 members of Congress, and a half-dozen gave speeches on her behalf. Her mistake, members of Congress argued to me afterward, was that her message was flat. Her campaign, and the speeches that day, made two points:

1. Black women powered the Democratic Party, and a black woman should be in leadership.
2. She cast a lone courageous vote in 2001.

There was universal acclaim for both points, but Lee didn't bother to make a case beyond that. Jeffries, meanwhile, made his case based on "generational change" and cited his ability to go toe-to-toe with Trump on cable. Implicit in his generational argument was that elevating him to caucus chair would put him in line for Speaker. And nobody in the room thought there was any chance he'd support primaries against incumbents (except, perhaps, against Ocasio-Cortez).

The votes were cast by secret ballot, and as the counting began, Crowley returned to the stage to say goodbye. On the night of his primary loss, Crowley queued up a song at his watch party — "Born to Run"

---

286   Three members of Congress in the room relayed this to me on the day of the vote.

— that he'd been playing for years at events and had planned to play at his victory party. Instead, he dedicated it to the insurgent who'd beaten him, Ocasio-Cortez, mispronouncing her name. As the votes to replace him in leadership were being counted, he again broke out in song. This time it was what multiple members said sounded like an Irish funeral dirge.

As he sang, one member of Congress leaned over and captured the mood of the room, saying quietly, "It's such a shame. This isn't right." The congressman looked up and realized — or, perhaps, pretended to realize — that he was talking to Ocasio-Cortez.

It took more than an hour, but when the votes were tallied, Jeffries prevailed 123-113. I found Lee in the hallway later that day and asked her about Crowley spreading the rumor about her check to Ocasio-Cortez. "Those rumors took place and that was very unfair," Lee said. "We're moving forward now."

She added, however, that the insinuation that she had supported Ocasio-Cortez during her primary against Crowley was patently false, because Lee wasn't even aware of Ocasio-Cortez's challenge. "I didn't even know he had a primary," Lee said of the under-the-radar contest that resulted in Crowley's startling loss.

While Lee had not encouraged primaries against her colleagues and had worked closely with party leadership in her time in the House, her iconoclastic image, rooted in that lone vote against authorizing the use of military force in the days after 9/11, meant that the caricature resonated, as Crowley no doubt knew it would. Indeed, it was a charge some Democrats in Congress were ready to believe — and some outside supporters of Lee were hoping was true — as Lee is something of a hero among the incoming class of outsider Democrats.

Rep. Pramila Jayapal said that when she was an anti-war activist and Lee cast her famous vote, it reshaped her thinking about what it was possible for a politician to do. For the first time, she considered getting into elected office herself, and when she did, she called Lee, who endorsed her immediately. "I take some issue with 'generational change' being just about age. I think it should be about ideas that resonate with young people across the country, and I think Barbara Lee is that person," a furious Jayapal told me after the vote.

Brian Higgins, a New York representative who backed Jeffries, suggested that Crowley had a hand in nudging Jeffries into the race against Lee. "To what extent, I don't know, but I do know that he's a mentor, and I think he helped him develop a strategy to succeed," Higgins told me. "Joe Crowley is the most popular guy on campus, with Democrats and Republicans."

Waleed Shahid, speaking for Justice Democrats, called Crowley's move "absolutely despicable" and all the more reason to continue targeting Democrats who undermine a progressive agenda. "This is exactly why we need more primaries — to have a Democratic Party that fights for its voters, not corporate donors," he said, though Crowley's move had put him in an awkward position. The despicable act was to associate Lee with Justice Democrats.

Rep. Dan Kildee of Michigan, and Rep. Debbie Wasserman Schultz of Florida also seconded Jeffries' nomination. After the election, Kildee told me that he had not heard that Lee had given money to Ocasio-Cortez's campaign, but said that it would indeed have been a problem for Lee if that message had circulated widely.

I noted to Kildee that Lee had made the contribution after the primary was over and asked if that changed his calculation. "It would be far less of a problem," he said. In other words, even a contribution to Ocasio-Cortez after Crowley had already conceded would still have been an issue in the minds of some House Democrats. "I know she did give her money and that it didn't sit well with a number of members. I doubt that's the reason she lost, though," said one Democratic operative who is close with Jeffries and supported his bid.

Crowley, following Jeffries' victory, congratulated him. "I've been honored to work alongside Hakeem as we both fought for the working and middle-class families of New York," he said in a statement. "As chair, I know he'll continue that fight and serve as a champion for all Americans by protecting their health care, their voting rights, and their livelihoods. I am incredibly proud that a fellow New Yorker and my friend will help lead the Democratic Caucus. New York, and the country, are in good hands with Hakeem."

Roughly half of Jeffries' campaign money had come from political action committees, including from the spheres of real estate, finance, law firms, entertainment, and the pharmaceutical industry. Jeffries has broken with Democrats to back Wall Street on key votes, including one high-profile measure written by Citigroup lobbyists in 2013. He has also been one of the most vocal supporters of charter schools in Congress and a close ally of not just Crowley, but New York Gov. Andrew Cuomo. A prominent supporter of Hillary Clinton during the 2016 campaign, he savaged her rival Bernie Sanders in particularly aggressive terms, dubbing him a "gun-loving socialist" who provided "aid and comfort" to Donald Trump.

Jeffries framed the election as a "contest of ideas." I asked what specific ideas he and Lee disagreed on during the campaign. "Well, the question for many was *How do we get the right mix of experience and gener-*

ational change. And I focused a lot on the work that I've done in the past with Blue Dogs, New Dems, and progressives; and with Republicans, at least as it relates to the criminal justice bill, and in a divided government context, made the case that I was reasonably well-positioned to get things done, working with Republicans in the House and in the Senate and with a Republican administration in the White House."

The election put Jeffries in line for Speaker, and as I stood in the hallway outside the caucus meeting, I couldn't help but think of "Terminator 2," with the liquid-metal android that reformed each time it took fire from Arnold Schwarzenegger. Justice Democrats and Ocasio-Cortez had taken the speaker-to-be out of leadership, but instead of replacing him with Barbara Lee, now Crowley's protegé was in line for the slot. The conversation on the left immediately turned toward challenging Jeffries in a primary, but that day it felt unmistakably like a game of whack-a-mole.

The game needs to change — or the players used to losing need to start playing by different rules. The act of civil disobedience inside Pelosi's office, which took place just two weeks before the leadership election, was as good a chance to flip the board as any.

By the time Ocasio-Cortez made her way inside Pelosi's office, protesters were already squatting every available square inch. She stood in the middle of them, with a bank of TV cameras just outside the door, and demonstrated what makes her such a confounding figure to the party establishment: *She wasn't there*, she said, *to cause trouble*, despite all evidence to the contrary. *No, she was there to help.* And here's the thing: She meant it.

"Should Leader Pelosi become the next Speaker of the House, we need to tell her that we've got her back," she told her young charges. The way to do that, she argued, was to capture the energy in the room and use it to push "the most progressive energy agenda that this country has ever seen."

Down the hall, I spied Drew Hammill, Pelosi's deputy chief of staff, somebody I'd known since at least 2007, when he worked in Pelosi's press office. He was red in the face, livid. "Can you tell them we support every single thing they're protesting us for?!" This was mostly true, I told him, but their specific demand centered on the creation of a new select committee dedicated to a Green New Deal, with the goal of producing legislation by March 2020, which would be ready for a hopeful Democratic — or perhaps democratic socialist — president the next year. But they also wanted the party's top leaders, and the chairs of committees that deal with climate change policy, to refuse contributions from fossil fuel companies. That, insisted Hammill, was out of Pelosi's control

— she can't make other lawmakers refuse money from any particular industry.

Legally speaking, of course, Hammill was correct, but what Ocasio-Cortez and the young people in the Cannon hallway wanted was a firm statement that Big Oil was quickly making the planet uninhabitable, and the industry had no business helping write legislation to address the crisis it has caused. That distinction cuts to the heart of the divide between longtime Democratic officials, even some of the most progressive ones, and the movement led by people like Ocasio-Cortez.

She did not stay to get arrested — and Pelosi told the police to let the young people go free, too. Leaving Cannon, I told Ocasio-Cortez that Hammill complained that they were protesting the wrong person, that Pelosi wants all the same things she does. "That is absolutely true," she said. "What this just needs to do is create a momentum and an energy to make sure that it becomes a priority for leadership."

Within days, the Green New Deal would find dozens of congressional supporters; within a few months it would become a resolution introduced in both chambers of Congress, dominate the political conversation, and receive endorsements from almost every serious Democratic presidential candidate for 2020. By May 2019, Democratic voters would tell pollsters that climate change was their top issue.

Ocasio-Cortez's day was just starting. Next on the agenda, she noted: a luncheon for the freshman class, hosted by Nancy Pelosi. "That should be interesting," she predicted.

Later that afternoon, Pelosi met privately with the Democrats on the Ways and Means Committee[287] to talk about the panel's 2019 agenda. The soon-to-be speaker laid out the year's agenda — infrastructure, a review of Trump's tax cuts — but then added one more item. "And we need to deal with the environment," Pelosi said, "because the teenagers want us to do something."

---

287   According to a committee member who was in the room.

Epilogue

The insurgent wave that crested in the Bronx, lifting Alexandria Oc-asio-Cortez to victory, had begun with a rock thrown into the water in 1983 Chicago, with the election of Harold Washington. It would be only fitting that the same wave crashed back down in Chicago, in 2019, wash-ing Rahm Emanuel out to sea.

One of Harold Washington's lieutenants, Chuy Garcia, had challenged Emanuel in 2015, and gave the mayor a scare from his left. It would lat-er emerge that Emanuel's team had suppressed horrifying video of the cold-blooded police killing of Laquan McDonald. He had buried it long enough to win reelection (Emanuel was first elected in 2011, after step-ping down as Obama's chief of staff), but it became clear that a third term was not in his future. In 2016, the Cook County prosecutor who fa-cilitated the cover-up was ousted by Kim Foxx, running on an aggressive reform agenda. In 2018, insurgents took on the beating heart of Chicago politics: county tax assessor. The position may sound mundane, but it produced the lubricant that greased the machine. An insurgent candi-date ran for the office in charge of assessing and collecting property tax-es in Chicago, and won a startling upset, which came along with other leftist pickups on the city council. Luis Gutiérrez retired from Congress, and Chuy Garcia, who had given Harold Washington's elegy, won the race to replace him.

Five members of the Democratic Socialists of America won city coun-cil races, producing enough socialists on the city's legislative body to form an actual caucus. Patrick O'Connor, the alderman who was Emanuel's City Council floor leader, had been in office for forty years. He was knocked out by a Latino democratic socialist. United Working Families, a sister to the Working Families Party that started in New York, backed an additional three successful leftist council candidates.

Bill Daley, who was the Obama chief of staff succeeding Emanuel, ran for mayor in 2019, hoping to succeed him again. Thirty-six years earlier, Washington had beaten his brother Richard Daley to become mayor. Daley finished a humiliating third; he didn't even make the runoff. Instead, two black progressive women, one openly gay and both outspoken opponents of Emanuel, would face off, with Lori Lightfoot clinching the nomination. This time, unlike in 1983, the machine didn't attempt to switch sides and back the Republican in the general election. People had dismantled it.

In 2019, "Fast Eddie" Vrdolyak, the alderman who had led the council wars against Harold Washington, pleaded guilty to tax evasion related to his looting of tobacco settlement money. At 81, he's hoping to avoid prison — and this would be his second time in the slammer. He pleaded guilty in 2008 to fraud.

Emma Tai, executive director of United Working Families, celebrated the victory. "Tonight, voters rejected Rahm Emanuel's legacy," she declared. "Chicago belongs to the people."

The people, however, have yet to claim control of the country as a whole, or even of the Democratic Party. It can be painful to think what could have been had Democratic leadership made different choices decades ago. What if Jesse Jackson's Rainbow Coalition had won that primary in Wisconsin and managed to clinch the nomination? Even if he had lost the general — as Dukakis did anyway — it would have shown future candidates that people power provides a genuine path to the nomination. "There would have been no room for Trump if we had democratized our economy," Jackson told me.

Instead, the notion of exciting the base and expanding the electorate was suppressed until it reemerged around Howard Dean in 2003 and 2004, then around Barack Obama's first presidential campaign. (We changed the rules in '88 which made possible for Barack to win. Under the '84 rules, Hillary would have been the winner, because we went to proportionality rather than winner take all," Jackson reminded me.) And finally, in a dramatic expression, behind Bernie Sanders in 2016. The eventual recognition that power for Democrats lies in people, not big money, transformed the 2020 primaries. No longer do candidates boast about locking down the most high-dollar bundlers, and the competition in fundraising is now who can raise the most money with the lowest average contribution.

Yet the party establishment can't be expected to simply hand over power. In 2019, the DCCC announced that it would blacklist any consulting firm who did any work for a challenger to an incumbent. Nancy Pelosi has reserved some of her most forceful language for the squad of Ocasio-Cortez, Tlaib, Omar, and Pressley. Omar and Tlaib — and Omar in particular — have faced withering attacks from their Democratic colleagues; Ocasio-Cortez has been called by a colleague "Nixonian," and much worse in private, where party honchos plot ways to bring her down. That's all before the president and a billion-dollar right-wing spin machine have had their say.

The final obstacle comes down to the people themselves. Democratic primary voters fancy themselves pundits. Jesse Jackson surged in the polls until he came close to winning. To be sure, some voters turned on him simply because they didn't want a black man in the Oval Office. Many others, though, believed that other people would be unwilling to elect a black man president, which meant he wasn't electable, which meant he needed to be stopped. Bill Clinton emerged from a deeply competitive primary, and persuaded Democrats that he and his Southern charm could put an end to twelve years of Republican rule. In 2004, Democrats preferred Howard Dean, but believed the military man, John Kerry, would be the smart pick to take on Bush in wartime. Like most strategic calculations made by Democratic primary voters, it was harebrained. The one risk primary voters took was going with their hearts and nominating Barack Obama. Hillary Clinton, perceived by the Democratic electorate to be electable, was everything but.

Headed into 2020, Sanders has a robust movement behind him, and Republicans I talk to in Washington believe he's one of the few Democrats who could give Trump fits in the key states: Pennsylvania, Wisconsin, and Michigan. His organizing operation would be able to register and turn out far more black voters in crucial cities like Philadelphia, Milwaukee, and Detroit, while he can also appeal to aggrieved working-class voters of all races who want someone to, well, drain the swamp. Elizabeth Warren, in many ways Sanders' ideological cousin, has demonstrated over the years that her message works with working-class voters, contrary to the D.C. conventional wisdom that widely dismisses her as an elite professor. But the pundit-voter who thinks of Joe Biden knows one thing for sure: That man is electable.

Biden was appropriately little more than a footnote in my chapter on the 1988 campaign. His 2008 campaign didn't end in disgrace, but merely faded into obscurity; his career was revived by Obama. Biden's contribution to the party debate has been to put himself on the wrong side of the issues with a startling consistency. One would think that just by chance, given a career that spans a half-century, he'd manage to get a few things right by accident. Even his most uncontroversial accomplishment, the Violence Against Women Act, was tucked into the Biden Crime Bill, which played a major role in juicing mass incarceration.

This book has been about how today's Democratic leaders, such as Chuck Schumer, Nancy Pelosi, Steny Hoyer, or Rahm Emanuel, are scarred from the political wounds they suffered in the 1980s and '90s. Even after Democrats took control of the House in 2018, making repeal of the ACA impossible, the party leadership continued arguing that any effort to advance Medicare for All risked the destruction of Obamacare. In May 2019, Pelosi warned that Trump might resist leaving office if he loses in a close election; therefore, the House should pull back on impeachment hearings and run to the center.

But the old-guard has company in their torment. Today's generation of young (and increasingly not-so-young) socialists recognizes the threat of fascism as real, but doesn't shrink from it, rallying behind the boldest possible platform. Their parents, haunted by Reagan and then the Gingrich wave of '94, worry that pushing for a progressive agenda will produce a backlash among the American public — an electorate they fear like an alien species meant to be pacified with moderation rather than won over with something robust.

Biden is just the man for that pacification project. The folksy Scranton man has managed to convince liberals that he's the guy who can talk to those white, working-class voters Democrats have been chasing since they took flight from the party half a century ago. Pete Buttigieg, the mayor of South Bend, similarly exploits liberals' lack of familiarity with rural culture to sell himself as the guy who can win the Midwest. Gone unmentioned is that he won a small mayoral election with roughly 8,000 votes — fewer than AOC won to beat Joe Crowley — and is running for president because he doesn't think Midwest voters will send him to the House or Senate.

Still, for a fearful party electorate, they feel safe in ways the wild-haired socialist and the woman from Harvard don't. Meanwhile, carbon concentration in the atmosphere rises, the oceans warm and acidify, the glaciers recede, the tundra warms, the rainforests shrink, coral reefs die off — and, according to the latest climate modeling, clouds themselves are at risk. In May 2019, the United Nations warned that the bottom was falling out. "The health of the ecosystems on which we and other species depend is deteriorating more rapidly than ever. We are eroding the very foundations of economies, livelihoods, food security, health and quality of life worldwide," said Robert Watson, chair of the UN's Intergovernmental Science-Policy Platform on Biodiversity and Ecosystem Services. "We have lost time. We must act now." If voters insist on being pundits, incorporating the climate crisis into their analysis ought to reorient their understanding of risk.

Trump's reelection isn't the only risk we as a people face. Indeed, it's not even the only political danger we face. In 1974, the Labour Party took power in the UK, with the country at a crossroads. A robust social movement looked to curb the power of banks, capital, and captains of industry, while democratizing the workforce and attacking sources of economic inequality. John Medhurst covered what happened in the next two years in his short but essential book, *That Option No Longer Exists: Britain 1974-76*. Finance fought back, and the moderate wing of the Labour Party won the internal struggle for power, implementing only meager reforms instead of the transformative ideas being pushed by a strong (but not-quite-strong-enough) left wing. Dissatisfied, the British public ushered in Margaret Thatcher, who had no such caution when it came to reshaping the country. Her dismantling of the welfare state and its working class was never inevitable.

If Democrats meet the public's demand for real change with something fake, the other side is willing to offer the real thing. The real risk of a Joe Biden nomination might not be that he could lose to Trump — though that is certainly plausible — but that he will beat Trump, fail to deliver, and open the door for a fascist who actually knows what he's doing. Playing it safe is going to get us all killed.

Acknowledgments

Depending on when you start counting, I've been writing this book for more than a decade, which means it wouldn't have been possible without the help of countless colleagues, editors, and sources both inside and outside Washington. I'm deeply indebted, as well, to people who've read my stories over the years — particularly people on the receiving end of my newsletter[288] — and written to me with criticism, ideas, tips, local insight, or background context. I've been able to keep up with the changing shape of the immensely complex Democratic coalition thanks in large part to these readers-turned-sources. Reporting for this book was done while I was covering the 2006 midterms for Washington Monthly, then while I was covering Congress for Politico in 2007 and 2008, then as I did the same at The Huffington Post from 2009 until 2017. Since then, I've been doing it at The Intercept, and I'm grateful to my editors at all of those publications for their guidance, and also for allowing me to use the reporting I did for this book. Particular thanks to editors Rebecca Sinderbrand and Rachel Morris at Washington Monthly; Carrie Budoff Brown at Politico; Arianna Huffington, Nico Pitney, Lydia Polgreen, Sam Stein, Amanda Terkel, and Nick Baumann at HuffPost; and Betsy Reed, Maryam Saleh, Roger Hodge, Ali Gharib, and Briahna Gray at The Intercept. I'm particularly grateful that they have allowed me to repurpose the reporting for this book, as it wouldn't have

---

288   It's called Bad News, and you should sign up. It's hosted at substack.bad-news.com and it's free.

been possible otherwise.

That reporting was often done in collaboration with colleagues, and many of the stories I referred back to in researching this book were co-bylined with colleagues like Terkel, Stein, Arthur Delaney, Zach Carter, Daniel Marans, Jen Bendery, Lucia Graves, Matt Fuller, Laura Barrón-López, Michael McAuliff, Aída Chávez, Akela Lacy, Lee Fang, and many people I'm forgetting to mention, but will remember the second this book goes to the printer.

This book was edited by Anne Fox, which makes for our third collaboration, though the first two came while she was Anne Marson. She edited me at my first reporting job at the Washington City Paper, and then I talked her into joining me later at Politico. Anne is meticulous, but also has an eye for the big picture, and this book wouldn't be readable without her. If there are errors that remain, it's because I was making edits up until the very last minute and slipped them past her.

My agent Howard Yoon has been providing helpful feedback on the concept for this book going back as far as 2009, and has become a good friend along the way. The folks at Strong Arm Press have been a dream to work with, including Alex Lawson, Troy Miller, Paige Kelly, and Alex Abbott, who (as far as I could tell) didn't miss a thing in fly-specking the manuscript. Thanks to Paige and Soohee Cho, our designer at The Intercept, for the cover design. Strong Arm Press, which I co-founded with Lawson in 2017, is built on the same premise that animates this book, that trusting in people rather than big money is both right and more effective in the long run. It's a publishing company that is funded by, and makes decisions collaboratively with, readers. Check it out at StrongArmPress.com, and if you'd like to become a member or hold a virtual or in-person event for this book, there's an easy way to sign up to do so.

I wanted to practice what this book preaches, and significant parts of it were crowd-edited by readers of my newsletter who took up the offer to take an early look at it, including Brandi Calvert, Janine Campbell, Linda Yoder, Vic Streiff, Michael Giardino, Stephanie Singer, Matt Totten, Richard Behan, Kim Hightower, Susan McCune, Jody Guth, and Vincent Flores. It was a thrill to open up the Google doc and see it teeming with people catching typos and flagging narrative holes. Acclaimed journalist Andrew Cockburn, who turns out to be a newsletter subscriber, caught a misspelling of Reagan (among other helpful notes). It takes a village.

Versions of the book were also read by Matt Stoller, Rich Yeselson, David Sirota, Briahna Joy Gray, Virgil Texas, Aída Chávez,, Maryam Saleh, Purva Rawal, George Grim, Cindy Quinn, Mimi Hook, Jess McIntosh, Thomas Neuburger, and Wendell Belew.

Belew, a top Democratic congressional staffer in the 1970s and 1980s, went on to be a high-powered lobbyist in Washington. Now retired from politics, he spends his days Voltaire-like, as a pre-K teacher's assistant at a D.C. public elementary school — a job at which he's spectacular, which I know because one of his charges is my daughter Virginia, who knows him as Mr. Blue. As Belew, he knew all the major players in the early chapters of this book, and was kind enough to read it and offer invaluable first-hand insight.

I benefited greatly from Brian Abrams' book *Obama: An Oral History*, which includes revelatory and newsworthy interviews with nearly all of the key players in the Obama administration, and has gotten far too little public attention. Abrams also provided me with a wealth of unpublished interview transcripts, which were immensely helpful. On top of that, he read the manuscript and offered meticulous notes that improved it in small ways, and bigger suggestions that improved it globally.

The chapter on the LGBTQ movement was written in collaboration with Kerry Eleveld, who I've been privileged to know for more than a decade, and is the author of *Don't Tell Me To Wait: How the Fight for Gay Rights Changed America and Transformed Obama's Presidency*. She covered Obama on the campaign trail and in the White House, interviewing him three times, including once in the Oval Office. She's now a Senior Political Writer for Daily Kos. It's normal in journalism to co-byline articles, or even books, but it's rare to co-byline an individual chapter. That's just one book convention I ignored with this one. Nobody knows the politics of the LGBTQ movement better than Eleveld, and the book is vastly improved by her contribution.

Writing this book without taking much time off meant that it was written heavily on buses or Metro rides, on my phone at the playground, and in downtime at home, and for that I owe a huge debt to Elizan Garcia and our kids, Iris, Sidney, Virginia, and George, who bore with me. All the promises I made about "after the book is done" are now coming due, and I even plan to honor some of them.

49030386R00239

Made in the USA
Middletown, DE
18 June 2019